PHYSICAL EDUCATION AND KINESIOLOGY IN NORTH AMERICA PROFESSIONAL & SCHOLARLY FOUNDATIONS

Edited, with introductory and concluding essays, by

Earle F. Zeigler
Ph.D., LL.D., FAAKPE, FSDMRDO (Hon.)
The University of Western Ontario
London, Ontario, Canada

With contributions in this order by

Laura J. Huelster, Ph.D., FAAKPE (dec.)
James S. Skinner, Ph.D., FAAKPE
Albert V. Carron, Ed.D., FAAKPE (C)
Susan L. Greendorfer, Ph.D., FAAKPE
Michael G. Wade, Ph.D., FAAKPE
Glynn A. Leyshon, Ph.D.
Marion J. L. Alexander, Ph.D.
Daniel G. Soucie, Ph.D.
Ann E. Jewett, Ed.D., FAAKPE
B. Don Franks, Ph.D., FAAKPE

STIPES PUBLISHING COMPANY
10–12 Chester Street
Champaign, Illinois 61820

Library of Congress Catalogue No.: 94-065402

Physical Education and Kinesiology in North America: Professional and Scholarly dimensions / editor, Earle F. Zeigler

p. cm.

Includes bibliographical references and index

1., 2., 3., 4., 5., etc. I. Zeigler, Earle F., 1919–

ISBN: 0-87563-495-8

Printed in the United States of America

10 9 8 7 6 5 4 3 2 1

STIPES PUBLISHING COMPANY
10–12 Chester Street
Champaign, IL 61820

Preface

The fundamental purpose of this book is to describe succinctly what the foundations of the field of physical education and kinesiology—recognized professional and disciplinary titles, respectively—consist of at the present time in North America. In providing a synoptic overview of the field, this volume has been prepared in such a way that it can meet the needs of at least four different groups of people: (1) those who are using it as an introduction to a field in which they are being prepared *professionally,* (2) those who are mature professional students and scholars and who are preparing for written and oral examinations at the master's and doctoral levels, (3) those who are already professional practitioners and/or scholars who wish to review a recent summary of the body of knowledge of the profession and the discipline, and (4) those who are using it from the standpoint of general education, as part of a broad liberal arts and science background.

Interestingly enough, it is very difficult to know just what name to give the field at present. It is called "sport and physical education" within the National Association for Sport and Physical Education, one of the allied professions of the American Alliance for Health, Physical Education, Recreation, and Dance. In Canada the professional association is still called the Canadian Association for Health, Physical Education and Recreation, but the term "physical and health education" prevails at the public- and secondary-school levels. "Physical education and sport" is still well recognized around the world, but the term "sport" is making strong headway.

In this book we are offering "physical education and kinesiology" as a "holding-pattern" term, to borrow from airline nomenclature, although it is true that the entire list of names that one will find applied to the field in North America is indeed a long one, number more than one hundred! Without listing them all, we still see physical education (by itself), kinesiology (at the university level by itself), human kinetics and physical education, sport and exercise sciences, physical activity studies, etc.

A text of this type offered to the profession at this time merits added justification. We believe that this volume has been conceived in such a way that it will meet the urgent needs of our field in the 1990s—and even on into the early years of the 21st century. Such a text must concern itself forthrightly and strongly with both the scholarly and "professional" foundations of our work—with the so-called subdisciplinary areas and with the concurrent subprofessional components that we all face. (An example of a subdisciplinary area is that called *functional effects of physical activity,* while an example of a concurrent professional component would be curriculum theory and program development that includes instructional methodology, also.)

Diagnosis of the present situation indicates that the field needs redirection and rejuvenation. The American Alliance for Health, Physical Education, Recreation, and Dance has now fully recognized that each of these terms represents separate professions that are also almost inextricably allied. In Canada there is a separate parks and recreation profession, but physical and health education remain closely intertwined. Dance educators are active within the Canadian Association for HPER. There is also a variety of separate subdisciplinary societies, and many scholars affiliate with more broadly based North American societies as well.

As the reader examines the table of contents, he or she will notice immediately that there is a balanced approach between the subdisciplinary areas of our field and what might be identified as the subprofessional or concurrent professional components. By this we mean that what many have called professional writing (e.g., curriculum theory investigation) will be regarded as scholarly endeavor—if it is well done—just as what many have considered to be scholarly, scientific endeavor (e.g., functional effects of physical activity) is regarded as professional writing too (writing that should ultimately serve the profession). Some may feel that this tends to redress the present imbalance too much, but we believe that our field, involved with lifelong developmental physical activity as it is, is indeed unique in this regard. Accordingly, we believe that the widening (psychological?) gap or rift in the field between the so-called scholars and the so-called practicing professionals should be significantly narrowed at the very least—and largely eliminated if we wish to move toward a relatively ideal state early on in the 21st century. If it is well received, this book may help to close the presently widening gap.

As part of this effort to close this gap or to reverse the direction of present movement, the Editor, with the earlier assistance of the late Dr. Laura J. Huelster, has developed a taxonomical table to explain the proposed area of scholarly study and research using our nomenclature (physical education and kinesiology terms only) along with the accompanying disciplinary and professional aspects. (See Table 1 below.). We agreed upon eight areas of scholarly study and research that are correlated with their respective subdisciplinary and subprofessional aspects in Table 1 below. Most importantly, the reader will note that the names selected for the eight areas *do not include terms that are currently part of the names, or the actual names, of other recognized disciplines* and that are therefore usually identified with these other (related) disciplines primarily by our colleagues and the public.

Table 1. Scholarly and Professional Dimensions of Developmental Physical Activity in Exercise, Sport, and Related Expressive Movement

	Areas of Scholarly Study & Research	*Subdisciplinary Aspects*	*Subprofessional Aspects*
I.	BACKGROUND, MEANING, AND INTERCULTURAL SIGNIFICANCE	-History -Philosophy -International & Comparative Study	-International Relations -Professional Ethics
II.	FUNCTIONAL EFFECTS OF PHYSICAL ACTIVITY	-Exercise Physiology -Anthropometry & Body Composition	-Fitness & Health Appraisal -Exercise Therapy
III.	SOCIO-CULTURAL & BEHAVIORAL ASPECTS	-Sociology -Economics -Psychology (individual & social) -Anthropology -Political Science -Geography	-Application of Theory to Practice
IV.	MOTOR LEARNING & CONTROL	-Psycho-motor Learning	-Application of Theory to Practice
V.	MECHANICAL & MUSCULAR ANALYSIS OF MOTOR SKILLS	-Biomechanics -Neuro-skeletal Musculature	-Application of Theory to Practice
VI.	MANAGEMENT THEORY & PRACTICE	-Management Science -Business Administration	-Application of Theory to Practice
VII.	CURRICULUM THEORY & PROGRAM DEVELOPMENT	-Curriculum Studies	-Application of Theory to Practice
	(General education; professional preparation; intramural sports and physical recreation; intercollegiate athletics; programs for special populations [e.g., handicapped] including both curriculum and instructional methodology)		
VIII.	MEASUREMENT AND EVALUATION	-Theory about the Measurement Function	-Application of Theory to Practice

Our position is that we must promote *our own* discipline of physical education and kinesiology (the term presently recommended) as described below, while at the same time working cooperatively with the related disciplines (to the extent that interest is shown in our problems). If we continue to speak of *sociology* of sport, *physiology* of exercise, etc., it will just be a matter of time before these other disciplines and professions awake to the importance of what we believe to be *our* professional task—the discovery, gathering, and dissemination of knowledge about, and the promotion of it to the extent that such promulgation is socially desirable, developmental physical activity through the media of exercise, sport, physical recreation, and expressive movement. It is our contention that the present trend, truly a debilitating fractionization, will in time, if unchecked, result in our developing profession being regarded as simply one more trade, and not a very important one at that.

However, our profession has the inherent potential to serve the high goal of enriched living and well-being for all people. It can provide an opportunity for the improvement of the *quality* of life and, additionally, there is now evidence that regular exercise throughout one's life will lengthen one's lifespan as well. Few other professions can make such a claim, but our profession can do this best with the help of our allied professions and related disciplines. Moreover, no other profession will do this *for* us, but because of our inactivity other professions and trades are now fulfilling some of our duties and responsibilities in a piecemeal fashion. This can only result in knowledge, competencies, and skills coming belatedly and ineffectively to help people improve the quality of their lifestyles.

What is needed right now, and is not presently available, is a steadily growing inventory of scientific findings about human motor performance (developmental physical activity) in exercise, sport, physical recreation, and expressive movement arranged as ordered generalizations to help our various professional practitioners in their daily work (be they teachers, coaches, scholars, laboratory researchers, managers, supervisors, performers, or others engaged in positions of a public, semipublic, or private nature (e.g., YMCAs and commercial fitness establishments)).

This text represents a beginning step in the direction of such an inventory of scientific findings. It is designed to meet the needs of North Americans primarily, although it has relevance for professional practitioners and scholars anywhere in the world. As mentioned above, it may be used for students beginning a period of professional training, for mature students preparing for comprehensive examinations, for professional practitioners on the job, or for those wishing to round out their general education. (It can also be studied profitably by students wishing to specialize in either health and safety education *or* recreation and park administration, but it has not been designed to meet their needs as an introduction to either of these developing professions. However, students intending to specialize in dance education as a developing profession could use it to advantage as an introduction because the focus in this volume is on human movement in exercise, sport, physical recreation, and expressive movement.)

What should go into this book was decided (1) by review of the historical development of the field in the twentieth century; (2) by consideration of the material that has been included in earlier, similar texts; (3) by careful observation of the strong trend that developed in the 1960s in certain quarters, a trend that has swung the pendulum too far in many instances in the direction of the related disciplines (and away from the consideration of our field's professional problems); (4) by review of the recommendations emanating from a variety of conferences devoted to undergraduate and graduate curricular analysis; and (5) by conjoint effort of the editor and the late Laura J. Huelster (who played a key role in many of these conferences and who along with the editor observed the occurrences of the past few decades with increasing concern).

In any analysis of this emerging field that traces the developments of the twentieth century, three categories or subdivisions of the field should be investigated: (1) the growing and potential body of knowledge being created by researchers and scholars drawing upon research methods and techniques of the *subdisciplinary areas;* (2) the similar development of knowledge emanating from the *concurrent professional components* of the developing field (as exist in all subject-matter fields to a greater or lesser extent); and (3) the knowledge becoming available from what may be called the *allied professions* (as may exist also in other emerging fields).

In this text, therefore, after a prologue in which the urgent need for a social relevance perspective for physical education and kinesiology is explained, the Editor presents an introductory chapter explaining the background, present status, and intercultural significance of the field in North America for which this present volume was designed. Then seven additional chapters are presented, all eight of which (together) offer succinct delineations of the fundamental subdisciplinary areas of the field as explained in Table 1 above. James S. Skinner discusses the Functional Effects of Physical Activity; A. V. Carron, the Social Psychological Aspects; Susan L. Greendorfer, the Sociocultural Aspects; Michael G. Wade, Motor Behavior; Glynn A. Leyshon, The Human Locomotor System; and Marion J. L. Alexander, Biomechanics: The Mechanics of Human Movement.

The last three chapters explain the various concurrent, subsumed professional components: Daniel G. Soucie discusses Management Theory and Practice; Ann E. Jewett, Curriculum Theory & Program Development; and B. Don Franks, Measurement and Evaluation. The editor offers a final prologue that summarizes, draws some obvious conclusions, and looks to the future.

In concluding these prefatory remarks, I want to remember and express continued appreciation to the late Dr. Laura Huelster (Illinois, Champaign-Urbana) for her ongoing encouragement and for the emphasis placed on the need for the profession's growth in a peaceful world. I wish to acknowledge further her assistance with the development of the proposed taxonomy for the profession and its body of knowledge used in the development of this text. I also want to express my gratitude and deep appreciation to the scholars who have contributed chapters to this volume. It should be made clear that these people have been selected because they are excellent physical educators and kinesiologists and are not necessarily a group of people reflecting the philosophical stance held by the editor. They are all outstanding scholars and outstanding professionals who are deeply concerned about the future of our field.

I must express gratefully my sincere appreciation and gratitude for the editorial and production assistance of Bob Watts, and the other good and helpful people at the Stipes Publishing Company. My association with them goes back almost 30 years, and it could not have been a better relationship. Anyone who has been in the role of text author knows that it is vitally important to receive excellent guidance and service throughout the entire process. Finally, to my wife, Bert, who reacts intelligently and frankly to my many requests for an "honest opinion." I want to repeat my appreciation and gratitude for such basic assistance dating back to the 1930s.

Earle F. Zeigler
The University of Western Ontario
London, Ontario, Canada N6A 3K7

DEDICATION

Physical education and kinesiology in North America is a profession dedicated to meeting the developmental physical activity needs of people of all ages, be they from normal, special, or accelerated populations. This book is dedicated to all those who envision the profession as a true vocation and who commit themselves to its mission of serving the public through the media of exercise, sport, play, and expressive movement in what we hope will be a free and peaceful world.

Contributors

Marion J. L. Alexander, Ph.D.
Faculty of Physical Education & Recreation Studies
University of Manitoba
Winnipeg, Canada

A. V. Carron, Ed.D., FAAKPE (Intern.)
Faculty of Kinesiology
The University of Western Ontario, Canada

B. Don Franks, Ph.D., FAAKPE
Department of Kinesiology
Louisiana State University, Baton Rouge

Susan L. Greendorfer, Ph.D., FAAKPE
Department of Kinesiology
University of Illinois, Champaign-Urbana

Laura J. Huelster, Ph.D., FAAKPE (deceased)
Department of Kinesiology
University of Illinois, Champaign-Urbana

Ann E. Jewett, Ed.D., FAAKPE
Department of Physical Education & Sport Studies, University of Georgia, Athens

Glynn A. Leyshon, Ph.D.
Faculty of Kinesiology & Department of Anatomy
The Univeristy of Western Ontario
London, Canada

James S. Skinner, Ph.D., FAAKPE
Department of Exercise Science & Physical Education, Arizona State University, Tempe

Daniel G. Soucie, Ph.D.
School of Human Kinetics
University of Ottawa, Canada

Earle F. Zeigler, Ph.D., LL.D., FAAKPE
Faculty of Kinesiology
The University of Western Ontario
London, Canada

CONTENTS

Prologue

A Social Relevance Perspective for Physical Education and Kinesiology

Earle F. Zeigler
Laura J. Huelster (dec.)

(*Editor's Note:* Many of the thoughts and ideas expressed in this prologue are those of the late Laura J. Huelster, Ph.D., FAAKPE. Accordingly, it is dedicated to Professor Huelster, University of Illinois, Champaign-Urbana, a friend, colleague, and professional leader who believed and worked for the theme underlying this prologue and the ideas expressed in this text.)

The world has become so threatening that all professions should now work assiduously to make a contribution toward the goal of world peace. Keeping in mind that bona fide professions have historically developed codes of ethics which included an obligation to work for both the public good and that of the profession, this clearly means that the sport and physical education profession has an obligation to foster and maintain societal values.

> The late Laura J. Huelster (1982, p. 1) pointed out that, . . . the survival of our society is threatened unless there is fitness to live the quality of life that deemphasizes war and promotes peaceful solutions to national and international social, economic, and political conflicts. . . .

She argued further that general education should include knowledge about the conditions of human societies that are conducive to minimizing wars and maximizing peace. Huelster stressed additionally that a willingness to accept and act upon that knowledge depends not only upon convincing evidence, but also upon having attitudes and ideologies that are compatible with it.

What should be included in general education should undoubtedly be reflected in professional education as well. This is apparent because the highly threatening world situation makes us aware of the urgent need for a practical response so that future generations will possess both the knowledge and the accompanying attitudes to bring about a peaceful, productive state in the world.

HOW CAN WE HELP WITH THE PROMOTION OF A TREND?

How can we as one profession, therefore, a professional field known now as sport and physical education in the United States (and as physical and health education in Canada), proceed to join in with any trend leading to such a future state? This question becomes poignantly vital when we appreciate that the need for such a condition of worldwide "social-self-realization" (Brameld, 1956, p. 272) is evidently not yet fully appreciated by a majority of the world population. When Naisbitt (1982) in his fascinating *Megatrends* explained that he and his Group have determined through research that 10 "new directions are transforming the lives" of people in the United States, the urgency of a vigorous quest for peace was seemingly not evident. The research technique employed by Naisbitt was that of monitoring selected publications carefully throughout the world to determine future trends. For example, this research pointed out that the United States was moving rapidly from an industrial society to an information society (pp. 11–38). Interestingly, however, as he postulated future trends for living, *there is no mention made of a trend toward the pursuit of world peace* so that this wonderful dream of an even better future *can* indeed be realized! Even in *Megatrends 2000* (1990), Naisbitt and Aburdene haven't found sufficient evidence of a strong quest for peace on the part of humankind. They do state, however, that,

> The 1990's present a new world view. The cold war ended in the last years of the 1980's, and the arms race has been slowed, perhaps even halted. The postwar period of nationalism and ideological cold war is over, and a new era of globalization has begun. . . . (p. 14).

These are optimistic sentiments, of course, but keep in mind that this book appeared before the almost unbelievable developments in eastern Europe with the USSR, the Gulf War crisis caused by Iraq's harsh conquest of Kuwait, and Yugoslavia's "ethnic-cleansing" period.

We must understand, of course, that the sport and physical education profession would assuredly not be alone if it were to move forthrightly in this direction both within the educational system and in the larger society where public and private programs of sport, exercise, and physical recreation are sponsored. For example, there exists already a group called "Concerned Philosophers for Peace" within the American Philosophical Association that in April, 1988 sponsored a joint meeting with another group named International Philosophers for the Prevention of Nuclear Omnicide in Cincinnati, Ohio. In a paper made available earlier (1983), Allen explained the situation as "Either/Or: How Should Philosophers Respond to the Threat of Nuclear War and the Arms

Race?" He was quite correct with his question to his colleagues, and we in the sport and physical education profession also face an either/or situation. *Either* we accept the challenge to respond to this unique, potentially devastating world situation, *or* we continue as usual with our programs of promoting *physical* fitness and presumably *positive* aggression in highly competitive sport (which somehow often emerges as *negative* aggression).

INTERRELATED ASSUMPTIONS FORMING THE THEORY

Based on the assumptions, therefore, (1) that unrestrained aggression in the world and potential nuclear devastation is forcing us to reconstruct our social environment, (2) that rational plans for peaceful resolution of conflicts are available that can move nations from ongoing wars to peaceful resolution of disputes, (3) that societies have before and can presently change their values, institutions and systems, and (4) that a *will for peace* will depend on the people's desire for it because of the attitudes, ideologies, and behaviors inculcated as they mature, Huelster (1982, p. 2) has provided us with a logical, sequential rationale that, if adopted, could lead or guide the profession toward a considerable re-orientation of its recommended program. By this we mean that the knowledge, competencies, and skills promoted in developmental physical activity in sport, exercise, and related expressive activities could well be re-arranged to offer quite different input, thruput, and output resulting in a markedly different product at the delivery stage.

In regard to Assumption No. 2 immediately above—that rational plans for peaceful resolution of conflicts are available—one example was recommended in the Special Session on Disarmament held by the United Nations in the late 1970s. Representatives of 149 nations adopted a set of principles for international disarmament strategy. There were recommendations for balanced and gradual reductions of armaments with the recommendation that the money saved be directed to the establishment of an international peace force and for the promotion of the well-being of people everywhere. In retrospect, we ask, "Why did this plan fail?" The answer is that leaders from the now-divided USSR and the USA were elsewhere at that very moment agreeing to a three percent increase in armaments! Today we can breathe a slight sigh of relief because these two "superpowers" are indeed involved in negotiations leading to massive disarmament. Of course, a cynic would argue that the underlying reason for such moves is more economic than ideological.

We appreciate that significant social changes do not come about overnight (Assumption No. 3 immediately above). For example, for thousands of years, slavery had been an accepted social practice throughout the world. When ancient Athens was in its so-called Golden Age, the population of the city was about

300,000—*260,000 slaves* and *40,000* freemen! And it was only a little more than 100 years ago that the U.S.A. had its Civil War, and even today racial prejudice still prevails in many quarters. Look further at the improving, but still terrible, situation in South Africa right now. However, overall *changes have been made,* and we must continue to work for a more wholesome world culture in all regards—although we do understand that progress has never been a straight-line affair.

Assumption No. 4 above is a truly difficult one to bring about—the assumption that a will for peace will depend on the people's desire for it because of the attitudes, ideologies, and behaviors inculcated as they mature. In his investigations on this subject, Eckhardt (1972) measured personality traits and social attitudes with the finding that dominant factors were compassion (loving, merciful drives) and compulsion (cruel, merciless drives). Love appears to be the fundamental ingredient of compassion, whereas hate is the feeling basic to compulsion. Building on Eckhardt's research, Alcock (1976) discovered that most of his subjects highly desired happiness and a world at peace, and further that honesty and courage would be needed to attain these goals. Huelster (1982, p. 10) summarized what this all adds up to as follows:

> Those among us who want to promote peace apparently need to confront and correct imbalances and inconsistencies in our *compassionate* attitudes and behaviors. We would need to promote conditions to minimize war by the nonviolent means of knowing the conditions for peace, and taking stands on them through petitions, demonstrations, and supporting legislation on disarmament and economic and political justice. We would also need to commit ourselves to the related problems of reducing populations, improving the welfare of the poor and the oppressed, and improving our ecology. Increased people-power is needed to pressure political leaders to take national and foreign actions in support of enduring peace.

This is obviously going to be extremely difficult to bring to pass in the United States and Canada at this time, not to mention in other sections of the world. Further, we in the profession of sport and physical education—especially the men—are going to "swallow mighty hard" before we put ourselves on the line for a futuristic, noncombative orientation such as this statement implies is necessary. Yet, does this evident fact mean that we shouldn't try to bring about change?

GENERAL EDUCATION FOR PEACE

One would think that a *fifth assumption* (No. 5), the idea of "general education for peace," would be relatively simple to introduce into the educational system. However, such will probably not be the case. There has been a tradition of keeping organized religion out of public institutions, and this separation of church and state is undoubtedly a good thing. However, the end result has been unfortunate from one standpoint: we have resultantly and concurrently kept discussions of ethics and moral values out of the schools and universities as well. We worship the god of value-free science that provides knowledge in the form of scientific facts that presumably adds up to improved living and a higher level of technology. But, we might ask, what good is all of this value-free knowledge going to do us if we end up with a desolate planet characterized overwhelmingly by radiation and nuclear fall-out? Thus, it would appear that we need both, what we call *value-free knowledge* and also what might be called *value-prone knowledge.* The former will give us the knowledge upon which we can call prior to the making of value-oriented decisions—decisions that some day may provide a high quality of life for all people everywhere!

What this adds up to is that a steady, strong theme will have to be injected into our entire general education program right up through the second year of university at least. This will be difficult to bring about right now when the hue and cry is for higher test scores, ratings that designate achievement levels in language, reasoning, conceptual, and mathematical skills. Also, there is no doubt but that the concept of "general education" is in the doldrums because of the overriding demand for professional knowledge, competencies, and skills to be used in a high-paying position. As I see it, advocates of liberal arts and science curricula would be well advised to stress, and then measure the attainment of, the general and specific life competencies that their general education programs produce.

EXPERIENCES BASIC TO PEACE IN THE SPORT AND PHYSICAL EDUCATION PROGRAM

A *sixth assumption* (No. 6) should be consideration of our role both (1) within our general education program and (2) within our professional preparation efforts for people who will subsequently "profess" developmental physical activity in sport, exercise, and related expressive activities for all people of all ages and conditions both within schools and universities and in the society at large. Providing experiences basic to peace in the sport and physical activity program—here is really where the "going will really get rough." (Once again, we believe that this will be more difficult with the men than with the women in our field.) How indeed are we going to promote personal and social traits leading more in the direction of *compassion* and considerably less in the direction of *compulsion* as explained by Eckhardt and Alcock above? This will be especially difficult in highly competitive sport for men, and now will also be quite difficult for women too. It may be a bit easier in Canada than in the United States—with the exception of Canada's national sport, ice hockey. In that instance the name of the game has been INTIMIDATION and VIOLENCE (with all letters capitalized)! To make matters worse, it is so obvious that even a recent beer advertisement (Karlsberg) jokes about the fact that we have exported this violent North American style of play to the rest of the world!

Our problem appears to be that we—undoubtedly strongly influenced by social forces, of course—have let so much of this get out of hand. Highly competitive sport, as now practiced at all levels in North America, amateur, semiprofessional, and professional, has increasingly become our momentary substitute activity as we seemingly move ahead to eventual warfare on a grand scale. We are presently functioning in competitive sport with an operational philosophy that daily promotes and rewards the following type of statements, questions, and actions: "get him before he gets you"; "the watchword is *intimidation*"; "call on the good foul when you need it to win"; "isn't it thrilling to watch the 'black gladiators' in the basketball arena and on the gridiron?"' "the hell with the spirit of the rules"; "drugs and doping are necessary to achieve superior performance and *win*"; "it is okay to cheat so long as you are not caught"; "winning may not be the only thing, but it beats the hell out of whatever comes next"; and so on *ad infinitum.*

As a former athlete and coach of three sports, the author wants to win just as much as the next fellow, and perhaps a bit more. He doesn't like "good losers" in sport or in the rest of life—that is, people who give every evidence of not much caring about the struggle or the quest for "the good life," one way or the other. However, even this professional is finding himself increasingly turned off by what occurs so often in competitive sport. Yet one can become extremely happy, almost ecstatic, because there is a Wayne Gretzky in professional hockey and an Isiah Thomas in professional basketball, for example. As Metheny (1965, pp. 41–42) sought to explain, what we should be promoting above all is the concept of "the good strife" rather than the "bad strife" examples we see around us every day.

Paradoxically, the word "competition" literally means to strive *with* rather than *against* according to the established letter and spirit of the rules. Even the word "contest" has a similar implication. It means to *testify with another* rather than *against* him or her. We need to arrange our competitions so that both the winners and the losers in a "good strife" gain from the experience. They have tested "themselves within the rules by doing their best against opponents who also did their best" (Huelster, 1982, p. 17). Competition characterized by "good strife" remains the ideal for which we should be striving.

And so we can still argue idealistically that highly competitive intercollegiate and interscholastic athletics can be justified inside the realm of sport and physical education if—and this is a very big IF!—positive educational goals characterize the good strife. The late Laura Huelster reluctantly disagreed with this position (1982, p. 17). She agreed that it might still be possible in Canadian inter-university sport, but that it is much less so in the United States—and particularly so in the top 100–150 universities who rely so heavily on gate receipts to maintain their enterprises. As she stated:

> Pressures from alumni and university communities to have winning teams is at the point at which success in recruitment of superathletes determines the amount of financial support in grants-in-aid funds, and there is little freedom for recruited athletes to make curricular choices. It is increasingly being realized by universities that their athletic systems have little to do with their educational systems.

She even recalled an earlier statement (p. 17) where Zeigler had argued that, "in the classification of athletics in the continuum of *players,* from amateurs to semiprofessionals to professional athletic *workers,* it is undoubtedly true that intercollegiate athletes in football and basketball in the U.S.A. can be classified as semiprofessionals" (1979, p. 204). Thus, we are forced to ask rhetorically, "What *should* we do?" "What *must* we do in light of the world situation?" "What *can* we do in the final analysis?"

THE POSSIBLE FUTURE SITUATION

What *can* we do "in the final analysis?" A relatively few professionals are moving in Dr. Huelster's direction on this point, but are not yet ready to concur with her that, "except for the basic sport skills in SPE programs, highly competitive athletics should be outside the realm of SPE . . ." (p. 17). Perhaps it is inevitable that it will end up that way in our educational system, but there are many who still feel that *we should and must work for* "the good strife" in competitive sport at all levels from children's competitions to the Olympic Games and even professional sport (is there a still difference here between the last two named?). However, time is running out on the United States, and Canada seems to be "inclining" similarly because the trend toward *compulsive* attitudes and behaviors is outstripping any efforts in the direction of promoting what Eckhardt and Alcock called *compassionate* attitudes and behaviors in the world social structure—and this appears to be especially true in highly competitive sport.

As members of the established profession (NASPE) in the United States—the situation is significantly better in Canada—we should not continue to "run away" from highly competitive sport. When the issue was raised at an international meeting recently, the writer was told, "We don't have any problem with intercollegiate sport on our campus; they're over there!" The immediate reaction should be to ask, "What are *we* doing over there? Isn't sport an integral part of the "life blood" of our field?" However, this splintering is what has happened on what may be called the "worst" campuses. The sport and physical education unit, now employing a variety of presumably academically sounding titles (e.g., kinesiology, human kinetics, sport and exercise science), has completely disassociated itself from competitive sport—and that's the way they both like it, but for different reasons.

One approach that an honorable, courageous profession could employ to reverse the prevailing situation, including the trend toward separate educational units and facilities, is to meet the matter directly by "declaring itself in" on the struggle to improve the quality of experience that is taking place in all parts of the program that we are offering in developmental physical activity. We should state boldly—when and where such a condition exists—that highly competitive sport has become so excessive and corrupt that it is actually perverting society. We should be joining forces with others on campus and in the community who want competitive sport to help us achieve true educational goals—not pervert them and society in the bargain. When the time has arrived that intercollegiate sport can topple university presidents and governors, we know that the time has come for the people to speak—if it isn't already too late.

And now, to move this argument up a notch to the level of Olympic sport, the appointment by Olympic officials of George Steinbrenner of the New York Yankees, for example, to straighten out some of their troublesome problems relative to drug issues and human relations is evidence of the lack of solid, constructive leadership at the upper levels of this phase of competitive sport in the United States. Steinbrenner unfortunately has set a continuing example of how not to administer sport—avowed professional or otherwise—and how not to deal with athletes and coaches at any level! (See "Playboy Interview: George Steinbrenner," <May 1991> *Playboy,* 38, 5:63–80, 171 for an enlightening discussion of Mr. Steinbrenner's philosophy of life and sport.)

We all understand that the compulsive-competitive elements in sport and physical education have steadily assumed a more primary role in the program, whereas it is the compassionate-cooperative qualities that need development if we hope to have an influence and perhaps bring about a change in people's attitudes and behavior leading to less social strife at home and enduring peace on an international level. Unfortunately, however, this would typically be *a new social approach* for our profession. There has been an effort by some to adapt older games so that they become newer, more cooperative contests with no losers and games where collective scores are kept (Orlick, 1978, pp. 159–175). However, we can readily understand that making activities such as this popular will be an uphill struggle with both members of the profession and most of our students or clients.

There seems to be no other way to get at this problem, however, other than by (1) selecting a wider body of activities of an individual and dual nature where *cooperative effort* is stressed more than *competition,* and (2) doing everything in our power to lessen the *aggressive behaviors* so evident in many of our team sports, while at the same time rewarding behavior that evidences fair play, sportsmanship, and living up to the spirit (as well as the letter) of the rules. In other words, we need lesson and coaching plans and teaching strategies that will emphasize and possibly heighten the compassionate attitudes and behaviors toward oneself and the people with whom one is playing. For example, even in Canadian hockey the teams line up after a game and shake hands and exchange a few words with members of the other team. Why couldn't that become a common practice in all competitive sport starting with the "collision" sports such as football, wrestling, and (now even) basketball?

Our North American (largely U.S.A.) "mentality" and attitudes in competitive sport could well be compared with some of the non-aggressive attitudes and behaviors displayed in selected other countries from an international standpoint (e.g., the "friendship approach" evident earlier in China). On the other hand, not so very long ago the ex-British Prime Minister Margaret Thatcher felt constrained to call for an urgent report on ongoing weekend violence by British soccer fans in Stuttgart, Federal Republic of Germany, amid a new wave of anger and shame at the notorious behavior of the country's soccer fans abroad (*The London <Ontario> Free Press,* June 14, 1988, p. C2). The important idea to keep in mind, of course, is that we *don't continue to export our aggressiveness* as happened, for example, with our forcing European countries and the USSR to employ violence and intimidation when they played hockey against us. There are some hopeful signs even here, however, as evidenced by the 1988 action taken by the Ontario Minor Hockey Association toward eliminating violent checking into the boards in hockey, a practice that has too often resulted in very serious neck and spinal injuries to young players (*The London <Ontario> Free Press,* June 14, 1988, p. A1).

SPECIFIC PROGRAM RECOMMENDATIONS FOR SPORT AND PHYSICAL EDUCATION

Keeping in mind (1) that our program should be directed to developmental physical activity in sport, exercise, and related expressive activities for people of all ages and conditions, and (2) that there is an urgent need to elevate compassionate-cooperative behavior to a level never deemed necessary before while discouraging and downplaying excessive violence, intimidation, unsportsmanlike conduct, and ignoring the spirit of the rules, what specific recommendations can be made at this time? Building on and adapting the tentative "principles," recommended by Huelster (1982, p. 19), the following recommendations are offered for serious consideration:

1. We should stress continually the cooperative elements and the need for more cooperative play in competitive games and sports.
2. We should reward through a variety of forms of recognition those who epitomize the qualities of fair play and sportsmanship that we wish to encourage.
3. We should make every effort to cope with overly aggressive competitive behaviors by redirecting them into more responsible cooperative ones. (In this regard, the profession should be exerting direct pressure on rules-making bodies to make sincere efforts to eliminate undue violence and aggression from their sports.)
4. We should insert the concept of "individual freedom" to a much greater extent in sport and physical education programs by encouraging students to select freely the motor skills and play forms they want to learn. (Understand that this recommendation does not apply to the student who seemingly doesn't want to be involved and possibly thereby improve his/her quality of life by developing such knowledge and competency.)
5. We should broaden program offerings to include more basic and exploratory motor skills such as (a) exercise patterns for physiological and/or psychological benefits, (b) body mechanics and relaxation techniques, (c) swimming and water safety knowledge and techniques, (d) lifetime individual and dual sports, (e) risk sports, and (f) expressive movement activities including folk, social, and modern dance.
6. We should, while developing such program offerings as in No. 5 above, use teaching and coaching strategies involving task-setting and problem-solving whenever appropriate. In the process, we should help students and clients to set performance-attainment goals beyond their expectations so as to promote the development of self-confidence.

CONCLUDING STATEMENT

There are many social forces or influences which have become persistent historical problems that impact upon society and education directly (Zeigler, 1988, pp. 255–292). These problems are identified as (1) the influence of values and norms, (2) the type of political state, (3) the influence of nationalism, (4) the influence of economics, (5) the impact of organized religion, and (6) the need for ecological awareness. Recently Zeigler added two more social forces to the growing list of persistent problems: (7) the impact of science and technology, and (8) the need for a search for world peace.

It will be inordinately difficult to convince the sport and physical education profession to follow enthusiastically the recommendations that have been made here. It will be especially difficult to persuade the many sport coaches to do not identify primarily with the organized sport and physical education profession. Nevertheless, the goal of improved international understanding and eventual world peace is so vital, so all-compassing as we think of present trends and what may happen in the twenty-first century, that we should all think this subject through for ourselves with great care. As so often seems to be the case, we can't simply leave it to the other fellow to do this for us. We must work and strive freely, consciously, and openly as true professionals to employ sport and related physical activity serving humankind. Any other choice is unthinkable.

REFERENCES

ALCOCK, N. Z. (1976). *The logic of love.* Oakville, ON: Canadian Peace Research Press.

ALLEN, PAUL III. (1983). Either/or: How should philosophers respond to the threat of nuclear war and the arms race? Unpublished paper made available at the annual meeting of the American Philosophical Association, Boston, MA, Dec. 28–29.

AMERICAN PHILOSOPHICAL ASSOCIATION. (1988). *Proceedings and addresses of The American Philosophical Association,* D. A. Hoekema, (Ed.). Newark, DE: Univ. of Delaware for the APA.

BRAMELD, T. (1956). *Toward a reconstructed philosophy of education.* NY: Dryden Press.

CRESSMAN, J. (1988, June 14). Minor hockey gets tough on boarding. *The London Free Press,* p. 1.

VIOLENCE ALARMS THATCHER. (1988, June 14). *The London Free Press,* p. C2.

ECKHARDT, W. (1972). *Compassion: Toward a science of value.* Oakville, ON: Canadian Peace Research Institute Press.

HUELSTER, L. J. (1982). Social relevance perspective for sport and physical education. In *Physical education and sport: An introduction* (E. F. Zeigler, Ed. & Au.). (pp. 1–22). Philadelphia, PA: Lea & Febiger.

METHENY, E. (1965). *Connotations of movement in sport and dance.* Dubuque, IA: W. C. Brown.

NAISBITT, J. (1982). *Megatrends: Ten new directions transforming our lives.* NY: Warner Books.

NAISBITT, J. & ABURDENE, P. (1990). *Megatrends 2000: Ten new directions for the 1990's.* NY: Wm. Morrow.

ORLICK, T. (1978). *Winning through cooperation: Competitive insanity—cooperative alternative.* Washington, DC: Acropolis Books.

PLAYBOY INTERVIEW: GEORGE STEINBRENNER. (May 1991). *Playboy,* 38, 5:63–80, 171.

ZEIGLER, E. F. (1979). *Issues in North American sport and physical education.* Washington, DC: American Alliance for Health, Physical Education, Recreation, and Dance.

ZEIGLER, E. F. (Ed. & Au.). (1988). *History of physical education and sport* (Rev. ed.). Champaign, IL: Stipes Publishing Co.

A POSTSCRIPT

Choosing a Career—Speaking Generally

If you are reading these words, you have probably already chosen a career in the profession of sport and physical education—or are thinking very seriously about it. We who wrote this foundations text are vitally concerned with helping to promote the optimum development of this field. Now I (as editor of this text) will ask you to spend a few moments reviewing at least some of the reasons why you may have expressed an interest in what I now refer to as physical education and kinesiology (or developmental physical activity in sport, exercise, and related expressive activities).

With a topic such as career selection, we encounter a great deal of confusion on the part of many different people, students included. Society is steadily becoming more complex with greater role differentiation. It has been estimated that there are 20,000 to 25,000 different occupations from which a person could conceivably choose. We are told, however, that young people are often reluctant to choose some of the newer occupations (e.g., ecology, ethnology, city planning). Why is this so? Lack of information? Insufficient courage? Pressure by parents or friends? Influence of the media? Unwillingness to accept a lifestyle that has not been experienced previously? It is difficult to respond to this question, but my own pet theory is that people tend to follow what they feel is the tried-and-true route because they are not provided with enough opportunity in advance to "stick their necks out without getting their heads chopped off" (adapted from Zeigler, 1990).

Each decade seems to bring about a change in emphasis, a reordering of priorities, a difference in approach on the part of students. At one point individualism seemed to be in vogue, and then there seemed to be a greater trend toward conformity and a desire to choose the generally accepted occupations. Upward of 50 percent of college students when asked are undecided. I typically ask new students in an introductory course to write down what they expect to be doing with their life 10 years hence, and I get the wildest answers from a significant percentage of them and rather stereotyped answers from the rest. This bothers me considerably, but it is difficult to know what to do about the ideas and attitudes that seem to prevail.

I cannot escape the feeling that students are not particularly excited about their careers. However, they do seem to be really concerned about the type of lifestyle they are going to be able to afford. A few students want to "find themselves," but many more seem to fit into a continuing pattern from the mid-1970s and 1980s—a period when young people usually early on became part of the "me generation." "How much will I make at the job?" "What are the hours?" "How long must I go to school to be able to qualify?" I often get the idea that a young person wants to start at the top and work up! And then there is the question that many interviewers dread when a young person is being interviewed early in his or her career. "What kind of a pension plan does this organization have?"

Some young people want a lifestyle, while others want to find meaning in their work. Some are anti-business, while others want to make the most money as soon as possible. Some are really eager to enter a profession, and others are just looking for a job. Some want to perform a public service, but others are not interested in helping their fellow humans. Some want hard science-oriented programs, while others lean to the social sciences and humanities. Some are realistic in the everyday sense, whereas others are (non-philosophical) idealists of the first order. Some want to be generalists; others are inclined toward specialization as soon as possible. Some have distorted ideas of reality, but others have had "hard slugging" for a number of years already. All in all, what we find is interesting but also quite disturbing to those who have already found their purpose in life. (Far too few have really developed a life purpose to which they are passionately committed!) Perhaps counselors should not worry. Maybe it is wise to shop around a bit. We used to say, "Try it out; after all, you're not marrying the job" (the latter clause implying a sense of finality and permanence that seems to have vanished in today's world).

Choosing a Career—Speaking Specifically

A person who is thinking carefully about choosing an occupation or career should make an effort to examine the proposed field under certain categories or subheadings: (1) definition of the occupation, (2) history and importance, (3) nature of the work, (4) working conditions, (5) qualifications necessary for entry and success, (6) preparation needed, (7) opportunities for advancement, (8) remuneration and security, (9) advantages, (10) disadvantages, (11) how to get started toward the occupation, and (12) related or allied organizations. Quite obviously, the entire book could be filled with extensive discussions of each of these categories and appropriate related questions. I do not intend to follow such an approach, however, because there is so much basic material about the past, present, and possible future of the profession that must be covered. I do urge, nevertheless, that several class periods be assigned to discuss at some length the various questions that are raised below. The reader will appreciate that the answers to these many questions will vary and perhaps change often, depending upon the state or province in which a discussion takes place. Some of the answers are self-evident, whereas others will require more specialized knowledge, a reasonable amount of which your instructor will most assuredly possess. There is definite value in asking representative members of the sport and physical education profession to make brief presentations to the class about their particular position, and this can be followed by a question-and-answer period. (At this point I must express appreciation to my colleagues over the years, notably people in both the sport and physical education profession and the recreation profession, who have contributed many ideas to this type of class procedure.) The following questions (and others) should be considered under the categories presented above:

Definition of the Occupation. Sport and physical education is a profession where qualified, professionally trained personnel, either within the educational system or in society at large, help people of all ages and conditions to become involved with developmental physical activity in sport, exercise, and related expressive activities. That sentence is quite a mouthful, I confess; so I ask you, "Do you feel that you presently have a good idea of what the profession of sport and physical education is all about? (If not, please read Chapter 1, the introductory chapter immediately following, right now and return to the questions in this category.) Has the prevailing confusion about terminology disturbed you? Considering the specific purposes for which we are (and should be) preparing men and women, where do you think you would fit best? Does this thought appeal to you?

History and Importance. What do you know about the history of sport and physical education generally, and what do you know specifically about what has been happening in the 20th century here in North America? (If you feel inadequate here, please read Chapters 1 and 3 before proceeding—and perhaps the Epilogue.) How does this profession serve society? Is it ultimately important? How many people, male and female, are employed in this field locally, statewide or provincially, regionally, and nationally? Is the number involved increasing or decreasing? Is there a wide geographical distribution of workers involved in the field?

Nature of the Work. What does a person involved in the various aspects of the profession do (in each of the following areas listed)? As a teacher? As a coach? As an administrator/manager? As a gifted performer? As a fitness specialist in industry? As a camp director? As a sports information director? As an aquatics specialist? As a sport and physical education consultant? As a government specialist? As a university professor? As a scholar and researcher? (The list is almost endless; name some other specializations that you know.) Consider a typical day of one of the above. How much time is spent in physical activity? How much time might involve so-called mental activity? Or both combined? Is the work highly repetitive, or is it varied? Is the work stimulating, or is it boring? Are there (a reasonable number of) new problems or challenges to solve?

Working Conditions. Is the work carried on indoors or outdoors? Are you sitting or standing most of the time? Are the working conditions generally sanitary? How many hours do you work (daily, weekly, annually)? At what time of day? Do you always work with others, or is some of work done alone? What kind of fellow workers will you have? Are the work itself and the working conditions well organized? Are there hazards to you or others? Do you and your fellow workers belong to one or more professional organizations or societies? What purposes do they serve? Does the profession have a creed? A code of ethics? What are the opportunities for recreation, for vacation?

Qualifications Necessary for Entry and Success. What physical qualities are necessary for the profession—strength, endurance, coordination, flexibility, height, weight, good hearing, good eyesight, etc.? What degree of intelligence is needed? Does this vary within different types of specialization within the profession? Is a high level of emotional stability required? What other personality traits are desirable or required—initiative, persistence, leadership, willingness to cooperate, etc.? Are there any special aptitudes or attributes required?

Preparation Needed. What general education and specialized professional preparation are necessary or desirable? How can you discover the best colleges and universities from which to obtain undergraduate and/or graduate preparation? Is an internship or apprenticeship necessary or desirable? What university degrees will you need now or in the future to be fully qualified? Approximately how much money will all of this cost? Are scholarships and/or fellowships available for those with high academic qualifications, for those with exceptional athletic ability, and for those students with bona fide financial need? Where can you find out about such scholarships/fellowships and other information? Will you need any special equipment to get started in this occupation (either at university or after graduation)?

Opportunities for Advancement. What types of positions are available for teachers, coaches, performers, administrators, supervisors, teachers of teachers or coaches or both, scholars and researchers, an alternate career opportunity (such as sports business management, aquatics director, athletic specialist, camp director, sports author, sports artist, etc.)? At what age do you enter any of these occupations? How do you go about entering them? Which of these are blind-alley occupations in the sense that advancement possibilities are limited? If there are levels of advancement in one or more of these occupations, how long must be spent typically at the various levels? Does a particular specialization within the field seem to be overcrowded? Is the entire field overcrowded? In which of these positions will there be an opportunity for supervisory or managerial responsibility (perhaps after a period of service)?

Remuneration and Security. What annual earning may you expect at first at any of these positions? When you become experienced, what are the average annual earnings? What is the range of salary you might expect? Which of these positions can you remain with for your entire life? How often are you paid (weekly, monthly, etc.)? What provisions are there for pensions and possible early retirement? What other compensations are there (i.e., life insurance, dental insurance, unemployment insurance, bonuses, illness or disability benefits, vacation periods, etc.)?

Advantages. In connection with one or more of the occupations listed above, what would you say are the main *advantages* of this position (e.g., service to mankind, salary, working conditions, opportunities for advancement)?

Disadvantages. In connection with one or more of the occupations listed above, what would you say are the main *disadvantages* of this position (e.g., salary, repetition of duties, working conditions, period of professional preparation, status of the profession)?

How to Get Started toward the Occupation. Which subject-matter areas are vital for background prior to specialized professional preparation for one or more of these occupations? Are there hobbies and other activities that would help to prepare you for such involvement? Is there part-time or summer employment that would help prepare you? What type of extra reading might be of assistance in strengthening your background?

Related or Allied Occupations. If it turns out that you become interested in looking elsewhere for your occupation, what other professions are similar with respect to the nature of the work (e.g., health education, safety education, driver education, related disciplines, recreation management, park administration)? Are the working conditions of any of these markedly different? What differences are there in regard to personal qualifications (e.g., recreation director)? What differences are there in regard to professional preparation (e.g., health education)? Finally, if you do not complete the entire period of professional preparation required for full acceptance for one or more of these positions, what opportunities are there for those with lesser qualifications?

Concluding Statement. In this postscript to the prologue, you, the reader, were asked to consider (or perhaps reconsider) the bases upon which you may have tentatively chosen your career. You were asked to respond, and perhaps discuss with your peers and the class instructor, your and their reactions to a great many general and specific questions. With these experiences behind you, you are now ready to move ahead to a full introduction to the professional and scholarly foundations of physical education and kinesiology in North America. If you finally decide to cast your lot with us to work for the future development of the profession, we wish you every success. May the journey also be both pleasant and profitable!

Chapter One

Background, Meaning, and Intercultural Significance

Earle F. Zeigler

In this opening chapter the stage will be set for the remainder of this text about the profession of physical education and kinesiology in North America viewed from the standpoint of its professional and scholarly foundations. In the Prologue, based on the inspirational thought of Laura J. Huelster, the urgent need for the profession to adopt a perspective of social relevance was stressed. Now in this chapter we will take a look at the 20th century history of physical education in the U.S.A. largely, with pertinent references to Canada where appropriate. (The term "physical education" will be used generically). We will also seek to say something about the meaning of these developments, as well as to place them briefly in international perspective.

This is an interesting but also a frightening time to be alive. The "future shock" affecting us currently has occasioned strong waves of nostalgia in many people who seem to want the dubious security of the good ol' days. Those days will never return, as we all recognize when we think about this possibility soberly. The task that we face is to prepare ourselves for the complexities of the impending future in the years immediately ahead. Such a recommendation is actually nothing more or less than the philosophical stance known as positive meliorism, a position that affirms that society has an innate tendency to improve and that people should strive consciously to bring about a steadily improving societal condition. To me this makes much more sense than subscribing to either blind optimism or despairing pessimism.

The world has become a much more complicated place during the 20th century, of course, but as we can already see it will become infinitely more complex in the years ahead. Succinctly put, right now the world appears to be divided into three major trading blocs: (1) the Pacific Rim dominated by Japan,

(2) the European Community dominated by Germany, and North America dominated by the United States of America.

THE INTERNATIONAL SCENE

With the dissolution of the Union of Soviet Socialist Republics (USSR), Russia and the remaining communist regimes will be severely challenged as they seek to convert to more of a capitalistic economic system (with "tinges" of socialism thrown in). Additionally, a number of other multinational countries are giving every indication that ethnic strains exist (e.g., Yugoslavia<!>, China, Canada).

Western Europe is facing a demographic time bomb even more than the United States because of the influx of refugees from African and Islamic countries, not to mention refugees from starvation in countries of the former Soviet Union and Africa. It appears that the European Community will be inclined to appease Islam's demands. However, the multinational nature of the European Community will tend to bring on economic protectionism to insulate its economy against the rising costs of prevailing socialist legislation.

We can expect China and Radical Islam to become increasingly aggressive toward the Western culture of Europe and North America. At present, Islam is replacing marxism as the world's main ideology of confrontation. For example, Islam is dedicated to regaining control of Jerusalem and to forcing Israel to give up control of land occupied to provide protection. (China has been arming certain Arab nations, but it is difficult to be too critical in this regard when we recall that the U.S.A. has also been arming selected countries when this was deemed in its interest.) In addition, as Hong Kong is absorbed into Communist China, political problems seem inevitable in the Far East as well. Also, the probability of North Korea building nuclear bombs exacerbates the Pacific Rim situation greatly. Further, there is the ever-present fear that small nations and terrorists will somehow get nuclear weapons too. Finally, a growing Japanese assertiveness in Asian and world affairs seems inevitable because of its extremely strong financial position. Yet the flow of foreign capital from Japan into North America has slowed down somewhat because Japan is being confronted with its own financial crisis caused by inflated real estate and market values. Yet there would be a strong reaction to any fall in living standards there. Interestingly, the Japanese work ethic is being tarnished by the growing attraction of leisure opportunities.

Despite the United Nations, United States-led incursions in the Middle East in the Gulf War and into Somalia for very different reasons and other similar situations on the horizon (e.g., Yugoslavia and Sudan, respectively), there is reason to expect U.S. retrenchment brought on by excessive world involvement and enormous debt that will inevitably lead to a decline in economic and military influence. And yet the evidence points to the strong possibility that the developing nations are becoming ever poorer and more destitute with widespread starvation setting in.

THE NORTH AMERICAN SCENE

Living in the West, it seems that a prevailing concept of cultural relativism will be increasingly discredited as the 1990s witness a sharp clash between (1) those who uphold so-called Western cultural values and (2) those who by their presence are dividing the West along a multitude of ethnic and racial lines. This is occasioning strong efforts to promote fundamentalistic religions and sects characterized typically by decisive right/wrong morality.

The economic situation in North America is creating a great many problems. Massive budget deficits at the national and state levels are creating a fiscal crisis (e.g., California's "IOUs"; Ontario, Canada's "Social Contract"; President Clinton's effort to reduce the massive U.S. deficit). Tax burdens on consumption will cause increased concern throughout North America as debts mount and household wealth declines. As the United States seeks to elevate its health-care standards, citizens will undoubtedly be faced with higher taxes of varying types in an effort to pay the health-care bill and to reduce the national debt at the same time. Canada is also facing serious financial problems with its ballooning national debt and its level of social benefits that are somewhat higher than the United States.

Despite agreements on the subject of what is being called "free trade"—the North American Free Trade Agreement does appear to be needed in the final analysis—unemployment is proving most difficult to bring under control. Protectionism will undoubtedly retard economic free trade. In Canada there isn't even free trade among the various provinces! With NAFTA finally approved, the need for job creation at the governmental level will grow as the seemingly necessary "free trade concept" moves from north to south proceeding from Canada to Mexico. Social entitlements to citizens (e.g., social security, Medicare, Medicaid), including the "welfare state concept" will be challenged severely. These developments all have import for older citizens; retirement at age 65, especially early retirement at 55, may still be available (the "Golden Handshake"), but government, businesses, and people themselves will find it necessary to keep people working longer to pay the requisite taxes to pay all of the bills. And yet the rich are getting richer, and the poor are getting poorer! "Workfare" seems destined for implementation. However, for those who can escape, the migration away from the big cities will continue as infrastructures continue to deteriorate along with rising terrorism and crime rates.

IMPLICATIONS FOR PHYSICAL EDUCATION (KINESIOLOGY)

I have reviewed the international and North American scenes at this point because education at all levels, and physical education in turn, are also facing crises from without and within. The level of support for education is diminishing, and yet at the same time the pressure is on to maintain high academic test scores in comparison with youth from other lands. There is a thrust toward school privatization caused by declining test scores and people's desire to provide safer environments for their children as the breakdown of public order continues. These developments have occasioned a traditionalist or essentialistic philosophy of education to surface more strongly. A "return to essentials" approach is prevailing, especially insofar as the hard sciences and mathematics are concerned.

All of this points indirectly to that fact that our profession will continue to fight an uphill struggle in the years ahead (as it was doing when I entered the field half a century ago!). Well, as we understand, progress is never a straight-line affair, and the pendulum does swing to the right and the left and never seems to stop in the middle. So now, as I am of necessity winding down my years in the field, physical education—and art and music too—are still facing a severe, uphill struggle. Where physical education, for example, once was required, it is now often fighting to remain as an elective offering at many schools, colleges, and universities in various states and provinces. And yet now we also have the evidence that, in addition to enabling a person to live life *more fully,* steady involvement in the right kind of developmental physical activity will help a person to *live longer.*

It will be our professional responsibility and task as our world—this "closed planet" that we call Earth—moves inexorably toward the 21st century to figure out how to best communicate to all people what our professional goals are. Interestingly, the concept of "communication" has now risen in importance to the point at which its significance is paramount if world society as we know it is to continue indefinitely. The late Isaac Asimov told us that, along with the increasing tempo of civilization, a fourth revolution is now upon us. It is a different type of revolution from those we are accustomed to on the basis of history. What is referred to here is the fourth revolution *in the area of communication* that is in certain specific ways making the world a type of global village (1970, pp. 17–20). Moving from (1) the invention of speech to (2) the invention of writing, (3) the mechanical reproduction of the printed word, and now to (4) relay stations in space, all people on earth are being confronted with a blanketing communications network that will make possible personal relationships hitherto undreamed of by our forebears.

This development will have great implications for all levels of education in every country and resultantly will be highly significant for all types of sport, dance, play, and exercise in society. This will place a new urgency on the topic of international and comparative analysis. Such urgency is needed, according to Asimov, because the world is now faced with a race. The race is "between the coming of the true fourth revolution and the death of civilization that will inevitably occur through growth past the limits of the third." Here we are presented with a theory, of course, but there is a warning for us that is startling—we must have vastly improved means of communication and put them into use so effectively that the signs of present breakdown will be eliminated.

We can all understand that our world society is indeed precarious for a variety of reasons—wars, poverty, hunger, disease, technology, disturbance of ecological balance. Nevertheless, here in North America, and in certain other advanced countries in the world, we find ourselves semi-comfortably ensconced in a changing society that has been grounded in the Judeo-Christian view of humanity and nature. This society—and now the entire world appears to be adopting Western world science and technology—tends to function on the basis of a series of what Schwartz (1971, pp. 15–16) called *unstated axioms of science* whose truths are accepted as an act of faith. In these statements he theorized that the universe is orderly, and that this order can be discovered by humans who will gradually learn to express it in mathematical relations and quantities. Although nature may be perceived to a degree through music, art, and poetry, for example, he theorized further that only science will provide the means to master nature through observation and experimentation of observed "facts" independent of the observer. Any secondary qualities observed are not measurable and thus are not real in the same sense.

This Western-world, scientific, and technological assumption is that all things on Earth are here for humankind to discover and use through the employment of reason. As conducted, science should be "neutral, value-free, and independent of morality and ethics." In the process such knowledge will free humans, who are not fundamentally depraved, from "ignorance, superstition, and social ills." Accordingly, in the final analysis, the "good life" on Earth can be both defined and attained by humans using their reason to achieve such status.

A HISTORICAL OVERVIEW OF THE NATURE OF THE HUMAN

Even though we may have arrived at a point at which we are prepared to accept these unstated axioms of science (indicated immediately above) as roughly analogous to those assumptions, theory, or both upon which we are grounding our lives, there is still considerable controversy and confusion concerning a definition of the nature of man and woman on a historical time scale. At approximately the mid-century mark, Morris (1956) presented a fivefold chronological series of definitions, including analyses as (1) a rational animal, (2) a spiritual being, (3) a receptacle of knowledge, (4) a mind that can be trained by practice, and (5) a problem-solving organism. Within such a sequential pattern, the primary function of the field of physical education and kinesiology could well be to help this problem-solving organism move efficiently and with purpose in such aspects of people's lives as sport, play, exercise, and related expressive movement. Such experience would occur, of course, within the context of humans' socialization in an evolving world (Zeigler, 1975, p. 405).

A more comprehensive analysis of the nature of humans was offered a bit later by Berelson and Steiner (1964, pp. 662–667). They traced six images through recorded history more from the standpoint of the behavioral sciences (as compared to Morris's philosophically oriented definitions). The first of these was the so-called *philosophical image* in which the human of the ancient world distinguished virtues through the employment of reason. This was followed by what was termed the *Christian image* in which the concept of "original sin" and possible redemption through the transfiguring image of God was possible for those who controlled their sinful impulses. The third delineation was the *political image* of man and woman during the Renaissance in which the human, through the introduction of power and will, managed to take greater control of the social environment. In the process, sufficient energy was liberated to bring about many political changes, the end result being the creation of embryonic national ideals that coexisted with somewhat earlier religious ideals. During the eighteenth and nineteenth centuries an *economic image* emerged that provided an underlying rationale for the individual's economic development in keeping with the possession of property and personal items along with improved monetary standards. There were early efforts to equate the concept of "individual good" with that of the "common good." At the same time, the third basic political division, that of class, was more sharply delineated and generally understood.

The early twentieth century saw the development of a fifth image, the *psychoanalytic image* that introduced another form of love hitherto largely misunderstood—the ego and self. The instinctual impulses were being delineated more carefully than ever before. An effort was made to understand the role of childhood experiences in people's lives and how these and other nonconscious controls often ruled their actions because of the frequently incomplete gratification of basic human drives related to libido and sex. Finally, because of the rapid development of the behavioral sciences, Berelson and Steiner postulated the *behavioral science image* of man and woman. This view characterized the human being as a creature who is continually and continuously adapting reality to his or her own ends. In this way the individual is seeking to make reality more pleasant and congenial—to the greatest possible extent *his* own or *her* own reality.

THE INFLUENCE OF PIVOTAL SOCIAL FORCES

There have been at least five, and probably six or more, social forces that have influenced the world's cultures for better or worse. Accordingly these social forces have influenced our views regarding the present or potential nature of the human being (Brubacher, 1966; Zeigler, 1977, pp. 6, 20–21). These social forces may be regarded also as persistent historical problems because they have been around since the development of primitive societies, and they will probably be present on into the distant future (or until a utopian state of affairs, perhaps rendering them more or less static in nature, is achieved).

These pivotal social forces, influences that I have also regarded as persistent historical problems to be confronted by societies and their many collectivities, will be described only briefly at this point:

1. *Values and norms.* The persistent problem of values and norms seems to possess a watershed quality in that an understanding of those objects and qualities desired by people through the ages can evidently provide significant insight into this particular problem—and also into most if not all of the other recurring problems that will be discussed. (A problem used in this sense, according to its early Greek derivation, would be "something thrown forward" for humans to understand and possibly resolve.) For example, throughout history there have been innumerable statements of educational aims (or values), and almost invariably there was a direct relationship with a hierarchy of such values present in the society under consideration. As another example, physical education (and kinesiology) has been viewed as curricular, co-curricular, or extra-curricular.
2. *Politics.* The influence of politics, or the type of political state, has affected the kind and amount of education offered in a society. Education has varied, depending upon whether a particular country was a monarchy, an aristocratic oligarchy, or some form of democracy. A philosophically progressivistic educational approach can flourish only in a type of democratic society. Conversely, a philosophically essentialistic or traditionalistic type of education, with its definite implications for physical education, may be promoted successfully in any of the three types of political system.
3. *Nationalism.* The influence of nationalism (or patriotism) on education and on physical fitness and sport is obvious. If a strong state is desired, the need for a strong, healthy people is paramount. There have been many examples of this type of influence as far back as the Medes and Spartans and as recently as many twentieth century European and Asian powers.
4. *Economics.* The influence of economics has been most significant throughout history. The field of education has prospered when there was a surplus economy and declined when the economic structure weakened. Educational aims have tended to vary, depending upon how people made their money and created such

surplus economies. Advancing industrial civilization has brought an uneven distribution of wealth, and this in turn has meant educational advantages of a superior quality for some. Education "of the physical" can be promoted under any type of economic system. In largely agrarian societies considerable physical fitness can be gained simply through manual labor. In industrial (and now in post-industrial societies) some means has to be developed whereby all will maintain at least an "irreducible minimum" level of physical fitness and health. The more individual freedom in a society, the more difficult a government will find it to demand that all citizens, male and female, be physically fit.

5. *Religion.* The influence of organized religion on education has been very strong throughout history, but there is evidence that the power of the church over the individual is continuing to decline in the twentieth century. In the Western world the Christian religion should be recognized for the promulgation of principles in which humans were considered valuables as individuals. Today, however, for several reasons a society must decide to what extent it can or should inculcate moral and/or religious values in its public schools. It seems reasonable to state that Judaism and Christianity have both hampered the fullest development of physical education and sport in modern times and earlier, but it is also true that a number of religious leaders are modifying their earlier positions as they realize the potential of wholesome sport and physical activity as spiritual forces in people's lives.
6. *Ecology.* The influence of ecology has been felt in a recognizable and significant way only since the early 1970s by North American society, so it is understandable that very little attention has been paid to the growing environmental crisis by those in the non-scientific fields in society, including those in social science and humanities disciplines within education and also the field of physical education and kinesiology. Although this problem has not been with us to a similar degree of intensity over the centuries as the five forces listed above, now it is definitely here to stay. Ecology is usually defined as the field of study that treats the relationships and interactions of human beings and other living organisms with each other and with the natural (or physical) environment in which they reside. In this respect the physical educator/kinesiologist has a unique role to play in helping individuals to understand and implement the developing body of knowledge about developmental physical activity into their lives at all stages. In this way our field can make a contribution to "total fitness" based on a goal of international understanding and cooperation.

(Some would argue at this point for the inclusion of other social forces. For example, science and <accompanying> technology, viewed as being complementary, may now be considered a strong social force. Another social force is undoubtedly the yearning for peace in a troubled world beset by innumerable ethnic and religious conflicts presently. <This takes us back to the major theme of the Prologue that was inspired by the deep concern of the late Professor Huelster.> The influence of education on society may also be regarded as a significant social force. More recently, sport itself has mushroomed to a point in this culture at which it too has to be reckoned with as a social force—perhaps too strong a one as we view its recent development with considerable concern.)

THE CLASH BETWEEN ECOLOGY AND ECONOMICS

Because of the urgency of the ecological crisis, it seems wise to highlight this particular persistent problem at this point. It should be made clear that citizens of our North American society especially, whether from the United States, Canada, or Mexico, will very soon be faced with a decision—the need to decide between a continuous-growth economic policy and a no-growth one. Strangely, the political leaders of the three nations don't seem to be aware of the need for such a decision as they move ahead with the North American Free Trade Agreement in an effort to compete economically on a worldwide basis. According to Murray (1972, p. 38), this is simply not an either-or matter.

Unfortunately, however, even today the very large majority of citizens don't have a real understanding about the urgent need for such a decision. Even if they understood that a number of scholars are indeed recommending a no-growth policy, they would probably not believe them anyhow or even pay much heed to their advice. Is the United States, for example, not the land of capitalism and democracy where a steadily increasing gross national product is one of the best indicators of economic prosperity? And are not heavily populated Communist China and Russia and her satellites, for example, not moving in the same direction economically? Citizens are apt to wonder, therefore, if it is simply a case of the optimists saying, "full speed ahead, if we ever hope to reduce unemployment and poverty," and the pessimists responding with the idea that population and economic growth are on a "collision course" with the twenty-first century—that is, they must become steady-state, if it is not already too late. This brings us back to the concept of "positive meliorism" mentioned earlier—a position that would indicate the urgent need for careful investigation of this issue and dilemma along with concomitant awareness of this planet's ecological plight.

Lest the reader think that this situation is being overly dramatized, a further summarizing explanation will be included at this point. It is now almost a quarter of a century past the time when Murray (1972) first issued his warning. He had examined the concepts of "growth," "movement of materials," and "competition" in his comparison of these conflicting models. The ecologist's rule in regard to growth implies that a system will eventually collapse unless it stops growing at some point and recycles; secondly, he is concerned with the biogeochemical cycles operating within nature—the movement within ecosystems for life. Here the serious problem being created by what we call the "modern human" is that both people's food requirements and the demands of the vast technological progress are simply not being recycled in such a way as to sustain even a steady-state situation indefinitely. In other words, the movement of materials is largely in one direction—for the temporary service of the earth's population that has been expanding exponentially.

The other fundamental rule of ecology relates to a third concept of "competition." The implication here is that sooner or later competition excludes some of the competing agencies (or species). This means practically that if two organisms are competing for an exhaustible resource (and which resource is not in a closed system?), one of the competitors will be eliminated by its rival "either by being forced out of the ecosystem or by being forced to use some other resource" (p. 64). Thus, we must ask, for how long can the human race expect to proceed with a basic contradiction between the economic theory explaining that competition is supposed to maintain diversity and stability systems and an opposing theory based on the ecological model described above that has been tested in both natural and laboratory situations?

Other notes of gloom and doom could be sounded at this point, but most of us have heard or read so much by now about local, regional, national, and international problems of greater or lesser magnitude that we are actually beginning to reject such negative information subconsciously. Obviously this could become disastrous before long, especially if all of the grim tidings have not truly alerted us sufficiently and created the motivation to do something right away about the rapidly deteriorating situation. Once again we are faced with the reality of the concept of "positive meliorism"—striving consciously to bring about a steadily improving ecological status in the world. The late Norman Cousins (1974, pp. 6–7) sounded just about the right note with ample volume and clarity when he argued that perhaps "the most important factor in the complex equation of the future is the way the human mind responds to crisis." Citing Toynbee's famous challenge-and-response theory, Cousins asserted further that it is now up to the world culture, and the individual nations and societies within it, to respond positively, intelligently, and strongly to the challenges that are besetting it at the end of the twentieth century. He concluded by declaring that "the biggest task of humanity in the next fifty years will be to prove the experts wrong" (p. 7). Twenty-five years have elapsed since this statement, and the experts haven't been proved wrong yet.

THE STATUS OF EDUCATION

Shifting our focus now from the society in general back to the subject of education in particular—no matter which level you may wish to consider—the reports being received are anything but encouraging. Something seems to have happened to the schools, colleges, and universities (in North America at least), to the learning process that is taking place within them typically. The schools accept that bright-eyed youngster at the age of six years (or sooner), almost invariably eager and ready to learn, and then in so many cases he or she is "turned off," and the desire to learn is quite thoroughly blunted within a few short years. The youngster is indoctrinated into what is, for lack of a better term, called the modern way. This usually involves excessive drill and repetition, competition, speed, dull lectures, tests, quizzes, memorization, numerical grades, mastery of much useless information, and various types of overt and covert discipline. All along the way, a work-hard-to-get-ahead approach is being instilled, the idea being that this will somehow pay off financially when the young adult emerges from the formal educational system at the end of the entire schooling process (if he or she happens to get that far). This will enable the man, woman, or married couple to purchase sooner or later (usually sooner if one listens to the easy credit arrangements with fairly high interest available) all of the good things that presumably characterize a high standard of living.

All of this did indeed add up to one of the highest standards of living in the world—based on acquiring material possessions fashioned in an advanced technological age. The recommended plan for all seems to have been to get an education so that a person can make enough money to achieve this presumed high standard despite the difficulties that have been besetting the North American economy in recent years. Now we are finding that the former "American and Canadian dream" is becoming somewhat of a nightmare for the typical family—to the extent that this idyllic unit still exists. Families are having trouble making ends meet even with both spouses working to bring in two incomes (or in one case one is unemployed and stays home to care for the children because of the scarcity of qualified day care).

The man or woman (or both) still want to keep up with relatives, friends, and business associates who are seeking the same goals (i.e., ability to purchase all of the modern conveniences becoming increasingly available < "don't pay a cent until next June!" > because of the technological advancements made largely in this century). Somehow such advantages are going to improve the quality of life, although most of us would be hard pressed if we were asked to explain just how such a level of "conspicuous consumption" is going to achieve the desired state for us. (At this point I cannot resist mentioning the plight of people in the Third World nations, who are overworked physically and underfed <while exactly the opposite is the case for most of us>, and reproducing at a much higher rate than people in the developed nations.)

My own analysis of the situation is that we have largely lost track of what education should be all about. The presumed deficiencies of the educational system are evaluated as such depending to a large degree on what the evaluator believes the long range goals and specific objectives of the educational system should be. Even when a program is evaluated in as objective a manner as possible, the results often indicate inadequate curriculum content and poor instructional methodology. In the final analysis, the desired knowledge, skills, and competencies should be spelled out carefully at the outset and then evaluated annually and comprehensively prior to advancement or graduation. In my opinion this is where the often glaring inadequacies surface.

What is truly disturbing is that we should be doing a better job of teaching children and young people to think logically and how to act ethically on the basis of democratic values and norms. We should also be teaching students how to develop active, healthy bodies and how to maintain such a state through physical activity much of which should be *joyous!* Further, we should be helping young people to develop a life purpose so that maximum energy for living may be gained and maintained. However, for a variety of reasons these vital topics are not being introduced at the appropriate time, and we do not follow through to help them achieve desirable educational objectives to the extent that this is possible.

Most of us have become quite familiar with Toffler's several volumes of warning and exhortation about our changing society. His concept of "future shock" (1970) seems to be most apt, but so few seem prepared to examine the educational values and norms by which they function daily in any depth. Far too many want to "circle up the wagons" so that the "slings and arrows" of changing times will not cause us harm while we wait for the "U.S. cavalry to bring us aid from the rear." The good old times are gone; they will never return. What people will need are problem-solving, heuristic abilities that will enable them to adapt and adjust to the changing times and the seemingly increasing tempo of civilization.

Take the case of the university, for example. In 1969 Gould told us "the modern university has never been more necessary and central to our national life than it is today," and yet "we must also say in the next breath that no other major institution in this country is now so open to disbalance and in so precarious a state of health." These words were spoken at the end of a very difficult decade for colleges and universities—the 1960s, but who is prepared to argue validly that the 1970s and 1980s were that much better, and that the 1990s will see many of the major problems of this institution resolved? Assuredly the students were ever so much less sullen and openly mutinous in the 1970s and then, almost unbelievably, they were typically positively "angelic" in the 1980s. One wonders how such a transformation came over the maturing generation in such a relatively few years. But now in the 1990s, the situation may become quite different again as the pendulum swings in the opposite direction because of the overall financial crisis that has developed. Today we find that students are far from being blissfully happy about the university experiences they are receiving, but yet political clout through vigorous public support has not been apparent in any quarter. The legislators know that the public would not pay much attention to us no matter how loud the protest might be. One is forced to conjecture why the status—not the salaries—of university personnel seems so much lower in North America when studies inform us that the professoriat ranks very high in, for example, the Federal Republic of Germany.

What Gould was telling us above at the end of the 1960s decade, what he was recommending, was that our colleges and universities should be more democratic, more concerned with social problems, more alert to students' justified demands, and more critical of our own performance (especially as teachers). Many of these recommendations have indeed been heeded, to recognizable degrees at least. Nevertheless—and I think there is a relationship here—the social forces have been such that the educational pendulum has steadily swung farther to the right again in the direction of so-called educational essentialism. I view this as disturbing from several standpoints, but the social forces are so great that one hardly dares to speak in favor of inclining to educational progressivism, an almost mythical condition or state that brings immediate opprobrium and which was never really understood and certainly not implemented except in isolated instances.

However, let us put this old argument aside for the present. Of significance now is the prognostication of Toffler (1970, pp. 353–378) and others about education in the future sense. As I indicated above, he also affirmed that "one of our most critical subsystems—education—is dangerously malfunctioning. Our schools face backwards toward a dying system, rather than forward to the new emerging society. Of course, any student of educational history understands that the schools have never been in the vanguard, that they have never led the way in society. And as long as they are dependent on the public purse through taxation, there is no reason to believe that matters will change significantly. Nevertheless, Toffler's farsighted thoughts expressed several decades ago now seem to ring true today—that people preparing for tomorrow's world, those "who must live in super-industrial societies . . . will need new skills in three crucial areas: learning, relating, and choosing" (p. 367). Our task will be that of seeking to provide the answers to the following questions: learning what, relating to whom, and making what choices?

THE STATUS OF PHYSICAL EDUCATION AND KINESIOLOGY

As might be expected, the field of physical education and kinesiology has not escaped from the serious malaise that has permeated the very fabric of society today. We in this field have one of the most blurred images in the entire educational system! (I suppose it could be argued conversely that our image is *crystal clear* to the public. People think we are involved with competitive sport, dull exercise, and casual physical recreation.) This blurred image, to which I referred, probably occurred originally because of the many conflicting educational philosophies extant in each of the 60 state and provincial educational systems on this North American continent (excluding consideration of Mexico at this point). Our image with its fuzzy boundaries continues today for essentially the same reason and, of course, because of considerable individual and collective confusion.

At the beginning of this opening chapter, I listed some unstated axioms of science whose truth we accept. What has been troubling me for several decades is that the field of physical education and kinesiology has also been proceeding generally—despite the fact that many do not accord us full curricular status—on the basis of its own unstated axioms. For example, I think that many of us, be we professional practitioners or university scholars and researchers, believe that physical education and kinesiology (considered as an entity) is viewed as so important by people of all ages in our society that the future of the field in our schools is guaranteed forever—no matter whether true professional status is acquired or not. Lest you think that I am being too harsh, I believe there are other unstated axioms that could be listed too. However, let us allow just this one to suffice as a basis for what follows.

By now you no doubt sense that I have serious concerns about what the emerging profession of physical education and kinesiology needs to accomplish in the foreseeable future. (Frankly, I'm not certain how long beyond the year 2000 our grace period will extend.) I truly believe that we will need to move strongly and forthrightly during the 1990s decade than we have ever done in the past. My diagnosis of the present situation is that the field of physical education and kinesiology as we have known it and promoted it is seriously ill. Many people recognize the symptoms of the illness, but most of the group teaching and coaching within the field do not comprehend the severity of the malady that has gradually infected the profession. (I must confess also that, as these words are being written, many people are seriously concerned about the *entire* educational enterprise as well.)

At least the American Association for Health, Physical Education, and Recreation had the wisdom to substitute the word *alliance* for *association,* and a bit later added the word *dance* to the overall title (AAHPERD). Further, we are also witnessing the struggling emergence of an entity called the National Association for Sport and Physical Education within the AAHPERD as presently constituted along with an accompanying unit called the Association for Research, Administration, Professional Councils, and Societies. Both of these groupings relate to what was previously, and is still today to a large degree, known as physical education; so, there is considerable overlap of membership within these two separate associations. My concern is (1) that the membership of these associations is relatively speaking so small that it is nowhere nearly representative of the total field and (2) that the quality of the endeavor viewed objectively from all standpoints must become much higher in the foreseeable future. (By this latter statement, I am in no way denigrating the efforts of those involved professionally within NASPE and ARAPCS; I am simply stating the fact that support from the profession has not been sufficient for these associations to be influencing the field nationally to become more effective and efficient.)

In Canada there has not seemed to be the urgency to change the name of the Canadian Association for Health, Physical Education and Recreation, although there have been fairly recent recommendations that such be done. Some of the same problems mentioned above prevail in Canada, also. However, health education has not emerged as a separate profession; so in the public and secondary schools the subject-matter is still largely known as "physical and health education." Also, recreation and parks administration is a separate profession. Further, a great many secondary schools teachers and coaches identify more with their provincial teachers' federations than they do with the national physical education association. Additionally, CAHPER has made a bit of inroad into the Province of Quebec, but for many years those physical and health educators who are concerned with professional affiliation have formed their own separate organizations. Of course, there is the ever-present need to promote more effective bilingualism than exists at present.

It appears that there is an urgent need throughout North America for the application of the techniques of normative and analytical philosophizing to be directed basically to sport, exercise, and related expressive movement. Such endeavor is long overdue when we consider our bewildered public often seeking to comprehend—or simply ignoring!—what we mean by the conglomeration of terms presently in use such as movement studies, health, parks administration, campus recreation, leisure studies, physical education and sport, sport and exercise science(s?), recreation, rehabilitation education, applied life studies, dance, kinanthropology, kinanthropometry, recreaology, safety education, driver education, physical fitness, movement education, human motor performance, ergonomics, exercise studies, sport studies, physical activity studies, human kinetics, kinesiology, anthropokineticology (the late Fritz Hubbard's tongue-in cheek addition to the list), and, last but not least, the interesting combination of Latin and Greek roots known as homokinetics. If we in the field can laugh at this sampling of terms and combinations thereof in use, just think what people in other disciplines and professions and the public must think.

To make matters more complicated, while the above developments have been taking place, a large and frightening rift has become apparent between the people in the field with one or more of a number of subdisciplinary orientations and those with what might be called a professional orientation. Still further, there is a split between those with heavier involvement in the biophysical aspects of the field and those with a scholarly interest in the social sciences and humanities subdisciplinary aspects (social psychology, philosophy, management theory, etc.). Yet despite these controversies of a spoken and unspoken nature, the competitive athletics-oriented ones among us (the coaches!) continue on their merry way toward an open future because of our culture's increasing "love affair" with highly competitive sport.

In an effort to improve the clarity of this historical analysis of the 20th century in North American physical education and its allied professions, and thereby to communicate the present status more effectively, the following explanation through the use of a series of diagrams may assist the reader to understand what has happened since 1900 (Zeigler, 1979b, pp. 9–19). My hope is that physical education/kinesiology will now sharpen its focus and delimit its aims and objectives as it seeks to serve humankind more efficiently and effectively in the 21st century.

A DIAGRAMMATIC REPRESENTATION OF THE 20TH CENTURY DEVELOPMENT OF PHYSICAL EDUCATION/KINESIOLOGY

Stage 1—Physical Education—circa 1900–1930. In this analysis of the emerging physical education field at the beginning of the 20th century within the public education system primarily, three subdivisions (or categories) of the field will be traced as follows:

1. The *potential body-of-knowledge* as characterized by its subdisciplinary areas (e.g., anatomical and physiological aspects)
2. The *concurrent professional components* of the developing field such as exist in all subject-matter fields (e.g., curriculum, methods of instruction)
3. The *potential allied professions* (e.g., health education, competitive athletics)

(See Figure 1.1 below; note that the subdisciplinary names in diagrams use the names of other disciplines (e.g., physiology, psychology), but that toward the end of the study a recommendation is made to employ only those names that do *not* "give our field away" to another established discipline.)

Figure 1.1 seeks to describe the situation for the period extending from app. 1900 to app. 1930 (or Stage 1). It indicates that the subdisciplinary areas are "blurred" and almost indistinguishable within the center of the circle depicting physical education. It is true that professional students of that time received instruction in anatomy and physiology, as well as in chemistry and physics, prior to the required professional physical education courses identified, for example, as physiology of exercise, kinesiology, anthropometry, physical examination and diagnosis, massage, history of physical training, emergencies, and medical gymnastics (Oberlin College *Catalogue* for 1894). However, the strong point to be made here is that there were (1) basic science courses and (2) professional physical education courses. Instruction in the so-called "academic courses" was almost completely lacking. It was true, very importantly, that certain professors (instructors) had areas of specialization (e.g., Fred Leonard in physical education history; Delphine Hanna in medical gymnastics), but the very large majority of these people *saw themselves as physical educators*—not

Figure 1.1 Stage 1—1900–1930

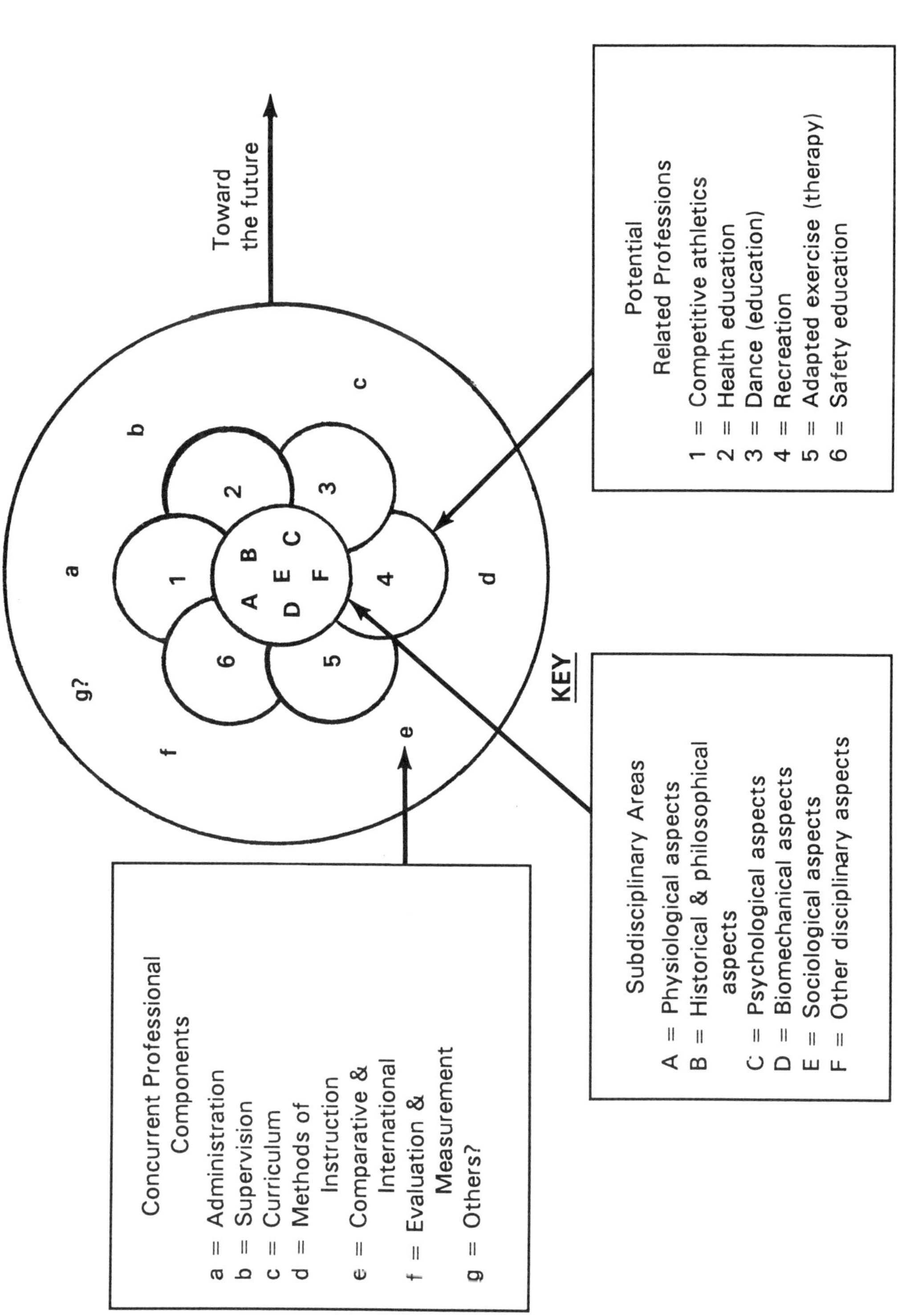

as specialists in some other disciplinary subject-matter within the college or university. (*N.B:* We need to mention the "M.D. phenomenon" in our early history. For example, a person such as James H. McCurdy, M.D., recognized that our embryonic profession needed people with "scientific ability who will increase our knowledge with reference especially to bodily growth, to personal hygiene, to physiology of exercise, etc." <McCurdy, 1901, pp. 311–312>.)

The "potential allied professions" were also "blurred" and almost indistinguishable within the center of the circle depicting physical education in Figure 1.1. For example, in the *Wellesley College Catalogue* for 1910, athletics (no. 1 under potential allied professions) is included in the requirements for the Bachelor of Arts degree in Physical Education under the heading of "Professional Courses" by virtue of a two-hour course in "organized sports," a three-hour course in "athletics" (presumably track and field), and a three and one-half hour course in "outdoor games and athletics." Health education (no. 2) is included as "Reg. A. B. Hygiene" for one hour, and dance (education) (no. 3) is listed as "dancing" for one or two hours. Recreation (no. 4) could conceivably by regarded as *physical* recreation insofar as sports activities were offered within the physical education curriculum. Adapted exercise (therapy) (no. 5) appeared as "corrective gymnastics and massage" for one hour. Finally, the only reference to safety education (no. 6) was a course experience called "emergencies" for one hour. Thus, if you will check Figure 1.1 above again, you will note (1) that the subdisciplinary areas (A, B, C, D, E, and F) are very close together in the center of the core depicting physical education as a field; (2) the potential allied professions (shown as 1, 2, 3, 4, 5, and 6) are firmly attached, or closely spaced next to, the core of the diagram; and (3) the concurrent professional components (a, b, c, d, e, f, and g) are simply indicated as belonging in the larger circle (similar to the way that they will be shown in subsequent diagrams).

Stage 2—Physical Education—circa 1930–1960. In Figure 1.2 below, which represents roughly the period from 1930 to 1960, we find that there has actually been considerable change within the field still known as "physical education." However, the subdisciplinary areas are beginning to emerge from the core depicted in Figure 1.1 above. The typical tests and measurements course, for example, was gradually characterized by an improved laboratory experience, often largely physical fitness/exercise physiology in nature. These were soon supplemented by motor learning and kinesiological laboratory experiences as well. There was kinematic analysis of human movement in sport and exercise, but the first doctoral study involving kinetic analysis had not yet been carried out. Sport and physical education sociology had not yet appeared on the scene, nor had the social psychological analysis of sport and physical activity surfaced to any recognizable extent.

Figure 1.2 Stage 2—1930–1960. (See Figure 1.1 for explanatory key.)

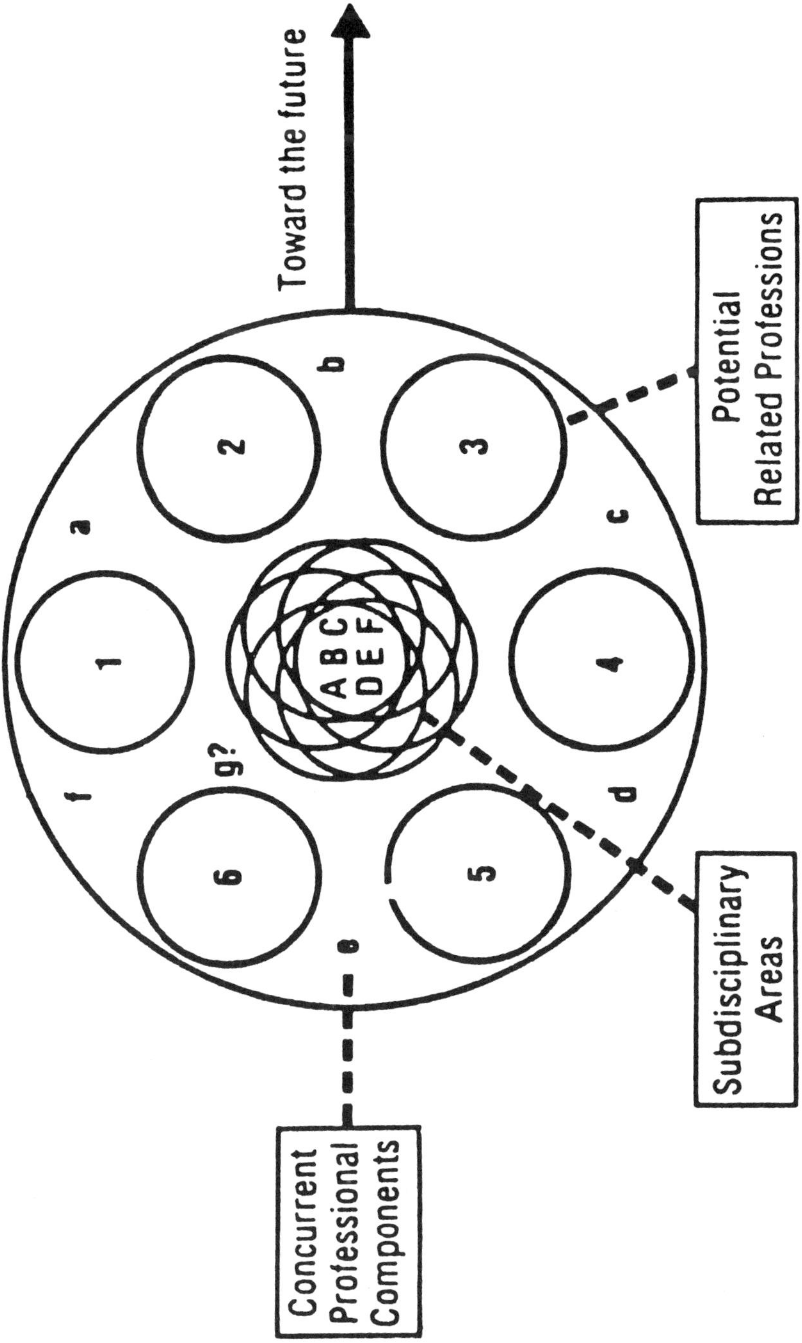

There were a great many historical and biographical theses, but by and large the historical studies were not characterized by the use of an interpretive criterion to evaluate the evidence that had been gathered. The biographical studies were interesting and usually substantive, but the subject of such an investigation typically emerged with such a large halo around his/her head that one wondered whether there had been a second coming of the Lord! Early philosophical studies were not impressive, although in the mid-1940s and the fifties they improved and were similar to studies being carried out in educational philosophy. Occasionally the question was being asked by scholars like C. H. McCloy, and especially about the "softer side" of our field (as it is often unfortunately called), as to how long a field could expect to prosper as a profession when the bulk of its research was carried on through the medium of doctoral study.

Shifting attention to the designated "concurrent professional components," there were a large number of doctoral studies that could be characterized as administrative in nature. Many of these were helpful and provided useful information, but as Spaeth reported, "there is an almost total lack of theoretical orientation in the design of research and interpretation of the findings in the sample of administrative research studied." She stated further, "the administrative research lacked the methodological rigor necessary for contributions to the development of scientific knowledge about administrative performance" (Zeigler and Spaeth, 1975, p. 44). With exceptions, of course, much the same can probably be said for the studies carried out in the components identified as "supervision," "curriculum," and "instruction."

It is important to keep in mind, however, that these are usually types of investigation employing a variety of techniques under descriptive research methodology. In such cases it is often not possible nor desirable to emerge from these studies with a coefficient of correlation or a multiple correlation—not to mention results available from employment of a factor-analysis technique. International and comparative research in sport and physical education was practically non-existent from the standpoint of the use of even relatively complex social science methodology and accompanying techniques. The final category listed here ("measurement and evaluation") was viewed more as part of the subdisciplinary efforts of our scientists. It was therefore tied in with those interested in the physiological, kinesiological, and psychological aspects of physical education. Today it is being used more as a tool subject that may be used by almost any researcher in the field carrying out an investigation based on the natural sciences, the social sciences, or even the humanities.

Finally, then, in this period from 1930 to 1960, the "potential allied professions" will be considered briefly. Examination of Figure 1.2, which is called Stage 2, indicates that the "allied professions," which were firmly attached to (and literally part of) physical education, have now moved out of its inner core. By 1960, these potential allied professions—i.e., competitive athletics, health education, dance (education), recreation, adapted exercise (therapy), and safety education—have clearly established their own identities. Indeed, in some cases they have even established a separate identity within the field of education, not to mention any recognition that had been accorded to them by the public.

Stage 3—Physical Education (and Sport)—circa 1960–1970. Many people can recall vividly the events of the 1960s both within society in general and within physical education specifically. Our graduate study programs were attacked by Conant; responded to by Esslinger on our behalf; and the field developed an incomplete understanding of the need for a substantive body-of-knowledge to undergird our professional efforts. A notable undertaking, still operative in an altered format, was the Big Ten Body-of-Knowledge Project as conceived by Daniels and followed through to fruition by McCristal and some of us who were present at the time. The subdisciplinary areas included in this undertaking were (1) sociology of sport and physical education; (2) administrative theory; (3) history, philosophy, and comparative physical education and sport; (4) exercise physiology; (5) biomechanics; and (6) motor learning & sport psychology (Zeigler, ed., 1975, p. 292). The subdisciplinary areas shown in Figure 1.3 below are similar, the only difference being that certain subdisciplinary areas are indicated as concurrent professional components (e.g., administrative theory). The significant point to be made, however, is that the subdisciplinary areas themselves have moved from the central core of physical education in the earlier diagrams to a position not unlike the positions held earlier by the potential allied professions. These subdisciplinary areas (e.g., so-called sociology of sport) were indeed moving strongly away from physical education toward the end of the 1960–1970 decade. The position of sport sociology, soon followed by other subdisciplinary societies being established, reminded one of the "floating apex" of Peter Principle notoriety. They had gone off to function by themselves without any undergirding organizational support of the mother discipline of sociology. Thus, it was essentially unrecognized by the societal entities that they purported to describe—i.e., sport or sociology.

Further examination of Figure 1.3 in regard to the movement of the potential allied professions shows that all six of the fields have moved further in the direction of establishing their own identity even within educational circles. It is impossible to describe *precisely* where each of these professions concerned was located, but it was clear that further movement away from the field of physical education had been taken.

Examination of the concurrent professional components for the period from 1960–1970—components which by their very nature are inextricably linked to the professional development of physical educators—brings to light some interesting developments as well. For example, we saw the introduction of a

Figure 1.3 Stage 3—1960–1970. (See Figure 1.1 for explanatory key.)

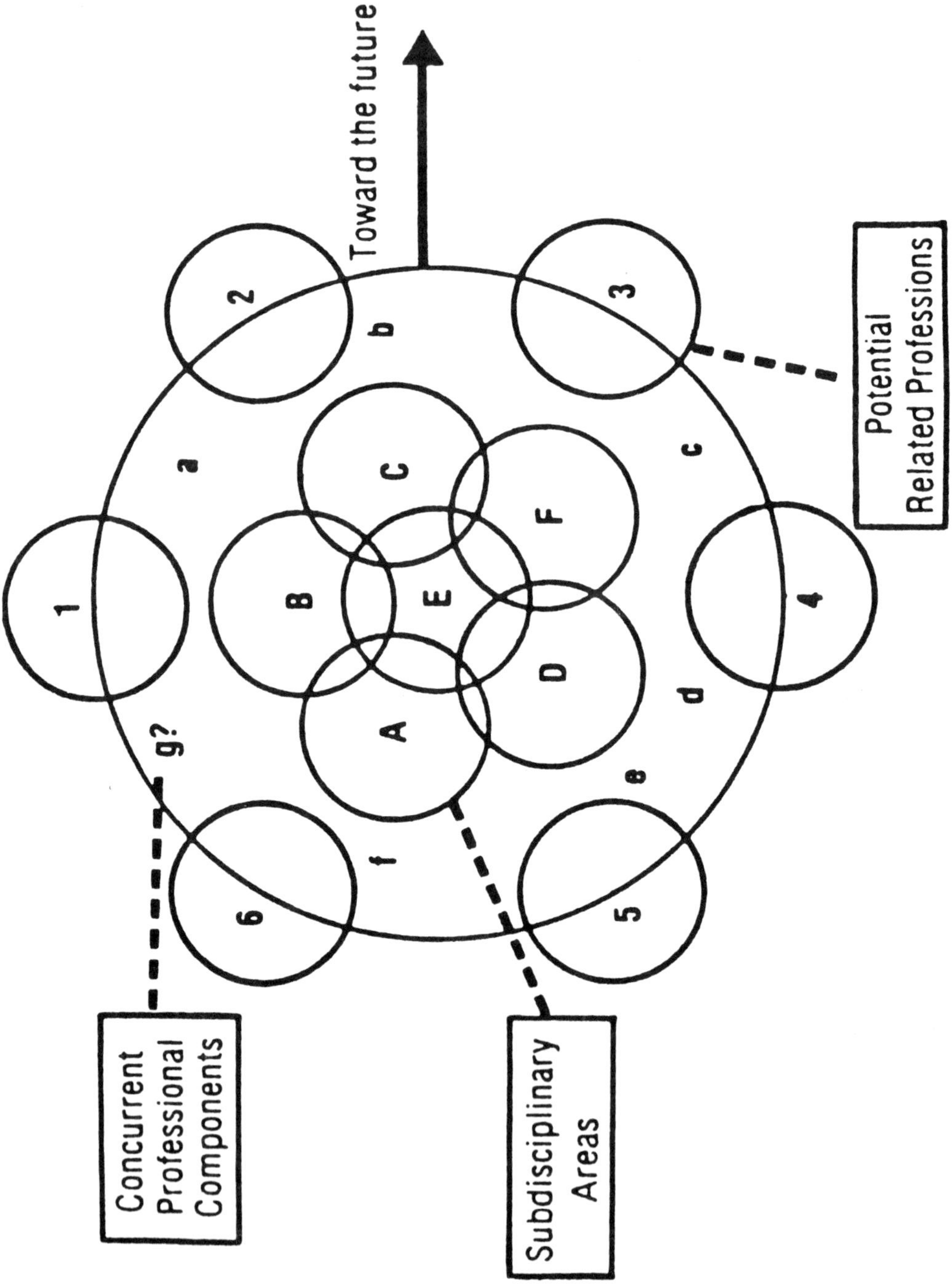

more theoretical orientation in these topics on the part of a relatively few graduate programs. Typically, the concept of supervision had merged more completely with the larger realm of overall administration. The subject of curriculum (i.e., program development) received somewhat more attention generally, and several scholars led the way in giving this topic a more theoretical orientation than previously. The same can be said for the topic "methods of instruction," but this professional component did not receive noticeably more attention during this decade. (A few professors reacted to what they considered to be the overemphasis of the subdisciplinary orientation by a very small segment of the total population of physical educators in the United States. As a result, they cast their lots with what they called a "professional preparation" approach to both undergraduate and graduate education in the field. It could be argued that this "move" was simply an improved, more precise approach to what the large majority of college and universities had been emphasizing for decades.)

Stage 4—Physical Education (and Sport)—circa 1970–1990. Stage 4, as explained in Figure 1.4 below, treats the period from 1970 to 1990 and, as we can readily appreciate, it is extremely difficult to gain a true perspective on the happenings of this most recent 20-year period. Nevertheless, some of the developments that began in previous decades did indeed continue along apace, and so several reasonably accurate observations may be possible.

For example, the subdisciplinary areas that were moving strongly away from involvement with physical education at the professional-conference level have continued with their movement in the direction of the respective mother disciplines (e.g., sport history and sport philosophy). However the movement of those who called themselves sport philosophers was "sharper" in nature, whereas the North American Society for Sport History still provides a "comfortable atmosphere" for those with an historical interest in physical education to convene. This trend has continued despite the fact that the very large majority of these people received their graduate training in what were called physical education units and—where some money was still available—received their travel funds from the same units as well.

Also, although many within the larger professional associations in both the United States and Canada have been aware of this departure of many scholars, it has been difficult to know whether to ignore this development or to attempt to reverse it. We did witness the inauguration of a number of subdisciplinary *and* subprofessional "academies" with the larger professional groupings. In the United States, the professional association (AAHPER), recognizing the impact of the term "sport," established the entity now known as the National Association for Sport and Physical Education. (It should be noted at this point that the large majority of conferences held on other continents, including those with a

Figure 1.4 Stage 4—1970–1990. (See Figure 1.1 for explanatory key.)

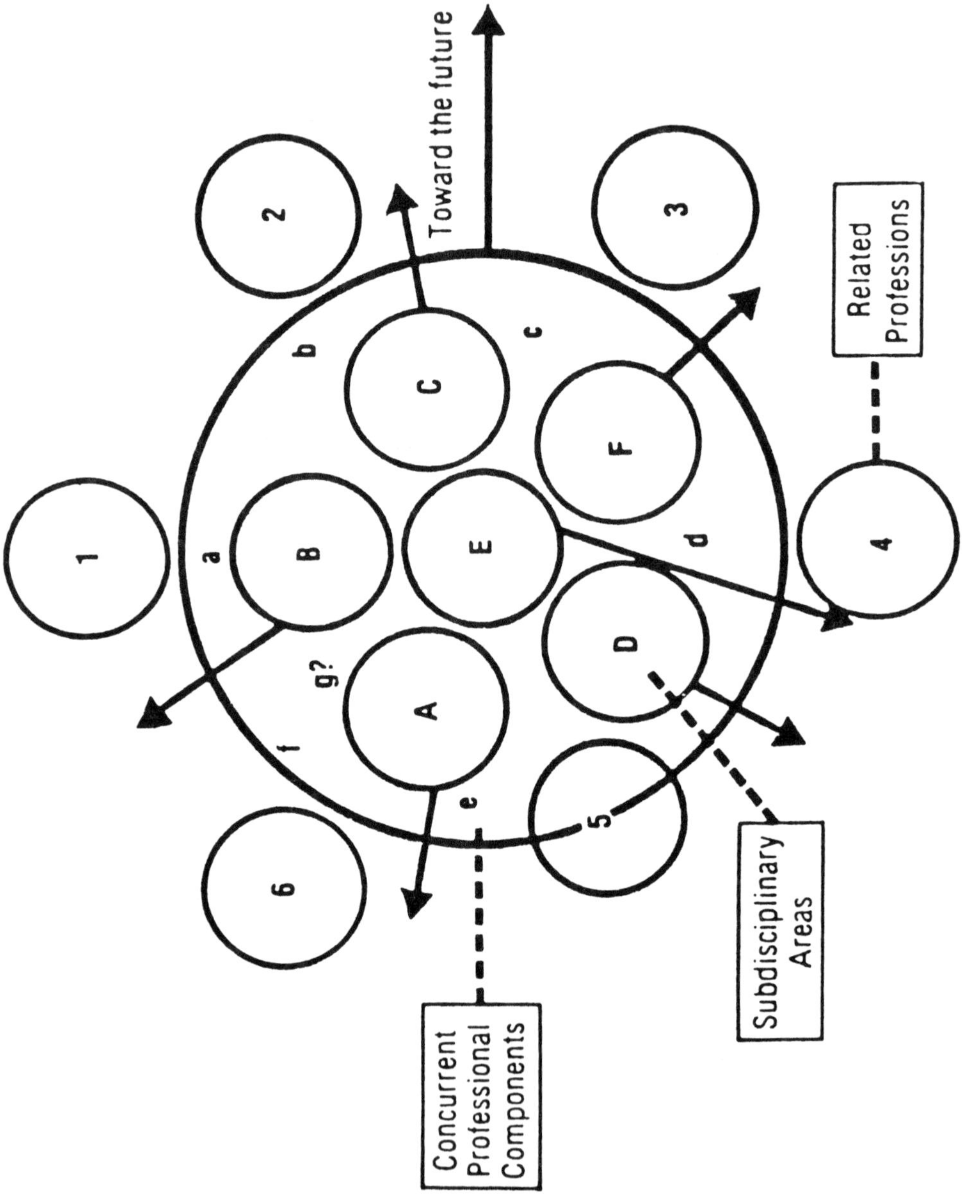

worldwide orientation, typically employ the word "sport" in their terminology in one way or another along with the term "physical education.")

Viewed from an overall basis, it can be argued that the six potential allied professions have almost completely consolidated their positions outside of the domain of physical education at the college and university level, although this has not yet been possible officially at the lower educational levels. The American *Association* for Health, Physical Education, and Recreation recognized this independent growth of the allied professions by changing its name to the American *Alliance* for Health, Physical Education, and Recreation. Then, just before the turn of the 1980s decade, the Alliance Board of Governors officially added the word "dance" to the official title and AAHPER became AAHPERD. This action culminated a period in which a number of dance units within colleges and universities moved, or sought permission to move, out of the physical education unit per se to some other educational entity on campus. Thus, whether the topic is about competitive athletics, health education, dance (education), recreation (education), safety education, or even adapted exercise (therapy), it became obvious that most of those people who came to relate primarily to one or the other of these allied professions want to be free from what they identify as the "fizz ed stigma."

During this most recent period, there doesn't appear to have been a considerable amount of change in the concurrent professional components shown in Figure 1.4 as Stage 4. The term "management" began to gain acceptance in the latter half of the 1970s, and then really began to supplant the term "administration" as sport management curricula burgeoned in the 1980s. However, it was only after the establishment of the North American Society for Sport Management and its official journal in the latter half of the decade that there was some evidence of the need for improving both the theoretical and practical components of professional preparation in this aspect of the field. Also, a small, stalwart band of curriculum theorists continued to strive for careful investigation into the intricacies of this aspect of our professional program. Further, and fortunately for those interested in professional preparation, including curriculum or program development and instructional methodology, higher education institutions are continuing their drive for an improved level of instructional competency by all professors, a move that was sparked by the clamor of students in the 1960s and which has been perpetuated by the continuing aim to please occasioned by the ongoing financial constraints that began in the 1970s and the accompanying need to preserve the student head-count, constraints that seem even more constricting at the beginning of the 1990s.

The remaining two professional components to be considered within Stage 4 are "international and comparative" and "measurement and evaluation." There is a small, loyal group of professionals keeping the former area alive within the

Alliance (and ICHPER), as well as a second small international group functioning within the International Society for Comparative Physical Education and Sport. However, the amount of scholarly investigation carried out in this aspect of our professional endeavor must be categorized as slight throughout the 1970–1990 period. This is truly an indictment of our professional growth at a time when we should be moving toward more not less involvement with our colleagues abroad. However, there is no doubt but that a good deal of cross-fertilization does occur within the subdisciplinary societies at international meetings. Yet, there is no mechanism for the knowledge engendered at all of these conferences to be transmitted to professionals everywhere in a useable fashion.

Measurement and evaluation, typically packaged earlier in the required tests and measurement course, was still an important part of undergraduate professional preparation in physical education at the end of the 1970s, but during that decade it became diffused in many programs at the graduate level into the various subdisciplinary or subprofessional streams available. During the 1980s a similar development was occurring at the undergraduate level as well. There are some universities that offer it as an area of specialization at the graduate level, and there are universities who maintain a "measurement and evaluation professor" (i.e., allot a percentage of this person's workload) to service students and/or professors needing advice insofar as research design and statistical techniques are concerned. The feeling seems to be that it is a physical impossibility to do a good job of packaging the research methodologies and the multitude of accompanying research techniques under one specific course. There is some merit in this argument, but I believe that the student is being short-changed and resultantly does not understand the "big picture" in regard to scholarly research.

Stage 5—Physical Education and Kinesiology—circa 2000. We have finally arrived at the point where we are in a position to conjecture *about,* and possibly prescribe *for,* the future of the field of physical education and kinesiology as we struggle ahead toward the turn of the century. By combining these two terms in this way, the current position seems to be that "physical education" is what the professional practitioner does, and kinesiology (or the study of movement) is where the undergirding knowledge resides. (See Figure 1.5 below.)

(Before moving ahead, it will be necessary to retrogress for a moment to Figure 1.3 <Stage 3—1960–1970> above where it was explained that the subdisciplinary movement at that point began to move significantly away from what might be called the "central core" of the physical education profession. It was at that point that Cyril White, now an Irish sport sociologist, offered the idea in a discussion paper that our field might be moving from a *multi-discipline* to a *cross-discipline* on the way toward becoming an *interdiscipline* <Zeigler, 1975, pp. 350–51>. However, he postulated that the profession's "future development to interdisciplinary level will require a far greater degree of

Figure 1.5 Stage 5—A Proposal for the Future of Physical Education & Kinesiology

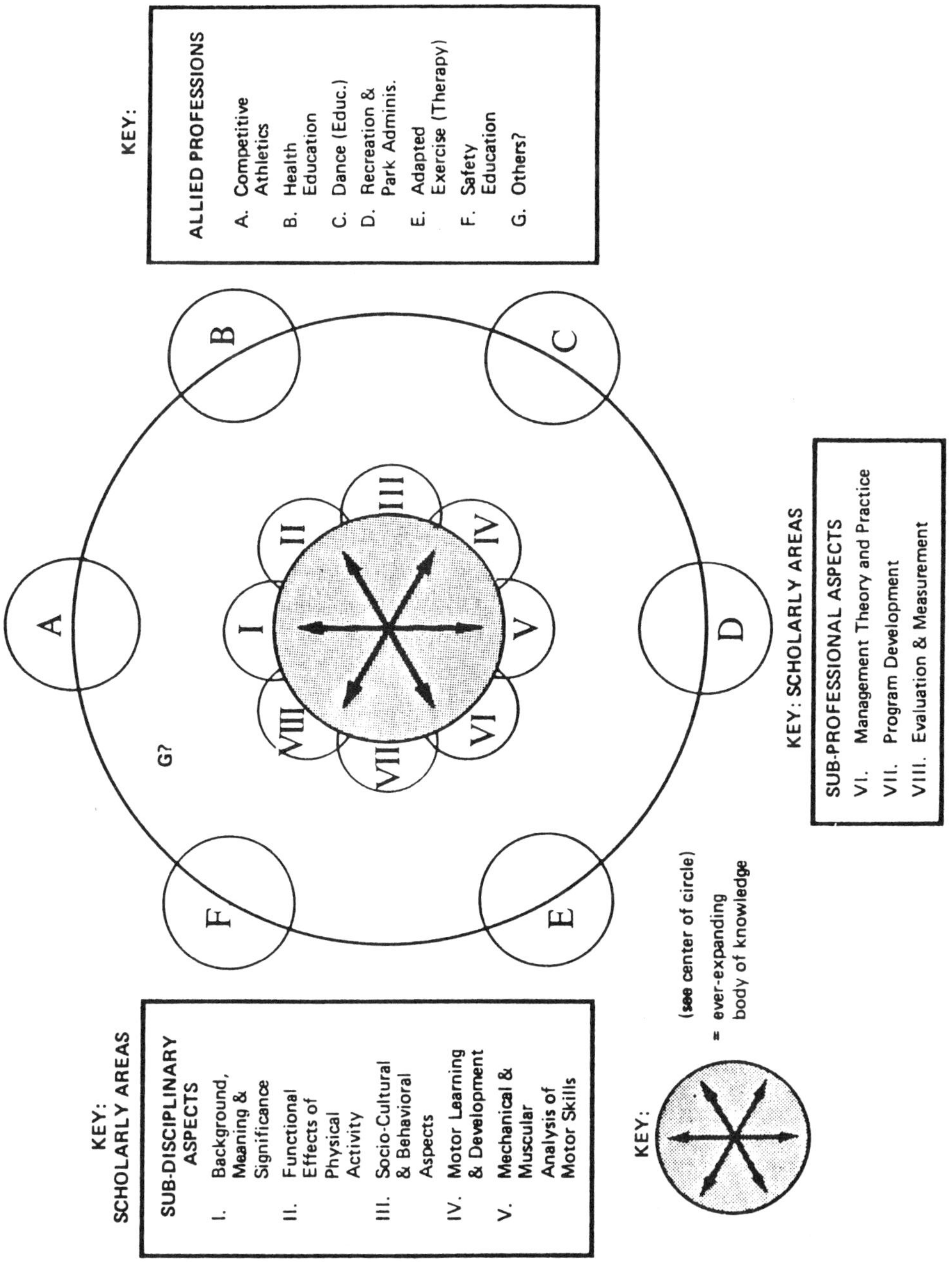

sophisticated research abilities and orientations than the field at present possesses." The idea was intriguing, but it simply was not happening that way at that time, and thus seemed completely out of phase with the development taking place. Interestingly, somewhat later in a chance discussion, Philip Sparling <then of Georgia Tech> opined that we were moving in the opposite direction. Time has shown that Sparling was indeed correct in his judgment!)

To compound further what is already a complex situation, I believe strongly that we as a field are not moving rapidly enough to what may be called true professional status. Those of us functioning in the public schools probably feel that we will be sheltered indefinitely by the protective arm of the teaching profession. They and others in the field may believe that society will not recognize our field as that profession which should be the leading force in human motor performance in exercise, sport, and related expressive movement. Whatever the facts in the matter may be, there is no escaping one discouraging fact that—despite our *unique* mission—we are, along with art and music typically at the bottom of the totem pole in educational circles. Additionally, we are presently slowly missing the opportunity to become the profession of which we are capable and along with this omission are thereby typically deprived of any accompanying social recognition and support.

It is for these reasons, therefore, that this Stage 5 (Figure 1.5 above) is being postulated here for the profession's consideration. Then, if certain vigorous steps were taken by the American Academy of Kinesiology and Physical Education, the National Association for Sport and Physical Education (along with ARAPCS, NAGWS, and ICHPER <as an outgrowth internationally from AAHPERD>, and the National Association for Physical Education in Higher Education, it is conceivable and possible that by the year 2000 (or shortly thereafter) that a strong trend would be recognized that would soon lead to a much stronger profession undergirded by a body-of-knowledge generated by the scholars and researchers of our *cross-discipline* that is well on the way to becoming an *interdiscipline.* (Obviously, it would be wise to include Canada and Mexico in the development of any such scheme if it were to be considered truly as a movement that is North American in nature.)

This recommended development is explained in Figure 1.5 above. The reader will notice immediately as the diagram is examined that the *sub-disciplinary areas,* instead of continuing along with their movement for greater identification with the *related* disciplines, have been persuaded to function more strongly *within* the field of physical education/kinesiology and are firmly attached to the profession's core—explained as a developing body-of-knowledge about the theory and practice of movement (or developmental physical activity) in exercise, sport, and related expressive movement. Obviously, persuading all three of these groupings (AAKPE, NASPE, and NAPEHE) to move solidly and soundly to a position of direct alliance or affiliation will be a tall order, but it could be done by means of persuasion, encouragement, influence, and even "bribery" if necessary.

If the *subdisciplinary areas* of our to-be-hoped-for cross-discipline/interdiscipline can be brought to conform with the proposal made in Figure 1.5, what about the *concurrent professional components?* In this instance we are fortunately not in a position where we would have to retrieve these elements from other professional organizations far removed from our midst. Our task here is to simply follow the lead to a greater extent of those scholarly people who have played leadership roles in curriculum and program development, professional preparation, instructional methodology, measurement and evaluation, comparative physical education and sport, and management theory. If their investigations are well executed, such scholarly efforts need to be recognized equally along with the work of those in the subdisciplinary areas. Thus, these components have been left importantly within the circle that describes the total field of physical education/kinesiology.

The present situation cries out the following to occur: (1) the scholars and researchers of our field identifying and working strongly with the professional associations and (2) the leaders of the professional associations recognizing that the future of the profession *requires* the sound knowledge undergirding that the scholars and researchers can provide. As matters stand now, neither set of groupings (guided by their own leaders) sees the need for such a development clearly. We have done a bit of hand-wringing over the dispersion that is occurring, but the leaders haven't made it clear to all concerned that the profession needs a concerted effort to assure a future that embodies professional status of a higher order. Frankly, as matters stand now, keeping all of the characteristics typically ascribed to a full-fledged profession in mind, the field of physical education is a "glorified trade" with the potential to become a true profession when it organizes itself sufficiently to provide its practitioners with tenable theory about human movement based on ongoing high-level scholarly endeavor. Further, any such resultant body-of-knowledge should be made available in the form of *ordered generalizations* that can be readily understood and applied by our professional practitioners.

Within AAHPERD we are, of course, faced with the continuing problem of our relationship with what have been described as the (potential) *allied professions*. The Alliance has made steady progress in this regard, and on October 1, 1992 implemented a three-year transition to full implementation of a new organizational model "intended to maximize autonomy of functioning for the national associations (the Alliance program arm), maintain autonomy for the district associations, and at the same time preserve the Alliance umbrella and the potential for synergistic mission accomplishment inherent in such an organization" (*UPDATE,* April, 1993, 1). This plan should insure that these related professions stay firmly allied to us. We can do this best, of course, (1) by making the members of these associations (e.g., the National Dance Association) feel completely at home within the Alliance and by demonstrating through our actions that we are proud of the early role that physical education played in assisting them to develop to the point where separate professional status was the next feasible step for them to take; (2) by improving the quantity and quality of our own scholarly endeavor so that they will feel proud to be allied with us; and (3) by relating in cross-disciplinary fashion to those scholars in each of these related professions at those points where joint research effort can be rewarding to all involved.

A MODEL FOR THE OPTIMUM DEVELOPMENT OF A PROFESSION CIRCA 2000

I would now like to recommend a model (Figure 1.6 below) that may be employed for the profession's optimum development. (This model could also be gainfully employed by all of the allied professions, and, for that matter, *any* profession.) None of us can be certain what most of us will be calling the field in the future. Personally, although I remain loyal to the established physical education profession, I regard *sport and physical education* and (internationally) physical education and sport as holding-pattern terms. What we really need is a term that explains to the public (and to ourselves) what our function truly is. We seek knowledge and understanding about purposeful human movement (or motor performance) in such activities as exercise, sport, physical recreation, and related movement. (Perhaps, as suggested by the late Seward Staley of Illinois years ago, we should invent an acronym such as UNIROYAL, a term that was adopted for one brand of tires some time ago.

The model in Figure 1.6 includes the following subdivisions: (1) societal values and norms, (2) an operational philosophy for the profession, (3) a developing theory embodying assumptions and testable hypotheses, (4) professional, semiprofessional, and amateur (volunteer) involvement as practitioners, (5) professional preparation and general education, and (6) scholarly endeavor and disciplinary research.

Societal values and norms are placed at the top of the model. This is based on the theory that a society's values and norms have a watershed quality, that in the final analysis progress will be made toward their achievement, and that they exert control and conditioning over the lower levels in the social system as the culture moves gradually and unevenly toward what may be considered progress. Directly below in the model is the overriding philosophy of sport and physical education (our current name!) in a society, or the values according to which the profession conducts its practice. At this level we appreciate that, especially in a democracy, pluralistic philosophies are permitted to exist (Zeigler, 1977, pp. 7–9).

Figure 1.6 A Model for Optimum Development of a Field Called "X"

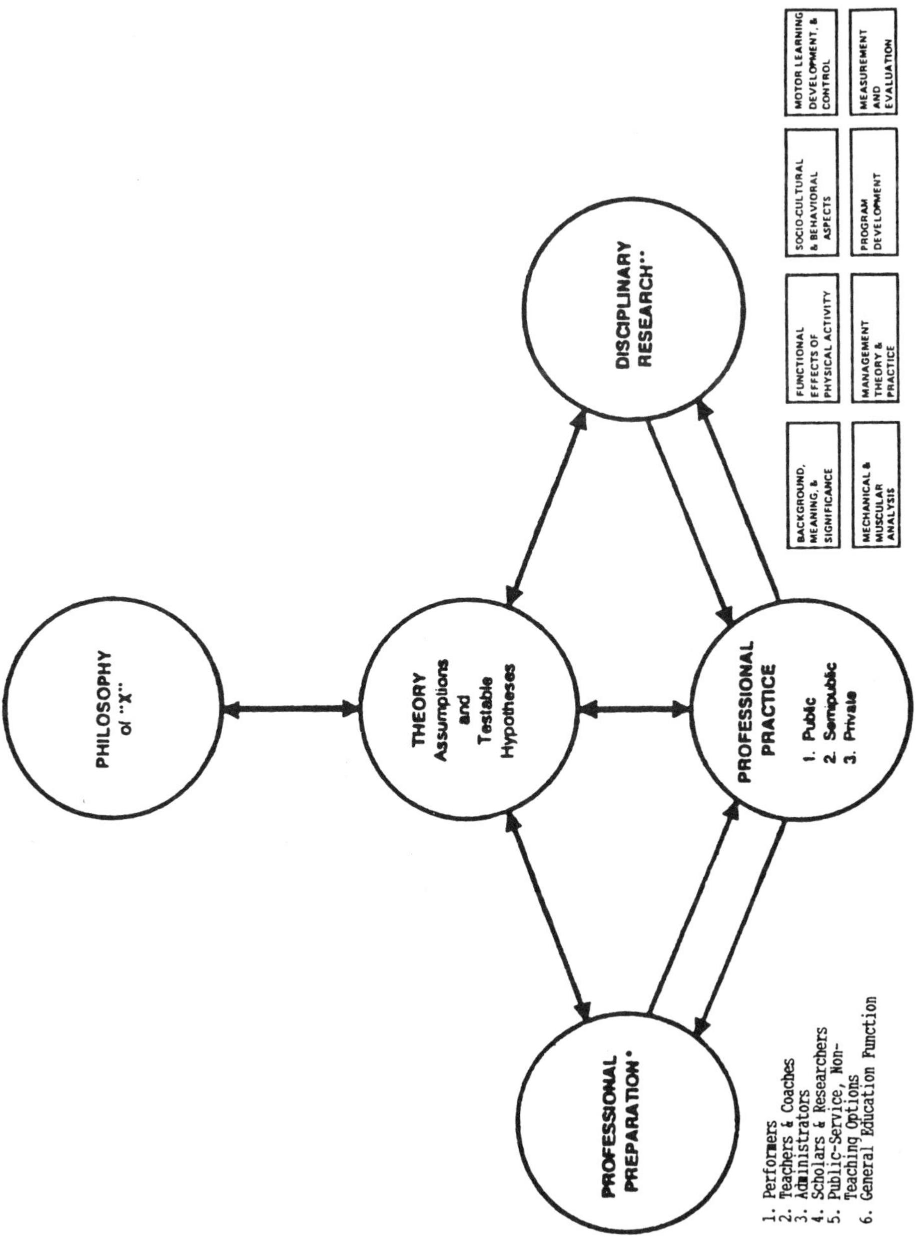

The third level involves the assumptions and testable hypotheses of steadily evolving theory underlying the profession—a knowledge base upon which professional practice is predicated and executed. This theory should comprise a coherent group of general and specific propositions that can be used as principles to explain the phenomena observed in developmental physical activity in exercise, sport, and related movement.

The fourth level in the model is depicted as professional, semiprofessional, and amateur (volunteer) involvement in the practice of the profession. This is subsumed under the categories of public, semipublic (or semiprivate), and private involvement or practice. To the left of this is the area of professional preparation and general education. Professional preparation should include (1) the performer, (2) teachers/coaches, (3) administrators/managers, (4) teachers of teachers/coaches, (5) scholars and researchers, and (6) alternative professional careers. So-called general education should now be elevated so that it is regarded as part of a broad liberal arts and science background rather than merely as a "service" course. To achieve this it will be necessary to provide a sound educational experience in the theory and practice of human motor performance in exercise, sport, and related expressive movement.

To the right at the fourth level is the area of disciplinary research and scholarly endeavor. The reader should note carefully that for the future the late Laura Huelster and I are recommending a complete changeover from the use of terms belonging to related fields (e.g., physiology, sociology). Further, the so-called subprofessional areas are included right along with the subdisciplinary areas as legitimate aspects of developmental physical activity for various types of scholarly investigation. Thus the subareas included in Figure 1.6 are (1) background, meaning, and intercultural significance, (2) functional effects of physical activity, (3) sociocultural and behavioral aspects, (4) motor learning and control, (5) mechanical and muscular analysis of motor skills, (6) management theory and practice, (7) curriculum theory and program development, and (8) measurement and evaluation.

RECOMMENDATIONS AND OBSERVATIONS

In drawing this first chapter to a close, I would like to make (1) some *specific recommendations* which, if carried out, could insure the future of physical education/kinesiology in the 21st century, and (2) some *general observations* about the culture at large and the international scene:

Specific Recommendations. Based on what has been reported in this historical analysis of physical education/kinesiology in the 20th century, can it be stated arguably that the field through its own efforts has indeed undergone a significant process of modification? Can it also be stated that the field has simply been in the unfavorable position of being buffeted about by all of the various social forces of the 20th century? One might ask whether we have more than our share of "that vast majority who either watches things happen, or doesn't even know that anything is going on." Whatever the answer to these three questions may be, I feel constrained to ask further at this juncture, "could we possibly take control of our professional destinies?" Is there a chance that we could soon become somewhat more able to make things happen in our field within education and within the larger society? In other words, are we as a profession willing to accept the idea of, and then assist in the forging of, a behavioral science image of man and woman as people who are continuously adapting reality to our own ends to the greatest extent possible?

After lengthy consideration of the subject over a period of many years, I do feel able to state firmly that we have definitely undergone a process of considerable modification. I use the term "modification" deliberately, rather than the terms "change," "alteration," "variation," "transformation," "conversion," or "transmutation." By this I mean that we are definitely tending to restrict, limit, or qualify what it is that *we*—in what is called sport and physical education by NASPE and kinesiology and physical education by the Academy (AAKPE)—should be doing professionally. Nevertheless, we have also indubitably reached the point in our professional development where we MUST sharpen our focus. I state this, because my fear is that this process of modification is occurring too slowly. In the meantime, other social forces are arising; are crowding us and delimiting our development in various undesirable ways; and are, in the process, often buffeting us unmercifully. The following, then, are some of the changes that are occurring.

1. Because in the past the field of physical education has sought to be "all things to all people," *we now don't know exactly what we stand for.* Pretty soon we won't even be certain whether push-ups and jogging still belong to us. What ever happened to Arthur Steinhaus's "principal principles" of physical education? Where does our major thrust lie?
2. *All sorts of name changes are occurring* to explain either what people think we are doing or should be doing, not to mention how they can camouflage the "unsavory" connotation of the term "physical education." Thus, we are becoming kinesiology, human kinetics, ergonomics, sport management, sport studies, kinanthropology, or what have you?
3. The advent of Sputnik (1958); the subsequent "race for the moon" and how this affected education, science, and technology; Conant's devastating criticism of the presumed academic content of our curricula (1963); and the subsequent almost frantic drive for a body-of-knowledge based on solid scientific and scholarly investigation for the field have placed us in a curious position as a profession—*we really don't know where or what our body of knowledge is.* Nowhere is it available

to us in a series of ordered principles or generalizations based on an accepted taxonomy of subdisciplinary and subprofessional specializations.

4. *We are not supporting our own professional organizations anywhere nearly sufficiently,* either at the state or provincial, or national levels in either the United States or Canada. As a result, they are struggling with insufficient funding and are thereby incapable of meeting the many demands being made by the practitioners.
5. *An ever-widening gap is developing* between what might be called the related-discipline sport societies and the established profession of physical education—i.e. those people who belong to the National Association for Sport and Physical Education, ARAPCS, NAGWS, and ICHPER in the United States. (The same sort of gap was developing in Canada between the Canadian Association for Health, Physical Education and Recreation and the Canadian Intramural Recreation Association, but recently because of financial constraints the Federal Government has mandated a partial merger. However, sadly, the Canadian Association for Sport Sciences has recently moved even further away from the field of physical education by changing its name to the Canadian Society for Exercise Physiology. The journal has also been changed from *Canadian Journal of Sport Sciences* to *Canadian Journal of Applied Physiology,* thereby narrowing its scope enormously.) Also, we find the North American Society for the Sociology of Sport, the Philosophic Society for the Study of Sport, the Association for the Anthropological Study of Play, the North American Society for Sport History, the American College of Sport Medicine, and many others who for the larger part could seemingly care less, to put it bluntly, what happens to the profession of physical education along with its programs at the elementary and secondary levels of education. It was very interesting to note the recent plea by Sparks (1992, 1, 10–11) in which he also asked our "specialists" to consider integrating more closely with the profession.
6. Despite the fact that the College Entrance Examination Board in the United States in the early 1970s established a commission that eventually *recommended much greater weight and consideration in entrance requirements be allotted to certain important qualities and attributes over and above the traditional verbal factor and mathematical factor* (e.g., sensitivity and commitment to social responsibility, political and social leadership, ability to adapt to new situations), there is no evidence that we have stressed, or even understand to any degree, whether physical education majors possess originally or subsequently achieve knowledge, competence, or skill in any of the total of nine vital components as recommended by the CEEB. In Canada there never was any question in this regard: The academic average is now the one deciding factor in decision-making in regard to university entrance, and in Ontario, for example, there is talk of bringing back provincial-level examinations and standardized testing along the way.
7. *Another unacceptable series of "internal" gaps* has developed among (a) the people in physical education concerned with the bioscience aspects of the field; (b) those investigating the social science and humanities aspects of the discipline; (c) a third group concerned with the professional preparation of physical educators and with investigation concerning what might be called the subprofessional aspects of the field (e.g., curriculum, instructional methodology, supervision, management); (d) a group of professionals promoting professional training in sport management; and (e) the professional practitioners in the field where divisions often exist among the physical educator, the coach, and the dance teacher.

8. *A further disturbing development is taking place.* For several reasons, at least one of which is our fault, the highly influential and volatile area of competitive sport has become a playground for several of our allied professions, as well as for an increasing number of people in what we call our related disciplines. Many of these people became aware of the ever-increasing popularity of exercise programs and competitive sport, and are tackling "our" problems in a piecemeal fashion, often without a full awareness of sport and physical education's total (claimed!) domain and outlook. Here we are referring to the relatively recent, close identification of the recreation profession with highly competitive sport and fitness, the interest of health educators in exercise science, the involvement of physiotherapists in adaptive or special physical education, the developing relationship between business administration and sport management and/or intercollegiate sport, and, of course, the gradually awakening interest of historians, philosophers, sociologists, psychologists, anthropologists, physiologists, medical professors, biomechanics specialists, etc. in competitive sport. All of these people could readily help our mission without seeming to ignore us or put us out of business at the same time.
9. Steadily, but surely, because physical education has been struggling to acquire an "academic image" since it was criticized so sharply by Conant in the early 1960s, *a larger wedge than ever has been driven between physical education and intercollegiate athletics.* (Of course, that relatively small, but highly visible, segment of intercollegiate sport that may be called "big-time, commercial, intercollegiate athletics" has been subject to all sorts of abuses throughout this century and is to all intents and purposes out of educational control.) This has been a highly unfortunate development for us and, I do believe, for them, too. A relatively small group of pressure-driven administrators and coaches has used us and many of their colleagues in other disciplines as well, not to mention the unethical way in which many so-called scholar-athletes have been sacrificed along the way (e.g., the extremely large percentage of black athletes who have not graduated). This has been most unfortunate for all concerned.
10. Finally, and such a listing as this always seems to include 10 items, *I detect an uneasiness or malaise no doubt brought on by the developments of the past 25 years.* Possibly the most crucial aspects of the modification that I claim we are undergoing are the beliefs of those who seem ready and willing to write off physical education. Also, there is evidence that some within the field are losing their *will to win.* In the final analysis this latter conclusion could be the most devastating of all the aspects of modification indicated above.

General Intercultural Observations. In addition to including some political and social observations about world development early in this chapter, I felt it necessary to include some "general intercultural observations" with more direct implications for the physical education/kinesiology field before concluding here. There are a relatively small number of physical educators and a minute number of coaches with what I would call an international orientation in relation to their chosen profession, but I'm concerned that the vast majority in the United States especially who feel that "if anything worthwhile is going to happen, it will be here," and that "it had better be made available in English if I am to be expected to read it." This may sound harsh, but it is my considered opinion that far too much of this attitude prevails, and it does not bode well for the 21st century.

For this reason it is important that the International Council for Health, Physical Education, and Recreation (sponsored by AAHPERD) has for decades now continued to strive to broaden our horizons. Also, the inauguration of the International Society for Comparative Physical Education and Sport in 1968 in Israel marked the beginning of a second thrust in this direction. It is through efforts such as this that we in this profession may be able to assist civilization to move a bit faster toward what Glasser (1972) identified as "Civilized Identity Society" in which the concern of humans will again—as he theorizes—focus on such concepts as "self-identity," "self-expression," and "cooperation." Postulating that so-called "primitive society" societies ended in a great many areas several thousand years ago as populations increased sharply and some countries considered it necessary to take essential resources from neighboring societies, he argued that a "civilized survival" situation ensued. Now for the continuation of life on this planet, with ecological dictates and presumed economic requirements clashing sharply, it is possible—but not probable—that humankind may re-enter what Glasser called civilized identity society again.

Encouragement to move in this direction comes from the findings of Kaplan (1961, pp. 7–10) who over three decades ago found even then certain "recurring elements in the various world philosophies." Despite continuing warfare on earth—29 major ones in the current year—Kaplan theorized that there are indeed four recurring themes of rationality, activity, humanism, and preoccupation with values present in the leading world philosophies.

For reasons such as the above, I have been promoting for 20 years the fundamental importance of three concepts as we move toward the twenty-first century: the concepts of "communication," "diversity," and "cooperation." First, the concept of "communication" has now become vitally important because what the late Isaac Asimov (1970, pp. 17–20) called a "fourth revolution" has occurred in this area. We now witness its presence every day! The world has moved from the invention of speech, to writing, to mechanical reproduction of the printed word, and now to relay stations in space creating a blanketing communications network that will make possible a type of international personal relationship hitherto undreamed of by men and women.

Interestingly, this development has fantastic implications for the profession of physical education and sport, making it mandatory that we view this aspect of our task in a new light. Basically, the world *MUST* "win this race"—that is, this vastly improved means of communication must be employed to foster international goodwill and cooperation rather than as a means to promote global conflict.

Second, the concept of "diversity"—the state or fact of being different, unlike, or diverse—must be fostered as well. We are a diverse lot—now both here *and* abroad, and we simply must come to understand this diversity ever so much better than we do at present. It is at this point that the struggle between the world's leading ideologies comes into focus. Communists—both before the collapse of the U.S.S.R. and still at present in China and elsewhere—argue that humankind in social settings must pass through four stages: from agrarianism to capitalism to socialism and, finally, to ideal communism. Presently, hovering presumably somewhere between the second and third stages, we can observe that China, for example, has completely stifled the concept of "diversity" in their culture. So the question is whether we can ever have a world in which all people could be "significantly diverse" if they wish. Must we eventually have a type of operant conditioning (à la B. F. Skinner) involving behavior modification so that people's actions are regulated more stringently than ever before because of overpopulation, aggressive tendencies, and many other deterrents? This is the major issue that will have to be addressed in the not-too-distant future, and we can only hope that this crucial issue can be worked out peacefully (Skinner, 1971).

Third, the concept of "cooperation" must be paramount in our planning for the future along with the other two concepts mentioned above. Cooperation implies working together for a common purpose or benefit. As the world grows "smaller," we must pay ever so much more attention to international relations. This will be vital within society generally, as well as between cultures. The field of education can lead the world in this respect. Our specific concern is how this applies to the field of physical education and sport as we develop new plans and extend the horizons for cooperation in the various aspects of endeavor among individuals, groups, and societies on earth—and maybe someday in space.

As we contemplate this "Third Wave" world, what will this mean to us who are interested in human motor performance in sport, exercise, and expressive movement for people of all ages who might be classified as "accelerated," "normal," and "special" populations? We have our responsibilities in our own countries, of course, to help people understand the need for, and opportunities in, human motor performance of a correct and desirable nature throughout their lives. Our role is to so guide general education that all will comprehend that healthful and enjoyable physical activity is necessary to promote (1) circulo-respiratory efficiency, (2) joint flexibility, (3) adequate muscular strength, and (4) the development and maintenance of correct, functional segmental alignment of bodily parts to foster health, functional efficiency, and aesthetic movement.

As we look outward to all parts of the world, however, we need to devise a step-by-step approach for the description, interpretation, comparison, and evaluation of prevailing patterns of human movement from a cross-cultural standpoint. As matters stand now in the United States especially, many travelers' tales have been told, but very little educational borrowing has been carried out. A number of other countries have been more cosmopolitan than we in this regard, and their relative progress is significant. Admittedly, a certain amount of international cooperation has occurred, but language barriers, economic shortages, a resurgence of unwise nationalism, and other barriers have hampered development. Many come to North America to learn, but very few of us have the desire to go elsewhere to learn, much less the language capability to profit from such an experience or the funds to support the venture. In summary, what is needed is an international strategy for a worldwide cross-cultural comparison, a step-by-step analysis of the prevailing patterns of human movement in sport, exercise, and expressive movement. Only in this way will it be possible for the profession to reach its potential on a worldwide basis in the future.

CONCLUDING STATEMENT

Above I have argued that the profession is neither dead nor quiescent, but that it has definitely been undergoing serious modification throughout the course of the 20th century. I believe it can be further argued successfully that our profession—sport and physical education in the United States (i.e., physical education and kinesiology) and physical and health education as it is called by a significant number in Canada—has not been growing and developing as rapidly and strongly as it should be in a society where the idea of "change" must now become our watchword. It is difficult to refute the thought that change is here to stay. Our problem seems to be that we are "ill" ("running a slow fever," one might say) and that many recognize the symptoms, but that they don't appreciate the serious nature of the illness and are therefore unwilling to take drastic action in an effort to effect a cure.

I wish that I were able to say that I had overstated the 10 developments above that seem so disturbing to me. They indicate a serious modification of what (in perhaps rosy retrospect) seemed to be physical education's earlier halcyon state at the turn of the 20th century. Other problems and issues could be recounted by some with a different perspective. I wish that I could simply shout "April Fool" and be done with it. Alas, such is not the case. In my opinion these problems represent accurately the modification that our profession has been undergoing.

What should we do—perhaps what *must* we do—to ensure that the profession will move decisively and rapidly in the direction of what might be called *true* professional status? Granting that the various social forces will impact upon us willy-nilly, we must determine what we can do collectively in the years ahead that will bring about the best possible solution to the continuing efforts of all those men and women who throughout the 20th century have had a deep commitment for the future of all that physical education/kinesiology stands for in serving as a highly valuable component of human life.

Without attempting to enumerate specifically where any stumbling blocks might confront us as we strive to move ahead strongly in the 21st century, I would like to propose four major processes (March and Simon, 1958, pp.

129–131) that could be employed chronologically as we seek to realize our desired objective as follows:

1. *Problem-solving.* Basically what is being proposed here is a problem for our profession to solve or resolve. We must move as soon as possible to convince others of the worthwhileness of our plans for rejuvenation. Part of our approach includes assurance that the objectives are indeed operational (i.e., that their presence or absence can in most cases be tested empirically as we progress). In this way, even if sufficient funding or unanimous approval were not available—and it well might not be—the various parties who are vital or necessary to the ultimate success of the field would at least have reached considerable consensus about the field's objectives. However, with a professional task of this magnitude, it is possible, and quite probable, that consensus will not be achieved at the outset.
2. *Persuasion.* For the sake of argument, then, let us assume that many of our objectives on the way toward the achievement of long-range aims are not shared by the others whom we need to convince, people who are either inside our own profession or are in allied professions or related disciplines. On the assumption that the stance of the others is not absolutely fixed or intractable, then this second step of persuasion can (should) be employed on the assumption that *at some level* our objectives will be shared, and that disagreement over subgoals can be mediated by reference to common goals.

   Note: If persuasion were to work, then the parties concerned can obviously return to the problem-solving level (No. 1 above).
3. *Bargaining.* We will now move along to the third stage of a theoretical plan on the assumption that the second step (persuasion) didn't fully work either. This means obviously that there is still disagreement over the operational goals proposed at the problem-solving level (the first stage). Now the profession has a difficult decision to make: do we attempt to strike a bargain, or do we decide that we simply must "go it alone" without the help and approval of—say—our allied professions, related disciplines, or the public?

   The problem with the first alternative is that bargaining implies compromise, and compromise means that each group involved will have to surrender a portion of its claim, request or argument. The second alternative above may seem more desirable, but following it may also mean eventual failure in achieving the final, most important objective.

   Note: We can appreciate, of course, that the necessity of proceeding to this stage, and then selecting either of the two alternatives, is obviously much less desirable than settling the matter at either the first or second stage.
4. *Politicking:* The implementation of the fourth stage (or plan of attack) is based on the fact that proposed action of the first three stages has failed.

   The participants in the discussion cannot agree in any way about the main issues. It is at this point that the organization (or professional association) involved has to somehow expand the number of parties or groups involved in consideration of the proposed objectives and the overall plan. The goal is, of course, to attempt to include potential allies so as to improve the chance of achieving the final desired objective. Employing so-called "power politics" is usually tricky, however, and it may indeed backfire upon any group bringing such a maneuver into play. However, this is the way the world (or society) works, and the goal may well be worth the risk or danger involved.

Note: Obviously, we hope that it will not be necessary to operate at this fourth stage too frequently in connection with the highest type of development for our profession. Politicking is often divisive and time-consuming and, at times, does more harm than good.

Finally, what we professionals with a humanistic orientation should be thinking is that life has everything to do with succeeding at the level of *doing one's best* as we strive to be "creatures who adapt reality to our own ends, who transform reality into a congenial form, and who make their own reality." This concept of the ideal way to live explains that not everyone catches the brass ring on life's carousel. Most of us had better enjoy the ride for its own sake, or we may end up believing that life has no meaning at all. Finally, in this shrinking world we had better do all that we can to encourage others to control the world population and to live together peacefully—or else this "noble experiment" of humankind may have well been in vain. . . .

REFERENCES AND GENERAL BIBLIOGRAPHY

AMERICAN ALLIANCE FOR HEALTH, PHYSICAL EDUCATION, RECREATION AND DANCE. (1962). *Professional preparation in health education, physical education, recreation education.* Report of national conference. Washington, DC: Author.

AMERICAN ALLIANCE FOR HEALTH, PHYSICAL EDUCATION, RECREATION AND DANCE. (1974). *Professional preparation in dance, physical education, recreation education, safety education, and school health education.* Report on national conference. Washington, DC: Author.

ASIMOV, I. (Oct. 24, 1970). The fourth revolution. *Saturday Review,* 24:17–20.

BERELSON, B., & STEINER, G. A. (1964). *Human behavior.* New York: Harcourt Brace Jovanovich.

BOOKWALTER, K. W., & BOOKWALTER, C. W. (1980). *A review of thirty years of selected research on undergraduate professional preparation physical education programs in the United States.* Unionville, IN: Author.

BRUBACHER, J. S. (1966). *A history of the problems of education* (2nd ed.). New York: McGraw-Hill.

BRUBACHER, J. S. (1969). *Modern philosophies of education* (4th ed.). New York: McGraw-Hill.

CANADIAN ASSOCIATION FOR HEALTH, PHYSICAL EDUCATION AND RECREATION. (1966). *Physical education and athletics in Canadian universities and colleges* (pp. 14–21). Ottawa: Author.

COMMAGER, H. S. (1961). A quarter century—Its advances. *Look,* 25, 10 (June 6), 80–91.

CONANT, J. B. (1963). *The education of American teachers* (pp. 122–123). New York: McGraw-Hill.

COSENTINO, F., & HOWELL, M. L. (1971). *A history of physical education in Canada.* Don Mills, Ont.: General Publishing Co.

COUSINS, N. (Aug. 24, 1974). Prophecy and pessimism, *Sat Rev. WORLD,* 6–7.

COWELL, C. C. (1960). The contributions of physical activity to social development. *Research Quarterly,* 31, 2 (May, Part II), 286–306.

ELLIOTT, R. (1927). *The organization of professional training in physical education in state universities.* New York: Columbia Teachers College.

FLATH, A. W. (1964). *A history of relations between the National Collegiate Athletic Association and the Amateur Athletic Union of the United States (1905–1963).* Champaign, IL: Stipes. (Includes a foreword by E. F. Zeigler entitled Amateurism, semiprofessionalism, and professionalism in sport: A persistent historical problem.)

GLASSER, W. (1972). *The identity society.* NY: Harper and Row.

GOULD, S. B. (Sept. 23, 1969). The academic condition, *The New York Times,* 30.

HESS, F. A. (1959). *American objectives of physical education from 1900 to 1957 assessed in light of certain historical events.* Doctoral dissertation, New York University.

JOHNSON, H. M. (1969). The relevance of the theory of action to historians. *Social Science Quarterly,* (June), 46–58.

KAPLAN, A. *The new world of philosophy.* Boston: Houghton Mifflin.

KENNEDY, P. (1987). *The rise and fall of the great powers.* NY: Random House.

KENNEDY, W. F. (1965). *Health, physical education, and recreation in Canada: A history of professional preparation.* Unpublished doctoral dissertation, Teachers College, Columbia University.

LAUWERYS, J. A. (1959). The philosophical approach to comparative education. *International Review of Education,* V, 283–290.

LAZERTE, M. E. (1950). *Teacher education in Canada.* Toronto: W. J. Gage.

LEONARD, F. E., & AFFLECK, G. B. (1947). *The history of physical education* (3rd ed.). Philadelphia: Lea & Febiger.

LIPSET, S. M. (1973). National character. In D. Koulack & D. Perlman (Eds.), *Readings in social psychology: Focus on Canada.* Toronto: Wiley.

MCCURDY, J. H. (1901). Physical training as a profession. *American Physical Education Review,* 6, 4:311–312.

MEAGHER, J. W. (1958). *A projected plan for the re-organization of physical education teacher-training programs in Canada.* Unpublished doctoral dissertation, Pennsylvania State University.

MEAGHER, J. W. (1965). Professional preparation. In M. L. Van Vliet (Ed.), *Physical Education in Canada* (pp. 64–81). Scarborough, Ont.: Prentice-Hall of Canada.

MERGEN, FRANCOIS. (1970). Man and his environment. *Yale Alumni Magazine,* XXXIII, 8 (May), 36–37.

MORRIS, V. C. (1956). Physical education and the philosophy of education. *Journal of Health, Physical Education and Recreation,* (March), 21–22, 30–31.

MORROW, L. D. (1975). *Selected topics in the history of physical education in Ontario: From Dr. Egerton Ryerson to the Strathcona Trust (1844–1939).* Unpublished doctoral dissertation, The University of Alberta.

MURRAY, B. G. JR. (1972). What the ecologists can teach the economists. *The New York Times Magazine,* December 10, 38–39, 64–65, 70, 72.

NAISBITT, J. (1982). *Megatrends.* NY: Warner.

NEVINS, A. (1962). *The gateway to history.* Garden City, NY: Doubleday.

NOAH, H. J., & ECKSTEIN, M. A. (1969). *Toward a science of comparative education.* NY: Macmillan.

OBERLIN COLLEGE *Catalogue* (1894).

PATON, G. A. (1975). The historical background and present status of Canadian physical education. In E. F. Zeigler (Ed.), *A history of physical education and sport in the United States and Canada* (pp. 441–443). Champaign, IL: Stipes.

PROCEEDINGS OF THE 6TH COMMONWEALTH CONFERENCE. (1978). *Sport, physical education, recreation proceedings* (Vols. 1 and 2). Edmonton, Alberta: University of Alberta.

ROYCE, J. R. (1964). Paths to knowledge. In *The encapsulated man.* Princeton, NJ: Van Nostrand.

SCHWARTZ, E. S. (1971). *Overskill: Decline of technology in modern civilization.* NY: Times Books.

SKINNER, B. F. (1971). *Beyond freedom and dignity.* NY: Knopf.

SPAETH, M. J. (1975). Administrative research in physical education and athletics. In *Administrative Theory and Practice in Physical Education and Athletics* (E. F. Zeigler & M. J. Spaeth, eds. & aus.), p. 44.

SPARKS, W. (1992). Physical education for the 21st Century: Integration, not specialization. *NAPEHE: The Chronicle of Physical Education in Higher Education,* 4, 1:1–10–11.

TOFFLER, A. (1970). *Future shock.* NY: Random House.

UPDATE (April 1993), 1. (Newsletter of the Alliance for Health, Physical Education, Recreation, and Dance, Reston, VA).

VAN VLIET, M. L. (Ed.). (1965). *Physical education in Canada.* Scarborough, Ontario: Prentice-Hall.

WELLESLEY COLLEGE *Catalogue* (1910).

ZEIGLER, E. F. (1951). *A history of undergraduate professional preparation in physical education in the United States, 1861–1948.* Eugene, OR: Oregon Microfiche.

ZEIGLER, E. F. (1962). A history of professional preparation for physical education in the United States (1861–1961). In *Professional preparation in health education, physical education, and recreation education* (pp. 116–133). Washington, DC: The American Association for Health, Physical Education, and Recreation.

ZEIGLER, E. F. (1968). *Problems in the history and philosophy of physical education and sport.* Englewood Cliffs, NJ: Prentice-Hall.

ZEIGLER, E. F. (1975). Historical perspective on contrasting philosophies of professional preparation for physical education in the United States. In *Personalizing physical education and sport philosophy* (pp. 325–347). Champaign, IL: Stipes.

ZEIGLER, E. F. (Ed. & Au.). (1975). *A history of physical education and sport in the United States and Canada.* Champaign, IL: Stipes.

ZEIGLER, E. F. (1977). *Physical education and sport philosophy.* Englewood Cliffs, NJ: Prentice-Hall.

ZEIGLER, E. F. (1979). The past, present, and recommended future development in physical education and sport in North America. In *Proceedings of The American Academy of Physical Education* (G. M. Scott (Ed.)), Washington, DC: The American Alliance for Health, Physical Education, Recreation, and Dance.

ZEIGLER, E. F. (1980). A systems approach to the development and use of theory and research in sport and physical education. *Sportwissenschaft,* 10, 4, 404–416.

ZEIGLER, E. F. (1980). An evolving Canadian tradition in the new world of physical education and sport. In S. A. Davidson & P. Blackstock (Eds.), *The R. Tait McKenzie Addresses* (pp. 53–62). Ottawa, Canada: Canadian Association for Health, Physical Education and Recreation.

ZEIGLER, E. F. (Ed. & Au.). (1982). *Physical education and sport: An introduction.* Philadelphia: Lea & Febiger.

ZEIGLER, E. F. (1983a). Relating a proposed taxonomy of sport and developmental physical activity to a planned inventory of scientific findings. *Quest,* 35, 54–65.

ZEIGLER, E. F., & BOWIE, G. W. (1983b). *Developing management competency in sport and physical education.* Philadelphia: Lea & Febiger.

ZEIGLER, E. F. (1986). Undergraduate professional preparation in physical education, 1960–1985. *The Physical Educator,* 43(1), 2–6.

ZEIGLER, E. F. (1986). *Assessing sport and physical education: Diagnosis and projection.* Champaign, IL: Stipes.

ZEIGLER, E. F. *et al.* (1988). *A history of physical education and sport.* Champaign, IL: Stipes.

ZEIGLER, E. F. (1988). A comparative analysis of undergraduate professional preparation in physical education in the United States and Canada. In Broom, E., Clumpner, R., Pendleton, B., & Pooley, C. (Eds.), *Comparative physical education and sport, Volume 5.* Champaign, IL: Human Kinetics.

ZEIGLER, E. F. (1989). *Sport and physical education philosophy.* Carmel, IN: Benchmark.

ZEIGLER, E. F. (1990). *Sport and physical education: Past, present, future.* Champaign, IL: Stipes.

Chapter Two

Functional Effects of Physical Activity

James S. Skinner

One of the best ways to study how the body functions is to increase the demands on its various parts and then see how they adjust. No mechanism is better suited for this than exercise. Muscles can increase the turnover of energy 80 to 90 times their resting rate for a few seconds and 20 to 25 times the resting rate for several hours. By contrast, the highest "non-exercise" rate can be seen in nude persons sitting in a room where the temperature is below zero. When these people shiver uncontrollably, their metabolism is only four times greater than that seen at rest. While it may be argued that shivering is a form of exercise, the comparison is clearer when one considers that the same amount of energy is required to walk at the moderately fast pace of 3.5 mph.

Each of the many forms of occupational, leisure, and sports activities places specific demands on the various systems of the body. Exercising continuously for 20 to 30 minutes, for example, requires *immediate responses* by the nervous, muscular, cardiovascular, respiratory, hormonal, and thermoregulatory systems. There are even responses at the cellular level. In short, physical activity puts demands on almost all parts of the body. Likewise, training produces a number of *chronic adaptations* that are specific to the kind of training involved. These adaptations occur in all the systems mentioned above. By studying how the body responds to and recovers from the many types of physical activity, as well as how it adapts to the many kinds of training programs, a better understanding of bodily function can be obtained.

It should be remembered that these adjustments do not occur without good reason. If the reader can perceive and understand the logic of these modifications, then the study of the functional effects of physical activity can be simple, stimulating, interesting, and satisfying. These are the objectives of this chapter.

DEFINITIONS

Two terms are often used and need to be defined. *Work* is the amount of force applied over a distance; it is not related to time in any way. *Power* is the amount of work applied per unit of time. Thus, if 50 kg is lifted 2 m, then 100 kg·m of work is performed (regardless of how much time was needed to do it.) If the same 50 kg is lifted 2 m once every 3 seconds or 20 times/min, then a power output (PO) of 2000 kg·m/min (50 × 2 × 20) is performed.

In oversimplified terms, *exercise* is a form of physiological stimulation of the body. In this sense, exercise can be considered any form of physical activity "involving movement, maintenance of posture or expression of force by muscles" (Knuttgen, 1976). The performance of exercise requires the response of a number of functions within the body. The degree to which each of these functions is needed depends on the intensity, duration, and frequency of the activity, as well as on the specific characteristics of the activity performed. In other words, specific forms of exercise produce specific responses in specific people, i.e., identical exercise stimuli produce different responses in different people and even different responses in the same person at different times.

Training is the adaptation (chronic response) by the body to the repeated physiological stimulation of exercise. Adaptation is produced only in those parts of the body that are stimulated to respond (principles of overload and specificity) and is generally of two kinds: structural and functional. Structural adaptations are characterized by changes in the number and/or size of the functional units within each bodily system involved, while functional adaptations are characterized by modifications in the function of these systems. Muscular hypertrophy as a result of strength training is an example of a structural adaptation, and the reduction in heart rate seen at a given PO after endurance training is an example of a functional change. Generally speaking, functional adaptations occur earlier, but are also lost sooner. Structural adaptations take longer to achieve, but also last longer when training is decreased or is stopped; the time required to reverse a structural change also depends on how long it had been present.

The term *physical fitness* implies many things to many people. Its importance to individuals varies during their lifetime and can be influenced by the type of activity they usually do, as well as by their motivation to do that activity. Fitness can also be specific to individuals, depending on the physiological challenges that they will meet in their life. Thus, a marathon runner and a weight lifter both need high levels of specific components that are a part of overall fitness; namely, endurance and strength, respectively. Even though the marathon runner may not be strong and the weight lifter may not have much endurance, each athlete is "fit" to do those activities he/she likes. For this reason, a concise definition of physical fitness is not presented. In general terms, however, many changes occur in the body with regular activity. With the increase in the maximal capacity for work or power that usually occurs, there is a greater energy reserve. As a result, the same amount of work or power feels easier because it is less strenuous in relation to the increased maximum. If a person's maximum is high enough, daily tasks and pleasures can be done without fatigue, sufficient energy reserves will be available to meet unexpected emergencies safely, and enough extra energy will be available to enjoy leisure time.

There is a close relationship between physical fitness and the study of the functional effects of physical activity. Lamb states that

> the improvement in physical fitness could be defined as the application of the principles of exercise physiology to the improvement of man's response and adaptation to life's physical challenges. . . . It is unfortunate that many persons do not see the connection between exercise physiology and physical fitness, for better physical fitness programs could be designed to meet an individual's specific fitness needs if knowledge gained from studies of exercise physiology were more frequently applied to the design of fitness programs. (1978)

The study of the functional effects of physical activity is therefore related to the description and explanation of the acute responses and chronic adaptations of the body to single or repeated bouts of exercise. It is the factor of specificity that makes the study of these functional effects so complex, challenging, and interesting.

PRESENT STATE OF KNOWLEDGE

Basic Concepts. It is important that the reader be aware of certain basic concepts of how the body functions in order to understand this chapter. Examples will also be given throughout to clarify these concepts and to demonstrate how they are used in the study of the physiological functions during exercise.

1. The energy that is used for the functioning of every living cell in the body is produced by chemical reactions. These reactions are either aerobic (occurring in the presence of oxygen) or anaerobic (without oxygen).
2. A given amount of PO requires a given amount of energy, regardless of whether the energy is produced aerobically or anaerobically. If sufficient amounts of energy are not available, the exercise intensity will be reduced.
3. The relative contribution of these two forms of chemical reactions depends on the type, intensity, and duration of exercise.

4. If there are differences in pressure, concentration, or temperature between one part of the body and another, there will be a tendency for movement from areas of high pressure, concentration, or temperature to those areas with lower values in an attempt to reach an equilibrium.
5. The greater the differences in pressure, concentration, or temperature between two areas of the body, the greater the speed of this movement. If no difference exists, movement will cease.

Production of Energy. Energy needed for such bodily functions as muscle contraction, transmission of nervous impulses, and production of hormones is produced by the degradation of basic raw materials (oxygen, carbohydrates, and fat). For all practical purposes, protein is not used as a direct source for energy production. Proteins are used for the structural components of cells and are a major element of the enzymes that control the speed of different chemical reactions occurring in the cells. If more protein is eaten than is needed, the excess will be converted into either fat or carbohydrate.

Since we live in a sea of oxygen, there is usually not a problem of an adequate supply except at high altitude. After we eat, the stockpiles of the other raw materials are replenished. Fat is stored in fat cells, and all forms of carbohydrates (sugars, starches) are converted by the body to glucose, a simple sugar. This glucose is then transported in the blood to various parts of the body (muscle, liver, kidney, heart) where it is stored in the form of glycogen. Once these glycogen stores are filled, any excess glucose is converted to fat and stored as such.

During periods of fasting, liver glycogen is converted back to glucose and released into the blood stream. Glycogen cannot be released from muscle because the necessary enzyme for its conversion is not present. Thus, the liver is the main reservoir for glucose during fasting. This is an important mechanism for maintaining blood glucose levels, especially because the nervous system uses only glucose as fuel.

There are no such limitations on the release and utilization of fat by the body. A fat cell contains about 5% water, while each gram of carbohydrate is stored with 3 g of water. (It should be noted that other than sugar crystals, which are man-made, carbohydrates do not normally appear in nature without the presence of water (e.g., orange juice, syrup, potatoes, berries). As a result, fat can be stored in a more compact, easily transported form (9 kcal energy/g fat vs. 4 kcal/g for both carbohydrates and proteins) and is the body's major reservoir of potential energy.

Figure 2.1 is a schematic of the maximal amount of energy that a well-trained athlete can produce over time and of the relative importance of the aerobic and anaerobic mechanisms for energy production during exercise. For comparison, the energy requirement at rest is given a value of 1.

Figure 2.1 Total energy expenditure and the different sources of energy in relation to duration of exercise.

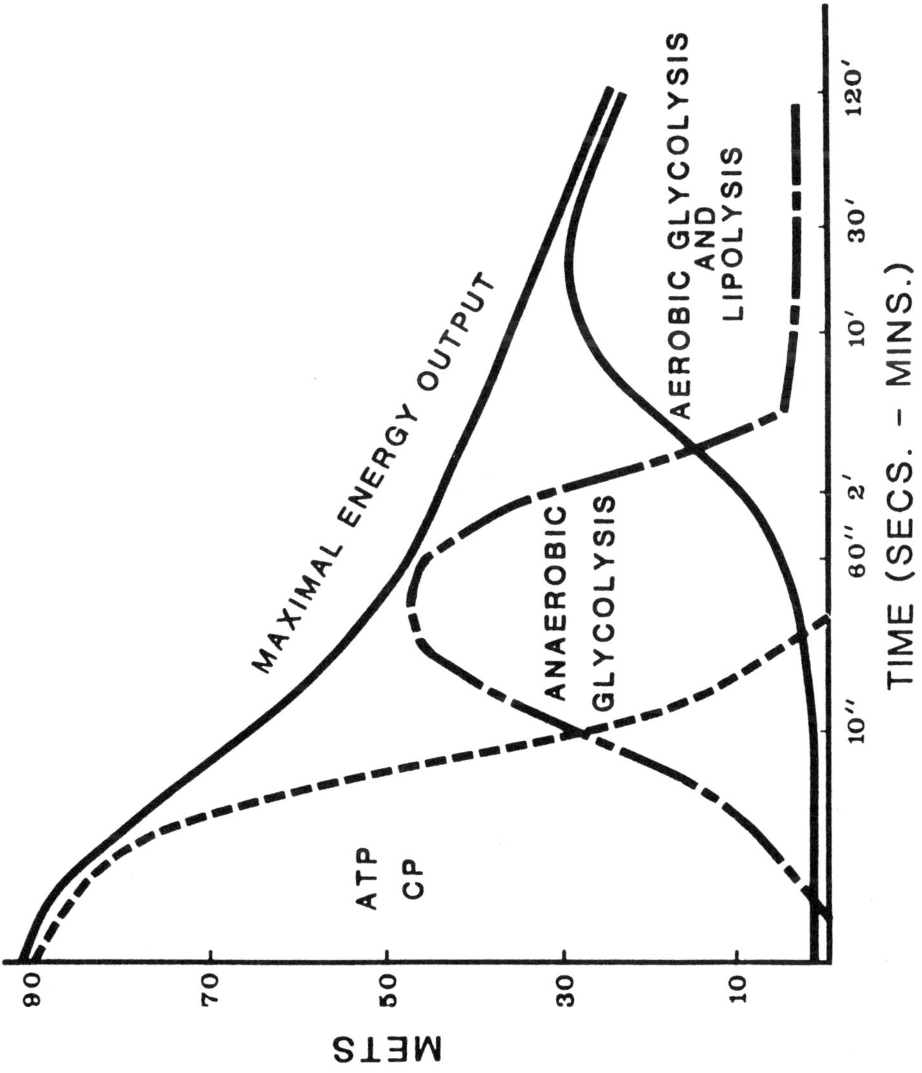

The body does store a very limited amount of energy in muscle for its immediate use, especially when energy is needed rapidly (e.g., at the onset of exercise or when going from walking to running). This energy is present in such energy-rich phosphates as adenosine triphosphate (ATP) and the form in which it is stored, phosphocreatine (PC). It is easy to understand the role of ATP and PC if one thinks of these limited reserves as a small battery that can provide energy until the body generates more ATP via aerobic or anaerobic chemical reactions. Even though ATP and PC are formed aerobically, their breakdown occurs very rapidly and does not require the presence of oxygen. They can be utilized for very brief periods during high-intensity exercise requiring energy levels that are 80 to 90 times the level normally found at rest (Fig. 2-1). As an example of the type of exercise that can be performed, it is possible to run at top speed for 8 to 10 seconds without breathing. During this time, the energy comes almost exclusively from that stored in the muscles.

Because these reserves are very limited, there must be a continuous re-synthesis of ATP if exercise is to continue. Although the aerobic system is the preferred, more efficient form of energy production, it takes time for the cardiovascular system to pick up and transport sufficient amounts of oxygen to the muscle fibers. As a result, only a fraction of the energy needed is provided by the aerobic mechanism at this time. A faster, emergency supply of energy is needed and this comes from the anaerobic breakdown of glycogen stored in the muscle. Depending on how hard the exercise is, and therefore how much energy is needed, the anaerobic mechanism can provide most of the energy for brief periods of 20 to 120 seconds. Because the re-synthesis of ATP takes more time, the supply of energy is not as great and can reach levels of only 30 to 70 times the energy requirement at rest (Fig. 2-1). Therefore, after running at top speed for 10 seconds, a runner has to slow down. This explains why an athlete cannot run 400 m as fast as he can 100 to 200 m, or why a weight lifter can lift more in one to two repetitions than he can in four to five lifts without a pause.

This emergency system has its disadvantages, however. Although the method is faster, lactate (LA) is produced during the anaerobic breakdown of glycogen. If too much LA is present in the muscle cell, it inhibits the efficiency of the aerobic chemical reactions. If this happens, not enough energy can be produced aerobically, and the person has to either slow down or use the anaerobic system more and more. The use of the anaerobic system is limited, however, by a person's tolerance to high levels of LA. For reasons that are still unclear, the accumulation of LA in the muscle and blood is associated with feelings of breathlessness, fatigue, and heaviness of muscles, forcing the person to stop.

The more efficient method for manufacturing energy is the breakdown of glycogen and fat in the presence of oxygen. Although this aerobic mechanism is slower, its advantage is that the supply of raw materials is essentially unlimited. As more and more oxygen is breathed in, picked up by the blood, pumped by the heart, and carried to the muscles where it is needed, aerobic reactions provide more and more energy. After 3 to 4 minutes, these aerobic reactions provide most of the energy needed. The longer the duration of exercise, the more important is the aerobic system. However, if the amount of energy required is greater than the slower aerobic reactions can provide (e.g., if the exercise intensity exceeds 60% to 80% of the average person's maximal aerobic power or $\dot{V}O_{2max}$) or if there is a sudden increase in the amount of energy needed, then the faster anaerobic system is once more activated as an emergency, back-up system. As can be seen in Figure 2.1, a highly trained endurance athlete can aerobically produce 20 to 25 times as much energy during prolonged exercise as he needs at rest.

It is a basic rule in exercise physiology that a given PO requires a given amount of energy, regardless of the source of that energy. The relative contribution of aerobic and anaerobic energy production depends on the type, intensity, and duration of exercise. Thus, brief, high-intensity, static, and intermittent activities that emphasize speed and strength tend to be anaerobic (using only CHO), whereas prolonged, low-intensity, dynamic and continuous activities that emphasize endurance tend to be aerobic (using both CHO and fat).

Based on findings from many studies, Skinner *et al.* (1989) proposed a classification system that included two aerobic, one mixed (aerobic and anaerobic), and two anaerobic types of activity. These five types include:

1. *Aerobic* activities requiring <65% to 80% $\dot{V}O_{2max}$ that can be continued for two hours or more.
2. *Aerobic* activities requiring <90% to 95% $\dot{V}O_{2max}$ that can be done for 10 to 60 minutes.
3. *Aerobic and anaerobic* activities requiring >90% to 95% $\dot{V}O_{2max}$ that can be sustained for up to eight minutes, but <200% $\dot{V}O_{2max}$ that can last up to one minute.
4. *Anaerobic* activities requiring 200% to 300% $\dot{V}O_{2max}$ that can be done for 20 to 45 seconds.
5. *Anaerobic* activities requiring 250% to 450% $\dot{V}O_{2max}$ that can be done for 1 to 10 seconds.

Figure 2.2 is a schematic diagram of this classification system, expressed as a percentage of the $\dot{V}O_{2max}$ for an average individual. The diagonal line in the upper figure shows that a given PO requires a given amount of energy. The areas below the diagonal represent an estimate of the relative contribution of stored energy (ATP and PC), anaerobic glycolysis, and aerobic metabolism at each PO. At low intensities requiring 75%–90% $\dot{V}O_{2max}$, most energy is derived from aerobic metabolism. As the intensity increases, the anaerobic system provides more and more energy until about 200%–250% $\dot{V}O_{2max}$. Finally, for activities requiring very high levels of energy (300%–400% $\dot{V}O_{2max}$), the phosphagens are the main source.

Figure 2.2 Schematic representation of energy needed, duration of exercise, and levels of blood lactate relative to power output. **A:** Energy needed, expressed as a percentage of the maximal aerobic power (VO_{2max}) and the relative contribution of aerobic metabolism, anaerobic glycolysis, and phosphagens (ATP and PC). **B:** Duration of exercise possible and the associated blood lactate level at the various power outputs. (ATP = adenosine triphosphate, PC = phosphocreatine.)

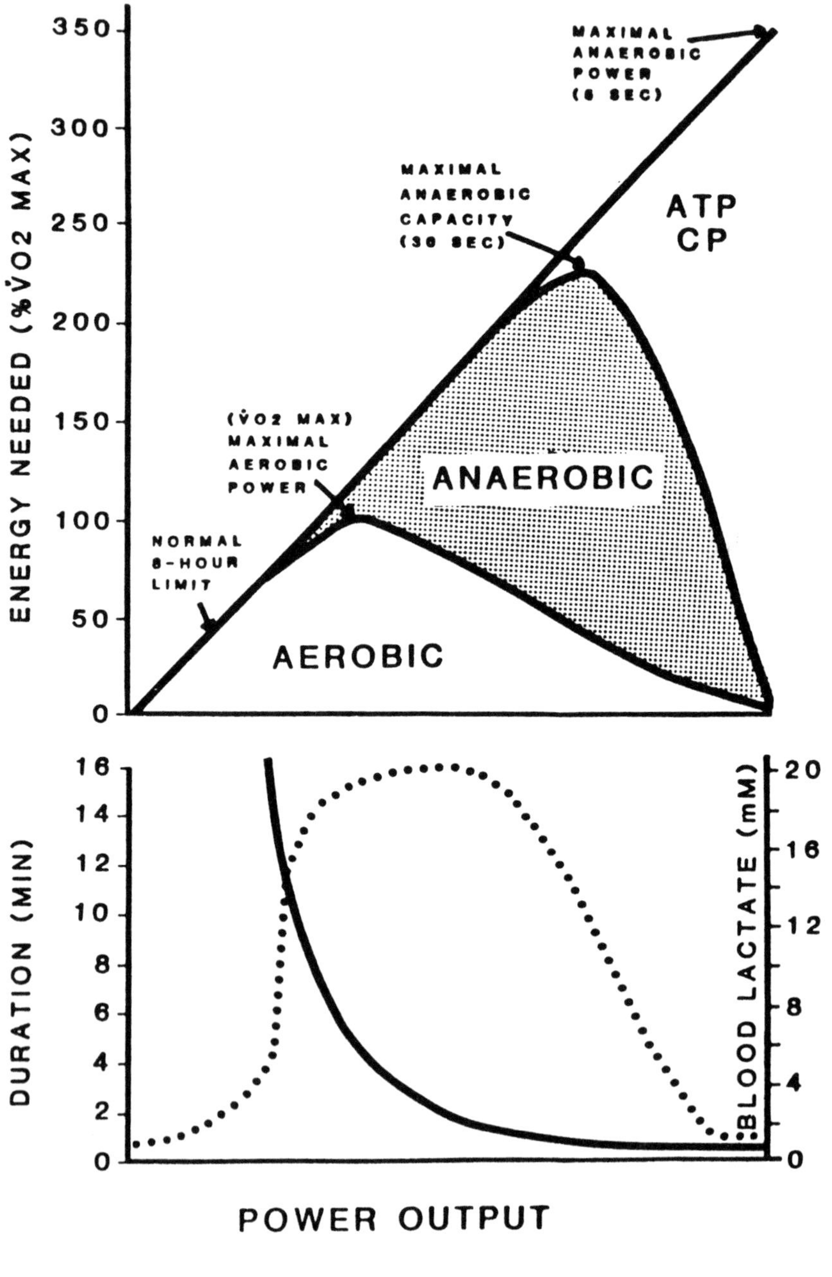

The solid curve in the lower part of Figure 2.2 depicts the maximal duration of exercise that can be done at each intensity. At low intensities, the energy source is primarily aerobic, and one can exercise for a long time. For example, it has been shown that one can work continuously at about 50% $\dot{V}O_{2max}$ for eight hours per day with no problems or fatigue. At the other extreme, if intensity is very high, then duration is very short because limited amounts of ATP and PC are available. For intensities that can be maintained for a maximum of one to eight minutes, energy is provided by both aerobic and anaerobic sources. As can be seen, there is a gradual transition from one source to another and no abrupt threshold.

The dashed curve in Figure 2.2 shows the association between blood LA levels and the various types of exercise. At low intensities and long durations, as well as at high intensities and short durations, low levels of blood LA are seen, suggesting that the energy sources are aerobic in the first case and phosphagens at the other extreme. The highest levels of LA are obtained during high-intensity activities lasting one to eight minutes that involve both the aerobic and anaerobic systems. Because both systems are providing energy, one can exercise long enough to accumulate high levels of LA.

From Figure 2.2, it can be seen that few activities are purely anaerobic or aerobic and these few occur only at the extremes of the intensity-duration continuum (e.g., sprinting and slow walking, respectively). Thus, intermittent activity can be aerobic (e.g., golf is low intensity) and prolonged activity can have anaerobic periods (e.g., sprinting in soccer).

Rest. Since the energy requirements of resting muscle are so low, all of the energy can be provided by the slower, more efficient aerobic mechanism. Fat is the preferred raw material for several reasons: (1) much more potential energy is stored as fat, while glycogen reserves are small and limited; (2) fat can be broken down only via the aerobic mechanism, while glycogen can be used in both aerobic and anaerobic reactions; and (3) by using more fat, glycogen stores are conserved in the liver (this is important for maintaining blood glucose levels) and in the muscle (muscle glycogen is the predominant fuel for anaerobic reactions during intense exercise). Both fat and carbohydrates are used for energy.

Onset of Exercise and Recovery. Once exercise starts, extra energy is needed right away. Because the aerobic system slowly increases its production of energy, there must be an emergency back-up system that will allow the body to function until the aerobic assembly line speeds up. This is the function of the anaerobic system.

By definition, oxygen is needed for aerobic reactions. Therefore, one way of determining the rate of aerobic energy production is to measure the amount

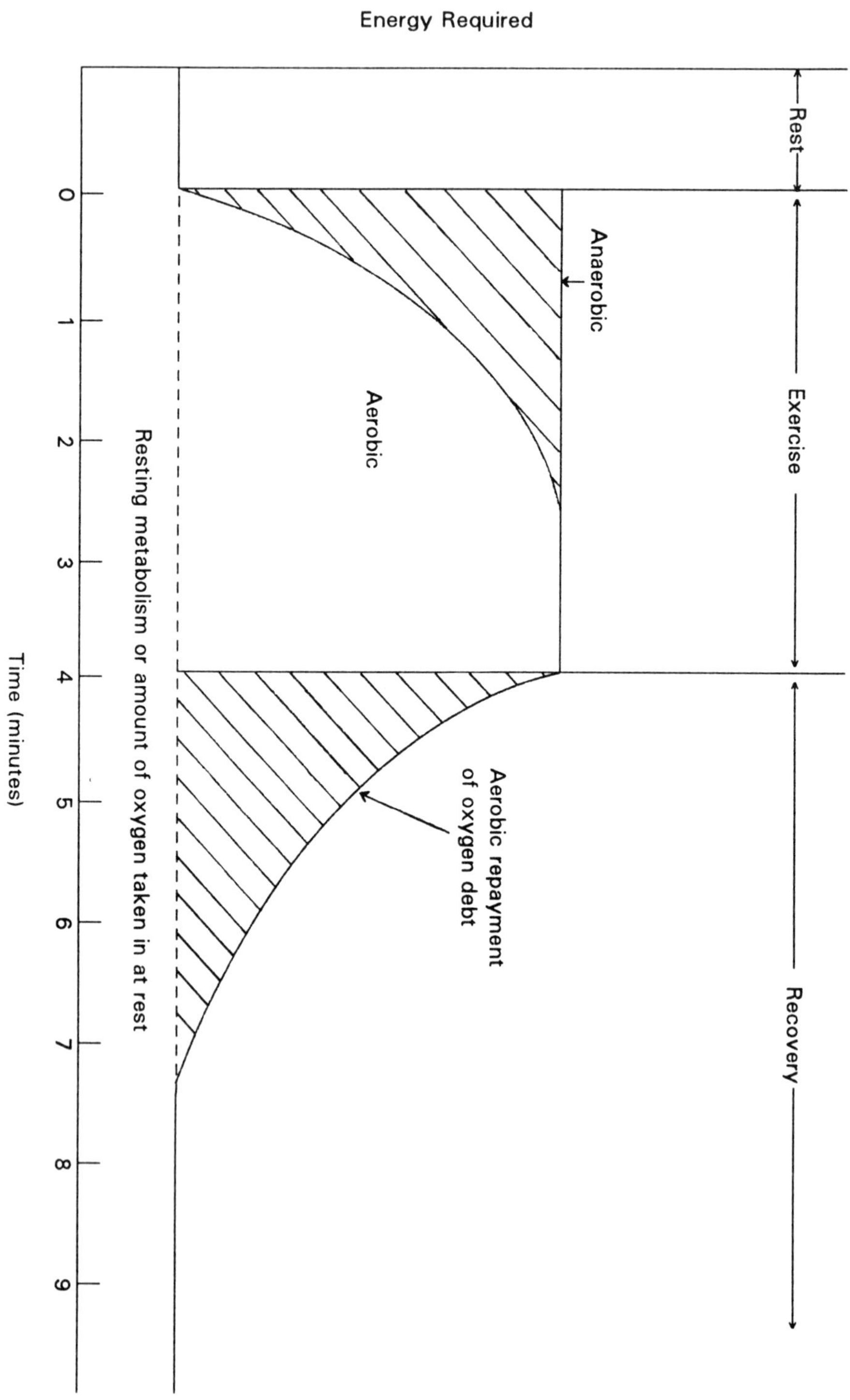

Figure 2.3 Energy required or amount of oxygen taken in by the body at rest, during exercise, and during recovery from exercise.

of oxygen taken in by the body. Figure 2.3 shows the typical course of oxygen intake ($\dot{V}O_2$) before, during, and after moderate exercise. At rest, only a small amount of energy or oxygen is used. Once activity starts and a given amount of exercise is performed, however, a given amount of energy is needed at all times; this energy requirement is represented by the solid horizontal line. The anaerobic system (ATP, PC and muscle glycogen) produces most of the energy at first until the aerobic system becomes activated. The shaded area on the left of Figure 2.3 shows the magnitude of this anaerobic energy supply. This is called the *oxygen deficit* and represents the amount of borrowed energy that must be repaid later.

With activation of the aerobic system, $\dot{V}O_2$ rises until there are no further increases after 3 to 4 minutes. This point is called the *steady state*, i.e., the amount of oxygen taken in is the same as the amount of oxygen being used to produce energy. It is at this point that $\dot{V}O_2$ is measured to determine the energy cost of an activity. Measures of heart rate (HR), blood pressure (BP), and respiration ($\dot{V}_E$) taken at this time also show a tendency to level off and stabilize. This fact is useful when testing people under standardized conditions and when prescribing exercise.

After exercise, HR, $\dot{V}_E$, and $\dot{V}O_2$ do not return immediately to their resting levels because one must pay aerobically for the energy borrowed from the anaerobic sources. The local supply of energy stored in the muscle (ATP, PC) must first be restocked for later use. In addition, the LA produced during the initial part of the exercise must be reconverted into glycogen. This conversion occurs in the muscle itself, as well as in the liver after the LA is transported via the blood. Since all of these chemical reactions require energy to proceed, an extra amount of oxygen must be consumed. This is referred to as paying off the *oxygen debt*. In other words, this is the amount of oxygen that would have been used during the first few minutes of exercise if it had been available, plus the extra oxygen needed for the elimination of LA. Like all debts, it takes longer to repay than it does to borrow, and one must pay a charge. In the case of LA, the energy can be borrowed in a few seconds, but the body requires about 15 minutes to eliminate one-half the LA produced. As well, there is an interest rate of about 24% (i.e., 24% more energy is needed just to convert LA back to glycogen). Thus, although the emergency anaerobic system is necessary and useful, it is more expensive to use.

Progressively Increasing Exercise. As the intensity of exercise rises, there is an increase in HR, $\dot{V}_E$, and $\dot{V}O_2$, as well as in the activity of other parts of the oxygen delivery and utilization system. There comes a point, however, above which the $\dot{V}O_2$ cannot increase, even though more work is being performed. This point is called the maximal aerobic power or $\dot{V}O_{2max}$ and is considered by some to be the best single indicator of "fitness" because it involves the maximal ability of many parts of the body to transport and use oxygen.

Figure 2.4 is a schematic diagram of some of the changes that occur in a normal, untrained person with progressively increasing exercise. There appear to be three phases during the transition from rest to maximal aerobic exercise. These phases are separated by the two vertical broken lines in the diagram.

Phase 1 occurs at exercise of low intensity. During exercise, more O_2 is being used by the working muscle, resulting in a greater difference between the O_2 content of the muscle and that of the blood passing by. This larger difference causes more O_2 to diffuse from blood to the tissue. Likewise, more carbon dioxide (CO_2) is being produced by the muscles and diffuses into the blood. As the blood is circulated back through the lungs, the greater concentration of CO_2 rapidly diffuses out, and more O_2 from the air diffuses into the blood to offset the low levels. This movement of gases is enhanced by the fact that exercise produces a greater difference in concentration (i.e., it uses more O_2 and produces more CO_2).

In order to increase $\dot{V}O_2$ and to eliminate more CO_2 ($\dot{V}CO_2$), the body increases its rate and depth of breathing for a more rapid turnover of air. However, it would make little sense to increase the turnover of air in the lungs if this rise in $\dot{V}_E$ were not accompanied by a rise in the rate of blood flow to carry the greater amount of O_2 to the tissues and to transport away the greater amount of CO_2.

The circulatory system responds in a number of ways to increase blood flow. The amount of blood pumped by the heart per minute (cardiac output) is related to the HR and the amount of blood pumped per beat (stroke volume). Both HR and stroke volume increase during exercise. During the period of contraction by the heart (systole), blood is pumped into the large arteries; the systolic blood pressure (SBP) reflects the force of this contraction. The diastolic blood pressure (DBP) is a measure of the pressure in the muscular-walled arteries during the period of relaxation (diastole). Because there is a drop in pressure within the circulatory system as blood is pumped from the large arteries to the smallest arteries (arterioles), to the capillaries, and then to the veins, blood will continue to flow in this direction. During continuous exercise, the heart pumps with greater pressure, while there is a drop in pressure at the arterioles and capillaries. This greater pressure difference produces a faster flow of blood away from the heart. The body can also control the distribution of blood flow to its various parts by selectively closing and opening the small arterioles. In this way, for example, blood can be diverted during exercise from the less active organs (kidneys, gastrointestinal tract) to the working muscles where it is needed more.

During the first few minutes of low-intensity exercise, fat cells release increased amounts of fat into the circulatory system, which is then transported to the working muscles. Because the rate of diffusion of fat across the cell

Figure 2.4 Typical values for untrained people during progressive exercise from rest to maximal oxygen intake.

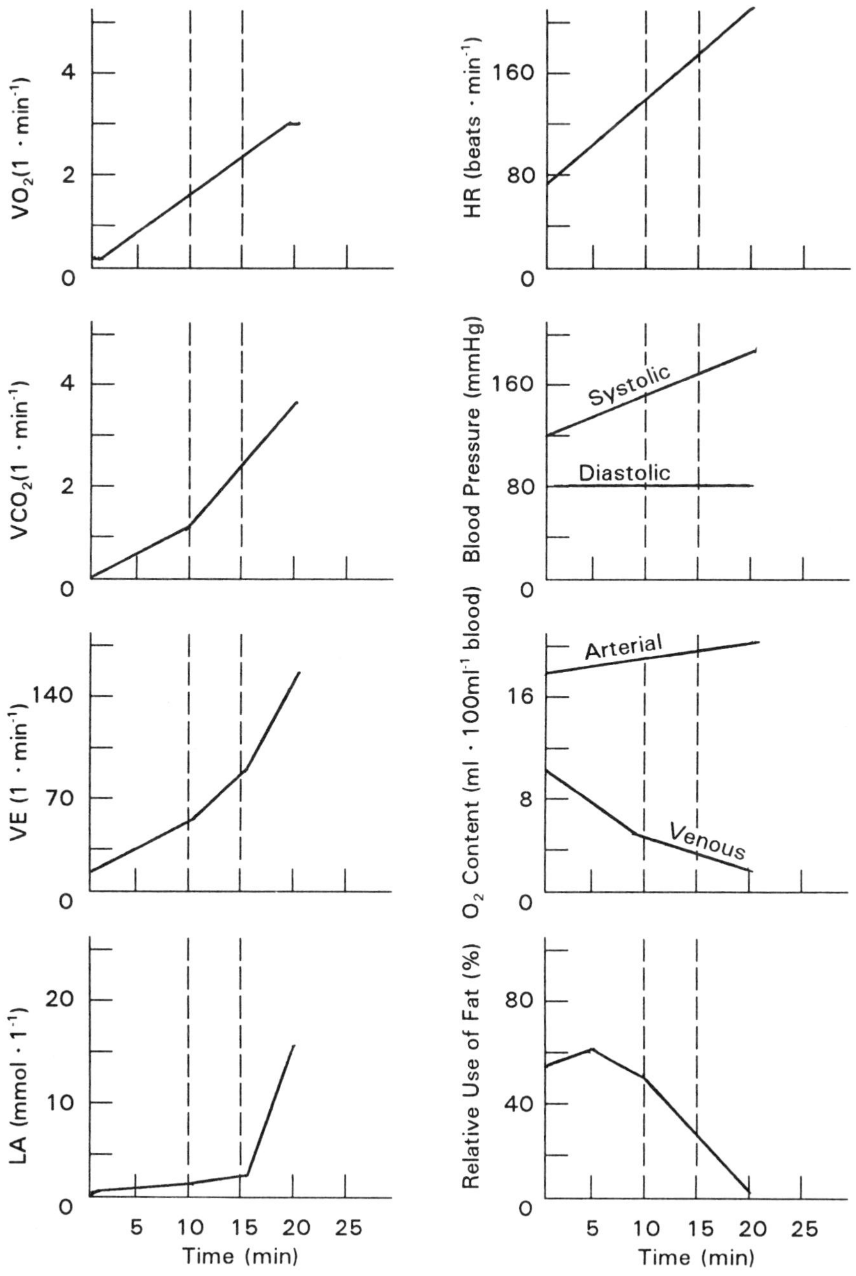

membrane is proportional to the difference in concentration, high levels of fat in the blood ensure a constant supply, making fat a major source of fuel for contracting muscles at low levels of exercise. Given the fact that fat can be metabolized only by aerobic chemical reactions, and that little or no LA is formed, there is little doubt that this first phase primarily involves aerobic metabolism.

As the exercise intensity increases and reaches a point around 50% $\dot{V}O_{2max}$ (phase 2), $\dot{V}O_2$, HR, and SBP continue to rise linearly, and there is an initial increase in LA to twice the resting levels. The acidity produced by LA stimulates the respiratory center, causing a nonlinear rise in $\dot{V}E$. Some excess CO_2 is also blown off, producing a disproportionate rise in $\dot{V}CO_2$ and eliminating part of the acidity caused by carbonic acid ($H_2CO_3 \rightleftharpoons H_2O + CO_2$). Since LA rises only a bit during this second phase, this respiratory compensation appears to be reasonably effective.

LA also has another effect in that its presence inhibits the breakdown and utilization of fat. The small amount of LA at this time probably initiates the reduction in fat utilization and the increased use of carbohydrates. Of course, the body does not switch over to the anaerobic system all at once but gradually shifts to produce energy faster. This transition seems to occur during the second phase. Above exercise intensities requiring about 70% $\dot{V}O_{2max}$, the aerobic system of most sedentary people cannot produce energy fast enough, and they must depend more and more on the anaerobic breakdown of carbohydrates.

With further increases in exercise intensity above 70% $\dot{V}O_{2max}$ (phase 3), the linear rises in HR, SBP, and $\dot{V}O_2$ continue until near-maximal exercise, at which time they begin to plateau. At the onset of this phase, blood LA increases very rapidly until $\dot{V}O_{2max}$ is attained. There is also a further disproportionate rise in $\dot{V}E$ and a continuous rise in $\dot{V}CO_2$ in an attempt to compensate for the marked rise in LA. At this point, however, the hyperventilation cannot compensate adequately. In addition, more and more of the $\dot{V}O_2$ has to go to the respiratory muscles performing the increased work of hyperventilation, and less is available for skeletal muscles performing intense exercise. More blood is also going to the skin in an attempt to eliminate the heat being produced during exercise. Thus, there is competition for blood at near-maximal and maximal levels of exercise. At this point, however, the heart has reached its maximal capacity to pump blood, and the control system for distributing blood flow cannot adequately supply blood to all parts of the body where it is needed at the same time. As a result, the person cannot do more exercise and has to stop.

The increased use of the anaerobic system at the higher intensities of exercise is not just a function of the speed with which energy must be supplied. It is also related to the amount of blood flowing to the working muscles. In order to sustain higher-intensity exercise, muscle contractions must also be stronger. However, when the muscle tension generated by the activation of more muscles fibers reaches 15% to 20% of the maximal force that that particular muscle can produce, the intramuscular pressure around the arteries exceeds the pressure within those arteries bringing nutrients to the muscle. The partial mechanical compression of the arterioles that follows causes a drop in blood flow and deprives the active musculature of a quantity of O_2. The anaerobic breakdown of glycogen stored within that muscle is then used to furnish some of the necessary energy. Once the muscle contracts at a force of about 60% of its maximal strength (and this occurs around the time of $\dot{V}O_{2max}$ in continuous, rhythmical exercise), then the supply of blood and O_2 to that muscle is completely blocked, and the anaerobic degradation of muscle glycogen is the only mechanism available for providing energy.

Thus, the third phase is characterized by the breathlessness, fatigue, and discomfort associated with high levels of LA. The rapid rise in LA seen at the onset of phase 3 partially explains why someone can run at a certain pace (e.g., at a speed requiring 70% $\dot{V}O_{2max}$) with no problem, but will become winded very soon after trying to run a bit faster (e.g., 80% to 90% $\dot{V}O_{2max}$).

In summary, phase 1 is predominantly aerobic, while phase 3 has large aerobic and anaerobic components. Phase 2 is a sort of transition between these two extremes. For a more detailed discussion of these phases, the reader is referred to the review article by Skinner and McLellan (1980).

It should be mentioned here that most sporting activities require both aerobic and anaerobic production of energy. For example, a soccer player performs aerobic exercise when running 20 to 30 minutes nonstop. If the activity were not aerobic, he could not run so long. Occasionally, however, he must sprint after the ball. During those brief, high-intensity intervals, he must draw upon his emergency, anaerobic sources once again.

Because of the high level of anaerobic energy production during activities at or near $\dot{V}O_{2max}$, most people can exercise at these intensities for only 6 to 10 minutes, the difference in duration being associated with the previous amount of exercise done, as well as with variations in state of training, motivation to continue, and tolerance to high levels of LA. Exercise can be done at intensities greater than $\dot{V}O_{2max}$ but for even shorter periods. Given the fact that the energy requirements are greater than the maximal amount that the aerobic mechanism can provide, it is apparent that a major portion of the energy must come from anaerobic sources.

As mentioned earlier, if one is just beginning to exercise, then the ATP and PC stored in the muscles are used first. If, on the other hand, a soccer player sprints all-out for the ball after running for 15 minutes, then the original stores of ATP and PC have already been exhausted and were replaced by the aerobic and anaerobic synthesis of ATP. Therefore, the maximal intensity and duration at which he can now work depends primarily on the rate of energy production by the anaerobic system, the amount of LA produced earlier, and his tolerance for high levels of LA. In general, however, the higher the intensity, the shorter will be the duration (see Figure 2.2).

Anthropometry. One of the axioms in physiology is that form and function are closely related. A concern in the study of physical activity, therefore, is how the performance of exercise may be influenced by the body structure and what influence physical activity may have on the body itself. Anthropometry, literally the measurement of the human, has been studied for many years to provide descriptive information in an attempt to explain, analyze, and understand humans and movement. The major aspects studied are size, proportion, shape, and composition of the body, each of which describes the body in a different manner.

Measurements of body size include such descriptive information as height, weight, and surface area, while measure of body proportion describe the relationship between height and weight and among lengths, widths, and circumferences of various body segments. It has been found that top athletes in some sports tend to have those proportions that biomechanically aid the particular performance required. In track and field events, for example, good jumpers tend to have longer legs in relation to their height, and good throwers tend to have longer arms.

Measures of physique use subjective terms to describe body shape rather than size to give an immediate impression of the overall appearance of an individual. The system used for body-shape classification (somatyping) looks at the relative contribution of three basic body types; namely, endomorphy (spherical, round, soft), mesomorphy (cubical, rugged, muscular), and ectomorphy (linear, fragile, delicate). Research by Tanner on Olympic athletes showed that they tend to be more mesomorphic, less endomorphic, and different from the normal population (1964). Interestingly, athletes in the same events were very similar to each other, regardless of their country of origin. In other words, athletes with a particular body shape tend to succeed in certain sports. Such information has been used to identify and direct youngsters into sports in which they can reach the greatest level of success. This does not imply that ectomorphic youngsters should not play football, or that endomorphs should not compete in distance events if they enjoy these activities. It suggests only that they will have less chance of reaching high levels of performance in them.

Much of the modern physical research in anthropometry involves the measurement of body composition, i.e., lean body mass (bone and muscle) and fat. In turn, because little or no change is seen in bone size (as determined by x-ray techniques and by measurements of bone widths, thicknesses, lengths, and circumferences), more research has focused on muscle and fat. With the problems of osteoporosis seen in older women and in some women athletes with eating disorders and amenorrhea, measures of bone mineral density are being performed increasingly.

Muscle mass can be quantified by measuring girths of various muscles. These measurements can then be compared with those from other people (athletes, patients, etc.) or with those from the same person after training, growth, or disuse. Given the fact that the number of muscle cells is generally determined at birth, any changes are related to alterations in the size of the individual fibers. Hypertrophy occurs after weight lifting because the muscles are specifically trained for strength development. The increased deposition of protein occurs in the actin and myosin filaments, those portions of the muscle directly involved in development of force during a contraction. Marked hypertrophy does not occur with endurance training, as the force of contraction is low in such sustained, aerobic exercise. As a result, the protein buildup that occurs is found in the enzymes (catalysts that control the chemical reactions in the muscle), as well as in the number and size of mitochondria (the sites of aerobic energy production).

Fat is the most variable tissue in the body and is distributed throughout the body, primarily under the skin and in the abdominal cavity. Measurement techniques include use of soft-tissue x-rays, skinfold calipers, and ultrasound to estimate the thickness of subcutaneous fat. Appropriate formulas are then used to estimate the total amount of fat. Total body fat and the pattern of body fat distribution are major interests in research on body composition.

It has been shown that fat patterning is genetically influenced and is different in both sexes, women having more fat on the upper arms and legs and men having more in the trunk. On the average, women are fatter than men. At age 20 years, 12% to 13% of a man's weight is fat, and a woman's is 18% to 20%. Later in life, at the age of 30 to 45 years, men have 18% to 20% fat, while women have 25% to 28%. Athletes in training have relatively little fat, males averaging 5% to 10% and females averaging 10% to 15%.

Because fat is a reservoir in which potential energy is stored, large variations can be found during growth, as well as in the continuum from inactivity to regular heavy training (or from starvation to overeating). Body fat can also influence the performance of various sports. For this reason, research results have also been used to predict a person's optimal weight and body composition for such sports as wrestling, boxing, and weightlifting.

Types of Skeletal Muscle Fibers. All skeletal muscle fibers are not the same. Similar to the situation discussed in relation to the types of energy production, there are fibers primarily used in activities requiring speed and strength (anaerobic), and there are fibers especially suited for endurance (aerobic) activities. These two types of fibers have been classified by the time required to complete a contraction. Thus, fast-twitch (FT) fibers can reach their peak tension after stimulation about twice as fast as slow-twitch (ST) fibers. Table 2.1 is a comparison of a number of structural and functional characteristics of these fibers. Once again, it should be obvious that form and function are closely related.

Table 2.1 Gross Distinction between Muscle Fiber Types

Characteristic	Slow-Twitch	Fast-Twitch
Size		
Innervating motor nerve	smaller	bigger
Muscle fiber	smaller	bigger
Recruitment		
Light exercise	some	none
Moderate exercise	more	some
Intense exercise	many	many
Contraction		
Speed	slower	faster
Tension developed	less	more
Content		
Myoglobin	more	less
Glycogen	same	same
Fat	more	less
Density		
Capillaries	more	less
Mitochondria	more	less
Enzyme Activity		
Myosin ATPase	less	more
Carbohydrate metabolism	less	more
Fat metabolism	more	less
Oxidation	high	low
Resistance to Fatigue	high	low

It can be seen that ST fibers are smaller and have a smaller motor nerve stimulating them. Because the smaller nerves are easier to stimulate and transmit a stimulus more slowly, ST fibers are primarily recruited for moderate levels of exercise, where less speed and strength are needed. ST fibers have more myoglobin (a small, localized reservoir of O_2), slightly larger intramuscular stores of fat (which can be metabolized only aerobically), more capillaries to bring O_2 to the fibers, plus more aerobic enzymes and mitochondria (the powerhouse of the cell that produces ATP aerobically) to use the O_2. As a result, low-intensity exercise can be performed for long periods, and these ST fibers are resistant to fatigue. On the other hand, FT fibers are bigger and have bigger motor nerves; this means that stronger, faster impulses are used for rapid, high-intensity contractions. The activity of the enzymes in these fibers is especially suited for this kind of anaerobic activity, as myosin ATPase is the enzyme involved in the rapid breakdown of ATP to provide energy, and the glycolytic enzymes are involved in the metabolism of glucose and glycogen. However, because FT fibers do not have a rich blood supply to bring nutrients and to carry away metabolic end-products (especially LA), they are easily fatigued. Interestingly, ST and FT fibers have similar levels of glycogen. Given that carbohydrates are used aerobically and anaerobically, however, a similar supply of readily available fuel should not be unexpected.

The recruitment of muscle fibers depends on the kind of activity being performed. At the onset of exercise of moderate intensity, FT fibers are selectively recruited to get things going (e.g., to overcome the initial high resistance on a bicycle ergometer). After a few seconds, the body is in motion, less force is required, and ST fibers take over. If the exercise continues for a long time, however, then more and more FT fibers are recruited as the glycogen stores in the ST fibers reach a low level due to sustained use. Once the glycogen reserves in FT fibers also reach low levels, the individual must either reduce the intensity (thereby allowing the slower aerobic system to metabolize more fat) or stop because of exhaustion. During progressively increasing exercise, as depicted in Figure 2.4, there is also preferential recruitment of specific fiber types. During phase 1, ST fibers are the main fibers being used. With increasing exercise intensity, there is a greater recruitment of FT fibers to provide more force. Many ST and FT fibers are used during phase 3.

All skeletal muscles have a mixture of ST and FT fibers. There is a wide range in the relative proportion of these fibers when all muscles are compared in the same person or when the same muscle is compared in different people. Within the same person, for example, ST fibers comprise 40% to 65% of the fibers in the gastrocnemius and 80% to 95% of those in the soleus. The reason for this difference should be clear when one remembers that the gastrocnemius is the larger muscle of the calf used for jumping, while the soleus is the smaller muscle of the calf located closer to the bone and is used while walking. The composition of the vastus lateralis muscle (lateral side of the thigh) can be very different among individuals. Although the normal average for ST fibers is 50% to 55% in both men and women, the proportion can range from 10% to 20% in successful male sprinters up to 90% to 98% in male distance runners. The values for women in the same events are 25% to 30% and 70% to 80%, respectively. The reason for the greater variation in men is unknown, but probably is related to the fact that more elite male athletes have been studied.

It appears that the relative proportion of the fiber types is genetically determined. Physical training does not seem to produce any change in proportion, only in the characteristics of the fibers. For example, endurance training will increase the oxidative potential of both ST and FT fibers by enhancing the capillarization, mitochondrial density, and activity of the aerobic enzymes of both fiber types.

Other Factors That Can Modify the Functional Effects of Exercise. If the preceding description of anthropometry, muscle fiber types, and the events occurring during exercise appeared to be logical and straightforward, then it has achieved the objectives of simplification, clarification, and education. The reader should now realize that the study of form and function is one of logic, and that nothing occurs within the body unless there is good reason. However, if readers are left with the impression that the structural and functional responses are simple and uncomplicated, then they should also consider the single and combined effects of some of the many variables and situations that can modify these responses. For example, there are differences when exercise is performed:

1. Rhythmically or statically
2. Intermittently or continuously
3. While lying or standing
4. With arms or legs
5. At altitude or underwater
6. In a hot (dry or humid) or cold environment
7. By different kinds of people, e.g.,
   a. by men or women;
   b. by children, adults, or the elderly;
   c. by an untrained person or an athlete who is specifically trained for that activity; and
   d. by a healthy person or one who has a disease that affects the ability to exercise (heart disease, emphysema, etc.)

Static versus Dynamic Exercise. Activities in our daily lives tend to be of two basic kinds, static and dynamic. Holding a suitcase while walking is an activity combining both of these. This simple classification of activity is based on the predominant type of muscle contraction occurring in a given muscle or group of muscles. A static or isometric contraction is one in which there is no apparent change in the overall length of a muscle, while a dynamic or isotonic contraction occurs when there is either shortening or lengthening of the muscle. Shortening of a muscle (concentric contraction) results when the force of contraction is greater than that of the resistance, and lengthening (eccentric contraction) occurs when the contractile force is less. There is also a special kind of dynamic contraction that can be produced only with a special device. In isokinetic contractions, this device allows only a constant rate of movement at all joint angles throughout the range of motion, regardless of the force exerted by the contracting muscle.

It should be mentioned that few daily activities are purely one type of contraction. For example, in the act of lifting a heavy weight, the first form of contraction is isometric since no movement will occur until there is enough force to overcome the resistance. During the lifting phase, the active muscle fibers are shortening and concentric contraction results. If the weight is held motionless at the top of the lift, contraction is once more isometric. When the weight is being lowered, the whole muscle is lengthening; this is considered an eccentric contraction, even though some fibers have to be shortened or the weight would drop rapidly. Once the weight is lowered and again motionless, a few fibers are still contracting isometrically.

Regardless of the relative contribution of each type of contraction to the total work performed, the effects on the body depend mainly on the intensity and duration of each. The general effects of dynamic exercise on various functions can be seen in Figure 2.4.

The effects of static of isometric exercise are quite different. At forces less than 15% to 20% of that seen with a maximal voluntary contraction (MVC), there is little effect on HR, $\dot{V}O_2$, SBP, or DBP, depending on the total size of the muscle mass involved (i.e., the total amount of work being done). A contraction at this intensity can be held indefinitely as the energy requirements are low, while the muscle blood flow is unchanged and more than adequate. As the intensity of contraction rises to 25% to 50% MVC, however, HR, SBP, and DBP increase rapidly, and the duration of the contraction progressively decreases along with muscle blood flow. In this case, the heart is attempting to nullify or overcome the progressive rise in intramuscular pressure and subsequent drop in blood flow by increasing its rate (HR) and force (SBP) of contraction. This sudden and marked rise in the work done by the heart is of little consequence to a normal person, but makes intense static exercise a high-risk activity for a cardiac patient who already has a weakened heart.

When the force of contraction exceeds 60% MVC, there is a complete blockage of blood flow to the muscle. Although a small amount of aerobic energy can be provided by the O_2 present in the muscle at the time of blockage, most of the energy must come from the anaerobic degradation of glycogen located within the muscle itself. As a result, the duration of exercise is very short, and the rise in HR, SBP, and DBP is greater and more rapid.

There is a gradual rise in $\dot{V}O_2$ at the onset of an isometric contraction, but it is less rapid than that seen with dynamic exercise (Fig. 2.4). Once the contraction has ended, there is an immediate increase in blood flow to those muscles partially or totally deprived of O_2, resulting in a brief but marked rise in $\dot{V}O_2$. The overall rise in $\dot{V}O_2$ is minor, however, as the duration of exercise is so short and the total use of stored energy is small.

Although there is a rise in HR, $\dot{V}O_2$, and SBP with high-intensity dynamic exercise, the increases in HR and SBP are less and the increase in $\dot{V}O_2$ is greater than those seen with static exercise because there are alternating periods of contraction and relaxation. During the period of contraction, the small arteries, arterioles, and veins are squeezed by the surrounding muscle fibers. The fact that they are emptied reduces the pressure in these blood vessels and accentuates the difference relative to the increased pressure at the heart and large arteries, resulting in an even greater blood flow during the period of relaxation. This explains why DBP does not rise as it does with isometric exercise. The alternating compression and filling of blood vessels ensures an elevated blood flow and thus adequate levels of O_2 and nutrients to the muscles that are working, allowing the person to perform more exercise for longer periods.

Intermittent versus Continuous Exercise. When exercise is done intermittently, it can be performed comfortably at high intensity for long periods. If the same amount of exercise is done continuously, the duration will be shorter. Thus, the two forms of exercise can be very different in their demands on the body.

Even though most occupational, leisure, and sporting activities involve intermittent exercise, more information is available on the effects of continuous exercise. Part of the reason is that once a physiological steady state is reached at a given submaximal power output, there are few changes in the variables normally measured, unless the exercise is continued for so long that body temperature rises or fatigue sets in. As a result, continuous exercise can be controlled, standardized, and described quite easily. In the case of intermittent exercise, however, there are many factors other than energy requirement that can influence response. Some of these are:

1. Duration of the exercise phase. High-intensity exercise can be performed for 1 to 15 seconds, using primarily the reserves of ATP and PC in the muscle (see Fig. 2.1). If the exercise is stopped, ATP and PC are replenished and become available for the next bout of exercise. If the same exercise is continued for 30 to 60 seconds, the anaerobic system is also stimulated and LA is produced. After continuation for more than 3 to 4 minutes (probably at a lower intensity), a steady state is reached and the aerobic system is a major supplier of energy. The duration of exercise is thus the most critical factor in high-intensity exercise, determining whether there will be high levels of LA in the blood, the accumulation of which is associated with fatigue and discomfort. By exercising at an intensity greater than $\dot{V}O_{2max}$ for only 20 seconds and then resting for 40 seconds, for example, one can continue to exercise for more than an hour without a major buildup of LA. If the same exercise is done for 60 seconds with 120 seconds of rest in between, exercise becomes more difficult after 30 to 40 minutes. Ice hockey teams have found that 1 minute on the ice with 2 to 3 minutes off is the most efficient schedule for their players. Done continuously, the same exercise would have to be stopped after 4 to 6 minutes and could not be continued at the same level until 8-12 minutes had passed.
2. Duration of the recovery (rest or low-intensity exercise) phase. Although LA can be produced in a few seconds, it takes about 15 minutes to eliminate one-half of the amount produced. With repeated intermittent exercise of sufficient duration and intensity, more LA will begin to accumulate. Thus, by the third period of ice hockey or the end of the second half of soccer, fatigue is present in poorly conditioned players and in those who pushed themselves too hard or too often. If low to moderate levels of exercise (less than 50% to 60% $\dot{V}O_{2max}$ and the point at which LA first begins to accumulate) are done during the recovery phase, as opposed to complete rest, then LA will be removed at a faster rate. The reason for this is that the blood flow to the muscle is higher, allowing more LA to diffuse from the areas of higher concentration in the muscle to the regions of lower

concentration in the blood. As well, ST muscle fibers can use the LA produced in FT fibers to produce energy aerobically.

3. Average intensity. The intensity of the exercise and recovery phases, as well as the average intensity of the two phases, will affect the responses to intermittent exercise. As with continuous exercise, intensity is a decisive factor for the sources of energy and the muscle fiber types being used.
4. Amplitude. If there is a big difference between the intensities of the exercise and recovery phases, the body will have to make more adjustments. Because of the delay in the body's ability to respond to varying intensities (see Fig. 2.3), however, the degree to which the responses will oscillate from one level to another depends on the duration of the exercise and recovery phases. For example, if the two phases are only 5 seconds each, oscillations will be small, and the responses will be very similar to those seen during continuous exercise at the same average intensity. On the other hand, if both periods are 3 to 4 minutes, then a steady state may be reached at the end of each phase. The greater the amplitude, the more time will be required to reach a steady state.

Thus, the responses to intermittent and continuous exercise can be very similar or quite different, depending on many factors (i.e., those mentioned above plus others). For a more detailed overview of intermittent exercise, the article by Saltin, Essén, and Pedersen (1976) is the most thorough.

Effect of Body Position. Changes in body position produce changes in the response to exercise. This is mainly due to gravity, which tends to force more blood into the lower parts of the body. While there will be little effect of gravity on the body when it is supine, there is an effect in the upright position.

The energy required to pump blood through the arteries to the extremities and to return the blood through the veins to the heart is much less while a person is lying down. Since the blood is more evenly distributed throughout the body, there will also be more blood returning to the heart. The amount of blood pumped per heart beat will then be greater, and fewer beats will be required to pump the same amount of blood per minute. In addition, the body does not have to use energy to maintain an erect posture. As a result, $\dot{V}O_2$, HR, and BP are lower at rest. In contrast to this, blood tends to pool in the large veins of the legs when the person is standing at rest. Less blood returns to the heart and more beats are required per minute to pump to the same amount of blood per minute.

Once exercise begins, a given PO requires a given amount of energy or O_2, regardless of body position. Except for the lower HR while the person is lying down, therefore, there is little difference in the body's responses. At about 40% $\dot{V}O_{2max}$, the flow of blood back to the heart is the same in both positions because of the pumping action of the muscles and the difference in HR disappears. As the exercise becomes more intense, however, there is a point at which standing is the more favorable position. This is true for two reasons. First, if the legs are slightly higher than the rest of the body (as would be the case while pedaling a bicycle in the supine position), gravity will tend to force more blood into the upper and middle parts of the body. As a result, more pressure must be generated by the heart to pump blood uphill to the legs. If it cannot provide enough pressure, then the legs work more and more anaerobically and have to stop sooner. Second, the efficiency of exercise is less while the person is lying down, meaning that more energy is required to do the same amount of external work.

Thus, the $\dot{V}O_{2max}$ is about 25% to 30% higher in a person who is upright (running) than in one who is lying down (pedaling a bicycle). Values for sitting exercise (bicycle) are about 10% less than those obtained while running; this is also partially caused by a difference in efficiency. It should be mentioned, however, that well-trained cyclists can do as well sitting as they can do running. This is a good example of the specificity of training.

Exercise Done with Arms versus Exercise Done with Legs. In turning the pedals of a bicycle against resistance, there will be differences in how the body responds to exercise done by the arms or legs. A comparison of the responses must consider three main factors: the absolute muscle mass involved, the relative intensity at which the muscle groups are working, and the efficiency with which they can work.

First, because the amount of muscle involved in pedaling a bicycle with the legs is so much more than with the arms, the legs can produce more power. It has been shown that the $\dot{V}O_{2max}$ with the arms is about 75% of that obtained with the legs, except in highly-trained athletes who have specifically trained their arms (e.g., kayakists and rowers whose values may reach 85% to 90% of the $\dot{V}O_{2max}$ obtained with the legs). Second, a smaller percentage of the muscle fibers in the legs will be contracting to produce the same power output on the bicycle. In other words, to perform a given level of submaximal exercise, the legs might be working aerobically with more ST fibers at 30% to 40% of the $\dot{V}O_{2max}$ attainable with the legs, while the arms will be working more anaerobically with ST and FT fibers at 75% to 80% of the $\dot{V}O_{2max}$ that the arms can attain. As a result, HR, $\dot{V}_E$, and LA concentration will be higher. Third, in order to pedal with the arms at a high intensity, it is necessary to stabilize the muscles of the trunk and shoulders with a series of isometric contractions. The isometric contractions cause the blood pressure to rise and inhibit the rapid breathing needed at this time. In addition, the arms are higher than the heart, so that blood must be pumped at a greater pressure uphill, causing both the SBP and DBP to rise. Because of a decrease in blood flow, LA will also be produced in the muscles contracting isometrically.

Combining arms and legs does increase the total amount of muscle mass that can be involved in an activity. It has been found, for example, that when arms provide 20% to 30% of the total power needed, then the work can be done for longer periods with less overall fatigue. Once the arms have to provide more than 30%, however, fatigue sets in more quickly. In such sports as rowing and kayaking, the strength and endurance of the upper body can be limiting factors for performance, while more work is done by the leg and trunk muscles in cross-country skiing.

Effects of Barometric Pressure. O_2 diffuses across the lungs into the blood and from the blood to the tissues because there are differences in its partial pressure. The partial pressure of O_2 (PO_2) is determined by multiplying the total pressure of all gases in the environment (barometric pressure) by the relative concentration of O_2. For example, if the barometric pressure of air at sea level and fully saturated with water (as is the case in the lungs) is around 710 mm Hg and O_2 comprises 21% of that total, then the PO_2 is 710 x 0.21 or 149 mm Hg. As the PO_2 of the venous blood is about 40 mm Hg, this difference is sufficient to drive O_2 from the lungs to the blood, raising the PO_2 in arterial blood to about 100 mm Hg. This blood then travels to the muscle, where the PO_2 is 40 mm Hg and the pressure difference causes O_2 to diffuse into the muscle cell.

If the PO_2 is changed somehow (either by altering the barometric pressure or the concentration of O_2 in the air), then the availability of O_2 will be affected. For example, if one goes to Mexico City (altitude of 7,600 feet), the barometric pressure drops to such an extent that the PO_2 at the lungs is only 110 mm Hg, and the driving force for the diffusion of O_2 is less. Similarly, the PO_2 in the Andes (14,000 feet) is around 84 mm Hg and only 42 mm Hg at Mount Everest (28,000 feet). Because of these reductions in barometric pressure, an effect would be seen only during exercise at Mexico City but *even at rest* up in the Andes. The only way one could exist at the top of Mount Everest would be to increase the concentration of O_2 by breathing from a tank of O_2.

Given the fact that a given amount of exercise requires a given amount of energy, the body has to use its anaerobic system more when less O_2 is available. Of course, this has no effect on those activities lasting only a few seconds or a few minutes, since the energy for these activities comes primarily from anaerobic sources. The longer the duration and the greater the need for O_2, however, the worse will be the performance. This was the case in the performances at the 1968 Olympic Games in Mexico City. When exercise is continuous at moderate altitude (5,000 to 10,000 feet), HR and $\dot{V}_E$ are higher, and more LA is produced. Interestingly, the same amount of LA is produced at the same relative intensity (e.g., at 75% $\dot{V}O_{2max}$), but since the $\dot{V}O_{2max}$ is reduced at altitude, a given power output represents a higher percentage of the maximum possible.

While altitude is associated with a drop in barometric pressure, there is a rise in barometric pressure of about 22 mm Hg for every foot that one is immersed under water; this increase is about 760 mm Hg or 1 atmosphere for each 10 m. At a depth greater than 1.5 feet, the external pressure on the chest will be such that it is not possible to inhale. That is the reason snorkels are less than 1 foot long. To go deeper, one needs a tank of compressed air with a regulator to compensate for the increased external pressure and to provide the air needed to exist.

Other than the sport of scuba diving, most activities in the water are carried out at depths of only a few feet, where the increase in barometric pressure is not the major change. What affects people more is the fact that they are in an environment where the force of gravity has been removed. As in the case of lying down, less energy is required to stand or sit, and the blood is now distributed more evenly throughout the body. With the increased external pressure on the body, the superficial veins are compressed so that more blood returns to the heart. Thus, HR and $\dot{V}O_2$ at rest will be lower.

During exercise in cool water, less blood goes to the skin to get rid of the heat being produced by the muscles and more blood is available to the muscles themselves. The HR is about 10 beats per minute lower in the water than while producing the same amount of power on land. The $\dot{V}O_{2max}$ in water is about 10% to 15% less; this is partially due to the increased resistance to breathing, thereby reducing the amount of air that can be ventilated. Also, the maximal HR is about 10 beats per minute lower. Interestingly, elite swimmers have a $\dot{V}O_{2max}$ in water similar to the level they have on land; this is another example of specificity of training.

Effect of Environmental Temperature. Considered as a machine, man has an efficiency of only 25%. That is, 25% of the energy obtained from food is used for chemical reactions, muscle contractions, transmission of nervous impulses, etc., while the other 75% is given off in the form of heat.

The temperature of the body is regulated very closely to stay within a few degrees of an optimal level so that none of the body's functions will be disturbed. This regulation is aided by the fact that the normal core temperature is 37° C (98.6° F), while it is 33° C (91° F) at the skin and usually 21° to 23° C (70° to 75° F) in most buildings. Since heat flows toward the area of low temperature, the body is constantly giving off heat if the room temperature is less than that of the skin. The greater the difference, the more heat will be given off. If the external temperature is less than 20° C (68° F), then the loss of heat can be reduced by adding more clothing; this insulates the skin from the air. On the other hand, if the external temperature is greater than 37° C, then the body gains heat.

The body has little difficulty regulating its temperature at rest in a comfortable environment. Once exercise begins, however, the body can produce 10 to 25 times as much heat for prolonged periods as it does at rest. Several mechanisms are available to eliminate this extra heat. When a fluid evaporates into a gas, heat is given off. For example, the evaporation of each liter of sweat

(2.2 lb water) causes the body to lose 580 kcal of heat. Evaporation is the main avenue for heat loss during exercise.

The regulatory system is also assisted by the bigger difference in temperature during exercise, as the core temperature rises because of increased heat production and the skin temperature drops as a result of evaporation of sweat from its surface. This greater temperature difference promotes the flow of heat from the core to the periphery. There is also more blood flowing to the skin to transport this heat. As a result, the HR rises in an attempt to supply blood simultaneously to the muscles and to the skin. The dilation of many blood vessels at the periphery causes a drop in BP.

At low levels of exercise and heat production, the body has little problem to adjust. This is not the case at higher intensities of exercise, however, when the demands for blood supply to the skin are so great that the amount available to the muscles is less and the person has to stop sooner. Thus, the $\dot{V}O_{2max}$ can be somewhat lower in a very hot environment, especially if it is humid.

An extra problem with exercising in a humid environment is that the skin is saturated with water when the air is 60% to 80% saturated. As a result, less sweat can be evaporated and less heat can be lost from the skin. The subsequent rise in skin temperature reduces the difference, and less heat flows from the core. Once the core temperature rises more than 3° to 4° F, disturbances occur in the body's functions. At this point, the person should (and usually will) stop exercising to avoid problems.

Problems can also arise when exercise of moderate intensity is done for more than 30 minutes, as in a marathon. The hotter the temperature, the higher the humidity, and the longer and more intense the exercise, the greater will be the loss of water. When more than 5% body weight is lost, the blood becomes less dilute, the concentration of minerals and electrolytes is altered, HR goes up, and the temperature-regulating mechanism is impaired. If exercise is continued, the sweating mechanism eventually stops in an attempt to preserve body fluids, such that body temperature rises quickly and heat stroke is imminent.

As long as body temperature remains near its desired level, few problems are created by exercising in a cold environment. In this case, the major problem is how to control heat loss. This can be done by adding more clothes (insulation) and by producing enough heat to maintain body temperature without sweating. Two winter sports amply illustrate this point. In downhill skiing, skiers wear heavier clothing to insulate themselves from the wind and cold mountain air. The intermittent exercise is generally adequate to keep them warm. By contrast, cross-country skiers wear less clothing since they produce much more heat during prolonged continuous exercise.

Heat loss can also be reduced by constricting blood vessels at the skin; this reduces the gradient between the skin and the environment and keeps more of the blood near the center of the body. With this vasoconstriction, there can be a rise in BP. If there is also an attempt to do intense, anaerobic work with the arms (e.g., shoveling a lot of snow in a short period) or intense, isometric exercise (e.g., pushing a stalled car), the combination of vasoconstriction, increased BP, holding the breath while straining, and intensive demands for energy may be too much for the heart of a middle-aged person with coronary artery disease. Doing mild, aerobic exercise for several minutes beforehand will result in dilation of the blood vessels to eliminate heat, and the aerobic system will be activated, thereby reducing the risk of a heart attack in such a person.

Comparison of Males and Females. Until adolescence, there is little difference in size or performance between boys and girls. This similarity ceases with the onset of puberty and the associated alterations in hormonal status. Aside from some obvious qualitative differences, females differ quantitatively in ways that affect their ability to exercise. Some difference may be more related to socio-cultural factors than to physiological ones, however. Not too long ago, women were not considered feminine if they engaged in physical activity. Thus, many girls did what was expected and became less active during and after adolescence. While this has changed, one must nevertheless consider these sociological factors when discussing possible physiological differences.

Women tend to be smaller and lighter than men. The composition of their weight is different in that they tend to have lighter bones, less muscle, and relatively more fat. The strength of their upper body is about 60% to 70% of that for men, while the strength of their legs is 75% to 85% of that for men. The lower values for upper-body strength may be more a reflection of the pattern of use and less of a physiological difference. For example, the difference in leg strength disappears when compared per unit of muscle in the legs. This suggests that the quality of the force development is the same, only that the quantity of muscle is less in women.

In respect to the aerobic system, women tend to have smaller hearts and a smaller volume of blood (both are related to their smaller body size), as well as less hemoglobin per unit of blood (hemoglobin is the carrier of O_2). Thus, a smaller heart has to beat more often during a standard amount of exercise to pump the same amount of O_2 to the muscles. Because men and women of the same age tend to have the same maximal HR, women will reach their maximal value sooner. This decrease in the ability to transport O_2 is matched by a concomitant drop in the ability to use O_2, i.e., it makes little sense to be able to use a large amount of O_2 if it cannot be delivered.

Accordingly, the $\dot{V}O_{2max}$ of women is less than that of men when reported as the total amount of O_2 consumed per minute; this is related to body size. The difference is less when the values are reported as the amount of O_2 consumed per minute for each kilogram of body weight (this reduces the effect of body weight) and becomes even less when the values are reported as the amount of O_2 consumed per minute for each kilogram of lean body weight (this minimizes the differences in body composition). When reported in this fashion, it shows that there are no qualitative differences in the ability of muscle in men and women to extract and use O_2.

Because of their smaller size and lower $\dot{V}O_{2max}$, women are at a disadvantage whenever they have to work against an outside resistance (rowing or cycling) or have to transport their own weight (running or jumping). The differences in performance tend to be less in swimming, where the extra fat and lighter bones help women float, thereby reducing the resistance and work involved in propulsion through the water.

Comparison of Children and Adults. Many people think of a child as a miniature adult. However, many of the functions in the bodies of children are not fully developed, and they cannot perform exercise as well.

Consider the three sources of energy production shown in Figure 2.1. Children are no different from adults in their ability to perform very intense activities for a few seconds. In other words, their ATP-PC system functions in much the same manner. Children do have problems, however, performing high-intensity exercise for 30 to 120 seconds. It seems that children have less of the enzyme needed to produce LA. As a result, they cannot supply as much energy with their anaerobic system and must slow down to allow the aerobic system to provide the required energy. The LA system develops during puberty. The systems for transporting and utilizing O_2 are not fully developed before puberty and put children at a slight disadvantage. Nevertheless, children are able to perform exercise of moderate intensity for moderate periods.

If the intensity becomes too high, there will be problems with the anaerobic mechanism of children. Likewise, if the duration of exercise is too long, there may be another problem peculiar to children. Relative to their body weight, children have a larger surface area. Since the surface is where heat exchange occurs, the greater the ratio of surface area to body mass (which produces the heat), the greater will be the exchange of heat with the environment. Thus, children lose more heat during long periods of exercise in a cool environment (e.g., swimming in cold water). Similarly, children will gain more heat if it is hot. Children also have less-mature sweat glands, so that loss of heat by evaporation is less effective.

Although children are not aware of these physiological differences, their pattern of play reflects them—that is, children tend to do activities of low to moderate intensity, with very short bursts of intensive activity. Part of this is also influenced by their shorter attention span. Only in competitive situations, especially with pressure from adults, do they attempt high-intensity exercise for any length of time.

Comparison of Young and Old Adults. Once maturity is reached (25 to 30 years of age), the effects of the aging process on a number of the body's functional and structural systems appear. Aging results in a loss in size, number, or both, of functional units within every system of the body, as well as a loss of function in those units that remain. As a result, aging can be characterized by a decreased ability to adapt to and to recover from physiological stimuli. It seems that the greater the intensity of the stimulus and the larger the number of physiological mechanisms involved in adjusting to that stimulus, the greater will be the loss of function with age.

As people age, there is a tendency for body fat to increase and for the number and size of both muscle fibers and nerve cells to decrease. This explains why older people are weaker, slower, and less powerful. Likewise, there is deterioration in those performances requiring the regulating and coordinating functions of the nervous system (e.g., balance, reaction time, agility, and coordination).

Changes in the respiratory system make it more difficult to supply adequate levels of O_2 to the body during intense exercise, but not at low to moderate intensities. The heart has to work harder to pump the same amount of blood, especially against an increased BP. When this is coupled with a decrease in maximal HR, it is evident that the maximal amount of blood that can be pumped per minute will also decrease. At the cellular level, there is a loss of functional units and a decrease in the activity of the enzymes associated with all three mechanisms for producing energy (i.e., ATP-CP, LA, and oxidation). When all these points are considered together, it is easy to understand why older people cannot perform as well in almost any kind of activity, except those of low to moderate intensity in which the energy requirements are easily met. If older people can select their pace, they usually have no problems. On the other hand, if the energy requirements are set too high by others, then they will have problems doing the exercise.

Because aging is characterized by a decreased ability to adapt, it stands to reason that the ability to train (adaptation to the repeated stimulation of exercise) will be less in the older person. Although studies have shown that older people can improve, their improvement tends to be less and requires more time.

It appears that training does not affect the aging process per se; that is, the *rate* of change in various functions is probably no different in an active or in a sedentary person. The difference between them is mainly related to the level of function existing at a given time. Well-trained persons who continue to train will be in better shape and have a greater functional capacity than others of the same age. The fact that their $\dot{V}O_{2max}$ at 60 years of age may be the same as that of a sedentary person 30 years of age does not mean that they are as young or that they have delayed the process of aging. It means only that they are well-trained 60-year-old persons whose body has undergone many changes and who are still capable of performing a lot of exercise.

The Effects of Training. It is generally accepted in physiology that a repeated, adequate stimulation (overload) of a system improves its ability to adapt to and recover from that kind of stimulus. This adaptation is the result of both structural and functional alterations within that system, the structural changes usually occurring later. There is also general acceptance of the principle of specificity (i.e., adaptations are specific to the various systems and their structural and functional units that are overloaded). Some examples will help clarify what is meant by specificity. Weight lifting is a brief, high-intensity anaerobic exercise stimulating the skeletal and neuromuscular systems, whereas marathon running is a prolonged, low-intensity aerobic activity that stimulates those systems involved in the transport and utilization of O_2. Specific training effects can be seen even in athletes who appear to stimulate the same systems. Even though runners, cyclists, swimmers, and cross-country skiers all may train for endurance, and all may have a high $\dot{V}O_{2max}$, athletes will excel in their particular activity. Similarly, runners, cyclists, and skiers will do better in activities requiring the use of the legs, while skiers and swimmers will be better in those requiring use of the arms. One can also find specificity in the same activity. In running, for example, a sprinter develops the ability to run fast for brief periods, an activity requiring high levels of strength and speed; all of these are associated with the development of the ATP-CP system. At the other extreme, marathon runners have the ability to run at moderately high intensity for prolonged periods, i.e., they have developed their aerobic system. Middle-distance runners are somewhere in between (depending on the intensity and duration) and have developed a high tolerance for the LA associated with the anaerobic system. What occurs, therefore, are specific modifications in the various mechanisms for producing energy.

Figure 2.5 diagrams what happens with training. The solid lines represent values in a sedentary person and are the same as those in Figure 2.4; the dotted lines show the effects of training. As an oversimplification, training causes an increase in the functional capacity of the various systems. With the higher maximum, the same absolute power output becomes relatively less strenuous (i.e., the intensity decreases). The $\dot{V}O_2$ is unchanged because the same amount of energy is needed, but there is a reduction in $\dot{V}_E$, $\dot{V}O_2$, HR, and SBP. As well, average sedentary people begin to produce LA at about 50% $\dot{V}O_{2max}$. After training, they are able to do more work before they attain 50% of their increased $\dot{V}O_{2max}$. This is due primarily to the functional changes in the aerobic system. With prolonged training, there will also be structural changes in the various parts of the aerobic system. As a result, they will now be able to work at 60% to 65% of an even higher $\dot{V}O_{2max}$ before their aerobic system is not supplying energy rapidly enough. Because fat is the preferred aerobic fuel, more fat is used at the same power output, thereby conserving the limited amounts of

Figure 2.5 Typical values for trained and untrained people during progressive exercise from rest to maximal O_2 intake.

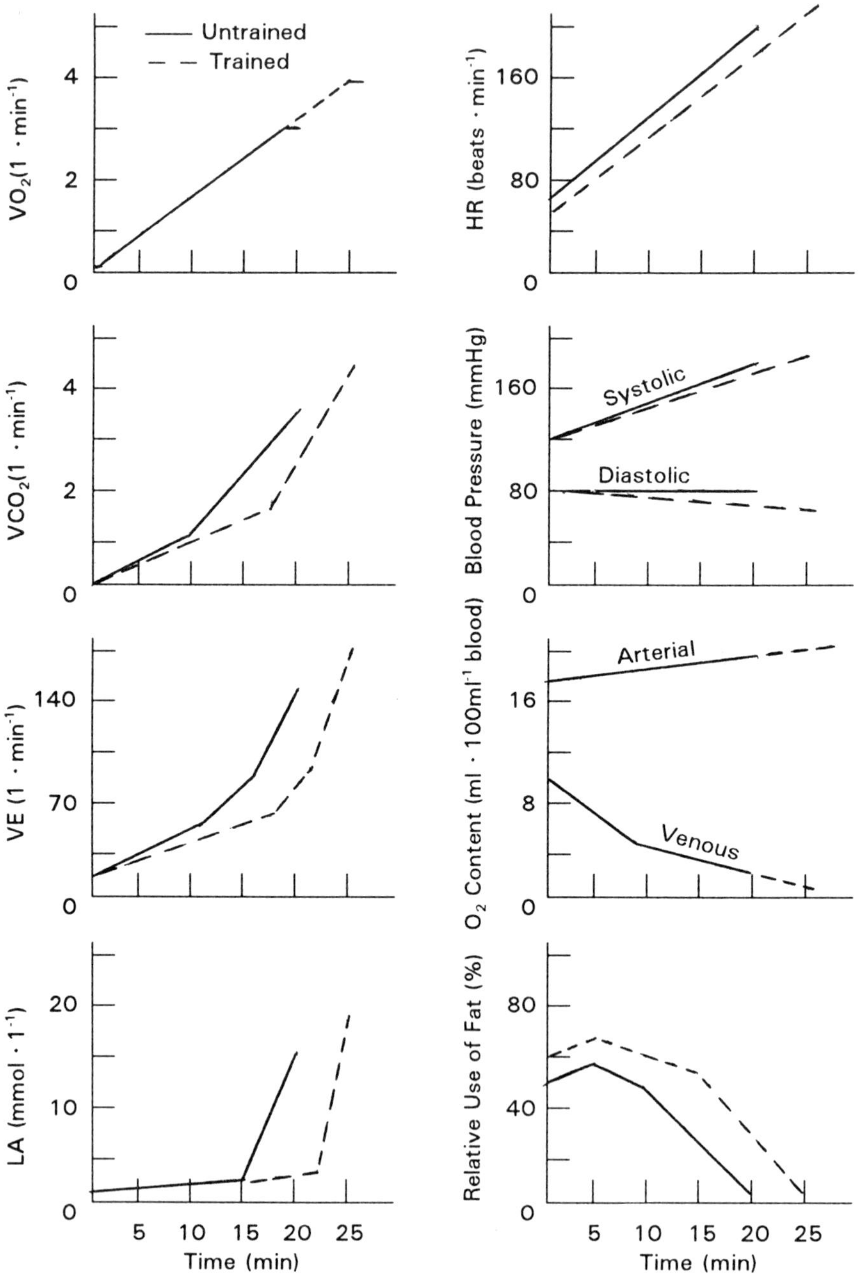

glycogen in the muscle and liver. Thus, a well-trained person is capable of exercising at higher relative power outputs, and at much higher absolute power outputs, than an unconditioned person of the same age and sex.

It should be mentioned that the body can adapt to inactivity as well as to training. It makes little sense to have the ability to produce large amounts of energy with any of the three mechanisms, if large amounts are seldom needed. The changes associated with prolonged inactivity are generally the opposite of those seen with training. A good example of this can be seen in the accelerated changes occurring in a leg that has been in a cast for 5 to 6 weeks.

Comparison of Various States of Health. A comparison of the effects of health vs. disease or medical problems on the ability to exercise is complicated by the large number and variety of health states. The fact that many people are also older and deconditioned when the symptoms and problems appear, makes such a comparison even more difficult.

In order to determine the effects of a particular state of health on the ability to exercise, one should first study the characteristics of that disease or medical problem to see which systems of the body or which mechanism for producing energy will be affected. For example, the ability to pump blood may be diminished in coronary heart disease, while emphysema alters the exchange of O_2 and carbon dioxide in the lungs. Both of these will affect the ability to do aerobic exercise of moderate intensity.

Knowing which systems have been affected, how they have been changed, and the role that each system plays during specific forms of exercise makes it easier to understand how a particular health state affects and is affected by exercise. Because of the complexity of the various states of health, however, the purpose of this section is only to alert the reader to the wide range of possible responses and not to discuss each of them in detail. For more information about various health states and exercise, the reader is referred to the book by Skinner (1993).

CONCLUDING STATEMENT

The study of the body is a fascinating subject. It is even more interesting to see how it adjusts to the stimulus of exercise and adapts to the influence of repeated exercise. Anyone who works in a profession in which physical activity plays such an important role should be aware of the theoretical and practical aspects of exercise physiology, the science that attempts to explain these responses.

It is a truism in all fields that the more one knows, the more one realizes that there is much more to know. In respect to exercise physiology, there are so many complex factors that can influence how a given individual might respond to a given amount of exercise on a given day that only general guidelines can be formulated. It is then up to the teacher, dancer, coach, or exercise leader to apply these guidelines in the manner that best suits the specific circumstances.

The study of exercise physiology is simplified, however, if one remembers that the responses are logical and specific. This, of course, assumes that there is adequate knowledge upon which to base a judgement. If the reader looks for and finds the logical modifications that should occur, then the study of exercise physiology can also be stimulating, interesting and satisfying.

REFERENCES AND SELECTED READINGS*

AMERICAN COLLEGE OF SPORTS MEDICINE. (1990). The recommended quantity and quality of exercise for developing and maintaining cardiorespiratory and muscular fitness in healthy adults. *Med. Sci. Sports Exerc., 22:* 265–274.

AMERICAN COLLEGE OF SPORTS MEDICINE. (1991). *Guidelines for exercise testing and exercise prescription* (4th Ed.). Philadelphia: Lea and Febiger.

ÅSTRAND, P. O., & RODAHL, K. (1986). *Textbook of Work Physiology* (3rd Ed.). NY: McGraw-Hill.

FOX, E. L., BOWERS, R. D., & FOSS, M. L. (1993). *The physiological basis for exercise and sport* (5th Ed.). Dubuque, IA: Brown and Benchmark.

HOLLOSZY, J. O. (1976). Adaptations of muscular tissue to training. *Prog. Cardiovasc. Dis., 43:*445–458.

KNUTTGEN, H. G. (Ed.). (1976). Neuromuscular mechanisms for therapeutic and conditioning exercise. Baltimore: University Park Press.

LAMB, D. R. (1984). Physiology of exercise. Responses and adaptations (2nd Ed.). NY: Macmillan.

MCARDLE, W. D., KATCH, F. I., & KATCH, V. L. (1991). Exercise physiology: Energy, nutrition, and human performance (3rd Ed.). Philadelphia: Lea and Febiger.

POLLOCK, M. L., WILMORE, J. H., & FOX, S. M. (1978). Health and fitness through physical activity. NY: Wiley.

SALTIN, B., ESSÉN, B., & PEDERSEN, K. (1976). Intermittent exercise: Its physiology and some practical applications. In E. Jokl, R. Anand, & H. Stoby (Eds.) *Advances in exercise physiology*. Basel: Karger.

SKINNER, J. S. (1973). Aging and performance. In J. Keul (Ed.), *Limiting factors of physical performance*. Stuttgart: Thieme.

SKINNER, J. S. (Ed.). (1993). Exercise testing and exercise prescription for special cases (2nd Ed.). Philadelphia: Lea and Febiger.

*This chapter was an attempt to summarize, synthesize, and simplify many facts. As such, it would have been difficult to read if references had been cited for even most of the points made. Therefore, the reader who wishes to know more is referred to any or all of these books and articles.

SKINNER, J. S., & MCLELLAN, T. M. (1980). The transition from aerobic to anaerobic metabolism. *Res. Q. Exer. Sport, 51:* 234–248.

SKINNER, J. S., NOELDNER, S. P., & O'CONNOR, J. S. (1989). Functional effects of physical activity. In A. J. Ryan & F. D. Allman (Eds.), *Sports Medicine* (2nd Ed.) (pp. 515–528). NY: Academic Press.

STRAUSS, R. H. (Ed.). (1991). *Sports medicine* (2nd Ed.). Philadelphia: W. B. Saunders.

TANNER, J. M. (1964). *The physique of the Olympic athlete.* London: Allen & Unwin.

WILMORE, J. H., & COSTILL, D. L. (1988). *Training for sport and activity* (3rd Ed.). Dubuque: W. C. Brown.

Chapter Three
Sociocultural Aspects of Kinesiology

Susan L. Greendorfer

Historically, scholars from several fields have taken an interest in the serious study of play, games, dance, exercise and sport. Since the mid-19th century anthropologists, sociologists, philosophers, and psychologists have recognized that these physical activity forms had cultural relevance and were part of the social and moral order. Moreover, many of these scholars suggested that forms and contexts of physical activity were cultural products intricately related to political, economic and social dynamics of society and were worthy of study (i.e., Tylor, 1878; Groos, 1901; Mead, 1934; Schiller, 1875; Stumpf & Cousins, 1947, 1949). Despite this early recognition, however, it wasn't until the mid-1960s that an academic specialty in physical education formally consolidated social science interest in play, games and sport into a legitimate area of study.

Several factors contributed to this consolidation. One was the growing awareness of organized sport as one of the most pervasive and salient social phenomena of the twentieth century. The growth and appeal of sport as a significant aspect of culture closely paralleled technological developments that led to mass production, increased amounts of leisure time, and creation of a middle class—all of which were outgrowths of the Industrial Revolution. Although some scholars documented this concurrent growth by the mid-1950s (Betts, 1974), many failed to recognize the significant impact that these developments were having on contemporary social life. The unprecedented growth of sport and its influence on patterns of social life became so taken for granted that they went virtually unacknowledged.

For instance, figures during the past two decades indicate that millions of individuals engage in sport directly or vicariously participate through mass media consumption; that sport is a dominant topic for conversation; and hundreds of thousands of people structure leisure activity and voluntary spending around sporting activities. At the same time, spectator team sports began to attract audience that numbered more than 100 million each year, and organized sport for youth became a big business, attracting more than 2 million children each year (Eitzen & Sage, 1989). It was this social context that motivated scholars from sociology and physical education to call for academic study of the role of sport in society and to begin to seriously consider the tremendous social, economic, and political significance that sport had in contemporary life.

While the presence of sport in society has changed little in type or form since the turn of the century, the subdiscipline that emerged from this call for the scholarly study of sport has undergone substantial transition during the past 30 years. Not only have there been shifts in subject matter focus, but methodological and theoretical approaches have also undergone dramatic shifts. Over this time frame, research attention has shifted from the phenomena of play, games, and sport to more generic forms of physical activity as the study of body practices—from what was initially called sociology of sport to what some are now labeling "cultural kinesiology." What was once a discipline-based specialty (e.g., sociology) now appears to be shifting to an interdisciplinary approach where boundaries between the social sciences and humanities (e.g., history, anthropology, literary analysis) are deliberately blurred.

To understand this transformation, students need to understand the historic development of sociology of sport as well as the types of research interests that have driven the development of knowledge in this area of study. This chapter attempts to provide such a foundation, describing factors that influenced the development as well as the transitions that have taken place in this subdiscipline. After this brief overview, the chapter outlines some recent debates that currently influence subdisciplinary interests, and follows with a brief discussion of how such debate has influenced recent research interests and approaches. The chapter concludes with a brief discussion of theoretical and methodological concerns that represent potential directions for future research.

DEVELOPMENT OF THE SUBDISCIPLINE

Despite the recognition of sport as a growing social phenomenon since the turn of this century, a call for the establishment of a legitimate area of study devoted to the serious study of sport from a social scientific perspective was not issued until the mid-1960s (Kenyon & Loy, 1965). The field of physical education responded to that call and eagerly welcomed sociology of sport into its curriculum. Unfortunately, this inclusion led to several misunderstandings and the outcome wasn't quite as expected.

Based on outward appearance, sociology of sport—the study of the regularity, and departures from it, of human social behavior in a sports context (Kenyon & Loy, 1965)—became an accepted sub-area in physical education by the early 1970s. Such favorable reception by the field of physical education, however, seemed to be based on two misunderstandings about the new subdiscipline: (1) that *any study* dealing with sociological variables or social issues related to sport would be acceptable, and (2) that the objective of the new subdiscipline was to promote the social development objective of physical education as espoused by such pioneers as Clark Hetherington, J.F. Williams, J.B. Nash and others (cf. Kenyon & Loy, 1965). Early position papers clearly distinguished what the nature and goals of sociology of sport were to be. The new subdiscipline was identified within the framework of science, not within that of education or physical education. Therefore, no attempt was made to link the "social benefits of physical activity" with the pursuit of scientific knowledge about sport.

In contrast to pedagogical considerations, the goals of the new subdiscipline were research oriented, focusing on theoretically based studies about substantive topics that would facilitate understanding of social processes (e.g., stratification, sport as a vehicle for social mobility) and of structural or organizational patterns (e.g., the relationship between cohesion and success; centrality of playing position and opportunities for leadership) in sport (McPherson, 1978).

To achieve this purpose, scholarly focus was on *sport* and the frame of reference to be used was sociology. The subdiscipline was further defined by its mode of inquiry: the use of sociological methods to study sport-related phenomena. Survey research, primarily in the form of questionnaires and interviews, along with field experiments and analysis of secondary data sets (e.g., sport data banks, guidebooks), became the most popular research techniques. What these techniques provided was an objective means by which empirical data could be gathered and statistically analyzed.

During the early stages of development, attention was on legitimating sociology of sport as an academic area of study. Even though primary focus was on the institution of sport, which may not have yet been considered as a serious topic of inquiry, the research approach rested on methods premised on the model followed by the natural sciences. This model stresses the importance of holding "value free" positions, being objective and collecting empirical data. This commitment to this model resulted in some immediate as well as long-range consequences. For example, although some interest in play and game phenomena did exist, few scholars studied these other physical activity forms and contexts. Perhaps play and games offered less conceptual and empirical clarity than sport did. In addition, the subdiscipline paid little attention to pedagogical or teaching-learning aspects of physical activity. Thus, what went on in physical education settings was virtually ignored and most noticeably excluded from subdisciplinary research.

Regardless of the reason, it was the growing dominance of sport in society that drew the attention of first-generation scholars, and early position papers in the subdiscipline focused on definitions of sport as well as descriptions of the nature and scope of sociology of sport. Although today the area of socio-cultural kinesiology/sport studies reflects diverse perspectives, early position papers advocated research strictly adhering to one perspective, that based on assumptions from the natural sciences (i.e., known as *structural functionalism* in the behavioral sciences and *logical positivism* in the natural sciences). The structural functionalist or positivist approach is based on natural science assumptions that sport as a social institution has *regularities in underlying patterns* of behavior and that such patterns can be *described, explained,* and *predicted.*

Although not as dominant today, this paradigm shaped the nature and type of research in the subdiscipline for 30 years, and research emanating from this perspective is characterized by empirical research studies which attempted to determine whether statistically significant relationships existed between aspects of sport behavior and aspects of other societal institutions such as the mass media, the economy, or politics. Early studies in sociology of sport could be classified according to general themes: (1) the study of basic social units (individuals, groups, institutions or societies), (2) fundamental social processes (socialization, stratification, discrimination), and (3) organizational structure (Kenyon, 1969; Kenyon & Loy, 1965; McPherson, 1975) as they related to some aspect of sport.

EARLY RESEARCH

More prominent examples of sport sociology research encompassed topics examining the relationship between sport and other social institutions such as education, politics, economics, and the mass media. With respect to these topics, it was assumed that because sport had been defined as a social institution (Loy & Kenyon, 1969), patterns within sport could be compared with patterns found in social institutions.

For example, research efforts related to politics consisted of descriptive studies which focused on the relationship between political ideologies of specific nations and examples of how sport served as a political tool for espousing such ideologies (cf., Lüschen, 1969; Riordan, 1977). Although early research on economics was also descriptive, it provided insight into the structure of professional sport and explained the complexities embedded in the definition of monopolistic practices, interstate commerce, and anti-trust legislation. Despite its failure to analyze political or legislative implications, this consideration of economics did shed insight into the complexities of athletes' salary structures, relocation of sport franchises, formation of player unions, and consequences of player strikes. Although attention was limited, some economic consideration was given to aspects of intercollegiate sport.

Sport and Social Institutions. One topic that received an inordinate amount of research attention was the relationship between sport and education. Debate over the effects of sport in the school led to several empirical studies which examined whether sport played a functional or dysfunctional role. To demonstrate that outcomes of participation were beneficial, researchers looked for factors which would demonstrate that athletic involvement of students was consonant with the goals of education. Empirical findings indicated that high school athletes not only earned higher grades than nonathletes (Buhrmann, 1972; Eidsmore, 1963; Schafer & Armer, 1968), but they also had higher educational aspirations (Lueptow & Kayser, 1973; Rheberg & Schafer, 1968) and tended to graduate at higher rates than did their nonathletic counterparts (Phillips & Schafer, 1971).

Although data from high school studies lent support to the position that sport was functional, findings at the college level suggested quite a different picture. Empirical findings suggested that college athletes tend to graduate at lower rates than nonathletes (Henschen & Fry, 1984; Webb, 1969); that graduation is less likely in "big time," revenue-producing team sports (Hauser & Lueptow, 1978; Henschen & Fry, 1984); and that athletes tend to earn lower grades or make less academic progress than nonathletes (Hauser & Lueptow, 1978; Sage, 1967; Spady, 1970; Webb, 1969).

One issue often linked to educational attainment is occupational attainment, which in itself encompasses the concept of social mobility, or the movement from one social class to another. Several popular beliefs about these relationships exist, the most notable being that sport provides athletes with opportunities for education that they would not ordinarily have, and that sport is a stepping stone to upward social mobility. Research findings suggest that both beliefs are myths.

As mentioned above, social mobility is defined as movement from one social class to another. When related to sport, the question is whether or to what extent sport serves as a vehicle for changing social class status. To address the issue, sport sociologists first examined the relationship between social class background and sport participation and found that sport participants, particularly college athletes, tend to come from the middle class and above (Loy, 1969; Sack & Thiel, 1979; Webb, 1969) and that the lower classes are not well represented in sport. Secondly, several studies demonstrated that sport achievement in college did not account for high-status attainment in terms of occupational prestige or earnings (Dubois, 1978, 1979, 1985; Sack & Thiel, 1979; Scoville,

1974; Spady, 1970). Consequently, researchers found little support for the "rags to riches" account of an athlete's rise from an impoverished background to an elite status in sport. If economic gains are made at all, it is at the peak of a playing career; moreover, any gains made seem to be temporary (Scoville, 1974; Spady, 1970). Researchers further suggested that if mobility did occur, it was due to educational achievement (i.e., earning a degree), not sport (Scoville, 1974; Spady, 1970; Webb; 1969).

Sport and Social Processes. The majority of studies dealing with sport and social processes tended to focus on two topics: (1) how individuals were socialized into or through sport, and (2) racial segregation and discrimination in sport. Theoretical frameworks borrowed from sociology or social psychology were instrumental in describing general patterns. More specifically, research on sport socialization leaned heavily on social-learning paradigms, while that on racial segregation used a theoretical framework on organizational structure of formal organizations.

Sport socialization. Social learning, the paradigm most frequently used for sport socialization research, assumes the presence and influence of others in the process of acquiring essential knowledges, skills, dispositions and values in order to become involved in physical activity. Theoretically, social learning is accomplished through the mechanisms of observation, modeling, reinforcement, feedback and practice, and the outcome of the process is assimilation and exhibition of observed motoric behavior in appropriate situations (Greendorfer, 1992; McPherson, 1981). Such notions were incorporated into a model which was used to explain how individuals become involved in sport and physical activity. Three clusters of independent variables (personal attributes, socializing agents, and socialization situations) influenced the dependent variable—active sport/physical activity involvement. Of the three clusters, primary attention focused on reference groups and significant other influence—that is, agents of socialization, who, because of their prestige, proximity, and power to distribute love, rewards, and punishment, either consciously or unconsciously influenced the sport socialization process (McPherson, 1981).

Findings revealed that active participation begins at an early age (i.e., 8 or 9 years of age); early participation brings a great deal of success; and young participants receive positive support from family, peers and teachers, each of whom influences participation within specific settings (Higginson, 1985; Kenyon & McPherson, 1973; McPherson, 1981). One of the most consistent findings is that the strongest predictor of participation during a later life-cycle stage (i.e., adolescence) is participation during the previous stage (i.e., childhood) (Greendorfer, 1983; McPherson, 1981). In addition, even though there are some general commonalities in the process of sport socialization, there are also some specific differences. For example, it seems that "significant-other" influence varies by sport and is differential over time or life-cycle stage (Greendorfer, 1983, 1992; Kenyon & McPherson, 1973; McPherson, 1981). Also, differences in the sport socialization process have been found relative to age, sex, and race.

In the case of males, for example, the school is the major socializing agency, particularly during adolescence, with teachers and coaches most important in stimulating interest in specific sports (Dubois, 1981; Higginson, 1985; Kenyon & McPherson, 1973; McPherson, 1981). Peer group influence and recognition or visibility are also important factors during adolescence (Greendorfer, 1977; 1983; McPherson, 1981). The family seems to generate interest in traditional spectator sports (Kenyon & McPherson, 1973; McPherson, 1981).

In the case of females the peer group is most influential during all three life-cycle stages, childhood, adolescence, and adulthood, with family influential only during childhood (Greendorfer, 1977, 1983). When the females were children, one or both parents were actively involved in sport. Finally, the school was influential only during adolescence, suggesting it was not initiating but perhaps merely reinforcing skills that girls learned elsewhere (Greendorfer, 1983).

Studies dealing with sport socialization of children have found that boys are more actively involved in physical activity and at an earlier age, and that they seem to be most influenced by fathers and had a higher value orientation toward sport (i.e., sport was more important to them). In contrast girls tend to be less active and receive more diffuse influence from each family member, and those young girls involved in physical activity seem to hold a higher value toward sport, perceiving themselves to be more skilled (Lewko & Ewing, 1981).

In one of the few studies of sport socialization by race, Greendorfer & Ewing (1981) concluded that race differences might be more profound than gender differences. Differences between African-American and white children suggest that two distinct mechanisms seem to be operant. African-Americans are more influenced by situational and contextual factors, such as availability of facilities and equipment (i.e., opportunity set) and value orientations of others, specifically peers, while whites are more influenced by specific significant others (i.e., family members, coaches) (Greendorfer & Ewing, 1981).

Although closely related to socialization into sport, *socialization through sport* consistently has been treated as a separate and isolated topic, with primary attention devoted to consequences of sport involvement which have been closely associated with the social objective of physical education. Despite the assumption that positive outcomes or benefits are gained through sport involvement, it seems there are few studies that support such notions, particularly if such global behaviors such as moral development (Bredemeier & Shields, 1985), leadership, character, good citizenship (Greendorfer 1987), and sportspersonship (Hodge, 1987; Rail, 1989) are concerned. Although some researchers have maintained that teamwork, cooperation, and other values (i.e., achievement, responsibility, obedience) inherent in children's sports and games can be carried over to social, economic, or political behaviors of adult life (cf., Lever, 1976, 1978; Roberts & Sutton-Smith, 1962; Webb, 1969), data tend not to support automatic transference of such social learning (Stevenson, 1975). Unfortunately, correlational findings have been interpreted as causal relationships; however, researchers have simply not been able to explain how transfer occurs, and why it occurs with some participants/athletes and not others (Greendorfer 1987, 1992). To date, no researcher has been able to identify the mechanism(s) through which the process of socialization through sport operates, if indeed it does.

Discrimination and racial segregation. Although the notion of racial segregation in sport originally used an organizational framework (Loy & McElvogue, 1970) to explain why few African-Americans became managers or coaches, by linking the centrality of playing position with leadership, later research seemed preoccupied with empirical findings rather than theoretical explanations. While these replications provided an excellent source of longitudinal data, the fact that the patterns remained relatively unchanged did not attract research attention. As a result the absence of social change was never explained, nor did it prompt a call for more in-depth analysis of ways in which the process of discrimination might be operating.

In their classic study on the topic of racial discrimination in sport, Loy & McElvogue (1970) extended Grusky's (1963) theoretical notions pertaining to the effects of formal structure on leadership. Grusky hypothesized that three dimensions of formal structure: spatial location, nature of the task, and frequency of interaction created two different types of positions—central and noncentral (or peripheral). In their explanation as to why no African-Americans were coaches or managers in Major League Baseball or the National Football League, Loy & McElvogue discovered that African-Americans were more likely to be found in noncentral positions (i.e., the outfield), while whites were be more likely to occupy central positions (i.e., infield and catcher). Their finding of underrepresentation of African-Americans in spatially central positions, and an overrepresentation in noncentral positions in both sports, provided empirical evidence along with a theoretical explanation that racial discrimination existed in sport.

As previously indicated, these patterns have remained virtually unchanged. In fact, the most recent data (*Center for the Study of Sport Digest,* 1993) demonstrate that African-Americans continue to be overrepresented in noncentral positions in Major League Baseball, the National Football League (i.e., running back, wide receiver, defensive back, and safety) and college football. In the professional sports, for example, African-Americans dominate at first base and in the outfield (76%), at defensive end (73%), defensive tackle (67%), defensive back (95%), wide receiver (88%), and running back (92%), while Whites dominate at pitcher (82%), catcher (87%), quarterback (94%), kicker (83%), and center (76%) (*CSSS Digest,* 1993).

While there is little disagreement over the existence of these patterns, there is considerable debate as to their interpretation. Generally speaking, the two most popular explanations offered are *stacking,* which is a discrimination hypothesis, and *differential socialization experiences,* which is a social psychological explanation that leans heavily on *role modeling.*

Stacking, a term describing the assignment to achieved positions on the basis of ascribed characteristics (Ball, 1973), is premised on the notion of racial stereotyping. This explanation holds that coaches have skill and ability requisites necessary to play each position, and that these skill characteristics are closely associated with racial characteristics. Accordingly, then, if good hands, speed, and instinct are needed to play a position—such as wide receiver—African-Americans would be more suited to that position, because it is assumed they are "naturally" fast and have good instincts and speed.

Although discrimination explanations have been the most widely accepted, an alternative explanation based on notions of role modeling also has gathered some research support. In keeping with this hypothesis, it has been argued that racial segregation was due to self-selection factors which results from differential socialization experiences. McPherson (1971) argued that African-Americans are socialized differently, have different world views, and develop different orientations and value structures because of these different socialization experiences. He suggested that since the most visible and successful African-Americans tended to be athletes, they served as heroes for black youth. Therefore, according to McPherson, in the attempt to emulate similar success young African-Americans desire to play the same position as their heroes. Although data from a study by Castine & Roberts (1974) provide some support for McPherson's hypothesis, as indicated above, various discrimination hypotheses are more widely accepted—regardless of whether they are based on economic (Medoff, 1977, 1986); institutionalized, or organizational decision making (Braddock, 1981; Anderson, 1993); or marginality-centrality (Phillips, 1991) factors.

ISSUES RELATED TO THE DEVELOPMENT OF THE SUBDISCIPLINE

The first 15 years of sociology of sport reflected such a healthy growth and development of interest that position and state of the art papers gave way to a proliferation of research studies. In addition to those topics previously discussed, researchers examined issues related to small groups (i.e., team effectiveness, cohesion); formal organizations (i.e., centrality and leadership, managerial turnover, formal and informal structure); the symbolic use of sport as a political tool; sport as it related to the mass media; the nature and function of sport in culture; sport subcultures; women in sport; and deviancy in sport—to mention only a few.

By the early to mid-1980s, several quarterly journals were flourishing (i.e., *International Review of the Sociology of Sport, Journal of Sport and Social Issues, Sociology of Sport Journal, Arena Review, Journal of Sport Behavior,* and second and third editions of several textbooks were published. Also during this period, several singly authored or co-authored textbooks began to compete with the popular edited anthologies. Unlike earlier anthologies, however, these latter publications consisted of more theory-based material. Although some authored texts continued to deal with subject matter topic by topic, a few authors attempted to integrate theoretical perspectives with empirical findings (cf., Loy, McPherson, & Kenyon, 1978). Unfortunately, however, these attempts were not representative of the literature. More invigorating for the subdiscipline was the fact that conferences served as forums for subdisciplinary development, and the rate of scholarly productivity seemed to attract interest of a new generation of sport sociologists whose professional preparation was steeped in a tradition of theory and methodology.

Marginalization. As suggested earlier, despite initial acceptance of the subdiscipline in the late 1960s—seemingly the result of a bandwagon effect—the relationship between sociology of sport and physical education became somewhat tentative. On the one hand, the subdiscipline had severed any connection with professional orientations, particularly those associated with the social objectives of physical education. On the other, it was not well understood by those in the bioscientific subdisciplines. Even though sociology of sport had adopted a theoretical and scholarly perspective similar to that held by the biosciences, the study of social behavior in sport or physical activity was viewed as something "suspect," mainly because these subdisciplines considered sociology, and to some extent psychology, as "soft" science. This sentiment led to subdisciplinary marginalization, a perspective which tends to view sociology of sport as not a mainstream or significant component of kinesiology.

Interestingly, initial marginalization by both physical education and sociology did not hinder the scholarly development of the subdiscipline. As productivity increased, subdisciplinary knowledge grew and the improved quality of research became quite evident by the mid-1980s. Early debates about theoretical research subsided; fewer studies that generated purely descriptive data appeared in the literature; and a large portion of the research became more reflective of theoretically driven empirical investigation. It was during this period that pleas for elevated levels of theory were heard, and some scholars began to more strongly advocate alternative ways of theorizing (cf., Rees & Miracle, 1986).

Despite this progress, however, the subdiscipline fell short of achieving the goal advocated by structural functionalist researchers: accumulating a solid foundation of knowledge from which to develop sophisticated theory about sport/physical activity-related phenomena (McPherson, 1978, 1986). Theoretical integration of facts simply did not occur, and theoretical explanations promoting an understanding of information gathered were not forthcoming. In short, there was little understanding of the myriad of empirical data collected, and few scholars attempted any type of theoretical synthesis.

RECENT ISSUES

It was during this developmental phase of the early to mid-1980s that sociology of sport became attractive to a number of scholars from fields other than physical education or sociology. Their inclusion into the cadre considerably broadened subject matter, opening domains previously not explored. For example, research attention began to shift toward topics such as: body culture, political economy of sport, sport and globalization, meanings of physicality, ways in which sport reproduces culture, and sport and gender relations. In addition, theoretical approaches other than structural functionalism began to gain greater appeal. This cross-fertilization of scholarly ideas from diverse perspectives and differing theoretical structures was not without cost, however. In fact it may be responsible for the most recent (and perhaps most serious) challenge faced by the subdiscipline—conflicting paradigms and approaches to the study of sport and physical activity.

Paradigmatic Structure and Conflicting Paradigms. Following Henry's (1964) call for a creation of physical education as an academic discipline, the entire field of physical education experienced transformation. Efforts were made to shift from a technical and professional focus to a theoretical and scholarly one. From the moment this shift began, the underlying perspective for generating subject-matter knowledge in physical education has been aligned with the goals and objectives of science (Newell, 1990). Scientific functionalism became the dominant paradigm in all subdisciplinary development in physical education. Moreover, the unquestioning belief in the status of quantitative, objective measurement of the physical and physiological functioning of the body became further entrenched when the field experienced its second transformation—to kinesiology.

This view of science as the ultimate approach to knowledge was also evident in the early position papers in the subdiscipline which advocated a natural science and positivistic (i.e., empirical) approach. Not only were the foundations of knowledge in sociology of sport to be rooted in assumptions of "normal science", but the goal was to generate an objective social science of sport. In fact, the social-science representation of the natural science model, structural functionalism, is based on assumptions of invariant processes in the social universe similar to those found in the physical and biological sciences. Structural functionalism sees reality (in this case, sport) as existing independently of human interpretation (Burrell & Morgan, 1979), and its primary goal lies in the discovery of facts.

By definition, then, the structural functional approach to the study of sport applied scientific methods to study human behavior in sporting contexts. Essentially, such research became the study of overt sport behavior because theoretical concepts (such as cohesion, centrality, segregation, significant other influence, etc.) were operationalized into objective behavioral indicators capable of quantitative measurement. Consequently, sociology of sport became an objective, cumulative, and technically grounded science, while knowledge pertaining to social behavior in sport and physical activity was viewed as the result of information about a world containing stable and impersonal experiences. This approach (i.e., positivism or structural functionalism) with its underlying assumptions dominated research in sociology of sport through the mid-1980s, and knowledge essentially consisted of facts and statistics about the relationship of a wide variety of variables and sport involvement (Sage, 1989).

Despite its dominance, however, structural functionalism had its critics. Although in the minority, some scholars objected to adopting a perspective which espoused value-free and objective research that stressed the importance of quantitative statistical analysis (Gruneau, 1976, 1978; Ingham, 1979; Melnick, 1975). They questioned whether human/sporting behavior could be meaningfully or effectively analyzed in a strictly objective manner. Criticizing structural functionalism as an overly mechanistic approach, they advocated alternative approaches that would examine sport more critically and would view sporting practice as a totality rather than of "fragmentary and decontextualized behavior" (Gruneau, 1976, 1978; Ingham, 1979). They objected to a perspective that did not view sport as socially constructed or from a broad cultural perspective. More specifically, they did not believe in examining or treating specific sport behaviors as "social facts." They maintained that sport was not a fixed concept or phenomenon located "out there" in reality. Rather, it was situated in a broad cultural and historic context, created by social conditions. To them, sport consisted of cultural messages and meanings that were interpreted or socially constructed.

Although this challenge to natural science assumptions of the subdiscipline received minimal attention during the early developmental stages of the subdisciplines, more recently it has been reissued with renewed energy. A larger number of scholars have begun to question the ontological and epistemological assumptions of the natural science model and its social scientific companion, structural functionalism (Bruce & Greendorfer, 1993; Denzin, 1989; Gruneau,

1988; Hargreaves, 1986; Ingham & Hardy, 1993; Hall, 1990). These scholars hold an alternative point of view: that reality is socially constructed, subjective and socially created. Contrary to structural functional assumptions, acceptance of a socially constructed reality denotes an acceptance of multiple realities—that is, different and competing explanations, understandings, and interpretations of reality exist, not one of which comprises "Truth" (Bruce, 1993a; Stanley & Wise, 1983). An example from this perspective is found in Sage's (1988) analysis of intercollegiate sport found on page 114.

This viewpoint not only takes the position that reality is *interpretive,* but it also maintains that interpretations of reality are subject to ideological belief systems. Scholars taking this perspective not only accept the social construction of reality, but they take the position that even social theory is a product of ideological beliefs—that ideas, concepts and theories are situated in and shaped by interpretations of situational and historical factors (Dunning, 1993; Gruneau, 1988, 1993; Hollands, 1984). These assumptions challenge those of positivism and structural functionalism, and the rise of this alternative school of thought has led to serious debate over legitimate theoretical and methodological directions for the subdiscipline (Bruce & Greendorfer, 1993; Nixon, 1993).

Whereas earlier discussions over alternative paradigms may have been challenges to positivism and structural functionalism (cf., Picou, 1979; Sage, 1979; Snyder & Spreitzer, 1979), they were not recognized as such at the time. Rather, they seemed to be explanatory position papers which simply maintained sociology of sport was a multiparadigm subdiscipline. Rather than representing their positions as challenges, *symbolic interactionism* and *hermeneutics* were presented as alternative perspectives (Harris, 1983, 1989) that emphasized different concepts and methods than structural functionalism. For example, instead of subscribing to scientific notions of explanation, prediction and control, these perspectives focused on the interpretive and interactional nature of social life, emphasizing shared understandings and frames of meaning within specific cultures.

Interpretive approaches emphasize a subjective approach to reality, one in which the sport experience is viewed as a product of perceptions and reflexive meanings as well as part of cultural formation. Methods of analysis involved observation, historical, and naturalistic techniques which sought to discover symbols, meanings, feelings, and perceptions that groups considered important aspects of sporting life (Adler & Adler, 1991; Bedker-Meyer, 1990; Harris, 1983, 1989). Research focused more on explanations emphasizing cultural meanings, subjective perceptions, and methods more suited to naturalistic settings (i.e., ethnography, participant observation) (Adler & Adler, 1991; Bedker-Meyer, 1990; Harris, 1989).

Another departure from positivism was critical social theory, which attempted to understand the social, cultural, and historic conditions of sport by focusing on issues of power and ways in which sport is used to perpetuate forms of domination. Emphasizing the role of power and tensions between groups in any society, critical theory viewed sport as a central part of general belief systems that influence political, economic, and ideological practices in society. From this perspective sport is viewed as a form of institutionalized social practice that promotes the interests of the dominant class.

The notion of *hegemony,* a key concept in critical theory, focuses on how dominant ideas come to be accepted as natural. As such, critical theorists would see sport as a vehicle for advancing values and meanings of dominant groups, and they would try to understand how values are transmitted through words, thoughts, ideas, and meanings which are part of the sports creed. *Ideology,* another key concept, fits practice with reality, creating a belief system that conveys meanings and ideas about sport. When applied to sport both notions are used to help critical theorists examine the ways in which images, ideas, and notions of success in sport are reproducing the ideology of social, political, and economic conditions of society (i.e., sport reproduces culture).

Consequently, advocates of a critical perspective would blur distinctions between topics of sport and culture, sport and politics, and sport and ideology, since it views sport as a cultural product central to all aspects of social life (Hargreaves, 1986). Although explanations of the critical perspective were clearly identified as action-oriented, political approaches interested in transforming sport—which definitely distinguished its objectives from the value-free orientation of positivism—these too were not viewed as representing serious challenge to structural functionalism during the mid-1970s, perhaps because the number of adherents was relatively small.

A reading of the most recent literature suggests that an increasing number of scholars have responded to interpretive and critical forms of theory (Dunning, Maguire & Pearton, 1993; Hall, 1990; Ingham & Loy, 1993; Messner, 1993). Moreover, they have more directly challenged the natural science model of research by presenting a wide-ranging and powerful critique of its ontological and epistemological assumptions (Sage, 1989). The fundamental or core issue or point is that any perspective subscribing to the notion that reality is subjective and socially created would argue that "objective" knowledge is unobtainable. It would hold that research is always subject to the researcher's consciousness, prevailing ideological beliefs, and historical conditions. As such, these alternative approaches would clearly reject positivist premises and would have difficulty accepting any knowledge based on such assumptions (Bruce, 1993b).

RESOLUTION OF THE DEBATE AND FUTURE DIRECTIONS

A resolution of this current state of affairs does not seem imminent, as sociology of sport continues to be divided over acceptability of normal science conventions for research, knowledge production, and knowledge diffusion. While future directions seem problematic at the present time, insights seem to be coming more from the perspectives of cultural studies, interpretive interactionism, critical theories, feminism, and political economy than from structural functionalism. Focus seems to be shifting toward theoretical approaches and subject matter that question distinct disciplinary boundaries.

Interestingly, the subdiscipline identified as "sociology of sport" seems to be shifting from one whose attention was solely devoted to the study of sport to one more inclusive of a broad range of physical activity phenomena. For example, the most recent research considers such activities as aerobics, recreational physical activity, exercise and fitness, and other generic forms of human movement. Although new names have been suggested for sociology of sport (e.g., cultural kinesiology; sociocultural kinesiology; physical culture and sport) to accommodate this shift, a name change does not yet seem imminent.

In contrast, recent research demonstrates that "sport" scientists have challenged and critically examined existing theory which rests on description, prediction, and explanation of social facts. Instead, interest has shifted to understanding and explanation of subjective meanings about sport and physical activity. Looking at recent research exploring the relationship between sport and education, we note that the preoccupation with grades, graduation rates, and other measures of academic success of athlete seems to have given way to alternative approaches (Adler & Adler, 1991; Bedker-Meyer, 1990; Bissinger, 1990; Foley, 1990).

For example, Adler and Adler (1991) took an interactionist perspective to examine the relationship between academic *and* athletic experiences of male basketball players. Their ethnographic study focused on the perceptions and reactions of athletes to their intercollegiate experience, and their observations and interviews revealed that most athletes became disillusioned with, and detached from, academics after beginning their college careers with idealistic intentions of graduating. Academic goals of athletes gradually eroded as athletic involvement increased. From interviews and interactions with basketball players, they discovered a number of factors played a role in the collective academic detachment and declining performance that transformed the athletes' college careers: (1) social, physical, and cultural separation from a wide variety of students; (2) shifting orientations from sport as recreation to sport as occupation; (3) philosophical shift toward increased commercialization and big business interests of intercollegiate sport; and (4) a growing cynicism over realizing educational objectives as unexpected problems arose in articulation of athletic, social, and academic spheres of the university.

Another example of the tendency toward paradigm shift can be seen in recent critical examinations which have viewed intercollegiate sport within the structural context of power, dominance, and the ideology of capitalism (Sage, 1988, 1990). In his analysis of intercollegiate sport, Sage (1988) viewed the college athlete as part of an inherently exploitative and unequal social arrangement created by commercialized interests and motivated by profit. Concepts from critical theory offered alternative interpretations that are contrary to traditional beliefs. For example, Sage viewed the notion of a sport scholarship as a deception, as a work contract hiring entertainers under the pretense of education. He further refuted ideological beliefs about scholarships that suggest student-athletes are beneficiaries of the generosity provided by institutions of higher education, when in fact they can be seen as forms of economic exploitation which establish a below poverty-level wage (Sage, 1988).

Obviously, this is a view of college sport not often found in the literature. Aided by critical theory, this alternative approach claims that focus on academic achievement of athletes deflects attention from the commercialized structure of athletic programs which do not function for the benefit of athletes. Also, measures such as Proposition 48 are mechanisms for blaming the victim, instead of identifying major problems inherent in the structure and philosophy of intercollegiate sport.

These examples reflect a shift in ways of knowing and the nature of knowledge that might be generated in the future. Although the literature in sociocultural kinesiology continues to reflect diverse perspectives of a multiparadigm subdiscipline, perhaps themes and theories contributing to the future body of knowledge will be more representative of critical and interpretive perspectives. Definite shifts seem to have already occurred in conceptualizing and framing the study of sport and physical activity. Instead of focusing on structural-functional notions of sport as a reflection or mirror of society and an expression of cultural values, a greater portion of the literature seems to view sport not only as a reproduction of culture, but also as a powerful and influential activity capable of reproducing cultural ideology.

As such, both culture and sport are viewed as social products originating and developing through human interaction. Both provide symbolic order and meaning to social life, and both are social constructions. Consequently, sport is viewed as a set of highly valued, institutionalized traditions and practices that serve as powerful socializers orienting us to symbolic cultural meanings. For example, performance and appearance in sport convey images and meanings about masculinity and femininity. Recent literature sees sport as a reproduction of dominant ideas and goals of society/culture; consequently, sport represents the interests and privilege of those in power (Dunning, Maguire, Pearton, 1993; Ingham & Loy, 1993).

Consideration of sport as a set of practices about the body which is socially and culturally constructed by dominant interests allows scholars to view sport as shaped and transformed by historical factors, as the product of historical conditions and the actions of social agents. Such consideration has broadened subject matter interests, and recent literature suggests the variety of ways in which sport reproduces the privileges of the dominant group and legitimatizes existing sets of social practices (Andrews & Howell, 1993; Dewar, 1993; Hargreaves, 1993; Ingham & Beamish, 1993; Maguire, 1993).

This literature views sport as central to an examination of interests and practices that manifest themselves along three major axes of oppression: race, class, and gender. From these perspectives, research focus has shifted to the ways in which these forms of oppression intersect with each other and with other modes of oppression (Dunning, Maguire, Pearton, 1993). Although sport sociologists have always demonstrated some interest in class, gender and race, more recent attention has focused on additional modes of oppression such as sexual orientation, age, and disability (Lensky, 1993). While the literature is reflecting a greater amount of theoretical attention to issues of race (Brooks & Althouse, 1993), consideration of race relations seems not to be developing theoretically at the same rate as that pertaining to gender and class.

Prospects for the future indicate that concern with issues of gender may take a new turn. Focus currently is on gender relations and the meanings of sport and their relationship to masculinity and femininity (Hall, 1990; Messner, 1993; Sabo & Messner, 1990), and the body as a social construction (Cole, 1993; Desaulniers, 1988). Theorists such as Foucault (1980) have invigorated recent investigation of the body as a neglected subject/object of study. In concert with this line of research, attention seems to be shifting to how the body is construed by the medical profession (Vertinsky, 1987, 1990) and the media (Duncan, 1992; Duncan & Hasbrook, 1988; Kane & Parks, 1992), and how it intersects with technology (Cole, 1993).

These alternative approaches have directed attention from the quantitative research tools advocated by structural functionalism towards more naturalistic approaches which include ethnography, participant observation, interview, media and film analysis, and (what is called) thick description (Bruce, 1993a; Denzin, 1989). Such methods are more suited for capturing the world from the point of view of the subjects involved in it. Not only do such methods allow greater visibility and voice to participants, but they attempt to capture meanings and understandings attached to and interpreted by people's lived experiences in sport and physical activity. Such approaches have been useful in better understanding media representations of lived experiences of athletes and the audience (Bruce, 1993a,b; Denzin, 1993). Personal history and biography have become more popular tools, as has critical deconstruction, which involves a process of outlining what already exists (e.g., analyzing ontological and epistemological assumptions embedded in sporting practices), and interpretively taking apart or dissecting a sport phenomenon in order to explain the sporting experience (Bruce, 1993b; Denzin, 1989).

These interpretive tools seem to be more prevalent in current research than in the past. Current thinking is that these methods facilitate a more complete understanding of lived experiences and meanings attached to the world of physical activity.

CONCLUSION

Substantial changes in scope, frames of reference, and methodology have occurred in what has traditionally developed as "sociology of sport." Although current debates over theoretical approach remain unresolved and the future directions of the subdiscipline seem uncertain, there has been a broadening of subject matter focus and research interest. In addition, despite the challenges to the dominant paradigm of structural functionalism, there are some consistent points of agreement. Most sociologists of sport (i.e., sociocultural kinesiologists) agree that studies of sport and physical activity that are not also studies of societies where physical activity takes place are studies out of context (Dunning, Maguire, & Pearton, 1993).

While objective studies of sporting and body practices have contributed valuable knowledge, they represent rather static, restricted, and limited insight. More recent approaches emphasizing the interconnectedness of past to present, the personal to the cultural, and human agency (i.e, personal action) to structure offer a potential for theoretical understanding that has not been present during the first 30 years of subdisciplinary development. The debate over ways of knowing has certainly expanded knowledge potential and broadened subject matter considerations.

While past debates over academic legitimacy and justification of social scientific study of sporting/bodily practices seem moot in light of the more recent turmoil over theoretical and methodological perspectives, they certainly indicate that the subdiscipline is alive and well. Moreover, despite its marginality, and despite the unknown outcome of current debates, most scholars in this area of study find the current state of affairs intellectually stimulating, exciting, and challenging. Most would agree that sociocultural kinesiology has been institutionalized and is here to stay.

REFERENCES

ADLER, P., & ADLER, P. (1991). *Backboards & blackboards.* New York: Columbia University Press.

ANDERSON, D. (1993, November). *Racial diversity on campus: A look at NCAA Division I-AA football coaches in 1991.* Paper presented at Annual Conference of the North American Society for the Sociology of Sport, Ottawa, Canada.

ANDREWS, D. L., & HOWELL, J. W. (1993). Transforming into a tradition: Rugby and the making of imperial Wales, 1890–1914. In A.G. Ingham & J.W. Loy (Eds.), *Sport in social development* (pp. 77–96). Champaign, IL: Human Kinetics.

BALL, D. (1973). Ascription and position: A comparative analysis of "stacking." *Canadian Review of Sociology and Anthropology, 10,* 97–113.

BEDKER-MEYER, B. (1990). From idealism to actualization: The academic performance of female students-athletes. *Sociology of Sport Journal, 7,* 44–57.

BETTS, J. R. (1974). *America's sporting heritage: 1850–1950.* Reading, MA: Addison-Wesley.

BISSINGER, H. G. (1990). *Friday night lights.* Reading, MA: Addison-Wesley.

BRADDOCK, J. H. (1981). Race and leadership in professional sports. *Arena Review, 5*(2), 16–25.

BREDEMEIER, B., & SHIELDS, D. (1984). Divergence in moral reasoning about sport and everyday life. *Sociology of Sport Journal, 1,* 348–357.

BROOKS, D., & ALTHOUSE, R. (Eds.). (1993). *Racism in college athletics: The African-American athlete's experience.* Morgantown, WV: Fitness Information Technology.

BRUCE, T. (1993a). *Women watching women's basketball on television: Audience resistance.* Unpublished Master's Thesis, University of Illinois, Urbana-Champaign.

BRUCE, T. (1993b). *Toward identifying criteria for interpretive research.* Unpublished manuscript, University of Illinois, Urbana-Champaign.

BRUCE, T., & GREENDORFER, S. L. (1993, November 4). *Postmodern challenges: Towards identifying criteria for social science research.* Paper presented at Annual Conference North American Society for Sociology of Sport, Ottawa, Ontario, Canada.

BRUMMETT, B., & DUNCAN, M. C. (1990). Theorizing without totalizing: Specularity and televised sports. *Journal of Speech, 76*(3), 227–246.

BUHRMANN, H. (1972). Scholarship and athletics in junior high school. *International Review of Sport Sociology, 7,* 119–128.

BURRELL, G., & MORGAN, G. (1979). *Sociological paradigms and organizational analysis.* Portsmouth, NH: Heinemann.

CASTINE, S., & ROBERTS, G. C. (1974). Modeling in the socialization process of the black athlete. *International Review of Sport Sociology, 9*(34), 59–74.

CENTER FOR THE STUDY OF SPORT IN SOCIETY DIGEST, (1993, Summer), *5*(1).

COLE, C. (1993). Resisting the canon: Feminist cultural studies, sport, and technologies of the body. *Journal of Sport and Social Issues, 17*(2), 77–97.

DENZIN, N. (1989). *Interpretive interactionism.* Newbury Park, CA: Sage.

DENZIN, N. (1993). *The lessons James Joyce teaches us.* Unpublished manuscript, University of Illinois, Urbana-Champaign.

DESAULNIERS, S. (1988, November). *Sport and the social construction of the gendered body.* Paper presented at Annual Conference of the North American Society for the Sociology of Sport, Cincinnati, OH.

DEWAR, A. (1993). Sexual oppression in sport: Past, present and future alternatives. In A. G. Ingham & J. W. Loy (Eds.), *Sport in social development* (pp. 147–166). Champaign, IL: Human Kinetics.

DUBOIS, P. (1978). Participation in sport and occupational attainment: A comparative study. *Research Quarterly, 49,* 28–37.

DUBOIS, P. (1979). Participation in sport and occupational attainment: An investigation of selected athlete categories. *Journal of Sport Behavior, 4,* 95–107.

DUBOIS, P. (1981). The youth coach as an agent of socialization: An exploratory study. *Journal of Sport Behavior, 4,* 95–107.

DUBOIS, P. (1985). The occupational attainment of former college athletes: A comparative study. In D. Chu & J. Segrave, & B. Becker (Eds.), *Sport and higher education* (pp. 235–248). Champaign, IL: Human Kinetics.

DUNCAN, M. C. (1992, November 6). *The politics of women's body images and practices of the ideological conflation of public and private in* Shape *magazine.* Paper presented at Annual Conference of the North American Society for Sociology of Sport, Toledo, OH.

DUNCAN, M. C., & HASBROOK, C. A. (1988). Denial of power in televised women's sports. *Sociology of Sport Journal, 5,* 1–21.

DUNNING, E. (1993). Sport in the civilising process: Aspects of the development of modern sport. In E. Dunning, J. A. Maguire, & R. E. Pearton (Eds.), *The sports process* (pp. 39–70). Champaign, IL: Human Kinetics.

DUNNING, E., MAGUIRE, J. A., & PEARTON, R. E. (Eds.) *The sports process.* Champaign, IL: Human Kinetics.

EIDSMORE, R. M. (1963). High school athletes are brighter. *School Activities, 35,* 75–77.

EITZEN, D. S., & SAGE, G. H. (1989). *Sociology of North American Sport* (4th ed). Dubuque, IA: Wm C. Brown.

FOLEY, D. (1990). The great American football ritual: Reproducing race, class and gender inequality. *Sociology of Sport Journal, 7,* 111–135.

FOUCAULT, M. (1980). *The history of sexuality: Volume I: An introduction.* New York: Vintage Books.

GREENDORFER, S. L. (1977). Role of socializing agents in female sport involvement. *Research Quarterly, 48,* 304–310.

GREENDORFER, S. L. (1981). Emergence of and future prospects for sociology of sport. In G. A. Brooks, (Ed.), *Perspectives on the academic discipline of physical education* (pp. 379–398). Champaign, IL: Human Kinetics.

GREENDORFER, S. L. (1983). Shaping the female athlete: The impact of the family. In M. A. Boutilier & L. SanGiovanni. *The sporting woman: Feminist and sociological dilemmas* (pp. 135–155). Champaign, IL: Human Kinetics.

GREENDORFER, S. L. (1987). Psychosocial correlates of organized physical activity. *Journal of Physical Education, Recreation, and Dance, 58*(7), 59–64.

GREENDORFER, S. L. (1992). In T. Horn (Ed.), *Advances in Sport Sociology,* (pp. 201–218). Champaign, IL: Human Kinetics.

GREENDORFER, S. L., & EWING, M. E. (1981). Race and gender differences in children's socialization into sport. *Research Quarterly for Exercise and Sport, 52,* 301–310.

GREENDORFER, S. L., & LEWKO, J. (1978). Role of family members in sport socialization for children. *Research Quarterly, 49,* 146–152.

GROOS, K. (1901). *The play of man.* New York: Appleton.

GRUNEAU, R. (1976). Sport as an area of sociological study: An introduction to major themes and perspectives. In R. Gruneau & J. Albinson (Eds.), *Canadian sport: Sociological perspectives* (pp. 8–43). Reading, MA: Addison-Wesley.

GRUNEAU, R. (1978). Conflicting standards and problems of personal action in sociology of sport. *Quest, 30,* 80–90.

GRUNEAU, R. (1988). Modernization or hegemony? Two views on sport and social development. In J. Harvey & H. Cantelon (Eds.), *Not just a game: Essays in Canadian sport sociology.* Ottawa: University of Ottawa Press.

GRUNEAU, R. (1993). The critique of sport in modernity: Theorising power, culture, and the politics of the body. In E. G. Dunning, J. A. Maguire, & R. E. Pearton (Eds.), *The sports process* (pp. 85–109). Champaign, IL: Human Kinetics.

GRUSKY, O. (1963). The effects of formal structure on managerial recruitment: A study of baseball organization. *Sociometry, 26,* 345–363.

HALL, M. A. (1990). How should we theorize gender in the context of sport? In M. Messner and D. F. Sabo (Eds.), *Sport, men, and the gender order: Critical feminist perspectives* (pp. 223–239). Champaign, IL: Human Kinetics.

HALL, M. A. (1993). Gender and sport in the 1990s: Feminism, culture and politics. *Sport Science Review, 2*(1), 48–68.

HARGREAVES, J. (1982). Sport, culture and ideology. In J. Hargreaves, (Ed.), *Sport, power and culture* (pp. 30–61). London: Routledge and Kegan Paul.

HARGREAVES, J. (1986). *Sport, power and culture.* New York: St. Martin's Press.

HARGREAVES, J. (1993). The Victorian cult of the family and the early years of female sport. In E. G. Dunning, J. A. Maguire, & R. E. Pearton (Eds.), *The sports process* (pp. 71–83). Champaign, IL: Human Kinetics.

HARRIS, J. C. (1983). Broadening horizons: Interpretive cultural research, hermeneutics, and scholarly inquiry in physical education. *Quest, 35*(2), 82–96.

HARRIS, J. C. (1989). Suited up and stripped down: Perspectives for sociocultural sport studies. *Sociology of Sport Journal, 6*(4), 335–347.

HAUSER, W., & LUEPTOW, L. (1978). Participation in athletics and academic achievement: A replication and extension. *Sociological Quarterly, 19,* 304–309.

HENSCHEN, K., & FRY, D. (1984). An archival study of the relationship of intercollegiate athletic participation and graduation. *Sociology of Sport Journal, 1*(1), 52–56.

HENRY, F. (1964). Physical education: An academic discipline. *Journal of Health, Physical Education and Recreation, 37*(7), 32–33.

HIGGINSON, D. (1985). The influence of socializing agents in the female sport participation process. *Adolescence, 20,* 73–82.

HODGE, K. (1988). *A conceptual analysis of character development in sport.* Unpublished doctoral dissertation, University of Illinois, Urbana-Champaign.

HOLLANDS, R. (1984). The role of cultural studies and social criticism in the sociological study of sport. *Quest, 36*(1), 66–79.

INGHAM, A. G. (1979). Methodology in the sociology of sport: From symptoms of malaise to Weber for a cure. *Quest, 31*(1), 187–215.

INGHAM, A., & BEAMISH, R. (1993). The industrialization of the United States and the 'bourgeoisification' of American sport. In E. G. Dunning, J. A. Maguire, & R. E. Pearton (Eds.), *The sports process* (pp. 169–206). Champaign, IL: Human Kinetics.

INGHAM, A. G., & HARDY, S. (1993). Introduction: Sport studies through the lens of Raymond Williams. In A. G. Ingham & J. W. Loy (Eds.), *Sport in social development* (pp. 1–19). Champaign, IL: Human Kinetics.

INGHAM, A. G., & LOY, J. W. (Eds.). *Sport in social development.* Champaign, IL: Human Kinetics.

KENYON, G. S. (1969). A sociology of sport: On becoming a sub-discipline. In B.J. Cratty (Ed.), *New perspectives of man in action* (pp. 163–180). Englewood Cliffs, N.J.: Prentice-Hall.

KENYON, G. S., & LOY, J. W. (1965). Toward a sociology of sport. *Journal of Health, Physical Education and Recreation, 36,* 242–243.

KENYON, G. S., & MCPHERSON, B. D. (1973). Becoming involved in physical activity and sport: A process of socialization. In G. L. Rarick (Ed.), *Human growth and development* (pp. 303–332). New York: Academic Press.

LEVER, J. (1976). Sex differences in games children play. *Social Problems, 23,* 478–487.

LEVER, J. (1978). Sex differences in complexity of children's play and games. *American Sociological Review, 43,* 471–482.

LEWKO, J. H., & EWING, M. E. (1981). Sex differences and parental influence in the sport involvement of children. *Journal of Sport Psychology, 2,* 62–68.

LOY, J. W. (1969). The study of sport and social mobility. In G. S. Kenyon (Ed.), *Aspects of contemporary sociology of sport* (pp. 101–119). Chicago: The Athletic Institute.

LOY, J. W., & KENYON, G. S. (Eds.) (1969). *Sport, culture and society.* London: Macmillan.

LOY, J. W., & MCELVOGUE, J. (1970). Racial segregation in American sport. *International Review of Sport Sociology, 5,* 5–24.

LOY, J. W., MCPHERSON, B. D., & KENYON, G. S. *Sport and social systems.* Boston: Addison-Wesley.

LUEPTOW, L., & KAYSER, B. (1973). Athletic involvement, academic achievement and aspiration. *Sociological Focus, 7*(1), 24–35.

LÜSCHEN, G. (1967). Interdependence of sport and culture. *International Review of Sport Sociology, 2,* 127–141.

MAGUIRE, J. (1993). American football, British society, and global sport development. In E. G. Dunning, J. A. Maguire, & R. E. Pearton (Eds.), *The sports process* (pp. 207–229). Champaign, IL: Human Kinetics.

MCPHERSON, B. D. (1975). Past, present and future perspectives for research in sport sociology. *International Review of Sport Sociology, 10*(1), 55–72.

MCPHERSON, B. D. (1978). Avoiding chaos in the sociology of sport brickyard. *Quest, 30,* 72–79.

MCPHERSON, B. D. (1981). Socialization in and through sport involvement. In G. Lüschen and G. Sage (Eds.), *Handbook of social science of sport* (pp. 246–273). Champaign, IL: Stipes.

MCPHERSON, B. D. (1986). Socialization theory and research: Toward a "new wave" of scholarly inquiry in a sport context. In C. R. Rees & A. W. Miracle (Eds.), *Sport and social theory.* Champaign, IL: Human Kinetics.

MEAD, G. H. (1934). *Mind, self and society.* Chicago: University of Chicago Press.

MEDOFF, M. (1977). Positional segregation and professional baseball. *International Review of Sport Sociology, 12,* 49–54.

MEDOFF, M. (1986). Positional segregation and the economic hypothesis. *Sociology of Sport Journal, 3,* 297–304.

MELNICK, M. (1975). A critical look at sociology of sport. *Quest, 24,* 34–47.

MESSNER, M. (1992). *Power at play.* Boston: Beacon Press.

NEWELL, K. M. (1990). Physical education in higher education: Chaos out of order. *Quest, 42*(3), 227–242.

NIXON, H. L. (1993, November 4). *A normal science imperative for sport sociology: Issues of objectivity, bias and knowing.* Paper presented at Annual Conference North American Society for Sociology of Sport, Ottawa, Ontario, Canada.

PHILLIPS, J. C., & SCHAFER, W. (1971). Consequences of participation in interscholastic sports: A review and prospectus. *Pacific Sociological Review, 14*(3), 328–338.

PHILLIPS, J. C. (1991). The integration of central positions in baseball: The black shortstop. *Sociology of Sport Journal, 8*(2), 161–167.

PURDY, D., EITZEN, D. S., & HUFNAGLE, R. (1985). Are athletes also students? The educational attainment of college athletes. In D. Chu, J. Segrave, & B. Becker (Eds.), *Sport and higher education* (pp. 221–234). Champaign, IL: Human Kinetics.

PICOU, J. S. (1979). Some comments on the growth of knowledge in sport sociology. *Review of Sport and Leisure, 4,* 1–9.

RAIL, G. (1989). *A social phenomenological study of physical contact in women's varsity basketball.* Unpublished doctoral dissertation, University of Illinois, Urbana-Champaign.

REES, C. R., & MIRACLE, A. (1986). *Sport and social theory*. Champaign, IL: Human Kinetics.

RHEBERG & SCHAFER, W. (1968). Participation in interscholastic athletics and college expectation. *American Journal of Sociology, 63,* 732–740.

RIORDAN, J. (1977). *Sport in Soviet society*. Cambridge: Cambridge University Press.

ROBERTS, J., & SUTTON-SMITH, B. (1962). Child training and game involvement. *Ethnology, 1,* 166–185.

SABO, D., & MESSNER, M. (1990). *Sport, men and the gender order*. Champaign, IL: Human Kinetics.

SACK, A., & THIEL, R. (1979). College football and social mobility: A case study of Notre Dame football players. *Sociology of Education, 52,* 60–66.

SAGE, G. H. (1967). *The academic performances of former high school athletes at college*. Unpublished paper, University of Northern Colorado, Greeley.

SAGE, G. H. (1979). Theory and research in physical education and sport sociology: Points of convergence and divergence. *Review of Sport and Leisure, 4,* 48–65.

SAGE, G. H. (1988, May). Power and ideology in intercollegiate sport. Paper presented at the R. Tait McKenzie Symposium on Sport, University of Tennessee, Knoxville, TN.

SAGE, G. H. (1989). A commentary on qualitative research as a form of scientific inquiry in sport and physical education. *Research Quarterly for Exercise and Sport, 60*(4), 25–29.

SAGE, G. H. (1990). *Power and ideology in American sport: A critical perspective*. Champaign, IL: Human Kinetics.

SAGE, G. H. (1989). A commentary on qualitative research as a form of scientific inquiry in sport and physical education. *Research Quarterly for Exercise and Sport, 60*(1), 25–29.

SCHAFER, W., & ARMER, J. M. (1968). Athletes are not inferior students. *Transactions, 5,* 21–26, 61–62.

SCHILLER, F. (1875). *Essays, aesthetical and philosophical.* London: Bell.

SCOVILLE, J. (1974). Labor relations in sports. In R. G. Noll (Ed.), *Government and the sports business* (pp. 185–219). Washington, D.C.: The Brookings Institution.

SNYDER, E., & SPREITZER, E. (1979). *The sociology of sport and the development of sociology: Present status and speculations about the future.* Paper presented at the Southwestern Social Science Association, Fort Worth, TX.

SPADY, W. (1970). Lament for the letterman: Effects of peer status and extracurricular activities on goals and achievement. *American Journal of Sociology, 75,* 680–702.

STEVENSON, C. L. (1975). Social effects of participation in sport: A critical review of the research. *Research Quarterly, 46,* 287–301.

STANLEY, L., & WISE, S. (1983). *Breaking out: Feminist consciousness and feminist research.* London: Routledge & Kegan Paul.

STUMPF, F., & COUSINS, F. W. (1947). Some aspects of the role of games, sports and recreational activities in the culture of modern primitive people. I. The New Zealand Maoris. *Research Quarterly, 18,* 198–218.

STUMPF, F., & COUSINS, F. W. (1949). Some aspects of the role of games, sports and recreational activities in the culture of modern primitive peoples: II. The Fijians. *Research Quarterly, 20,* 2–20.

TYLOR, E. B. (1878). On the game of Patolli in ancient Mexico. *Journal of the Royal Anthropological Institute of Great Britain and N. Ireland,* 116–131.

VERTINSKY, P. (1987). Body shapes: The role of the medical establishment in informing female exercise and physical education in nineteenth-century North America. In J. A. Mangan & R. J. Park (Eds.), *From fair sex to feminism* (pp. 256–281). London: Frank Cass.

VERTINSKY, P. (1990). *The eternally wounded woman.* Manchester: Manchester University Press.

WEBB, H. (1969). Reaction to Loy Paper. In G. Kenyon (Ed.), *Aspects of contemporary sport sociology* (pp. 161–178). Chicago: The Athletic Institute.

Chapter Four
Social Psychological Aspects

Albert V. Carron

The phenomena of sport and physical activity (which are referred to as *sport* in this chapter) have had a continuous significant impact upon our modern industrial society. This is vividly illustrated by a number of factors. For example, consider the amount of media coverage (radio, television, and newspaper, and magazine articles) devoted to sport. Do any other cultural events, including music or art, receive similar attention? Another example is the amount of time people spend in sport-related activities—either directly as participants or indirectly as spectators, coaches, officials, grounds keepers, concession workers, and so on. A third example is the significant financial expenditures associated with sport.

In light of the prominence of sport in our society, it is not surprising that there has also been a growth in interest in understanding issues concerned with the how and why of sport participation. An example of some of the questions that might come immediately to mind in regard to sport are: Why do so many people become involved in sport, either directly as participants or indirectly as sport consumers? What psychological and physiological variables are most closely related to performance excellence? Does a sport experience have any impact upon the social and personal or the anatomical and physiological growth and development of the child?

There are, of course, numerous other issues that have intrigued athletes, coaches, teachers, and researchers for a number of years. The athletes and their coaches and teachers have been interested in the how and the why of sport performance primarily in order to improve performance outcomes and to enhance the quality of the sport experience. While researchers have undoubtedly held similar concerns, they have been principally interested in setting out and analyzing theoretically based interpretations and explanations for sports activity

(Snyder and Spreitzer, 1975). Unfortunately, however, research progress, especially in the social-psychological dimensions has been slow.

Although Coleman R. Griffiths of the University of Illinois (C-U) published a textbook in the 1920s entitled *Psychology of Athletics,* historically the initial research interest in sport and physical education focused on the anatomical and physiological aspects, not on the social-psychological dimension. Not surprisingly, these early research emphases and interests were also reflected in physical education undergraduate curricula where the social-psychological aspects of sport, physical activity, and physical education received little or no attention (Gould, 1976).

Cratty (1973) highlighted these points with the following observations:

> Since before the turn of the century physical education major courses, the primary means of formal training for coaches, contained both practical and applied courses. Coaches were taught how to play and teach traditional sports activities on the one hand, and in addition they undertook various "scientific" courses in which they learned about some basic dimensions of human performance, knowledge of which would purportedly serve them later in good stead. For the most part, these latter courses were based on biomechanics and exercise physiology Until the late 1950's, courses dealing with the psychology of physical activity and the social factors that influence human movement in games and sport were largely absent.
>
> Since the early 1960's, however, interest in the psychological and social dimensions of human athletic endeavor has increased. . . .
>
> In the literature produced by physical educators, psychologists, social psychologists, and sociologists, there is some information that is indirectly relevant to many of the psychological and social dimensions inherent in athletic competition (pp. 4–5).

This increased emphasis on the social-psychological aspects of sport and physical activity in the 1960's and 1970's gradually led to its clear separation into a number of different (but interrelated) fields of interest including sociology, psychology, and social psychology. The latter two are combined in a general way to be the focus of this chapter.

DEFINITIONS

The principal focus of the social-psychological dimension is, broadly stated, *human social-psychological behavior in the context of sport and physical activity.* Although this definitional statement seems reasonably straightforward, it should be elaborated upon in order to outline (a) how the general social-psychological dimension differs from other general areas of science, (b) how the specific component areas within the social-psychological dimension (sociology, psychology, and social psychology) are different from one another, and, finally,

(c) what is meant by the term *behavior* in the definition "human social-psychological behavior in the context of sport and physical activity."

The Social-Psychological Dimension as an Area of Science. It is difficult to clearly distinguish between the various areas of science—to distinguish the social-psychological dimension from other dimensions. The boundaries between many areas of science are not easily differentiated. For example, it has often been suggested that a major difference between social sciences (such as psychology and sociology) and natural sciences (such as chemistry and geology) is that the former are concerned with behavior (and, as a result, are sometimes referred to as the behavioral sciences), while the latter are concerned with matter or material.

This suggestion is not only an oversimplification; it is essentially inaccurate. All science is interested in behavior. A chemist, for example, may be concerned with analyzing the behavioral properties of gases and liquids under different temperatures, while a geologist may be interested in assessing the behavioral changes that occurred in the earth's surface during significant periods in time. Similarly, the aggressive behavior demonstrated by a sport participant or the behavioral norms present on sport teams may be the subject of study for the social scientist.

Therefore, since all science is interested in behavior, broadly defined, the various areas of science are usually differentiated according to the *type of behavior* they study. From the above examples, it should be clear that the types of behavior focused on by the chemist, geologist, and the social scientist differ dramatically. And, as it has already been pointed out, the specific behavior that is the focus in the social-psychological dimension of physical education is human social-psychological behavior in the context of sport and physical activity.

A Distinction between Components of the Social-Psychological Dimension. Psychology has been defined by psychologists as the science of human behavior—the study of the complex forms of human behavior, including its integration, organization, and manifestation. On the other hand, sociology is considered to be the science of society—the study of human social behavior with emphasis on human interaction. Further, social psychology (which, as its name implies, lies midway between sociology and psychology) has been defined as the science of human behavior in social situations—the study of individual behavior and the social forces that influence it. All of these social sciences are similar and interrelated. Therefore by extrapolation, sociology of sport, psychology of sport, and social psychology of sport are all similar and interrelated. So how can these areas be distinguished from one another?

When areas of scholarly interest have a similar or an apparently identical focus, they are often differentiated on the basis of their *unit of analysis*. Thus, for example, the biologist, zoologist, and bacteriologist all have a similar general interest in animal behavior, but their respective specific units of analysis do differ.

In a discussion on the differences between psychology and sociology, VanderZwaag and Sheehan (1978) noted:

> In attempting to clarify areas of scholarly responsibility, two of the most difficult categories to separate are sociology and psychology. One simple way to emphasize the difference between them is to identify each discipline's unit of analysis. Because sociology studies interaction, the basic unit for the sociologist is two or more people. Formal sociological analysis involves the interaction between at least two people who can affect each other directly or indirectly. The basic unit of analysis for the psychologist is the individual. The effect of the social environment on the individual is the primary concern of the psychologist. (p. 171)

In terms of sport and physical activity, then, the sport psychologist might be concerned with the wrestler competing in intercollegiate competition, while the sport sociologist would be concerned with the interaction of the wrestler in the social environment (with the social environment being composed of the team, coach, officials, spectators, opponents, and so on).

Social Behavior in Sport and Physical Activity. A social scientist interested in sport and physical activity is curious about two general kinds of "outputs" that fall under the classification of social behavior. These are behavior and performance. *Behavior* is the individual's unique way of responding (thinking, feeling, acting, doing) to internal and external stimuli. Within this framework, the study of behavior includes the study of personality, attitudes, affect (emotions), cognitions (thoughts), and so on. Some questions about behavior that serve to illustrate this class of sport-related issues are: Are athletes more outgoing, extroverted, confident than nonathletes? Do female athletes more strongly support the concept of sportsmanship than do male athletes? What are the causes of hockey violence? Is a loss most distressing to a competitor when it results from a lack of ability, lack of personal effort, an opponent's good play, or, bad luck?

Performance is instrumental or goal-directed behavior that may or may not be effective. Within this framework, the study of performance includes an analysis of the factors that influence the quality and quantity of the athlete's output in games and competitions. Some questions about performance that serve to illustrate this class of sport-related issues are: Does the presence of spectators result in improvement or decrement in performance? Do children learn more quickly after observing the performance of a highly competent model? Does a team play better for an autocratic or democratic coach? Are cohesive teams more successful than noncohesive teams? It may be apparent that behavior and performance are highly similar concepts. Since the definition of behavior includes the concept of doing, performance is simply a very special type of behavior.

In the two sections which follow, some evidence from research which has examined behavior and performance in sport and physical activity from a social-psychological perspective is discussed. The first section focuses on individual psychology; the second on group dynamics.

INDIVIDUAL PSYCHOLOGY IN SPORT AND PHYSICAL ACTIVITY

Motivation. In any discussion of individual behavior in sport and physical activity, motivation is among the first topic that arises. Motivation, which is derived from the Latin word *movere,* to move, is the term used to represent the energy, the selectivity, and the direction for behavior. Although this seems to be relatively straightforward, individual motivation is exceedingly complex. Consider, for example, the definition advanced by Littman (1958):

> motivation refers to processes or conditions which may be physiological or psychological, innate or acquired, internal or external to the organism which determine or describe how, or in respect of what, behavior is initiated, maintained, guided, selected, or terminated; it also refers to end states which such behavior frequently achieves or is designated to achieve whether they are conditions in the organism or environment; it also refers to the behavior engaged in, or aspects of that behavior, in respect to the organization, occurrence, continuation, reorganization, or termination with regard to past or present or future organic or environmental conditions; further, it refers to the fact that an individual will learn or remember or forget certain material, as well as the rate or manner in which these processes occur and the ease or difficulty with which they are altered, as well as to some of the processes or conditions which are responsible for this behavior; similarly, it determines how or what perceptual and judgmental activities and outcomes will occur, as well as some of the processes and determinants of such activities and outcomes; similarly, it also refers to the fact of and the determinants of the occurrence and fate of affective processes; finally, it describes and accounts for various individual differences which appear in respect of the various behaviors, processes, conditions, and outcomes referred to above. Motivation refers to any one or more of the behaviors, conditions, processes, or outcomes in any combinations (pp. 136–137).

Coaches and teachers are constantly looking for ways to motivate their athletes/students. Where can they begin given the complexity of motivation? One approach I have suggested that coaches and teachers might consider is within a framework where motivated behavior is viewed as a result of contributing factors from within the individual and from within the individual's environment (situation) (Carron, 1984, 1993). This is only marginally useful, however, because as the Littman quote presented above suggests, the factors contributing to motivation are numerous and complex. Therefore, another useful distinction to bear in mind is that many of the factors that contribute to overall individual motivation—within the situation and within the person—cannot be readily influenced by a coach or teacher whereas others can. Thus, for example, an audience is a situational factor which has an impact on an athlete's motivation; it cannot be manipulated readily (if at all) by the coach. On the other hand, the nature of the practice situation is also a situational factor which has an impact on an athlete's motivation. Unlike an audience, however, changing the conditions of practice is directly under the coach's control. Similarly, the personality trait of need for achievement is a personal factor which influences athlete motivation. Because personality changes very slowly over time, it cannot be influenced readily by the coach. Conversely, intrinsic interest is a powerful source of motivation within the athlete that can be directly influenced by the coach. This framework is illustrated in Figure 4.1. An overview of some of the personal and situational factors which can influence personal motivation are outlined in Table 4.1.

Figure 4.1 A model for the study of individual motivation in sport and physical activity (Carron, 1984).

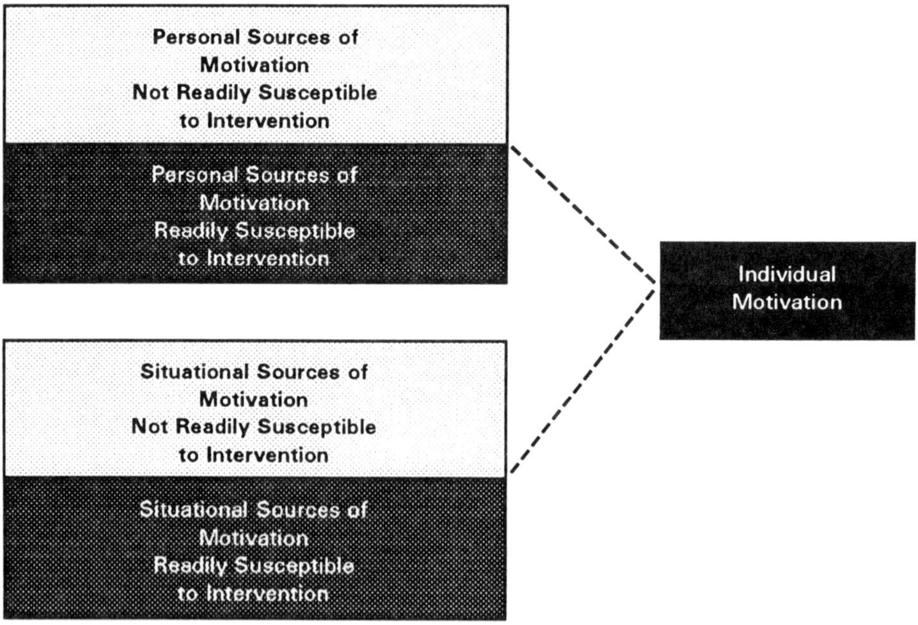

Situational factors susceptible to change. One fundamental assumption in education, business, industry, and sport is that the systematic distribution of *token rewards* is an effective way to motivate. The use of token rewards to

Table 4.1 Sources of individual motivation in sport and physical activity.

Location	Ability to Influence	Motivational Factor
Within the Athlete	Susceptible to Change	Personal Incentives Intrinsic Interest Self-Efficacy Causal Explanations
	Difficult to Influence	Trait of Anxiety
Situational Factors	Susceptible to Change	Token Rewards Goal Setting Practice Situation Social Reinforcement
	Difficult to Influence	Presence of an Audience Nature of Competition

control behavior has been referred to as contingency management—where a contingency is a relationship between a behavior and its consequences (Siedentop, 1978). The token rewards can be edible (e.g., food), social (e.g., verbal reinforcement), manipulable (e.g., access to special equipment), activities (e.g., access to free time), or possessional (e.g., trophies) (Martin & Hrycaiko, 1983). Research has shown that through the use of token rewards (1) undesirable behaviors can be eliminated, (2) desirable behaviors can be elicited, (3) individual performance can be improved, and (3) a spill-over effect often occurs in that non-targeted behaviors are often positively influenced (cf. Carron, 1984).

When *goal setting* is used in the athletic situation, it is also a powerful source of motivation (see Table 4.1). In fact, Locke and his colleagues (Locke, Shaw, Saari, & Latham, 1981) have stated that "the beneficial effect of goal setting on task performance is one of the most robust and replicable findings in the psychological literature" (p. 145). Goal setting works as a motivator because goals serve to direct the individual's attention and actions to important features in the performance situation, mobilize energy expenditure, prolong effort or persistence, and stimulate strategy development. Research has shown that (1) specific hard-challenging goals result in better performance than easy goals, do-your-best goals, or no assigned goals; (2) process and/or mastery goals (i.e., performance improvement) are more effective than outcome (i.e., win) goals; (3) subgoals should be used as a link to long-term goals; (4) supportiveness from the leader and goal acceptance by the participant contribute to goal-setting effectiveness; and (5) the positive effects of goal setting occur independent of age, sex, education, or personality (cf. Carron, 1984).

At elite levels in sport, *practice sessions,* by necessity, involve considerable repetition; this repetition can be draining both mentally and physically. People do get stale. Consequently, it is not uncommon for professional athletes who are returning from an injury and/or rest to play particularly well. Their motivation and interest are optimal. What their experiences and research evidence show is that (1) motivation can be increased through the introduction of novelty, a change of routine, and/or by providing special attention to the participant, and (2) the motivation and performance of participants in a slump can be improved by providing a "time-out" (cf. Carron, 1984).

When *social reinforcements* are used wisely in an athletic situation, they can be a strong source of motivation (see Table 4.1). Social reinforcements are all of the positive and negative comments and reactions made by coaches which serve to convey information of an evaluative nature to participants. Thus, social reinforcements can be verbal (e.g., praise or criticism) or nonverbal (e.g., smiles or frowns). Research evidence shows that social reinforcement is more effective (1) with younger rather than older children, (2) if it is administered by someone not well known to the recipient, (3) if it is administered by significant others of the opposite sex, and (4) with tasks that are simple, well learned, boring, or where feedback is not otherwise available (cf. Carron, 1984).

Situational factors difficult to influence. The presence of *spectators* is also motivating to competitors, but, of course, the presence or absence of others is largely outside personal control. The research in this area has been categorized as social facilitation research where social facilitation refers to "the consequences upon behavior which derive from the sheer presence of other individuals" (Zajonc, 1965, p. 269). A considerable number of investigations have been carried out on social facilitation, the earliest of which is attributed to Triplett in 1897. He used official data from the Racing Board of the League of American Wheelmen to compare cycling times under three conditions: *unpaced* (the cyclist raced alone against time); *paced* (the cyclist raced alone against time but in conjunction with a "pacer," a tandem bicycle manned by three or four confederates); and *paced competition* (the cyclist raced against another competitor, but both cyclists were paced). Triplett found that the paced and paced-competition conditions were 39.55 sec/mile and 34.4 sec/mile faster respectively than the unpaced condition.

Subsequent research evidence shows that the presence of others (1) influences motivation and performance, (2) improves performance in tasks that are simple or well-learned, and (3) causes a decrement in performance in tasks that are either very complex or not well learned. The nature of the audience is also important. An audience has more positive influence on the competitor's motivation if those present are (1) high in status and prestige, and (2) supportive (cf. Carron, 1984).

Our motivation is also strongly influenced by our *competitor* and/or the nature of the *competition.* Common sense tells us that it is very difficult to maintain motivation against an opponent who is either far inferior or superior in ability. A considerable amount of research has been undertaken to understand the nature of competition and its beneficial and harmful influences. This research indicates that competitiveness is learned because it (1) varies in intensity in individuals from different cultures and (2) increases in intensity as the child gets older. Because of the psychosocial development that takes place in young children, Passer (1984) has suggested that "children younger than 7 or 8 should be discouraged from participating in youth sport" (p. 58).

When competition is introduced, (1) early childhood success contribute to the development of the competitive drive, (2) individual motivation is optimal when the competitors are of approximately equal ability, and (3) individuals with high ability on the task generally improve but those with low ability generally show decrements in performance (cf. Carron, 1984).

Personal factors susceptible to change. One powerful source of motivation for our involvement in sport and physical activity lies in the *incentives* that we perceive to be present (Table 4.1). In 1976, Alderman and Wood identified what was referred to as the *incentive systems* for sport, that is, "what it is about the sport itself (particularly its nature and demands) that motivates a young athlete to persist in his participation" (Alderman, 1978, p. 52). The seven incentive systems in sport were identified as affiliation, aggression, excellence, independence, power, stress, and success—names that aptly summarize each one.

The *affiliation* incentive refers to the fact that children enter into sports to make friends or to maintain existing friendships through participation. The *aggression* incentive acknowledges the fact that some children use sport as a medium in which to intimidate others, while the *excellence* incentive reflects the motivation that people have to do something well (e.g., excel in sport). The underlying basis of the *independence* incentive is to do things alone without the help of others, whereas the *power* incentive reflects motives to influence and control others in the sport context. *Stress* incentives revolve around opportunities for excitement, tension, pressure, and action. Finally, *success* incentives are related to the desire for the extrinsic rewards in sport such as status, recognition, prestige, and social approval.

In order to determine the most powerful incentives for sport participation, researchers have used both the Alderman and Wood conceptual model and open-ended questionnaires. This research indicates that (1) the most consistently endorsed reasons for sport participation are affiliation, skill development, excitement, success and status, fitness, and energy release, and (2) the need for independence, power, aggression, and the influence of others (e.g., parents) are relatively unimportant reasons for sport involvement. Also, the bases for participation is remarkably similar (3) among females and males, (4) for individuals of different ages, and (5) for individuals from different cultures (cf. Carron, 1984). These conclusions, notwithstanding, one of the most interesting research findings to date is that there is no single dominant reason for involvement in sport and physical activity. Children have multiple incentives in any given sport, and the nature of their incentives generally varies across sports.

The reasons for sport and physical activity involvement are often categorized as intrinsic or extrinsic. Intrinsic interest stems from a motivation to participate in a task for its own sake—for the excitement, enjoyment and challenges which are an integral part of the task. On the other hand, extrinsic interest stems from motivation to participate in a task because of the rewards that have become associated with involvement in the activity. Many psychologists consider *intrinsic interest* to be the most powerful source of motivation for sport and physical activity involvement (Table 4.1). Deci (1975) has proposed that intrinsic interest is maximal when we have a sense of competence and when we are engaged in behaviors that are self-selected. This notion was substantiated by Halliwell (1978) who pointed out:

> the more people feel that their actions are self-determined and provide a sense of personal competence, the higher will be their level of intrinsic motivation. On the other hand, if people feel that they are being pushed around by others or if their performance results in constant failure and negative feedback, they will be less intrinsically motivated to participate in that activity (p. 68).

Research indicates that the intrinsic satisfaction associated with sport and physical activity is at its highest when the participant (1) has a sense of control over clear and challenging goals, (2) has no distractions, anxieties, or worries, and (3) is involved in an activity that is carried out for its own sake, not because of external pressures and/or rewards (cf. Carron, 1984).

A third personal factor contributing to motivation and highly susceptible to coaching influence is *self-efficacy.* Self-efficacy, which is defined as the strength of a person's conviction that he or she can successfully execute a behavior, carry out a task, or handle the responsibilities necessary to produce a desired outcome, is a situationally specific form of self confidence.

According to Bandura (1977), feelings of self-efficacy arise from four principal sources: performance success, vicarious experiences, verbal persuasion, and emotional arousal. Performance success is the strongest source of self-efficacy; nothing is as effective for confidence as personally experiencing success. Vicarious experiences—observing someone else being successful—also can increase confidence but the observed person must be perceived as similar (e.g., age, physique, ability level). Verbal persuasion (i.e., encouragement and reassurance from others), can be useful but it does have limitations. The confidence of a inexperienced diver on a tower is not likely to be changed substantially by reassurances from a coach that he/she has the necessary skill.

A fourth personal factor contributing to motivation is the *causal explanations* individuals use to account for successful and unsuccessful outcomes. The analysis of these causal explanations falls under a category of social science called attribution theory. Attribution theory is also referred to as common-sense or naive psychology because it is basically concerned with the "theories" that all of us use in everyday situations to understand, explain, and predict why particular events have occurred. For example, an athlete after competition, a student following an examination, and a person returning from a social engagement all share a common desire to understand why the particular outcome occurred.

Weiner (1972) proposed that when individuals attempt to account for an outcome they typically draw upon the four principal explanations illustrated in Table 4.2: ability, effort, the degree of luck experienced, and the difficulty of the task, assignment, or opponent. The first two are personal factors within the individual while the latter two are external factors over which the individual has no control.

Table 4.2 Weiner's (1972) model of causal attributions.

		LOCUS OF CONTROL DIMENSION	
		INTERNAL	EXTERNAL
STABILITY DIMENSION	STABLE	Ability	Task Difficulty
	UNSTABLE	Effort	Luck

It has been repeatedly demonstrated that individuals are extremely self-serving in their explanations for an outcome (Carron, 1980a). If the outcome was successful, the individual perceives the causes for this success to be personal—the level of personal ability and/or the amount of effort expended. On the other hand, if the outcome was unsuccessful, the individual perceives the causes for this to be outside of personal control—the amount of bad luck experienced and/or the extreme difficulty of the task.

Personal factors difficult to influence. An individual's personality can influence his/her choice of activities, the duration of time spent on those activities, and the intensity with which those activity are undertaken. But, since personality develops slowly over time, it is also not readily influenced by the actions of the coach.

One personality trait which has received considerable attention is *anxiety*. Martens (1977) identified a sport-specific anxiety which he referred to as sport competition anxiety: a tendency to perceive competitive situations as threatening and to respond to these situations with feelings of apprehension and tension. Research which has examined the relationship of the personality trait of anxiety to sport involvement indicates that (1) outstanding, average, and lesser skilled athletes do not exhibit inherent differences in either the general personality trait of anxiety or in the specific personality trait of sport competition anxiety, and (2) the degree to which athletes possess the specific personality trait of sport competition anxiety decreases with age and experience. When individuals are high in the specific personality trait of sport competition anxiety, they (3) worry more about performance and evaluations, (4) have higher feelings of stress in competitive situations, and (5) have lower self-esteem (cf. Carron, 1984).

Aggression. If motivation is among the first topics that arise in any discussion of individual psychology, aggression is among the second. However, aggression is one of the most misunderstood concepts. For example, one source of confusion concerns the term aggression and what types of behaviors it represents. Aggression, in the sense that it has been analyzed by social scientists (e.g., Bandura, 1973), is not a synonym for motivation, or assertiveness, or dominance; rather, it is a synonym for violence. As such, aggression is always a negative, undesirable behavior.

There is also some confusion about the causes of aggression in the sport context. In fact, there are essentially *three* myths that have arisen in regard to aggression by an athlete in a sport situation: (1) it is an instinctual response; (2) it is a natural byproduct of frustration; and (3) it serves as catharsis to drain away the tendencies toward future aggression (Carron, 1980b).

Smith (1974, 1978, 1979a, 1979b) has written extensively on the topic of aggression in sport, particularly on aggression in hockey. In an article entitled "Hockey violence: Interring some myths," he dismissed many of the fantasies (including the above three) that have developed around violence in hockey . His general conclusions are equally applicable to violence in baseball, basketball, football, and other sports. As Smith (1978) pointed out:

> Modern research repudiates instinct theory. Men—and beasts generally speaking—learn to be aggressive and use aggression for specific purposes, usually to get or keep something they want. Frustration theory has a scientific basis, but even its chief proponents don't claim that frustration always leads to aggression or that aggression is always caused by frustration. Anthropologists have shown that people in some societies simpler than ours are willing to suffer frustration indefinitely without ever resorting to aggression. Like most human behavior, responses to frustration are contoured by learning and culture. Violence in hockey undoubtedly is sometimes a response to frustration—but because it's tolerated, not because it's in our genes. Finally, there's almost no reliable evidence in support of catharsis (or "flush toilet") theory; on the contrary, numerous studies show that behaving aggressively, or viewing others behaving aggressively, tends to lead to more aggression, not less. (p. 142)

Violence in sport is a learned social behavior. Through the process of socialization the child learns to model and imitate the behavior of esteemed people such as parents, coaches, teachers, peers, and older, more skillful athletes (e.g., professional athletes). The learning of violence results from the observation, imitation, and social reinforcement of certain behaviors.

The development of aggressive behavior in the young athlete can occur in any (or all) of three ways (Bandura, 1973). The first is through *observational learning.* The athlete learns new patterns of behavior by watching others perform, e.g., a professional athlete's skillful, undetected use of an illegal elbow in hockey or basketball or the use of the hockey stick as a weapon might be two illustrations. The young athlete does not naturally acquire these techniques as part of some developmental process; they are learned responses.

Second, there is *disinhibition;* a model serves to strengthen or weaken inhibitions to particular behaviors. If a young athlete observes violent, illegal tactics, and these are either implicitly or explicitly condoned by coaches, parents, television commentators, teachers, and/or peers, there is a reduction in inhibition. The athlete has not only learned "how to" through observation, but also that it is an acceptable (possibly even approved) way of responding.

Finally, modeling influences behavior through *response facilitation.* Behaviors that are not illegal—aggressive rebounding in basketball, body checking in hockey, base running in baseball, tackling in soccer—are prompted or facilitated through the appearance of similar behaviors in esteemed models such as professional athletes. The result is that the behavior has a much greater likelihood of appearing in the young athlete's performance and then being expanded. Violence in sport can be eradicated if there is sufficient motivation on the part of sport policy-makers.

GROUP DYNAMICS IN SPORT AND PHYSICAL ACTIVITY

A sport team can be defined as a collection of individuals who possess a collective identity, have common goals and objectives, share a common fate, develop structured patterns of interaction and modes of communication, exhibit personal and task interdependence, reciprocate interpersonal attraction, and consider themselves to be a group.

When individuals are in group situations, there are two types of outcomes that can result from their involvement. These can be categorized as either *individual products* and *group products.* Insofar as the individual products are concerned, for example, membership in sport groups can contribute to individual feelings of satisfaction, personal conformity to behavioral norms, reduced anxiety, reduced independence, greater participation and adherence, and so on.

Insofar as group (or collective) products are concerned, for example, teams experience success and failure, develop a collective identity, and so on.

Figure 4.2 provides a useful way to look at group dynamics and examine the general categories of factors that influence group and individual products. As Figure 4.2 illustrates, the major influences can be categorized under the labels *member attributes* (or *group composition*), *group environment, group structure, group cohesion,* and *group processes* (Carron, 1988).

Group composition. Group composition refers to "the relationship among the characteristics of individuals who compose the group" (Shaw, 1981, p. 454). These characteristics can include the group members' physical size and body type, mental and motor abilities, attitudes, aptitudes, motives, needs, personality traits, and such social identifiers as age, education, religion, occupation, race, sex, and social status.

Jones (1974) carried out one of the most comprehensive studies on group composition and team success in sport. The focus in Jones' work was on how well individual ability predicts team success in a variety of different sports. The measures of individual ability he used were singles ranking in tennis, runs batted in and earned run averages in baseball, points assists and rebounds in basketball, and points for and against in football. The measures of team success were team rankings and won-loss records. Jones found that team success and individual ability were correlated .70 in men's tennis, .80 in women's tennis, .91 in football, .94 in baseball, and .60 in basketball.

Group environment. The group environment represents the situational, physical, climatic and/or geographical conditions which surround the group. These environmental conditions can be described from either an objective or subjective perspective. Thus, for example, the density in a practice facility (i.e., the number of athletes present per unit of space) would be an objective environmental factor whereas the athletes' perceptions of crowding would be a subjective environmental factor.

One environmental factor that has been studied extensively is the home advantage—the degree to which teams competing in a balanced schedule win over 50 percent of their home competitions. Research has shown that a home advantage (1) exists in all the major team sports, (2) is virtually identical in both college and professional for the same sport, and (3) varies widely across various team sports (baseball, 53.5%; football, 57.3%; ice hockey, 61.1%, basketball, 64.4%; and, soccer, 69.0%) (cf. Courneya & Carron, 1992). Also, a home advantage (4) is present in the individual sport of World Cup Alpine Skiing (the extent varies from discipline to discipline, between males and females, and between top-level and second-level skiers).

What are the causes of the home advantage? Considerable research has been undertaken but the picture is still unclear. Four possibilities suggested

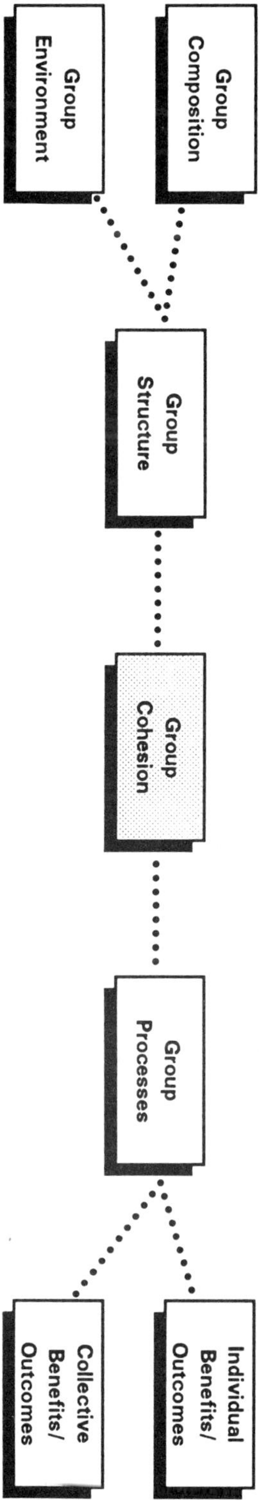

Figure 4.2 A model for the study of group dynamics in sport and physical activity (Carron, 1988)

include the home team's supportive crowd, the rules in some sports (e.g., batting last in baseball), the necessity for the visiting team to travel, and the home team's superior familiarity with its facility. Research undertaken on some of these factors has shown that the home advantage (1) does not result from rules factors , (2) is only minimally influenced by the fact that visiting teams must travel (and, therefore, are at a disadvantage), (3) is not influenced by the absolute crowd size (4) is influenced by crowd density (cf. Courneya & Carron, 1992; Agnew & Carron, In press).

Group structure (see Figure 4.2 again). According to Shaw (1981), there are four components which reflect the emergence of group structure: (1) group positions, i.e., the geographical place or location of group members; (2) status, i.e., the differences in power, prestige, and importance among group members; (3) roles, i.e., personal responsibilities within the group about which members have shared expectations; and, (4) norms, i.e., collective standards for behavior for which members have shared expectations. Group structure is a complex topic and space doesn't permit a full discussion. It might be useful, however, to consider one element of group structure—group position—and examine its relationship to an individual product (see Figure 4.1 again)—the personal rewards individual athletes receive.

Considerable research has shown that a player's position (e.g., catcher versus outfielder in baseball or running back versus lineman in football) can have a significant impact upon the probability of obtaining rewards and benefits. That is, individuals in some positions have a much greater chance of being elected captain, of being recruited as manager or coach after their playing career is over, and of being selected most valuable player.

Table 4.3 An overview of the relationship of playing position and organizational rewards in baseball (Adapted from Chelladurai & Carron, 1977).

Position		Managers & Coaches	Team Captains	Most Valuable Players
I	Catchers	·26.6%	21.4%	12.9%
II	Infielders	11.6%	9.9%	10.4%
III	Outfielders	3.6%	4.3%	6.4%

Table 4.3 contains data from a number of studies carried out on the sport of baseball. Similar studies have also been conducted with football (e.g., Sage, 1974; Massengale and Farrington, 1977); hockey (Roy, 1974); and basketball (Klonsky, 1978). In Table 4.3, the playing positions are subdivided into three categories: catchers, infielders, and outfielders. In terms of the organizational rewards, a catcher has a greater probability of being the recipient.

A number of explanations have been advanced to account for this phenomenon. Chelladurai and Carron suggested that this inequity in rewards and benefits is a function of two aspects of the athlete's playing position (1977). These were referred to as *task dependence* and *propinquity*. Task dependence refers to the fact that some positions in sport involve a considerable amount of task interaction while others do not. The catcher who handles the ball on almost every pitch can be contrasted in this regard with an outfielder who might not have any fielding chances in a full game.

Propinquity, the second dimension, consists of two combined attributes: *observability* (the extent to which the player in a position has knowledge of the ongoing action, including the locations and movements of those in other positions, the strategic decisions being utilized, and so on); and *visibility* (the degree to which the player is seen and watched by those in other positions on the field, including the opponents). Again, the catcher who serves as a highly visible defensive leader can be contrasted in this regard with an outfielder who is relatively removed from the hub of activity and plays a passive role in defensive decision making.

Chelladurai and Carron felt that positions in sport have different amounts of actual and ascribed status, prestige, and importance, depending upon the extent to which they possess propinquity and task dependence. The catcher is high in both, the infielder is average in both, and the outfielder is low in both. As a result, the organizational rewards and benefits are available to individuals in each of these three categories in decreasing degrees. This is highlighted in Table 4.3 (p. 140).

Group cohesion. Cohesion is a dynamic property which contributes to the tendency for a group to stick together and remain united in the pursuit of its goals and objectives (Carron, 1981). It is multidimensional in nature—that is, there are numerous "cohesions" which cause a group to stick together. For example, in some groups, the nature of social relationships is poor, but the members are highly task cohesive—committed and unified in the pursuit of the group's goals and objectives. In other groups, on the other hand, the group is highly unified in terms of its social cohesion, but its degree of cohesiveness in regard to its task is minimal.

My colleagues and I have undertaken a considerable amount of research to examine the correlates of cohesiveness in exercise groups and sport teams. Some generalizations resulting from our research with exercise classes are that (1) participants in more cohesive classes hold stronger perceptions that their group will be able to withstand the negative impact of disruptive events, and (2) perceptions of cohesiveness are strongly associated with improved adherence behavior. In short, participants who perceive their exercise class to be more cohesive have more confidence in their class's ability to overcome adversity.

They also demonstrate greater adherence in respect to absenteeism, punctuality, and drop-out behavior (cf. Carron, 1993).

In sport teams, the relationship between cohesion and performance is reciprocal—when a team is cohesive, it becomes more successful, and when it has been successful, it becomes more cohesive. The latter is the stronger of the two relationships. Athletes who have been on highly successful teams fondly recollect the feeling of camaraderie that developed. In turn, athletes who have been on highly unsuccessful teams recollect the lack of general rapport that was present and how happy they were to see the season end.

These subjective feelings have been supported by research by Carron and Ball (1977) and Bakeman and Helmreich (1975). Both studies were interested in determining which relationship was the stronger, i.e., cohesion leading to performance success or performance success leading to cohesion. Carron and Ball tested intercollegiate ice hockey teams, while Bakeman and Helmreich examined aquanaut teams that lived and worked in an underwater habitat. In both studies, it was observed that there was a considerably greater tendency for success to lead to cohesion than the reverse.

This is by no means an either-or situation. Martens and Peterson (1971) found that teams that were more cohesive were more successful, and, in turn, the more successful teams expressed greatest satisfaction with participation. On the basis of their findings, Martens and Peterson proposed that a circular relationship exists among cohesion, performance, and satisfaction.

Group size is also an important group variable insofar as feelings of cohesiveness are concerned. We have found that both dress roster size and action unit size are related to the athlete's perceptions of cohesiveness. In one study (Widmeyer, Brawley, & Carron, 1990, Study 1), we varied the size of the dress roster in a 3-on-3 basketball league from 3 to 6 and 9 members. Task cohesion was highest in the 3-person groups and lowest in the 9-person groups. Conversely, social cohesion was highest in the 6-person groups and lowest in the 9-person groups. In a second study, (Widmeyer, *et al.*, 1990, Study 2), we varied the size of the action unit in intramural volleyball teams from 3 to 6 and 12 members. Both cohesion and enjoyment were lowest in the 12-person groups.

Group processes. Group processes (see Figure 4.2 again) reflect the dynamic interactions associated with membership in groups. Team members communicate relative to task and social concerns, establish collective and personal goals, carry out group tasks and experience successes and failures, arrive at explanations to account for group events (including their successes and failures), develop personal and collective confidence, and so on.

One important group process that has received considerable attention is the emergence of *motivations and aspirations* in regard to group goals and objectives. No one would deny that individuals have aspirations and motivations. In addition, groups/teams also have aspirations and motivations—and these are more than the simple summation of the motivations and aspirations of the individual members. As Zander (1971) pointed out, the welfare of the group as a totality is a primary concern of individual members: "members often suppress any inclination to put their own needs first. . . . They concentrate instead on what the total group should do . . . what is 'good for the group'" (p. 2).

Zander identified two group-oriented motives. One, the *desire for group success,* is a disposition on the part of group members to feel pride and satisfaction with the group if it successfully accomplishes a challenging group task. The second, the *desire to avoid group failure,* is a disposition on the part of group members to feel embarrassment or dissatisfaction with the group if it fails on a challenging task.

While Zander (1978) reported mixed results from experiments carried out with groups in laboratory settings, in nonlaboratory research he found that groups with the greatest desire for group success showed the most effective performance. For example, a greater desire for group success was associated with more sales of insurance policies in the different districts of a large company (Bowers & Seashore, 1966), with more speed and skill when groups of military officers were on a 4 1/2 day trek in the snow (Thomas and Zander, 1959), and with more production on a factory assembly line (Zander & Armstrong, 1972).

The effect of success and failure upon group level of aspiration has been examined in a number of experiments with a variety of group tasks (Zander, 1971). The effects that success or failure have upon the aspiration that members have for their group follows a consistent pattern; that is, group success leads to an increase in group aspiration, and group failure, to a decrease. Further, the amount of absolute change is greater with success.

A second important group process that is evident in groups is the development of *collective efficacy.* Collective efficacy is similar to self-efficacy (which was discussed earlier) except that it is the strength of a *group's* conviction that it can successfully execute a behavior, carry out a task, or handle the responsibilities necessary to produce a desired outcome. Collective efficacy has a strong influence on group performance. In a laboratory study, we used a pretest manipulation involving bogus feedback about strength to obtain groups that differed in their collective efficacy (Hodges & Carron, 1992). These high and low collective efficacy groups were then placed in a competition against a confederate group where they experienced failure. It was found that the groups that possessed high collective efficacy showed an improvement in endurance performance following failure, whereas the groups with low collective efficacy showed a decrement.

A third important group process is the establishment of *team goals.* It was pointed out above that individual goal setting is associated with individual motivation and athletic success. So, it might be expected that groups would actively engage in collective goal setting. Interestingly, we have found that team goal setting is not well practiced. The overwhelming majority of team goals are general (>.70%) rather than specific in nature (Brawley, Carron, & Widmeyer, 1993). Also, advocates of goal setting have emphasized that process goals—specific behavioral strategies needed to achieve an ultimate objective—are far more effective than outcome goals—which is represented by the ultimate destination itself. (Thus, for example, a process goal might be to decrease opponent's shots on net in ice hockey by 10% per game; an outcome goal might be to win the league championship or win a greater percentage of games.) We have found that for practice situations, team process goals predominated (89.9%) whereas for competitions, the emphasis on process and outcome goals was approximately equal (Brawley, Carron, & Widmeyer, 1993a).

In another study (Brawley, Carron, & Widmeyer, 1993b), we examined the psychological consequences of athlete involvement in team goal-setting. On the basis of this research, we came to two conclusions: (1) with greater participation in team goal-setting, team cohesion is greater, and (2) when cohesion is high, athletes are more satisfied with their team's goals for practice and competition.

IMPLICATIONS FOR GENERAL EDUCATION

What implications does the social-psychological dimension of sport have for education? Learning that occurs in the actual school environment is of three general types: cognitive, psychomotor, and affective (VanderZwaag & Sheehan, 1978). Cognitive learning encompasses the traditional view of education with its emphasis on the development of intellectual skills such as the three R's. The psychomotor domain includes those learning experiences reflected in the development of skilled bodily movements through art, music, drama, industrial arts, and physical education. Finally, the affective domain centers around the acquisition of attitudes, values, and interests through the total educational curriculum.

Sport generally and the social-psychological dimension of sport have always been considered an essential medium through which affective learning can occur. Consider, for example, the objectives for athletic programs listed in *The Athletic Director,* a publication of the National Council of Secondary School Athletic Directors:

1. To provide opportunities for competition,
2. To provide activities that involve the whole school,
3. To instruct students in good health, personal hygiene, and safety habits,
4. To provide instruction in sport skills and to offer opportunities to improve those already acquired,

5. To provide opportunities for friendship development with both teammates and opponents,
6. To provide students with opportunities in leadership-training,
7. To provide opportunities for the development of good sportsmanship,
8. To provide opportunities for students to work in groups and to learn self-discipline for the overall benefit of that group,
9. To provide opportunities to learn to follow rules,
10. To provide the student with opportunities to gain satisfaction from self-sacrifice as a result of contributions to development of esprit de corps, a feeling of unity, belonging, pride in the team, team work, and the respect for authority,
11. To provide extended opportunities for grant-in-aid scholarships and professional athletic or associated careers for all participants,
12. To provide the general community with an understanding that the competitive athletic program has been designed to promote sportsmanship, citizenship, and a wholesome relationship between school and community,
13. To provide for opportunities to develop approved social patterns of conduct for both individuals and groups
14. To provide for opportunities to develop skills and attitudes that will lead to participation in sports throughout life, and
15. To encourage the development of the highest standards of moral and spiritual character.

It is apparent that the great majority of these objectives relate to affective learning, i.e., the learning of values, interests, and attitudes. In fact, it is the affective domain in which the social-psychological dimensions of sport have had their most significant impact. However, sport does not naturally contribute to the development of positive values, interests, and attitudes. As Orlick and Botterill (1975) observed, "sports are not inherently or necessarily good, as once supposed, nor are they inherently bad; rather they have the capacity to be either."

VanderZwaag and Sheehan have suggested that at least two important changes must be made before sport can serve as a social learning environment in general education:

> Both affect the teachers. *First,* teachers who are responsible for providing social learning experiences through sport must have the ability to do so. A good background in psychology, sociology, and social psychology (especially group dynamics) is indispensable. They must become applied social scientists to obtain productive results. Sport studies educators who are equipped with knowledge and skills acquired from the type of teacher-preparation program in sport studies are well prepared to provide social learning experiences through sport.
>
> *Second,* student expectations must be changed. Typically, students entering a gym class do not expect to be challenged to learn social behavior In many cases they expect to learn nothing at all—gym class to them is no more than "recess" or a "fun" class. It is absolutely necessary that teachers redirect these attitudes (1978, p. 260).

In short, teachers must become familiar with the social-psychological dimensions discussed previously. With an understanding of these dimensions, it may be possible to achieve a positive affective learning environment.

RELATIONSHIP TO AFFILIATED PROFESSIONS

What is the relationship of the social-psychological dimensions of sport to affiliated professions? Carron (1980b), in a discussion of the relationship of sport psychology to general psychology, suggested that:

> As a science, psychology is comprised of a number of subdisciplinary areas including the *developmental, clinical, social, personality, experimental,* and *educational.* Even minimal familiarity with these subdisciplines clearly shows that each has some relevance to the study of athletic behavior in sport. Thus, while many researchers in sport consider sport psychology to be another subdiscipline within general psychology, it seems preferable to consider it as a specific type of applied psychology which embraces aspects of all of the areas within psychology. Also, as an extension of this perspective, sport psychology can be defined as a study of the complex forms of human behavior in the specific context of play, games, and sport.

This same viewpoint is applicable to the social psychology of sport. Thirty years ago, Henry (1964), in a discussion on the evolution of physical education as an academic field of study, pointed out that physical education evolved because sciences such as sociology and psychology failed to view sport as a sufficiently significant social phenomenon for scientific inquiry. The result was the development of what can broadly be referred to as *sport sciences.*

Since the sport sciences are relatively young, the prevalent pattern has been to adapt theories and research strategies that originated in the parent discipline and test their application in the sport context. This is a natural, logical approach. However, it has now become apparent that, while there are some notable exceptions, theories of behavior that have their major application in general social settings are not particularly explanatory in sport settings. The development of theoretical explanations for behavior in sport is one of the major challenges facing researchers interested in the social and psychological dimension of sport.

CONCLUDING STATEMENT

The social-psychological dimension with its concern for the behavior and performance of individuals engaged in play, games, and sport plays a predominant role in physical education and athletics. For example, in terms of behavior, the perceived importance of the social-psychological dimension is clearly illustrated through an examination of the behavioral objectives listed for physical education and athletics. Sportsmanship, cooperation, social interaction, cohesion, and a variety of personality traits are frequently proposed as desired objectives of participation in sport. Whether they are developed or not is, of course, a function of the dynamics of the situation. Nevertheless, the sport environment does offer the potential if it is used effectively.

Gaining an understanding of the social-psychological dimension also has implications for sport performance. Ryder, Carr, and Herget (1976) analyzed the factors that could potentially affect future performance in track events. On the basis of their analysis of the performances of runners who held world records over the previous 50 years and the physiological parameters that affect sprint and endurance events, they concluded that the limits to future performance were psychological rather than physiological in nature. They also pointed out that the critical considerations were those affecting daily training, not those present in the actual event itself.

The suggestion by Ryder *et al.* (1976) notwithstanding, it is certainly premature to suggest that our understanding of the social-psychological dimension is highly advanced. It is true that we now have some insight into many issues. However, concentrated research efforts have only been initiated relatively recently, and the number of questions and issues that remain unanswered (or even unexamined) is considerable. This represents a target for social scientists in our field.

REFERENCES

AGNEW, G., & CARRON, A. V. (In press). Crowd effects and the home advantage. *International Journal of Sport Psychology.*

ALDERMAN, R. B. (1978). Strategies for motivating young athletes. In W. F. Straub (Ed.), *Sport psychology An analysis of athlete behavior.* Ithaca, NY: Mouvement.

ALDERMAN, R. B., & WOOD, N. L. (1976). An analysis of incentive motivation in young Canadian athletes. *Canadian Journal of Applied Sport Science, 1,* 169–176.

BAKEMAN, R., & HELMREICH, R. (1975). Cohesiveness and performance: Covariation and causality in an underseas environment. *Journal of Experimental Social Psychology, 11,* 478–489.

BANDURA, A. (1973). *Aggression: A social learning analysis.* Englewood Cliffs, NJ: Prentice-Hall.

BANDURA, A. (1977). Self-efficacy: Toward a unifying theory of behavioral change. *Psychological Review, 84,* 191–215.

BRAWLEY, L. R., CARRON, A. V., & WIDMEYER, W. N. (1992). The nature of group goals in sport teams: A phenomenological analysis. *The Sport Psychologist, 6,* 323–333.

BRAWLEY, L. R., CARRON, A. V., & WIDMEYER, W. N. (1993). The influence of the group and its cohesiveness on perceptions of group goal-related variables. *The Journal of Sport and Exercise Psychology, 15,* 245–260.

BRAY, S., & CARRON, A. V. (June, 1992). *The home advantage in alpine skiing.* Paper presented at the North American Society for the Psychology of Sport and Physical Activity Conference, Pittsburgh, PA.

CARRON, A. V. (1980a). *Social psychology of sport.* Ithaca, NY: Mouvement.

CARRON, A. V. (1980b). Sport psychology: Fact and fantasy. *Recreation Research Review, 8,* 28–37.

CARRON, A. V. (1981). Processes of group interaction in sport teams. *Quest, 33,* 245–270.

CARRON, A. V. (1982). Cohesiveness in sport groups: Interpretations and considerations. *Journal of Sport Psychology, 4,* 123–138.

CARRON, A. V. (1984). *Motivation: Implications for coaching and teaching.* London, Canada: Spodyn Publishers.

CARRON, A. V. (1988). *Group dynamics in sport.* London, Canada: Spodym Publishers.

CARRON, A. V. (June, 1993). *Group dynamics in sport.* Paper presented at the International Society for Sport Psychology Conference, Madrid, Spain.

CARRON, A. V., & BALL, J. R. (1977). Cause-effect characteristics of cohesiveness and participation motivation in intercollegiate hockey. *International Review of Sport Sociology, 12,* 49–60.

CHELLADURAI, P., & CARRON, A. V. (1977). A re-analysis of formal structure in sport. *Canadian Journal of Applied Sport Science, 2,* 9–14.

COURNEYA, K. S., & CARRON, A. V. (1992). The home advantage in sport competitions: A literature review. *Journal of Sport and Exercise Psychology, 14,* 28–39.

CRATTY, B. J. (1973). *Psychology in contemporary sport.* Englewood Cliffs, NJ: Prentice-Hall.

DECI, E. L. (1975). *Intrinsic motivation.* New York: Plenum.

GOULD, D. (1976). *The history of American sport psychology.* Unpublished manuscript, University of Illinois, C-U.

HALLIWELL, W. (1978). Intrinsic motivation in sport. In W.F. Straub (Ed.), *Sport psychology: An analysis of athlete behavior.* Ithaca, NY: Mouvement, 1978.

HENRY, F. M. (1964). Physical education—An academic discipline. *Proceedings* of National College Physical Education Association for Men. Washington, D.C., AAHPER.

HODGES, L., & CARRON, A. V. (1992). Collective efficacy and group performance. *International Journal of Sport Psychology, 23,* 48–59.

JONES, M. B. (1974). Regressing group on individual effectiveness. *Organizational Behavior and Human Performance, 11,* 426–451.

KLONSKY, B. (1978). The effects of formal structure and role skills on coaching recruitment and longevity: A study of professional basketball teams. In J. Loy, B. McPherson, & G.S. Kenyon (Eds.), *Sport and social systems.* Reading, MA: Addison-Wesley.

LITTMAN, R. A. (1958). In M. R. Jones (Ed.), *Nebraska Symposium on Motivation* (Vol 6). Lincoln, Nebraska: Nebraska University Press.

LOCKE, E. A., SHAW, K. N., SAARI, L. M., & LATHAM, G. P. (1981). Goal setting and task performance: 1969-1980. *Psychological Bulletin, 90,* 125-152.

LOY, J. W. (1972). Sociology and physical education. In R. Singer *et al.* (Eds.), *Physical education: An interdisciplinary approach.* NY: Macmillan.

MARTENS, R. (1977). *Sport competition anxiety test.* Champaign, IL: Human Kinetics.

MARTENS, R., & PETERSON, J. A. (1971). Group cohesiveness as a determinant of success and member satisfaction in team performance. *International Review of Sport Sociology, 6,* 49-61.

MARTIN, G. L., & HRYCAIKO, D. (1983). *Behavior modification and coaching: Principles, procedures, and research.* Springfield, IL: Charles C. Thomas.

MASSENGALE, J., & FARRINGTON, S. (1977). The influence of playing position centrality on the careers of college football coaches. *Review of Sport and Leisure, 2,* 107-115.

ORLICK, T. D., & BOTTERILL, C. (1975). *Every kid can win.* Chicago, IL: Nelson Hall.

PASSER, M. (1984). A psychological perspective. In M. R. Weiss & D. Gould (Eds.), *Sport for children and youth.* Champaign, IL: Human Kinetics.

ROY, C. (1974). *The relationship between centrality and mobility: The case of the National Hockey League.* M.S. Thesis, Department of Kinesiology, University of Waterloo.

RYDER, H. W., CARR, H. J., & HERGET, P. (1976). Future performance in foot racing. *Scientific American, 234,* 109-119, 1976.

SAGE, G. (1974). *The effect of formal structure on organizational leadership: An investigation of college football teams.* Paper presented at the National AAHPER Conference, Anaheim, California.

SHAW, M. E. (1981). *Group dynamics: The psychology of small group behavior* (3rd ed.).

SIEDENTOP, D. (1978). The management of practice behavior. In W.F. Straub (Ed.), *Sport psychology: An analysis of athlete behavior.* Ithaca, NY: Mouvement.

SMITH, M. D. (1974). Significant others' influence on the assaultive behavior of young hockey players. *International Review of Sport Sociology, 9,* 45-56.

SMITH, M. D. (1975). Sport and collective violence. In D.W. Ball and J.W. Loy (Eds.), *Sport and social order.* Reading, MA: Addison-Wesley.

SMITH, M. D. (1978). Hockey violence: Interring some myths. In W.F. Straub (Ed.), *Sport psychology: An analysis of athlete behavior.* Ithaca, NY: Mouvement.

SMITH, M. D. (1979). Social determinants of violence in hockey: A review. *Canadian Journal of Applied Sport Sciences, 4,* 76-82.

SMITH, M. D. (1979). Towards an explanation of hockey violence: A reference-other approach. *Canadian Journal of Sociology, 4,* 105-124.

THOMAS, E. J., & ZANDER, A. (1959). The relationship of goal structure to motivation under extreme conditions. *Journal Individual Psychology, 15,* 121-127.

TRIPLETT, N. (1897). The dynamogenic factors in face-making and competition. *American Journal of Psychology, 9,* 507–533.

VANDERZWAAG, H. J., & SHEEHAN, T. J. (1978). *Introduction to sport studies: From the classroom to the ball park.* Dubuque, IA: W. C. Brown.

WEINER, B. (1972). *Theories of motivation: From mechanism to cognition.* Chicago, IL: Rand-McNally,

WIDMEYER, W. N., BRAWLEY, W. N., & CARRON, A. V. (1990). The effects of group size in sport. *Journal of Sport and Exercise Psychology, 12,* 177–190.

ZAJONC, R. B. (1965). Social facilitation. *Science, 149:*269–274.

ZANDER, A. (1971). *Motives and goals in groups.* NY: Academic Press.

ZANDER, A. (1978). Motivation and performance in sport groups. In W. F. Straub (Ed.), *Sport psychology: An analysis of athlete behavior.* Ithaca, NY: Mouvement.

ZANDER, A., & ARMSTRONG, W. (1978). Working for group pride in a slipper factory. *Journal of Applied Social Psychology, 2,* 193–207.

Chapter Five

Motor Behavior

Michael G. Wade

Motor behavior is a subdiscipline area within the discipline of kinesiology. This chapter is written as an introduction to an important subdiscipline area of the scientific study of physical activity. I choose to call this kinesiology. Other terms that you may come across will be exercise science, exercise and sport science, and human movement science. Irrespective of the title of the discipline motor behavior is an important area of the kinesiology discipline. The reader should recognize that each section of this chapter could be a "chapter" itself! The idea here is to provide the student with a broad overview and provide key references and readings to encourage further study. The reader may note that sport and exercise psychology is not part of this chapter; yet, motor skill and motor behavior are important considerations to the study of sport and exercise psychology. This subdomain has developed to the point that it is discussed in a separate chapter in this book. Before reviewing the various elements that form the study of motor behavior, perhaps a word about physical activity in general and how the term motor behavior relates to physical activity would be appropriate.

Students who read further in the field of kinesiology will come across such terms as "motor activity," "motor fitness," "perceptual-motor activity," "motor skill," and a variety of other terms which employ "motor" as a prefix. In this context, the word *motor* would be defined as giving or producing motion; movement would be defined as the observable displacement of body parts. In this chapter, the study of *motor behavior* can initially is defined as the study of human movement—how movement skills develop, are learned, and are controlled.

Human movement skill is not random, but has both purpose and intent. A motor skill must always have a purpose: When we swing a bat the intention is to hit an object (a ball); when we throw a ball we intend that it comes close to someone or something. In the work place, we perform a variety of motor skills in producing goods and services. The surgeon uses his or her motor skills to repair or replace broken or malfunctioning body parts or organs. The dentist exhibits an array of motor skills in reconstructing or removing broken or decayed teeth. Thus, motor behavior is broad in the sense that it extends well beyond school-based physical education and sport on into the physical activity and action domains of industry, the military, and everyday living. Just as kinesiology extends beyond exercise and sport, the study of motor behavior is multidimensional and multicontextual.

OVERVIEW

The concept of skill covers wide range of motor, cognitive, and social domains. There are numerous definitions of skill. Guthrie (1952) provides one of the most parsimonious: "an ability to bring about some end result with maximum certainty and minimum amount energy" (p. 136). For our purposes the following will suffice: *Skill is that which minimizes the discrepancy between intent and outcome.* Connolly (1977) suggests that skill, in terms of behavior, is characterized as efficient, accurate, purposeful, economic, and precise. Motor *skill* is the ability to execute a movement in an optimal fashion, in that actions are organized and executed with economy (Elliot & Connolly, 1974). The study of motor behavior study is a subdiscipline of kinesiology in which the central focus is trying to find out *how motor skill is produced:*

1. How do we learn motor skills, and what are the variables that influence or mediate the learning?
2. How do we as humans control and coordinate our musculoskeletal system?
3. How do these skills develop in childhood and decline with old age?

As the word "behavior" indicates, the bias in motor behavior study has been toward the psychological sciences. The study of motor behavior and, more importantly, the study of human skills has its roots in experimental psychology. Many of the early studies of motor behavior were carried out by experimental psychologists who used the movement domain to better understand how people learn. At the end of the nineteenth century, Bryan and Harter (1887) carried out experiments on reaction time using a telegraph key. At the turn of the century, the famous American psychologist, Robert Woodworth, carried out a variety of experiments on movement behavior. For example, Woodworth (1899), in an attempt to find out the basic principles of fast arm and hand movements, was one of the first to study speed-accuracy trade-off. In the same year, Bryan and

Harter (1899) also introduced "plateau" as a learning phenomenon. The history of studying motor behavior was, in many respects, the history of early American experimental psychology. This introductory chapter cannot provide you with an in-depth history of motor skills research, but two good reviews are recommended for further reading: Adams (1987) and Newell (1990). In a similar vein, developmental psychologists were interested in the motor behavior of children to gain insight into the maturation of their nervous system and later development of language and thinking (Bayley, 1935; Gesell & Armatruda, 1941; McGraw, 1934).

From the end of the nineteenth century to the early twentieth century, psychologists had shown an interest in the study of motor skills. The artillery, tank, and aircraft technology and personnel training required to fight World War II gave enormous impetus to the study of motor skills. Since World War II, interest has grown steadily in the military, industrial, sport, and medical applications of motor skill learning. Along with these applied interests and the development of computer science, an intense effort has been mounted to better understand the origins of how skill is learned and acquired. This latter interest goes beyond the acquisition of specific motor skills and addresses fundamental questions on the biological and behavioral aspects of living systems, both their early development and their decline during advancing age.

THE SUBDOMAINS OF MOTOR BEHAVIOR

As one might expect of any field of study, different people have different interests in motor behavior. Within the subdiscipline of motor behavior, we have the three subdomains of interest: motor learning, motor control, and motor development. Motor learning specialists are those primarily interested in how people learn skills and the variables are that affect learning. A better understanding of these elements has implications for training people in better skill acquisition and maintenance. A second subdomain of research interest, motor control, has focused on constructing models and theories that can account for how movement and posture are controlled and executed seemingly on demand. Scientists in this area seek, often from a neurophysiological viewpoint, to describe and account for how we control and coordinate our skeletal system in order to maintain postural control and locomotion. A third subdomain stems from the view that, if one really wants to better understand how people learn motor skills, one ought to study the way children develop motor skills during their growth and maturation. This latter subdomain has traditionally been referred to as motor development. More recently, developmental issues in motor behavior have investigated both the product and process of changes across the whole life span, focusing not only on the acquisition of motor skills from birth through adolescence, but on the decline of motor skills as part of the aging process. In fact, these three subdomains of motor behavior are intercorrelated to some degree. Human motor behavior cannot be fully understood without holistically considering motor learning, control, and development. Motor control and learning are two sides of the same coin; one cannot study motor learning without knowledge of how motor skill is controlled and coordinated. Similarly, the study of motor control cannot ignore learning, because what is learned must be explained in part by motor control mechanisms.

Motor behavior as a subdiscipline of kinesiology addresses activities and questions in these three subdomains. The following discussion provides a sampling of research questions and studies typical in each of these three subdomains.

I. Motor Control

Motor control as an area of study that seeks an understanding of movements and postures from neurophysiological perspective. Basically, the study of motor control deals with levels of expertise in motor performance with "here and now" (Whiting, Vogt, & Vereijken, 1992). The question of how immediate motor problems are solved has received a great deal of attention from motor control researchers. In this chapter we focus more on the aspect of "movement" rather than postural control. From a mechanical engineering perspective, the human operator can be considered as a working system in which motor responses are produced and controlled by several system parts. There are two system modes of control, closed-loop and open-loop. Conceptually contrasting these two modes of control assists in our understanding, but we must recognize that human living systems are far more complex than these simplified models.

Closed-Loop and Open-Loop Control Systems. The simple closed-loop system begins with input about the system's goal to a reference mechanism, which samples the current output in the environment. That is feedback: information from the environment compared with the set or fixed value of the goal at the reference mechanism. An error is computed, if there is any difference between the intended and desired states and any error greater or smaller than the goal produces a decision on the basis of error reduction. The instructions from the executive level is sent to effector level (musculoskeletal system) to produce motor output. The outcome of the motor output (feedback), then, goes back to reference mechanism for further comparison. This process continues until the goal or a target is achieved. Central to closed-loop control is the role of feedback information and the role of the reference mechanism. Schmidt (1988) uses a home heating system and the role of the thermostat as a good example of a closed-loop control-system. Continuous skill (e.g., tracking task) fits a closed-loop concept in that, provided the speed of movement is relatively slow, feedback information can be sent to a reference mechanism for error detection and correction. Figure 5.1a illustrates a simplified diagram of a closed-loop system.

Figure 5.1 Loop systems: closed loop (a) and open loop (b).

a. Closed Loop

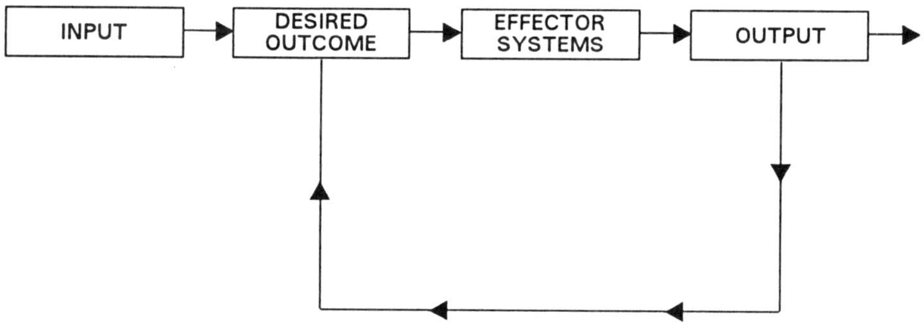

b. Open Loop

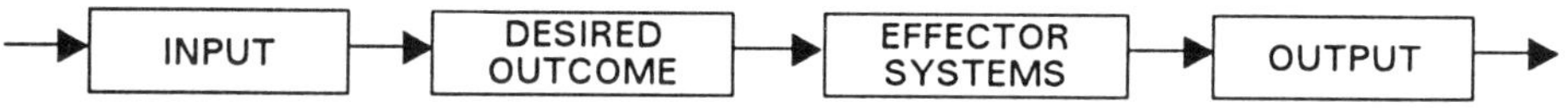

The open-loop control system (Fig. 5.1b) differs from a closed-loop control system because there is no reference mechanism ("thermostat") in the system. The instructions are preplanned and executed without consideration or use of a feedback mechanism. In other words, no feedback loop connects the executive level to the effector level between the input and output states. For example, you are asked to move a linear positioning lever 20 cm. in 200 msec; this rapid and discrete movement will be under open-loop control because the movement goal is structured in advance; and the movement time is too short to process feedback information during execution of the task. Quite often a skill that requires rapid execution does not permit the use of feedback because of the speed involved. Thus, rapid skilled tasks are usually under open-loop control and are pre-planned and executed without the use of engineering feedback.

Closed-loop and open-loop control systems, based on a mechanical engineering analogy, are provided to explain how control is functioning. It is possible that these two separate control systems share responsibility in human skill activity. Schmidt (1988) suggests that human motor control systems are not simple and should be regarded as combinations of both systems. Indeed, the above-mentioned motor control systems, using engineering analogy, functionally separate human operator and environment. The more recent ecological approach to the study of human motor behavior (discussed below) emphasizes the linkage between the human operator and the environment.

II. Motor Learning

Motor learning, according to Schmidt (1988), is "a set of processes associated with practice or experience leading to relatively permanent changes in the capacity for responding" (p. 346). The notion of a relatively permanent change in behavior in this definition makes distinction between "learning" and "performance." However, motor learning is inferred from performance. Since the turn of this century, experimental psychologists as well as motor behavior researchers have spared no effort in attempting to develop lawful and/or mathematical models to explain and predict human motor skill performance and learning. One of the very first and influential models was the information-processing model.

Information Processing. Much of the research that has gone on in motor learning has adopted a model that has its historical roots in experimental psychology and engineering psychology. Craik (1948), based on engineering analogy, suggested that information input, central computation, and motor output are the three main parts of his proposal of lawful explanations for human motor skill. This is the so-called information processing (IP) model; human beings are actively engaged with their environment as designated processors of all of the information that is so generated. All kinds of input come to us via our perceptual systems (our eyes, ears, sense of smell, sense of touch, and so on). As we move in and through the environment—on land, on sea, or in the air—a variety of environmental events generate input. To make sense of all these inputs, the organism must regulate and analyze it in the central nervous system. Psychologists for a long time have regarded humans as information-processing systems continuously sorting out the different inputs that come to us. Scientists build models to better understand how we accomplish this. Perhaps the best analogy of this information-processing is a telephone exchange. When one telephones a friend, the input that one generates by dialing the friend's number goes to some central location where it is then appropriately directed to the friend's house. The code that one used was a seven-digit number if the call was local, or more numbers if it was to another state or country. The caller provided this input, and a central location analyzed it and organized it to connect the call to the friend's telephone. Information processing is very similar in that one receives the input; some form of organization takes place; and an appropriate response is generated. Figure 5.2 is a simplified version of an information-

Figure 5.2 Simplified human information-processing model.

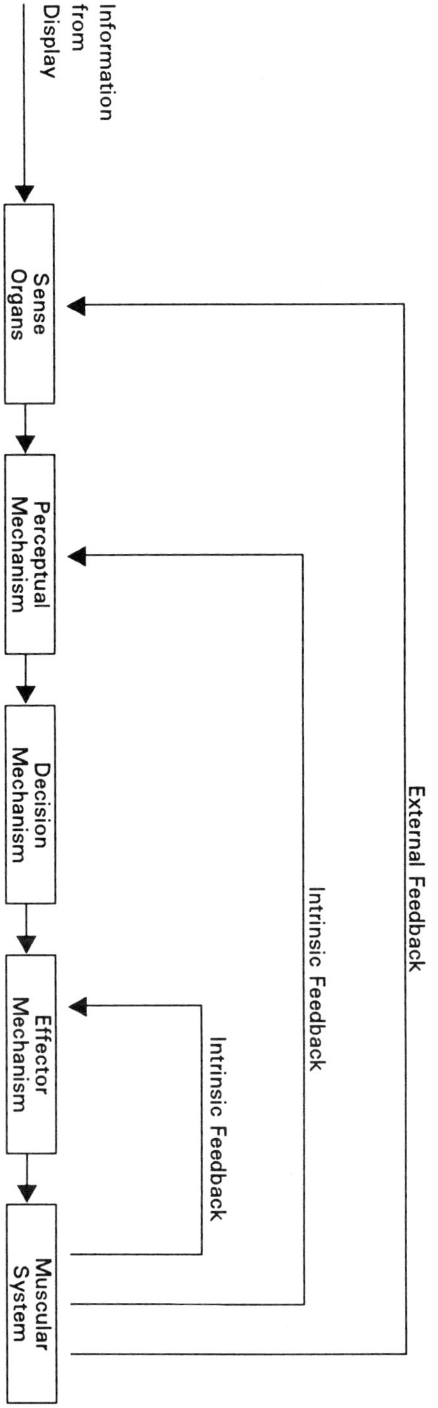

processing system. Note that the feedback loops from both within and without the system are part of this model.

The IP model is thought to work as follows. As an example, consider that an automobile is stopped at a highway intersection, and the driver must determine if an oncoming vehicle is approaching too fast, or is too close, to safely cross the intersection. The information coming in is primarily visual, and the driver must analyze that information and makes an appropriate decision either to proceed or to wait.

For the study of motor skills, the IP model has enabled motor behavior researchers to better understand how we produce skilled activity by identifying, isolating, and explaining primary mental processes. Motor behavior research has assumed the human operator to be a component system that processes stimulus information received from the environment and intrinsic feedback (kinesthesis). Because the information-processing activity is unobservable in the central nervous system, the processing activity is inferred from the overt movement products. This has been called "black-box" theory. Implicit within the information-processing model in the understanding of human motor behavior is the assumption that mental processes take time (Craik's term, "time-lag") and that different component processes require different amounts of time. For example, three stages of information processing are required: First, the stimulus identification stage; second, the response selection stage; and third, the response programming stage, can be experimentally manipulated in order to measure speed for specific stages of processing. In reaction-time research, reaction time (RT) is often used as dependent variable to infer the time needed for the mental processes to occur.

A typical experiment or study in a laboratory setting might well require a subject to move a stylus from a fixed point very quickly to a target when a light goes on. This experiment measures the speed at which one can move and accurately hit the target. The total time this takes is called *response time.* Response time comprises of reaction time (RT) and movement time (MT).

Figure 5.3 Schematic diagram of reaction time, movement time, and response time.

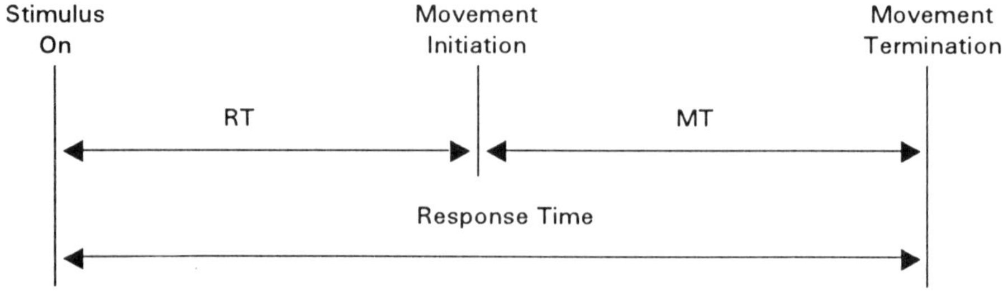

Figure 5.3 illustrates how response time is broken down. To the left of the diagram is the actual *reaction time:* the lapsed time between the onset of some stimulus (a signal or perhaps a light going on) and the subject initiating the movement. The *movement time* is the actual time that the subject takes from beginning the movement to the end of the movement. The reaction time takes up the smallest part of the response time, and the movement time (the actual movement of the limb) is the largest part of the response time.

Scientists interested in motor skills experiment with both reaction time and movement time. Reaction time is interpreted as the processing time, or the speed with which signals can move through the central nervous system when some kind of external command (stimulus) is given. The movement time (speed and accuracy) is also of interest, depending on the developmental level of the subject (young child, disabled person, or an older person), not only to determine the speed with which a person can make a movement, but also the accuracy required for the movement.

Over the years a great deal of research has been done to clarify the role played by reaction time, movement time, and accuracy in the acquisition of a whole range of motor skills. Young children, for example, react more slowly than adults. By the time we reach our late teens or early twenties, our average reaction time is about 220 milliseconds. We maintain this reaction time into the middle or latter half of our third decade. Reaction time then slowly gets longer as we get older. Reaction time has important implications for our ability to practice skilled behavior. Young children's slower abilities to "react" can place them in dangerous situations and can make them less skilled in game playing than an individual who has a more mature (faster) reaction time. Similarly, as we age we slow down, thus becoming more cautious in order not to place ourselves in danger. Although both children and elderly people have slow reaction times, children lack experience and can place themselves in danger without appropriate supervision. However, older individuals avoid harmful situations through caution, and thus remain generally safe. Unfortunately, this is not always true, since an older person driving a car may seem too careful and too slow to younger drivers. The frustration of younger drivers in regard to slower drivers can often generate impulsive, dangerous behavior.

Underlying the information processing model are two laws (Hick's Law and Fitts' Law) which are known for their predictions of human motor responses. First, Hick (1952) noted that there is a linear relationship between choice reaction time and Log_2 of the number of the stimulus-response alternatives. This is known as Hick's Law which states:

$$\text{Choice RT} = a + b[\text{Log}_2 (N)]$$

Here a and b are empirically defined constants, and N is the number of stimulus-response alternatives. The implication of Hick's Law to real-world, motor skill performance is the prediction that the more uncertain the environment, the longer it takes for a performer to make an appropriate decision before the initiation of movement. So, in tennis, for example, a serve will occasion a longer reaction time on the part of the receiver, if the server is capable of producing various types of serves. The other law is Fitts' Law (1954), which explains the relationship of speed accuracy trade-offs via the mathematical relationship between movement time and the index of task difficulty. The equation of Fitts' Law:

$$\text{Average MT} = a + b[\text{Log}_2\ (2A/W)]$$

Where a and b are empirically defined constants, A is amplitude, and W is target-width. Fitts (1954) had his subjects hold a stylus and reciprocally moved between two target areas. The average movement time was observed, while task difficulty was manipulated by changing either amplitude or target-width (or both). The index of task difficulty (ID) equals Log_2 (2A/W). Fitts found that movement time increased as the ID of the task increased. What these two laws tell motor behavior researchers is that established mathematical models provide a lawful explanation and prediction for complex human movements. While both of these so-called "laws" are not *always* reliable, they have provided the basis of generating a great deal of insight into motor skill behavior.

Theories of Motor Learning. To date, there are two designated theories of motor learning (Adams' closed-loop theory <1971> and Schmidt's schema theory <1973>) that have had important impact on the development of motor behavior knowledge. In fact, theses two theories provide insights about both motor control and motor learning. Adams proposed his closed-loop theory of motor learning in 1971 in an attempt to establish a theoretical base for motor learning research. The closed-loop theory is based on the concept of closed-loop control with an emphasizes the role of sensory feedback and knowledge of results (Adams, 1971). The closed-loop theory consists of two memory states: (1) memory trace, which is responsible for selecting and initiating a motor response (Adams considers memory trace to be a "modest motor program"); and (2) a perceptual trace, which is a reference mechanism that can be used to compare the movement being made with past experience (cf. Fig. 5.1a). According to Adams' closed-loop theory, the perceptual trace is responsible for deciding how the limb movement should be produced. Appropriate practice *with* feedback is critical for strengthening perceptual trace; lack of feedback will weaken perceptual trace. However, there are limitations to Adams' closed-loop theory. It was based on relatively slow, simple, limb-positioning movement tasks, and thus it was hard to generalize, in theory, to fast, discrete movement in which sensory feedback may not be necessary or available. Also, Adams' theory does not account for the way in which novel movements are produced. Schmidt's (1975) schema was, in part, a response to the problems inherent in Adams' theory. Central to Schmidt's theory is the concept of schema and generalized motor program. Every time, after a movement is completed, four sources of information (i.e., initial condition, response specification, sensory consequence, and response outcome) are stored and integrated to modify a general rule (or "schema") for a class of movements. A schema is defined as a set of rules which can be used to generate a movement-decision. The schema consists of both a recall schema and a recognition schema. The recall schema is responsible for determining the motor response, while the recognition schema evaluates the outcome of the movement. The evaluation is done by comparing the sensory feedback with the expected sensory feedback and making possible movement corrections or adjustments. Interestingly, one of predictions from Schmidt's schema theory is that variability in practice will promote schema development. Fortunately, the variability-in-practice hypothesis can be empirically tested by an experiment designed to compare variable practice against constant practice. We will discuss this idea more fully in the following section on practice.

Variables in Motor Learning. Research scientists interested in how we learn and perform motor skills devote considerable time to understanding how we process information when making skillful movement. When motor learning is viewed as a set of processes, many factors or variables can influence or mediate how we learn, how much we learn, how much we remember, and where we best acquire any particular skill. Some of the important variables that influence motor learning are explained below, such things as practice, knowledge of results (KR), transfer of training, and also stimulus response compatibility (to name but a few):

1. Practice

Correct practice helps make perfect! When we talk about practice, we are interested not only in what it is that we practice, but also how long we practice, and how the practice sessions are organized to optimize skill learning. All of us from time to time have interests, perhaps recreational or maybe at a higher level, in a variety of sports skills. When we participate in such activities, performing at our very best is often important for us. One way to improve performance is to practice. Golf, for example, requires a high level of skill in the sense that it requires a very small ball (1.68 inches in diameter) be hit over varying distances to a very small target. Players who practice the different components of this game diligently can produce quite dramatic increases in skill level, and thereby lower their score.

As with any activity, practice structure is important. We must decide *what* we are going to practice, *how long* we will practice it, and *what* the actual components are of any practice session should be. Scientists interested in the effects of practice, for example, study whether it's better to practice the complete skill to improve overall performance or to systematically divide the activity and practice each of the component parts. This is referred to as "whole practice" and "whole-part practice." Basically, in deciding whole/part practice methods, task organization and task complexity are important considerations. Part practice is more favorable for tasks with high complexity and low organization. The phenomenon of massed versus distributed practice is also important when considering motor skill learning. Rest interval is a key point for making a distinction between massed and distributed practice. The massed practice is defined as when the rest interval is less than, or equal to, practice interval. The rest interval in distributed practice structure is longer than practice interval. In a classic motor learning experiment, Stelmach (1969) compared the effect of massed and distributed practice on the learning of a ladder-climbing task. He found that during the original learning stage, the distributed practice group performed at a higher level than the massed practice group. However, after a four-minute rest interval at the end of the original learning phase, the level of motor skill learning was the same for the two groups when they were retested! The result clearly tells us that while the massed practice condition suppressed performance, it did not interfere with learning.

Recently, in the motor learning literature a topic called "contextual interference" has received attention from those scientists who are interested in practice scheduling. That is, for practicing several tasks, random practice and blocked practice can be considered. Random practice is when the order of task presentation is randomized with no two consecutive practice trials the same across the practice period. Blocked practice is when all the practice trials of a given task are the same before changing to another set of practice trials for another given task. The research results from both laboratory study with fine sequential motor skill (Shea & Morgan, 1979) and field study (Goode & Magill, 1986) with badminton-serving have shown that there is a positive effect of random practice. (Magill and Hall (1990) have provided a recent review on contextual interference effect in motor skill learning.)

One of Schmidt's (1975) schema theory of motor learning predictions is that variability of practice will improve skill learning in novel situations. To test a variability of practice hypothesis, the experiments are designed to compare constant practice with variable practice. In practice, a single task, constant-practice schedule is designed to practice only a single version of a task, while a variable-practice schedule is set to practice more than one version of a task. The positive effect of variable practice on motor skill learning can be attributed to schema learning (Schmidt, 1991).

So far we have discussed a number of practice conditions. However, Newell and McDonald (1992) suggest practice is a necessary, but not sufficient, condition for skill perfection. They argue that the *structure* of practice should be related to the constraints from performer, environment, and task that are critical to acquire task solutions to solve motor problems. In other words, performer and environmental variables should be considerations in scheduling practice.

Nowadays, we use a whole range of technologies to help with our practice, and perhaps the most common of these is the use of videotape replay. Video usage allows the person who is practicing the skill to view the outcome of the activity immediately after it has been performed. With the help of a coach or some other mentor, video permits immediate analysis of different elements of the movement and allows corrections to be made. Such new technology not only aids in the actual practice, but also helps scientists interested in the role of practice in skill learning to carry out a variety of experiments and investigations.

2. Knowledge of Results and Knowledge of Performance

Thorndike (1927) proposed a "law of effect" for instrumental learning. The law of effect emphasized learning through rewards and punishments which are feedback in nature. Since then the concept of feedback had been used in the study of motor skill acquisition. Manipulations of feedback in motor learning studies were quite popular during the post-World War II period. Central to the effect of feedback on motor learning is knowledge of results (KR), which is very much connected with the idea of practice. Knowledge of results (KR) is really part of a whole process that we call *feedback.* Information returns to the performer in one of two ways. The performer may be able to see the outcome of any particular activity, or the performer may feel the effects of any particular activity by feedback received from the joints and limb positions as he or she goes through the movement. This latter feedback is called *proprioceptive* or *kinesthetic feedback,* and this is how we "know" or "feel" we have made a mistake. For example, when we play softball, baseball, tennis, or any game that requires us to hit a ball of one kind or another, we know immediately from the "feel" of the bat or racket making contact with the ball that we have made a mistake. This is the important feedback we get from our limbs and the contact on the bat, both the "feel" of making a stroke at a ball and the sight of the outcome in terms of accuracy and distance achieved.

Feedback comes also from what an observer or a camera may tell us about our performance, and this is known as knowledge of performance (KP). Strictly speaking, KR is information about movement outcome regarding environmental goal, while KP is information about movement kinematics or patterning. Many experiments have been carried out that have investigated the importance of KR and KP in skill learning. Suppose, for example, that someone must perform an extremely accurate task without seeing the performance, but rather relying exclusively on information given by an observer. Research studies have used such experiments to gain a better understanding of the role of KR in learning. For example, one study may ask participants to move a lever over a particular distance, but the distance and the target are both hidden from view. A watcher can provide KR in one of several ways. For a young child, the instructions at the end of each trial may be as simple as "Too long, try it again," or "Too short, try it again," or "Hit!" For an adult, the instructions may become more complex, such as "Long by four points," or "That was short by three inches." With adult subjects, adding a number to the long or short descriptors adds more information to the KR and may, or may not, be advantageous to a learner. In general, young children do not appear to be able to use very specific KR, whereas the older learners can understand relatively complex KR. Clearly KR is an important variable in skill learning, and is the subject of a fairly large amount of research literature.

KP is most useful and effective in teaching situations. During the initial stage of motor skill acquisition, what learners need is to establish in a good movement pattern (that is, the organizations of temporal and spatial elements of the action). KP is important to motor skill acquisition in that it provides information about movement displacement, velocity, and acceleration for further corrections. For example, a typical form of KP in the tennis serve is "Your contact point to the ball was not at a peak "point," or "You did not rotate your shoulder while tossing the ball." Coaches can use KP very effectively in helping learners achieve better results.

3. Transfer of Training

Another important motor learning variable is called *transfer*. For example, tennis and badminton use similar skills. If playing tennis in the summer automatically improves a player's badminton game in the winter, this would be called *positive transfer*. If, on the other hand, playing tennis in the summer does not help, and may, in fact, hinder badminton expertise in the winter, this is a *negative transfer*. Virtually we cannot learn all the skills that we need through practice. In most of the cases, we transfer from what we have learned and practiced. Transfer of training is closely linked to the idea of practice; thus, it is also an important issue in studying motor learning.

4. Stimulus-Response Compatibility

Another item of interest in the study of skill learning is *stimulus-response (SR) compatibility*. This is the relationship between a particular stimulus in the execution of a skilled activity and the response required. The design of control panels in automobiles, ships, and aircraft, for example, use one application of SR compatibility to motor skill. To move to a car or an aircraft to the right, logically the operator turns the wheel or moves the joystick to the right. Similarly, to operate the undercarriage control lever in an aircraft, the logical movement is a downward movement for lowering the landing gear and upward for raising the landing gear. Quite often left-handed people have difficulty dealing with control panels designed by right-handed people simply because right-handed designers inadvertently design control panels for their own SR compatibility. Thus, a left-handed person would find the stimulus-response compatibility to be less than optimal.

While engineering design problems ostensibly have little to do with sport and physical activity, such activities apply to the domain of motor skill learning and motor control studies particularly in the broad area of human factors. Human factors studies investigate how best to optimize human performance in situations where the human being is controlling a wide range of mechanical systems. The findings of stimulus-response compatibility have provided great contribution for better design of safe workplaces and reducing human errors in human-machine operations. (Human factors are discussed later in this chapter.)

III. Motor Development

Motor development is the subdomain of motor behavior that studies changes in motor behavior across the lifespan. Despite this broad definition, a lot of research in motor development has focused primarily on development during the first 16 years of life. Until recently, research largely ignored the motor behavior of aging populations. Clark and Whitall (1989) suggest that the complete definition of motor development should include both the product and process changes across the lifespan and should provide a good review of the history of motor development research.

As noted, a great deal of motor development focuses on changes in the growth patterns of children from birth through adolescence to adulthood, and has produced an important descriptive record of the motor milestones of development. These *"motor milestones"* are the observed, expected ages at which children exhibit control of such skills as upright posture and the beginning of walking. They also relate to most of the variety of other important motor skill activities which are referred to in the motor development literature as the fundamental motor skills.

The motor cortex is one of the first parts of the brain to develop, and the research literature supports well the dire consequences if a young child does not experience physical activity that provides the opportunity to develop motor skills. The evidence strongly suggests that young children who are not provided the opportunity and encouragement to move freely around their environment and to discover the world around them through motor activity exhibit less than optimal development. Children, thus deprived of movement opportunities (e.g., as in play), do not fully discover their own ability to control and coordinate their bodies at their own growth rates.

Theories of child development recognize the importance of motor activity in the early development of the brain. Perhaps the most famous model is that of Jean Piaget (1952) in which stages of development include a sensory-motor stage. Early researchers in the field of motor development (Gesell, 1928; McGraw, 1934) emphasized that the motor development of children was closely tied to the maturation of the nervous system. Their developmental models hold that the motor milestones of children are a reflection of a developing nervous system that permits these motor activities to emerge. However, the contributions of these early researchers, while important, do not really provide us with any real insights as to how these different skill activities are produced or emerge in the developing child.

In the section above on motor learning, we discussed how the information processing model has made important contributions to understanding how people learn motor skills. These ideas about information-processing have also been applied to investigate the motor behavior of young children. Thus, an extensive literature is available, not only in psychology, but also in the area of motor development, on children as processors of information (Wade, 1976; Thomas, 1980).

Motor development researchers have tried to better understand how children solve motor problems by conducting studies that involve simple laboratory tasks such as moving a lever over a specific distance. They have also investigated the role of practice and knowledge of results as factors in young children's acquisition of skills. In addition to experimental tasks, scientists carefully monitor the developing skill to observe the transition from the reflex activities, present in a newborn child, to upright posture, general locomotion, and the skills of walking and running. These postural developments provide for a whole array of everyday motor skills.

Other research has focused on how children develop the ability to manipulate small objects in their hands and how they learn to make accurate reaching and grasping movement. A more detailed outline of the kinds of research that have been conducted on the development of coordination and control in the growing child, and also on the diminishing coordination and control of the sixth and seventh decades of life, is beyond the scope of this chapter. For an excellent review of this topic, see *Quest* (1989, Vol. 41), a special edition on motor development.

Motor development is an intriguing area of research in the subdiscipline of motor behavior study. Kinesiologists who study motor development come in close contact with child psychologists, child-care workers, and teachers, particularly those working in the kindergarten and elementary schools. For an up-to-date review of this subdomain see Wade and Whiting (1986).

RECENT DEVELOPMENTS: STUDYING CONTROL AND COORDINATION AS A SYSTEM

In the early 1980s a new and exciting way of understanding motor development began to appear in the research literature. This approach is often referred to as the "dynamical systems" approach. As discussed above, earlier theories of motor behavior hold that motor skills develop or emerge in children as the nervous system matures; thus, all of our motor skills are controlled by some sort of motor program, acting much like a computer. The *dynamical systems approach,* however, adopts the idea that motor skill patterns are already present in the newborn child, but appear at different stages in development as the physical growth progresses. Thus, height, weight, levels of muscular strength, bone growth, and so on, permit the appropriate levels of coordination and control to emerge. While the information-processing model has been a very important influence in the research on this topic, it is by no means the only model or paradigm that has provided impetus for researching motor skill learning. Recently, some motor behavior researchers (Beek, 1989; Beek & van Santvoord, 1992) have sought to identify invariant variables to better explain motor skill acquisition (e.g., learning how to juggle) using a dynamical systems theory approach.

Dynamical systems theory applied to the development of coordination and control is based on the concept that small changes in the organism can produce significant changes in motor behavior. Dynamical systems theory is based on nonlinear, thermodynamic principles found originally in physical biology. A dynamical systems perspective on skill development emphasizes movements, not centrally prescribed as cognitive science proposes, but emerging peripherally from the interaction among the organism, the task, and the environment. The theory behavioral form emerges in a self-organized fashion within a particular task and environmental context as the organism attempts to accomplish a task (Clark & Whitall, 1989). There are several concepts central to the dynamical systems theory for the development of movement skills. These concepts may seem complex, but the important point here is to gain a conceptual idea of "dynamical systems."

1. *collective variable* is a compressed dimension of the system. For example, in Thelen and Ulrich's (1991) study, the phasing of alternating steps on treadmill is a collective variable which should be first identified;
2. *control parameter,* which can be an organic or environmental variable that drives changes in the collective behavior of the system;
3. *attractor* concept shows stable and unstable states. Motor development across age is expressed by the stabilizing and destabilizing of attractors in a set of collective variables;
4. *phase shift* implies change, a transition period during an unstable state.

Esther Thelen, a psychologist at Indiana University, has reported some very interesting research with seven-month-old babies. Earlier developmental models held that the stepping reflex, essential to walking, does not appear in children until they reach an appropriate level of neurological development. Thelen (1986) has demonstrated that it is possible to elicit the stepping reflex (the walking pattern) in young babies long before they are strong enough to walk unaided. Thelen and her associates supported their baby subjects over a treadmill and added small weights to the babies ankles. This independent manipulation of the physical constraints on the child's muscular skeletal system produced a stepping pattern. Thus, Thelen's research appears to demonstrate that maturation is an insufficient reason to explain the pattern of the developing motor skills of young children. Thelen and Urlich (1991) have resultantly outlined seven steps in the dynamical systems approach to skill development:

1. Identify the *collective variable* of interest.
2. Characterize the behavioral *attractor* states.
3. Describe the dynamic *trajectory* of the collective variable.
4. Identify points of *transition.*
5. Exploit the instabilities at transitions to identify potential *control parameters.*
6. Manipulate the putative control parameters to generate *phase transitions* experimentally.
7. Dynamic accounts at many *levels of analysis.*

The dynamical systems approach focuses on developing theoretical ideas to explain *how* motor skill develops in living systems, rather than merely identifying the variables that affect the learning of a motor skill. The focus is on how the different parts of the system—such as the joints, the muscles, and the nervous system—coordinate to produce a desired outcome. All movements from walking or hitting and catching balls, to flying an aircraft, and to performing a complicated gymnastic routine can resultantly come under scrutiny.

This contemporary approach to the study of motor behavior has its roots both in physiology and psychology. Much of the thinking that originally produced this approach is attributed to the Russian physiologist, Nicolai Bernstein (whose work in the 1930s was not published in English until 1967). Bernstein's ideas have had enormous impact on modern theories of how we control and coordinate our bodies to produce meaningful skill behavior. His ideas require an elementary understanding of what in biomechanics we call "degrees of freedom." The *degrees of freedom* are the constraints placed on the system of bones, joints, and muscles of the human body that permit controlled movements such as locomotion, two-handed activities, and a host of other movement skills.

The following is an example that you can try. We wish to calculate the degrees of freedom available when we perform a right-arm reaching movement that involves the shoulder girdle down to the wrist.

1. At the shoulder girdle, movement is possible in three planes of motion: extension and flexion up and down; abduction and adduction out to the side and back toward the body; and rotation in a circular fashion. The shoulder girdle has three (3) degrees of freedom of movement.
2. At the elbow, only flexion and extension are possible. Thus, the elbow has only one (1) degree of freedom. The shoulder and the elbow together have four (4) degrees of freedom.
3. From elbow to wrist, the forearm can pronate and supinate (i.e., the hands can face up or down). The forearm thus has one (1) degree of freedom. The shoulder, the elbow and the forearm together total five (5) degrees of freedom.
4. At the wrist, the joint can flex and extend, as well as move from the medial to the lateral side. The wrist has two (2) degrees of freedom. The shoulder girdle, the elbow, the forearm, and the wrist, together total seven (7) degrees of freedom.

This seven (7) degrees of freedom is limited only to the bones of the shoulder girdle. If we consider all of the different muscles that are attached to our arm and shoulder, plus the many fibers making up each muscle, we quickly realize that the number of degrees of freedom controlling the performance of an ordinary activity, such as picking up a glass of water from a table and drinking from it, can be seen as a truly amazing feat requiring the control of thousands of degrees of freedom!

We perform many activities throughout our daily lives without conscious thought. However, all of these so-called "simple activities" require the organization and control of many degrees of freedom. To write a computer program to solve the coordination and control problem that such "simple" movements pose, and to perform each activity so effortlessly, is at best a very complex task and at worst an impossible task. No computer currently available can be programmed to perform such a complex activity. The miracle of human motor skill cannot be comprehended in terms of technical engineering or computer science. The robot machines that assemble automobiles, for example, can only approximate the complex movement skills that humans generate so effortlessly in everyday life.

We as humans control and coordinate our joint and muscle system. The question is then how our nervous system helps us to perform these activities. For movement science this is a most intriguing problem, one that researchers find both frustrating and very rewarding. The kinds of experiments that are performed in this particular branch of movement science usually require individuals to make relatively simple, coordinated movements. One such experiment involves swinging the leg, pendulum style, backward and forward at rates dictated by the individual, not by an experimenter. Thus, the rhythmic backward and forward movement reflects the performer's own "preferred" rate. The experimenter can make the leg (or pendulum) heavier to determine whether a "preferred" rhythm (or rate of movement) changes as a function of increased mass (weight) of the leg (pendulum) (See Figure 5.4).

The lower limbs of the human body act much like a pendulum of a clock. Thus, the idea with this kind of research is not to study movement activity related to some special kind of skill activity, but is rather to study naturally occurring activities that we see in everyday life such as walking or performing activities with our hands. Dynamical systems theory and the ideas expressed in Bernstein's "degrees of freedom" problem suggest that we solve movement problems by "discovering" the equation of constraints that allow the skilled action to emerge. This is a very different approach than the more traditional idea that a computer-type program is stored in our brain.

Modern computer games or other arcade video games often require the player to manipulate two levers at the same time to produce a particular outcome displayed on a computer graphics screen. This kind of bi-manual tracking, one which requires a player to move a target or cursor into a particular position, is of great interest to scientists studying motor skill acquisition since it reflects how individuals control and coordinate two limbs simultaneously. Such studies of control and coordination examine the kind of problem-solving behavior that goes on when a player must coordinate the movement of two arms and hands together in searching this so-called perceptual motor space (the area over which one can move to optimize the outcome of the game).

These searching strategies, and the relationships between the movements of the two hand-held levers, are problems of coordination and control. How a player solves these motor problems is often measured by using a three-dimensional high-speed video or film that can track both the actual movements of your limbs and the places that they visit to optimize the solution of this problem.

Figure 5.4 Added weights to the swinging leg during rhythmic movement.

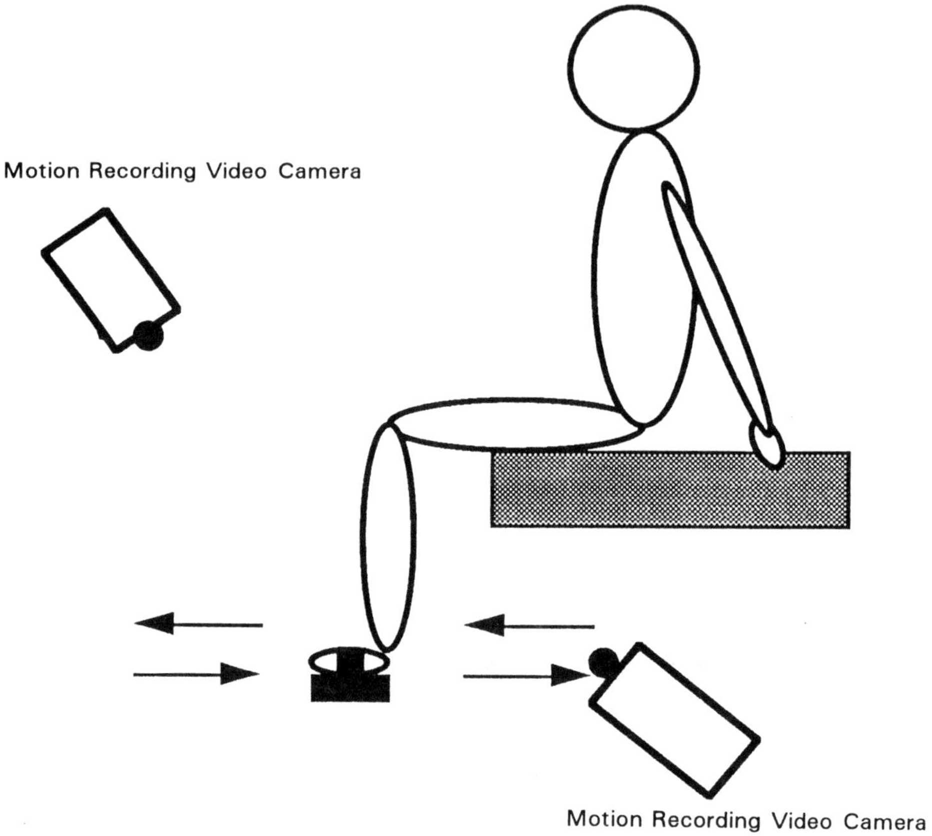

Rather than measuring the kinds of errors that one makes and recording them in milliseconds, as with reaction time experiments, coordination and control studies produce graphs or traces of the places where the limbs have moved. These tracks or plots are called the "kinematics profiles" of the actual movements.

ASSOCIATED AREAS OF STUDY

Adapted Physical Education

Individuals who are physically or developmentally disabled also have a need to use motor skills both in their daily lives and for recreation. Motor skill capacities and potentials for persons who are either physically or developmentally disabled comprise an area that has received considerable research attention . The development of educational programs to serve such populations is an area generally referred to as *adapted physical education.* Within the subdomain of motor behavior studies, research contributions in adapted physical education seek to better understand the relationship between the motor behavior of such individuals and the kinds of diagnoses that have been made. Another way of better understanding the motor behavior of such individuals is to contrast the performances that these individuals find extraordinarily difficult with the performance of the rest of the population. Hoover and Wade (1985) have provided a historical review on the applications of motor learning theory to individuals with mental retardation. Such comparisons allow a better understanding of the origins of the acquisition of motor behavior. Also, such comparisons permit researchers to devise better training methods to enable special populations to reach their full potential in the movement domain. Recently, an ecological approach to task analysis in adapted physical education was suggested to place performer, task and environmental constraints into consideration to optimize physical performance of children with physical challenges (Davis & Burton, 1991; Burton & Davis, 1992). Motor behavior research on disabled populations can be found in the *Adapted Physical Activity Quarterly.*

Human Factors

The term "human factors" is virtually synonymous in meaning with ergonomics, the only difference being that the first is used most frequently in North America, and the latter in Europe; however, they both share a common history. Human factors study showed a rapid growth during World War II. A variety of scientific disciplines were contributing to achieving an increase in the effectiveness of human skill performance. Basically, human factors research investigates the development of "people friendly" designed equipment and machine systems in the workplace. The goal of human factors is to "fit the job to the person," rather than making the person fit the job. Motor skill research contributes its knowledge to improve performance in the workplace. We all know that people have individual differences in their sizes, ages, shapes, and have certain physical and mental limitations. Through skill-analysis, tools and workplaces can be better designed to increase production as well as to prevent injuries. It is because human factors investigation is concerned mainly with human skill performance that kinesiology graduates find this an important area of professional growth.

Therapeutic Science

Motor skills' learning and performance aspects are important considerations in the professions of both occupational and physical therapy (OT and PT). It is important that the OT and PT professionals understand the physiological and psychological underpinnings of human movement. PT has its historical roots in physical education and, nowadays, many OT and PT professionals find that undergraduate degrees in movement science are excellent preparation to enter the therapy fields. Also, many OT and PT professionals are returning to the universities to take advanced degrees in movement science. Motor skills study is often an important area of study for both occupational and physical therapists.

Professional Societies and Journals

There are three major professional societies, the North American Society for the Psychology of Sport and Physical Activity (NASPSPA), the Canadian Society for Psycho-Motor Learning and Sport Psychology (SCAPPS), and the Association for the Advancement of Applied Sport Psychology (AAASP) for motor behavior scientists and sport/exercise psychologists in North American. Each of the three societies, the first two established in 1970s and the latter in 1980s, holds an annual meeting. Their research interests and fields of inquiry have produced different interests groups within the broad study of motor behavior. People interested in sport and exercise psychology still maintain an active participation in both NASPSPA and SCAPPS, but AAASP is a newer organization that specifically serves the interests of sport and exercise psychologists. There are also divisions of sport and exercise psychology in both the American Psychological Association (APA) and the American College of Sport Medicine (ACSM).

Motor behavior published research papers can be found in a wide range of publications. The following is not an inclusive list:

Adapted Physical Activity Quarterly
Canadian Journal of Sport Science
Child Development
Ergonomics
Human Factors

Human Movement Science
Human Performance
Ecological Psychology
Journal of Experimental Psychology: Human Perception and Performance
Journal of Experimental Psychology: Learning, Memory, and Cognition
Journal of Human Movement Studies
Journal of Motor Behavior
Motor Skills: Theory into Practice
Perceptual and Motor Skills
Research Quarterly for Exercise and Sport

SUMMARY

Some people study the *what* of motor skill behavior, and others choose to study the *how* and the *why*. This distinction is made not to imply that these different activities go on in a vacuum, but to recognize the research in motor behavior is a broad enterprise. Scientists who spend most of their time investigating problems of coordination and control are aware of the research that is going on in motor learning, in motor development, and about a host of applied motor problems. Similarly those individuals interested in the developmental issues surrounding the acquisition of motor skills also read the work of their colleagues in motor learning and motor control, as well as in sport and exercise psychology.

Thelen's experiments with young babies and the research involving the movement of limbs acting like pendulums at preferred rhythms are attempts to better understand how the motor system coordinates and controls movements, and whether we develop movement patterns that are natural and reflect individual preferred rates of motion. This chapter has separated the sections on motor control, motor learning, and motor development, but it should be emphasized that all of the research on motor behavior seeks to better understand how we control and coordinate our bodies in efficient way to move around our world, to perform our jobs, and to execute daily living skills, as well as to pursue recreational and physical activities for leisure and enjoyment. Thus, in a way, the terms *motor control, motor learning* and *motor development* are a little old fashioned; but they remain useful to delineate different areas of research interest.

Of course, it has not been possible to delve too deeply into this important subdiscipline area of our field. At the end of this chapter references for further reading are listed. Interested students should talk with their instructors and inquire in departments of sport and exercise science and/or kinesiology, or departments of psychology, and seek to speak further with professors who spend much of their professional time studying motor skill behavior. This may be an avenue some students may wish to pursue in their university degree program and beyond.

CRITICAL READINGS

KELSO, J. A. S. (Ed.). (1982). *Human motor behavior: An introduction.* Hillsdale, NJ: Lawrence Erlbaum.

SCHMIDT, R. A. (1991). *Motor learning and performance: From principles to practice.* Champaign, IL: Human Kinetics.

WADE, M. G., & WHITING, J. (Eds.). (1986). *Motor development in children: Aspects of coordination and control.* Dordrecht: Martinas Nijhoff.

REFERENCES

ADAMS, J. A. (1971). A closed-loop theory of motor learning. *Journal of Motor Behavior, 3,* 111–150.

ADAMS, J. A. (1987). Historical view and appraisal of research on the learning retention and transfer of human motor skills. *Psychological Bulletin, 101,* 41–74.

BAYLEY, N. (1935). The development of motor abilities during the first three years. *Monograph of the Society for Research on Child Development, 1,* 1–26.

BEEK, P. J. (1989). *Juggling dynamics.* Doctoral Dissertation. Amsterdam: Free University Press.

BEEK, P. J., & VAN SANTVOORD, A. A. M. (1992). Learning the cascade juggle: A dynamical systems analysis. *Journal of Motor Behavior, 24,* 85–94.

BERNSTEIN, N. (1967). *The control and regulation of movements.* London, England: Derganon Press.

BRYAN, W. L., & HARTER, N. (1897). Studies in the physiology and psychology of the telegraphic language. *Psychological Review, 4,* 27–53.

BRYAN, W. L., & HARTER, N. (1899). Studies on the telegraphic language: The acquisition of hierarchy of habits. *Psychological Review, 6,* 345–375.

BURTON, A. W., & DAVIS, W. E. (1992). Optimizing the involvement and performance of children with physical impairments in movement activities. *Pediatric Exercise Science, 4,* 236–248.

CLARK, J. E., & WHITALL, J. (1989). What is motor development? The lessons of history. *Quest, 41,* 183–202.

CONNOLLY, K. (1977). The nature of motor skill development. *Journal of Human Movement Studies, 3,* 128–143.

CRAIK, K. J. W. (1948). The theory of the human operator in control system: II Man as an element in a control system. *British Journal of Psychology, 38,* 142–148.

DAVIS, W. E., & BURTON, A. W. (1991). Ecological task analysis: Translating movement behavior theory into practice. *Adapted Physical Activity Quarterly, 8,* 154–177.

ELLIOT, J. M., & CONNOLLY, K. J. (1974). Hierarchical structure in skill development. In K. J. Connolly & J. S. Bruner (Eds.), *The growth of competence* (pp. 135–168). NY: Academic Press.

FITTS, P. M. (1954). The information capacity of the human motor system in controlling the amplitude of movement. *Journal of Experimental Psychology, 47,* 381–391.

GESELL, A. (1928). *Infancy and Human Growth.* New York: Macmillan.

GESELL, A., & C. S. ARMATRUDA. (1941). *Developmental diagnosis: Normal and abnormal child development.* NY: Paul B. Hoeber.

GOODE, S., & MAGILL, R. A. (1986). The contextual interference effects in learning three badminton serves. *Research Quarterly for Exercise and Sport, 57,* 308–314.

GUTHRIE, E. R. (1952). *The psychology of learning.* NY: Harper & Row.

HICK, W. E. (1952). On the rate of gain of information. *Quarterly Journal of Experimental Psychology, 4,* 11–26.

HOOVER, J. H., & WADE, M. G. (1985). Motor learning theory and mentally retarded individuals: A historical review. *Adapted Physical Activity Quarterly, 2,* 228–252.

MAGILL, R. A., & HALL, K. G. (1990). A review of the contextual interference effect in motor skill acquisition. *Human Movement Science, 9,* 241–289.

MCGRAW, M. B. (1934). *The neuromuscular maturation of the human infant.* New York: Hafner.

NEWELL, K. (1990). Motor skill acquisition. In M. R. Rosenzweig and L. W. Porter (Eds.), *Annual Review of Psychology, 42* (pp. 213–237). Palo Alto, CA: Annual Review.

NEWELL, K. M., & MCDONALD, P. V. (1992). Practice: A search for task solutions. In R. W. Christina, & H. M. Eckert (Eds.), *Enhancing human performance in sport: New concepts and developments* (pp. 51–59). (American Academy of Physical Education Papers, No. 25). Champaign, IL: Human Kinetics.

PIAGET, J. (1952). *The origins of intelligence in children.* NY: International University Press.

SCHMIDT, R. A. (1975). A schema theory of discrete motor skill learning. *Psychological Review, 82,* 225–260.

SCHMIDT, R. A. (1988). *Motor control and learning: A behavioral emphasis* (2nd ed.). Champaign, IL: Human Kinetics.

SCHMIDT, R. A. (1991). *Motor learning and performance: From principles to practice.* Champaign, IL: Human Kinetics.

SHEA, J. B., & MORGAN, R. L. (1979). Contextual interference effects on the acquisition, retention, and transfer of a motor skill. *Journal of Experimental Psychology: Human Learning and Memory, 5,* 179–187.

STELMACH, G. E. (1969). Efficiency of motor learning as a function of intertrial rest. *Research Quarterly, 40,* 198–202.

THELEN, E. (1986). Treadmill-elicited stepping in seven-month-old infants. *Child Development, 57,* 1498–1506.

THELEN, E., & FISHER, D. M. (1983). The organization of spontaneous leg movements in newborn infants. *Journal of Motor Behavior, 15,* 353–377.

THELEN, E., & ULRICH, B. D. (1991). *Hidden skills: A dynamical systems analysis of treadmill stepping during the first year.* Chicago: University of Chicago Press. [*Monographs of the Society for Research in Child Development, 56*(1)]

THORNDIKE, E. L. (1927). The law of effect. *American Journal of Psychology, 39,* 212–222.

THOMAS, J. R. (1980). Acquisition of motor skills: Information processing differences between children and adults. *Research Quarterly for Exercise and Sport, 51,* 158–175.

WADE, M. G. (1976). Developmental motor learning. In J. F. Keogh, & R. S. Hutton (Eds.), *Exercise and Sport Sciences Review* (pp. 375–379). Santa Barbara: Journal Publishing Affiliates.

WADE, M. G., & WHITING, J. (Eds.) (1986). *Motor development in children: Aspects of coordination and control.* Dordrecht: Martinas Nijhoff.

WHITING, H. T. A., VOGT, S., & VEREIJKEN, B. (1992). Human skill and motor control: Some aspects of the motor control—motor learning relation. In J. J. Summers (Ed.), *Approaches to the study of motor control and learning* (pp. 81–111). Amsterdam: North-Holland.

WOODWORTH, R. S. (1899). The accuracy of voluntary movement. *Psychological Review, 3* (Monograph supplement No. 2), 1–114.

Chapter Six

The Human Locomotor System

Glynn A. Leyshon

The human body is a machine of wondrous complexity capable of strong and violent movements or delicate and precise movements. This machine is made up of slightly more than 200 bones to which are attached better than 600 muscles. The latter produce movement under the control of the brain, whose complexities continue to defy understanding even after centuries of study. To properly appreciate the smooth and integrated functioning taken for granted in the body, let one aspect malfunction; the interdependence then becomes apparent. Suppose, for example, you suffer a mild but not uncommon condition known as jumper's knee or chondromalacia. The articulation (joint) between the thigh bone (femur) and shin bone (tibia) will malfunction. This will cause a limp, which causes muscles to contract differently; which in turn causes the stride to change; which affects the fashion the foot strikes the ground; and which in turn may cause other problems in the good leg or even the back.

To fully appreciate the movement of the human body, one must dissect it—if not literally, then figuratively. One needs to know the major skeletal parts, the major muscle groups, which nerves do what, and how the blood supply plays its role. In addition, an understanding of the heart and lungs and their role in movement is essential. Since no one part functions in isolation or apart from the others, all parts should be studied in their integrated roles; however, there is a critical point in the degree of the detail of all the systems beyond which lies only confusion. It is wise, therefore, to limit oneself to studying regions of the body, or segments, and linking them together later.

In studying any region or segment as it concerns movement, one looks at bone, muscle, nerve, and blood supply. No actual line of demarcation exists between segments, so it is necessary to keep in mind that the segments are a study convenience only.

PRINCIPLES AND TERMINOLOGY OF HUMAN MOVEMENTS

Prior to study of the human body as it functions one should have an understanding of certain basic anatomical principles and terminology.

Anatomical Position. In all references to the body it is assumed that the body is standing erect with palms facing forward (Fig. 6.1).

Terms of Direction. From the anatomical position, directions for the location of muscles, bones, etc., are given as follows:

medial: structures near the midline of the body or of the segment
lateral: structures away form the midline
superior: toward the head
inferior: toward the feet
anterior: to the front
posterior: to the rear
proximal: near the centre of the body
distal: away from the centre of the body

Reference Planes. In dissection, certain viewpoints are necessary to comprehend the relationship of various structures. Thus, for example, a limb may be cut through to show the relationship of the superficial muscles to the deep.

Sagittal plane: any plane parallel to the median plane
Frontal: a plane at right angles to the median plane
Transverse: a plane at right angles to both sagittal and frontal planes. Also called the horizontal plane.

Movements. While movements are varied and complex, they are basically some form or some combination of the following. The terms are related to the body in anatomical position.

Flexion: a decrease in the angle between two bones, e.g., bend the elbow
Extension: an increase in the angle between two bones, e.g., straighten the elbow
Abduction: movement away from central axis, e.g., lift arm laterally
Adduction: movement toward central axis, e.g., returning arm to the side
Rotation: movement around a long axis—lateral or medial rotation
Circumduction: an action including all of the above, as when the arm is swung in a full circle
Supination: palms turned forward

Figure 6.1 The human figure in the anatomical position. A, Anterior view; B, Posterior view.

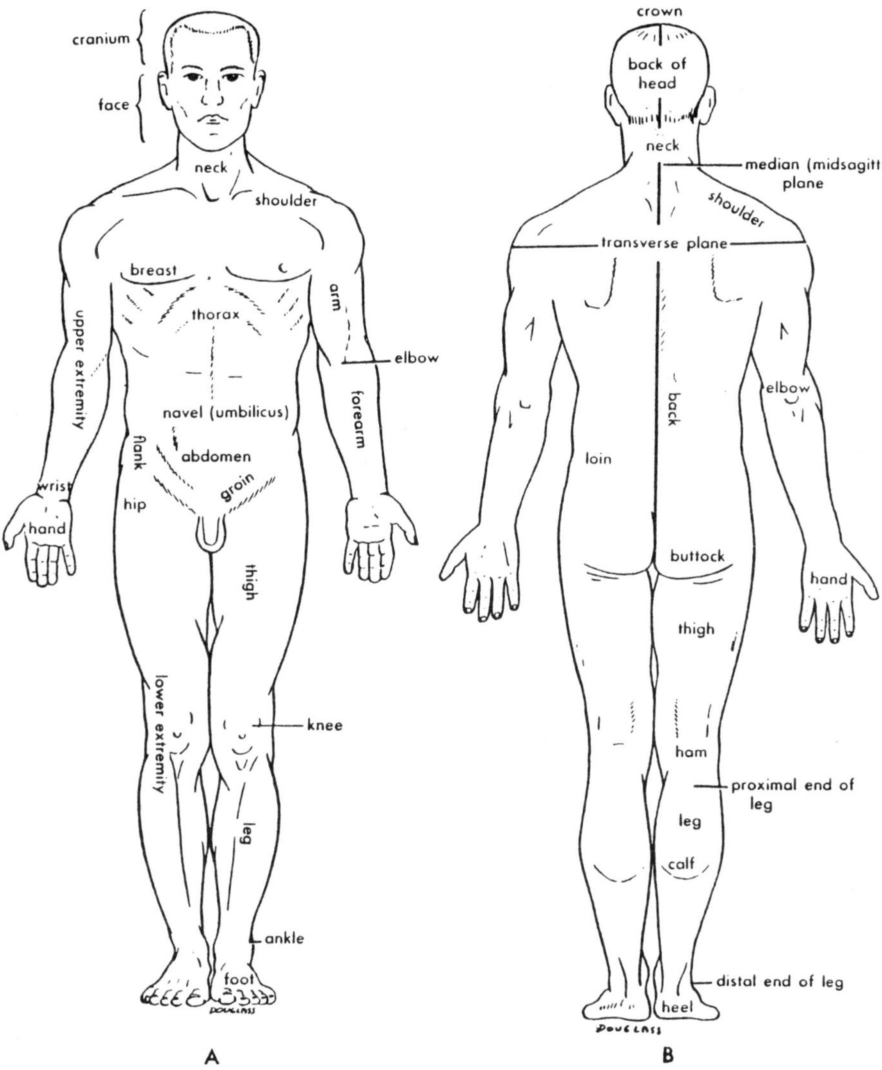

Pronation: the opposite of the above, i.e., palms facing backward
Inversion: rotation of the foot to turn the sole inward
Eversion: rotation of the foot to turn the sole outward

Muscle Fibres. Muscles, which constitute approximately one half of the body, are arranged in bundles of fibres. These fibre bundles, called fasciculi (singular, fasciculus), are arranged in various ways to afford maximum efficiency. In some muscles they are parallel; in others they converge to a centre line, and in yet others they are arranged to lie in several different directions. Since the fibres in the muscles resemble the forms in a feather, the word "penniform" is used to describe them (Fig. 6.2).

The reason for the various arrangements of fibers is to provide a maximum amount of force or direction with a minimum amount of volume. Tendons add necessary area for attachment of fibres, since bone itself would not provide half the surface area necessary. The fibres may insert into a central tendon running through the length of the muscle, or they may terminate in a tendon.

Attachments. Attachments of muscles are described on the basis of which end is stationary and which movable. The origin of a muscle is the stationary attachment, while the mobile end is the insertion. In the biceps, for example, the origin is the end closer to the shoulder, and the insertion is the end closer to the elbow. It should be noted that this naming is arbitrary. If one is hanging suspended from a bar and pulls himself upward as in a chinning exercise, the shoulder end of the biceps becomes the mobile portion, and the fixed attachment is now the elbow. This does not, however, change the accepted nomenclature of origin and insertion.

Names of Muscles. Muscles are named according to their shape, size, function, situation, direction, structure, or attachment. The following list illustrates this:

Shape: trapezius—shaped like a trapezoid
Size: gluteus minimus—the smallest gluteal muscle
Function: pronator teres—the round muscle causing pronation
Situation: pectoralis—the muscle of the breast
Direction: levator scapulae—the muscle that lifts the scapula
Structure: triceps—a muscle with three heads of origin
Attachment: sternocleidomastoideus—the muscle attached to the breast bone (sternum) and clavicle (cleido) and to the mastoid process

Nervous Stimulation. Nerves to the muscles contain motor (activating) and sensory (feeling) fibres in equal proportions. Each bundle of muscle fibres is supplied by a small branch from the main nerve. The branch ends in a motor

Figure 6.2 Various types of penniform muscles.

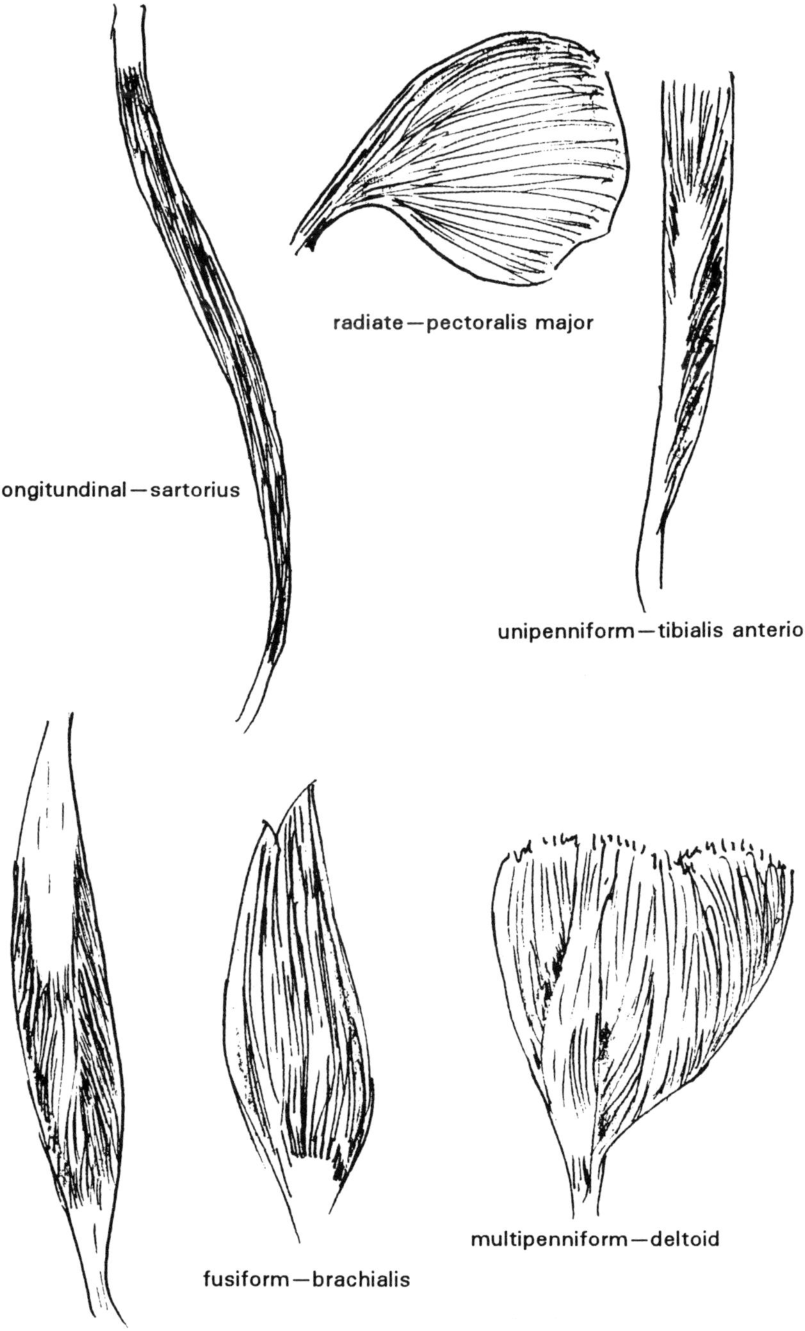

end plate on the surface of each muscle cell. In some muscles like the buttocks (gluteus maximus) there may be 200 muscle cells in a group. In others such as the fine muscles that move the eye, there may be as few as five. The nerve cell, its axon or arm, and its group of muscle cells form a motor unit.

The all-or-none law indicates that once a group of muscle cells is stimulated it must contract fully or not at all. Each motor unit obeys this law. Thus activity of the whole muscle is geared by the number, size, and power of its stimulated units. If a small number, of units is stimulated only a weak contraction is possible; if a large number, a strong contraction results. In holding an egg, one needs to exert enough force to keep from dropping it, but not enough to crush it. This means that only a very few groups of muscle cells are operating, but they are contracting to their maximum. Control is more precise in muscles in which there are fewer fibres to each motor unit.

By working in relays or shifts, motor units in a muscle can give continuous activity without fatigue during light work. As work get heavier, more motor units are called into action simultaneously until, for a maximum effort, all are called into play at once. Then the muscle fatigues very quickly.

The sensory nerve fibres have special endings called muscle spindles situated near the tendon of muscle. These sensory endings receive signals that are sent *out* of the muscle and to the brain. These signals initiate reflexes that coordinate and control muscular activity. The brain, for example, must know how much tension exists in a muscle or how many degrees of flexion have taken place in a joint to gauge how much more or how much less effort must be made by the muscle involved.

The sensory nerves providing the feedback are termed *afferent*, while the motor nerves providing stimulation are termed *efferent*.

Blood Supply. The skeletal muscles are the most richly supplied of all tissues. Since the muscles burn the calories necessary for movement it is only fitting that they receive an ample food supply. The major arteries and nerves travel together in a neurovascular bundle (Fig. 6.3), and thus each group of muscle fibres is assured of both a blood and nerve supply.

At each joint in a limb and at some other sites there are anastomoses. These represent alternate routes for the blood should major arteries become plugged or damaged. At the knee, for example, there are several alternate pathways leading from the thigh to the ankle.

The veins returning blood to the heart travel with the arteries deep within the muscle. They appear on the surface of the body as well, but without the accompanying arteries.

Contractions. Muscles shorten their fibres to cause movement in the limbs. When this occurs the insertion is brought closer to the origin (in most cases). There are, however, several types of contraction (Fig. 6.4). The most common

Figure 6.3 Summary of the circulation to the upper limb. Note the many anastomoses around the shoulder, elbow, and wrist joints.

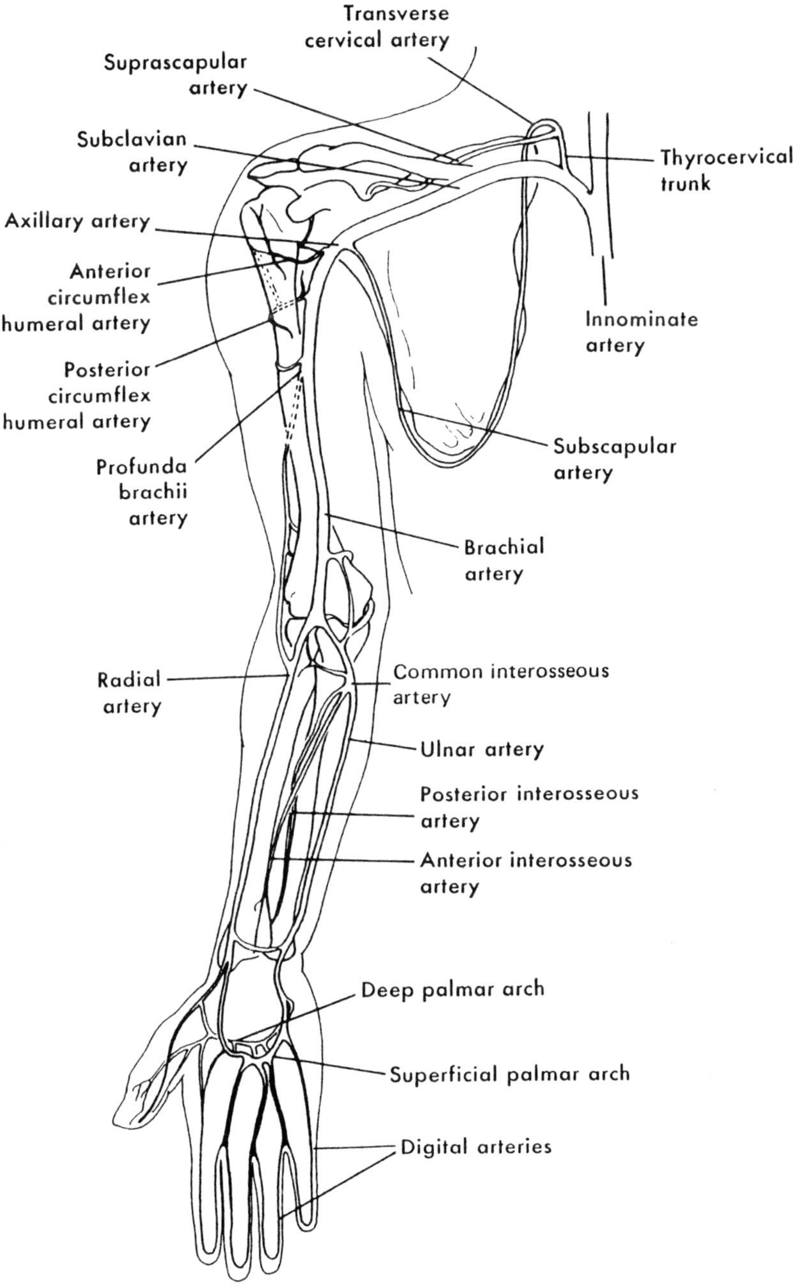

Figure 6.3 (con't) Diagrammatic representation of the brachial plexus.

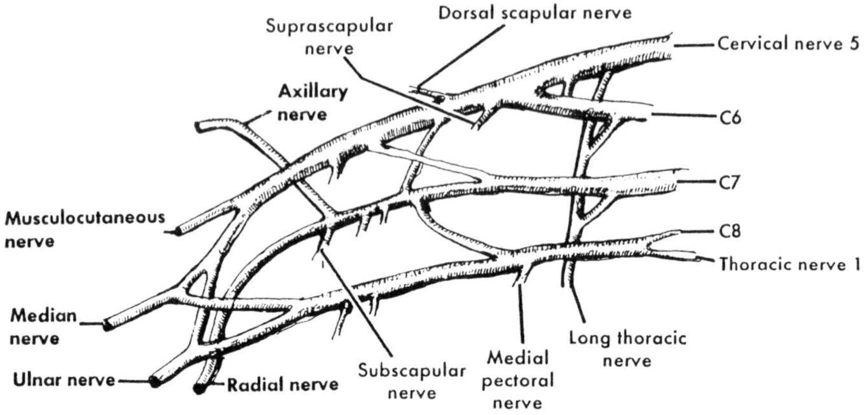

type of contraction is *isotonic*, and it is the type typical of most movements. Muscle fibres are drawn together because of nervous stimulation; the insertion is pulled closer to the origin; and the limb moves. Such is the process that occurs over and over again in the quadriceps and hamstrings, for example, in the act of walking. An isotonic contraction may be of two types—*concentric* and *eccentric*. The concentric contraction has already been described; the eccentric contraction is somewhat different. Lifting a heavy weight such as a suitcase uses a concentric contraction. Putting the suitcase down carefully requires an eccentric contraction of the same muscles. An eccentric contraction is one in which a muscle is slowly lengthened rather than shortened. The principle is used in weight training to put maximum load on a muscle group by having the lifter slowly lower a greater weight than he can lift with a concentric contraction.

In some cases a muscle contracts, but no movement takes place. Such a contraction is *isometric*. This state may occur because an object cannot be moved. In some instances movement may not be possible in the limb. Muscles cannot push; they can only pull. A person in a cast, for example, will be asked to contract the muscles even though he cannot move his leg or arm. The isometric contraction helps maintain strength in the muscle despite the lack of movement.

The final type of contraction is *isokinetic*. It is a laboratory-contrived type of contraction because it can be achieved only with a special machine, an isokinetic exerciser. In an isokinetic contraction the speed of movement of the limb is controlled throughout its full range of motion. When the limb moves under normal circumstances, as when the elbow is flexed, the first part of the movement is more difficult than the latter. Anyone who has performed the exercise known as a curl with a dumbbell can attest that the first few degrees of flexion are much harder to achieve than the last few. Thus in an isotonic concentric contraction, the greatest load is placed on the muscle at the beginning

Figure 6.4 Four different types of muscular contraction. A, Concentric; B, Eccentric; C, Isometric; D, Isokinetic

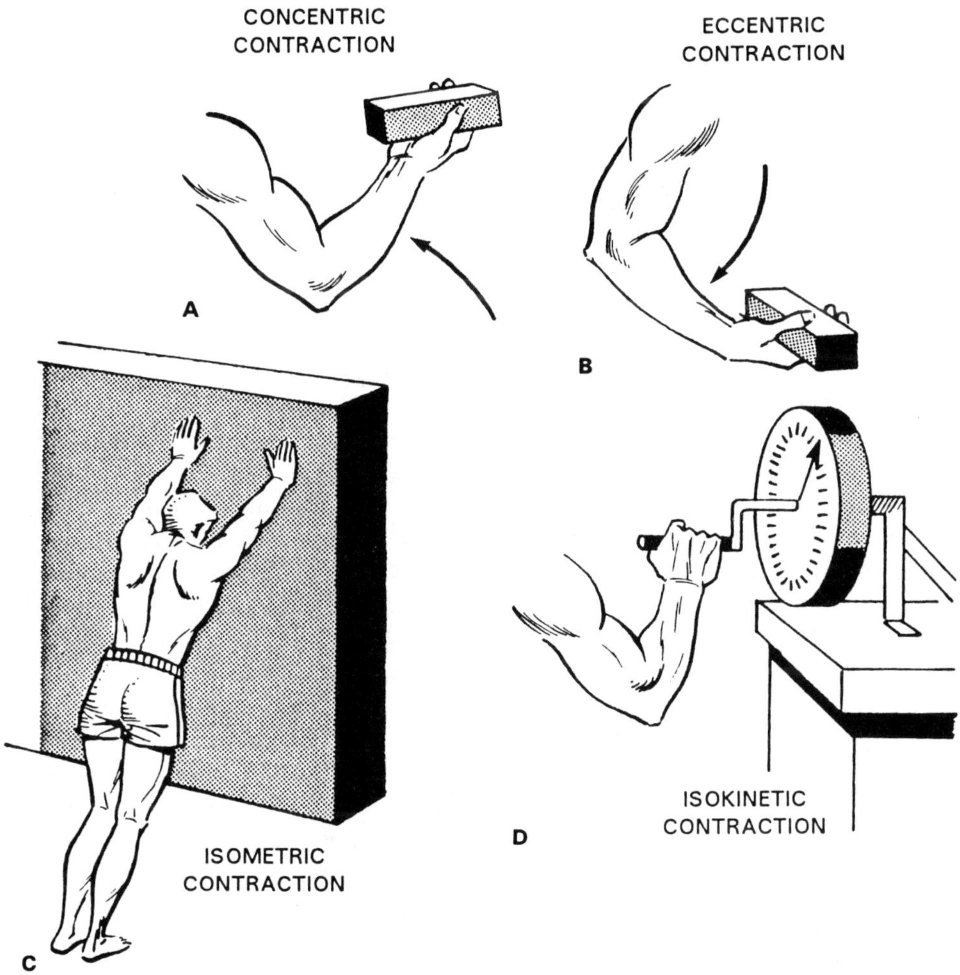

of the movement. An isokinetic contraction seeks to retain the same degree of resistance or load at any point in the movement, so that the last few degrees of flexion are just as difficult as the first few.

Lever System. The muscles move limbs according to a lever system that is based on a principle that muscles cannot push, they can only pull. Thus in any work or movement performed the muscle pulls (exerts force or power on) a bone (lever), which revolves around a joint (fulcrum); the weight (resistance or load) is at some point distal to the muscle.

There are three types of levers (Fig. 6.5), only two of which appear in any significant number in the body: Levers of class 2 are very rare; most of the levers are class 1 or class 3. In any class 1 lever the fulcrum is between the pull and the weight. The force applied is near the fulcrum and the weight is not far from the fulcrum; power is lost, but speed is gained.

In a lever of class 2 the weight is between the fulcrum and the pull. These levers have great mechanical advantage (a wheelbarrow is a good example), but they are often slow. The fact that the muscle insertions are usually close to the joints they move precludes most muscles from acting in a second-class lever, i.e., with the power acting far from the fulcrum.

In a lever of class 3 the pull is between the fulcrum and the weight. These are the most common levers in the body. The muscle in a class 3 lever operates at a mechanical disadvantage, but it is a lever of speed. The muscle is inserted close to the point (fulcrum) about which it moves; a rapid movement is produced even with little shortening of the muscle fibres.

Muscles' Roles. Muscles usually act in concert with others in a group. In fact, the body is established with the muscles grouped in mutually antagonistic sets. This means that for every flexor there is an extensor, for every abductor an adductor, etc., although this is not strictly true—there seldom being exactly three extensors opposing three flexors. It is only sensible that one should be able to return a limb from a flexed state to an extended one and vice versa.

Muscles are categorized as prime movers or agonists, antagonist or opposite movers, synergists or coordinators, and fixators.

Prime movers or agonists are primarily responsible for a particular movement. In flexion of the elbow the prime movers are the biceps and brachialis.

Antagonists act in opposition to the prime movers. In flexion of the elbow the antagonist is the triceps, used to extend the elbow.

Synergists are used to prevent any unwanted movement form occurring and to make fine adjustments necessary for accuracy and precision. In flexion of the elbow the forearm might pronate (turn over were it not for the synergistic action of certain muscles to prevent it.

Figure 6.5 The different classes of levers and examples of how they are represented in the body. A, Class 1; B, Class 2; C, Class 3; F = fulcrum; P = pull or force; W = weight or resistance.

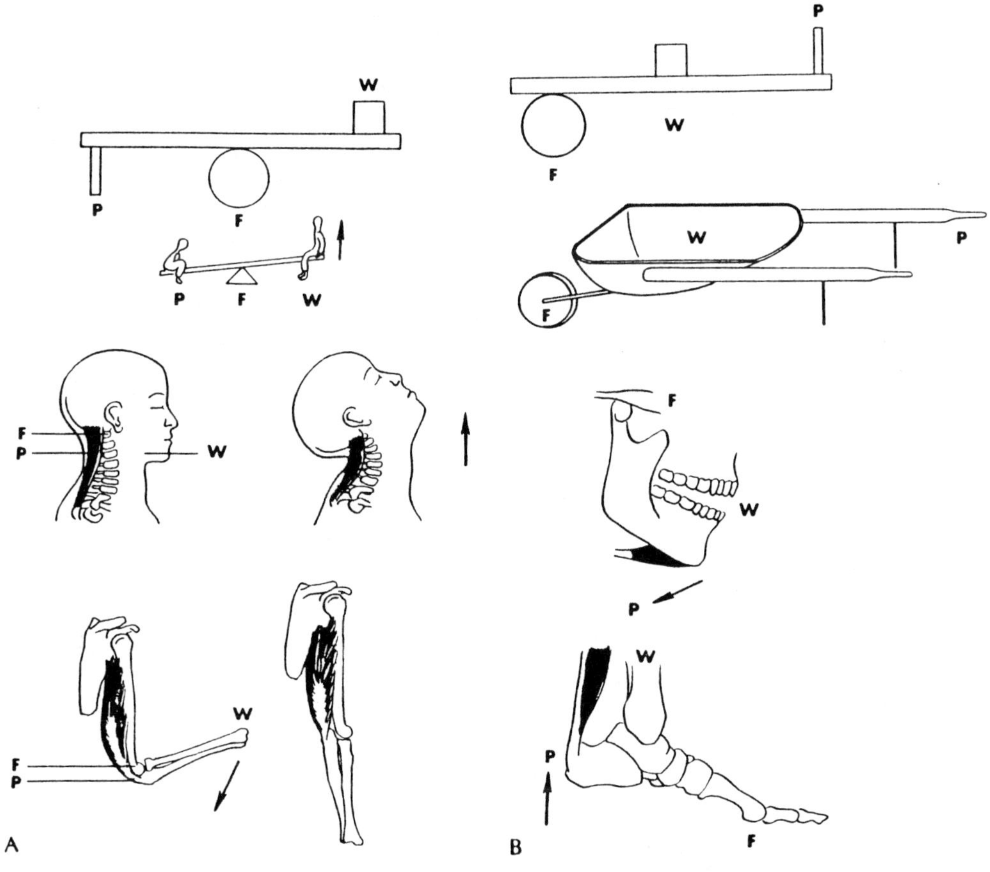

Figure 6.5 (con't)

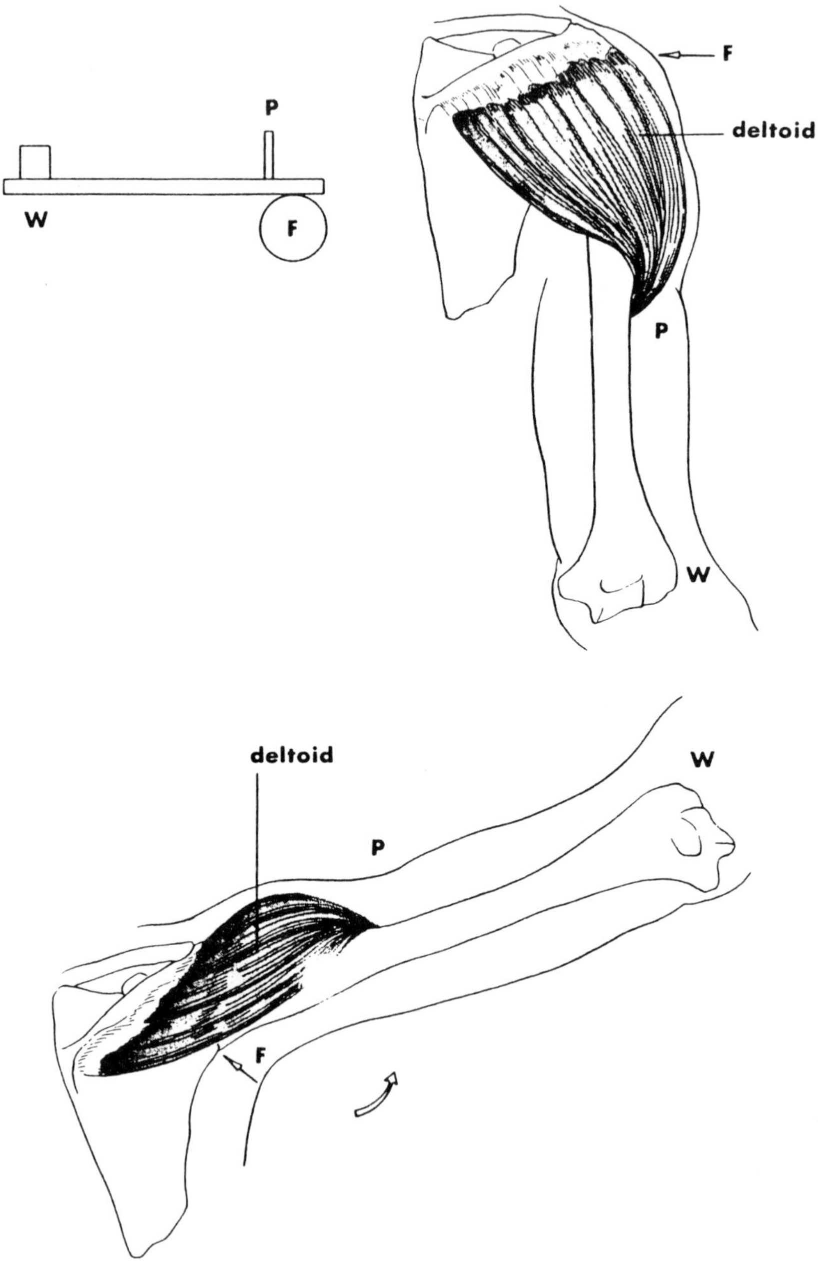

C

Fixators have nothing to do directly with the action, but "fix" the body or the limb. In flexion of the elbow it is often necessary to fix the shoulder joint to steady the elbow. Thus the shoulder muscles contribute to the working of the elbow flexors by holding the shoulder solid and providing a base against which the elbow flexors might work.

BASIC STRUCTURE OF THE UPPER LIMB

The human machine is capable of movement only because of the muscles acting on the articulated (jointed) skeleton. The most important body segments concerned with locomotion are obviously the arms and legs.

The study of the arm commences at the shoulder. The clavicle (collar bone) and scapula (shoulder blade), comprising the shoulder girdle, and humerus (bone of the upper arm), all function in movements at the shoulder. The attachments of ligaments (Fig. 6.6) and fascia as well as muscles insure that the arm is held in place.

Figure 6.6 Ligaments and capsule of the shoulder. Note the position of the ligaments that spring from the acromion and from the coracoid processes. The capsule has some slight thickenings that act as weak ligaments of the shoulder joint.

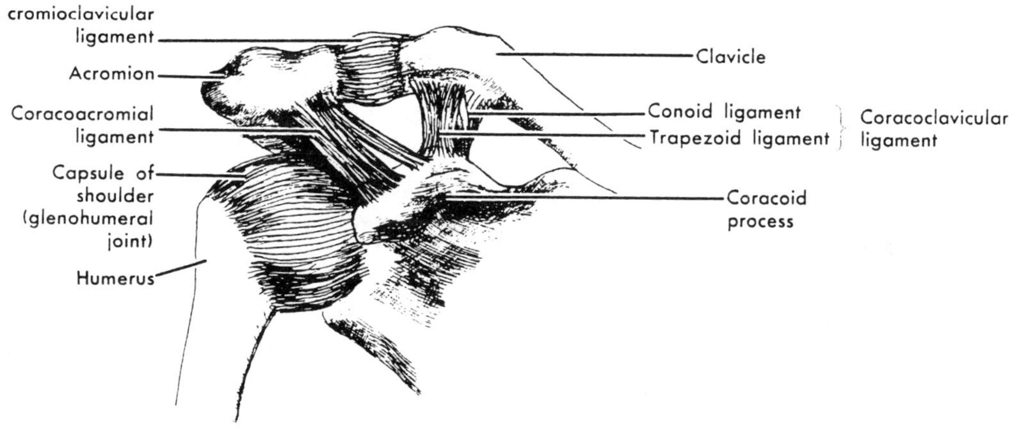

The shoulder joint is classified as a ball-and-socket joint, but the socket, or glenoid fossa, of the scapula is very shallow (Fig. 6.7). There are no ligaments of any significance attaching the humerus to the scapula; the main support of the joint comes from a capsule of heavy fascia that encloses both the head of the humerus and the perimeter of the socket. While the shoulder has lost most of its stability by virtue of the very shallow glenoid fossa, it has gained great mobility. Study of the shoulder joint and the hip joint will contrast the effects of a shallow socket (the shoulder) and a deep socket (the hip).

Figure 6.7 The scapula. **A** shows the posterior view of the right scapula, **B** shows the lateral view, and **C** shows the anterior view.

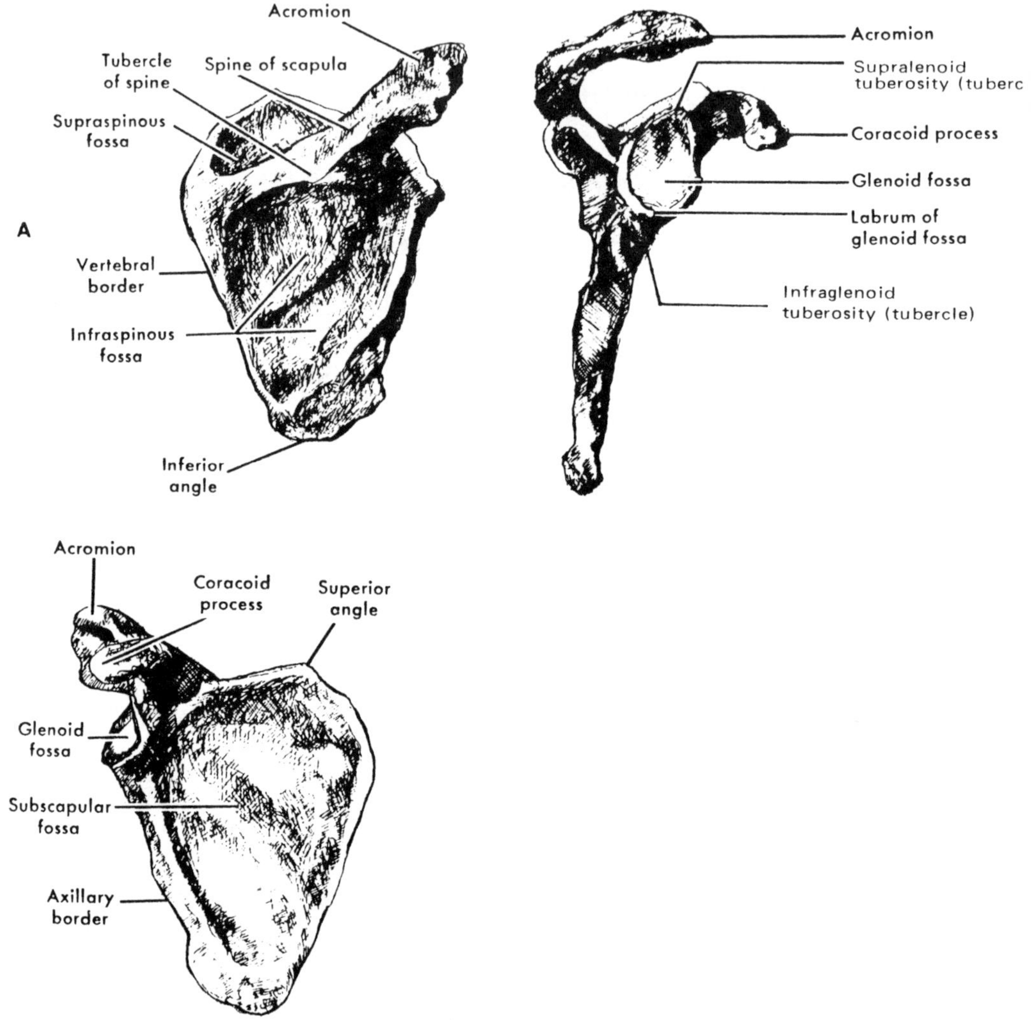

The shoulder joint, like all synovial joints in the body, is enclosed in a capsule lined with a special membrane called a synovial membrane. This membrane releases a thin fluid called synovia, or synovial fluid, that lubricates the joint much as oil lubricates moving parts in a machine. Also, the portion of the humerus and the glenoid fossa that articulate (come into contact) are coated with a very thin layer of cartilage, called hyaline cartilage, designed to protect the bony surfaces from the effects of friction.

Movement at the Shoulder Joint

The mobility at the shoulder is considerable. Swinging the arm in a circle is ample illustration. The movement forward is *flexion* of the shoulder, while movement backward is *extension*. Raising the arm laterally or sideways is *abduction*, and returning it to the body is *adduction*. Furthermore, the arm may be rotated on its long axis. Turning the thumb inward with elbow extended is *medial rotation*; turning it outward is *lateral rotation*. In swinging the arm in a wide circle, all of these movements are utilized; the combination of flexion, medial rotation, abduction, lateral rotation, and extension is *circumduction*.

Musculature of the Shoulder

The muscles that cause these movements are many, but the prime mover for all shoulder action is the deltoid (Fig. 6.8A). It is a large muscle, and coarse (making it suitable for injections), and it has three somewhat distinct sets of fibres (i.e., it is multipennate). These three sets of fibres allows it three distinct movements: (1) anterior fibres provide flexion; (2) posterior fibres provide extension; and (3) middle fibres provide abduction.

The origin of the deltoid is the clavicle, acromion, and spine of the scapula. The insertion of the deltoid is the deltoid tuberosity of the humerus.

Other muscles, of course, contribute to movement at the shoulder. Among the contributing muscles are the *rotator cuff* group. These muscles act as synergists (these are the muscles that prevent noncontributory movements) and have a special function. They act as dynamic ligaments to give the relatively weak shoulder joint support, which in other joints is furnished by the strong ligaments present. In addition they help movement by acting as synergists (coordinators). A lone person attempting to put a ladder into a vertical position has difficulty. As he attempts to lift one end higher, the opposite end moves away. An assistant, standing on the end of the ladder can hold it down, allowing the lifter to walk toward the assistant under the ladder and push it upward rung by rung as he advances. The rotator cuff muscles act in the manner of the assistant holding the end of the ladder; they hold the humerus in the glenoid fossa while the deltoid lifts the humerus. Were they not to do this job, the deltoid could pull the humerus straight up before the arm could be abducted.

It should be noted that adduction of the arm at the shoulder does not always involve the muscles antagonistic to the deltoid. Standing in anatomical position, one can abduct the arm and then simply relax the deltoid. Gravity will

Figure 6.8A The deltoid, a bulky triangular muscle shaped like an inverted Greek letter "D"—hence its name.

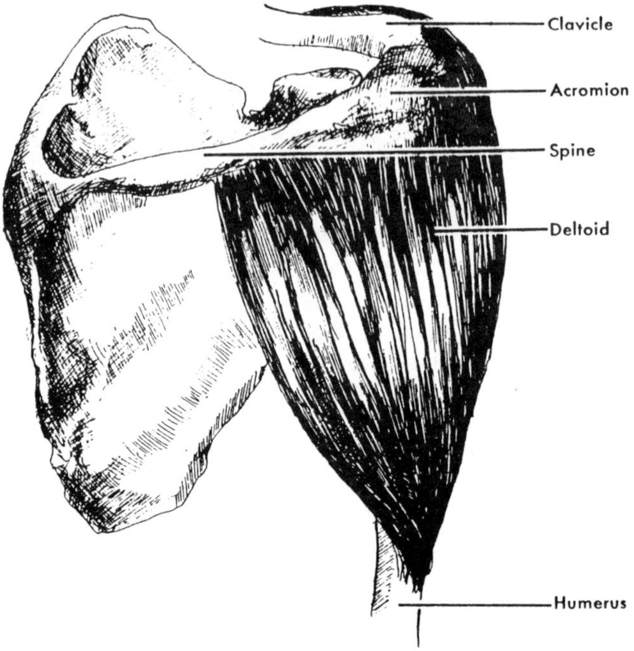

return the arm, or adduct it, to the side of the body. The antagonists (principally the pectoralis major and the latissimus dorsi) are used only when adduction is resisted. A gymnast performing the "iron cross" on the still rings must use the adductors to maintain his position.

Since the four rotator cuff muscles are beneath (or deep to) the deltoid, they must be relatively small (Fig. 6.8). All originate on the scapula and insert on the head of the humerus. The four muscles are the supraspinatus (above or superior to the spine of the scapula); infraspinatus (below or inferior to the spine of the scapula); teres minor (a round muscle and smaller than the teres major); and subscapularis (beneath the scapula).

Taking the first letter from each muscle provides the mnemonic, SITS. In addition to their function in assisting the deltoid, the rotator cuff muscles also provide medial and lateral rotation (i.e., on the long axis of the humerus).

Movement of the Scapula

Since the scapula is quite mobile, it must have opposing sets of muscles to move it and to return it to its original position. The following movements are those the scapula can assume:

1. Protraction. The scapula is drawn forward and around the rib cage as when reaching with the right hand to grasp the left shoulder.
2. Retraction. The scapula is returned from the above position or drawn back even farther as when standing at military attention.
3. Elevation. The scapula is raised as when hunching the shoulders.
4. Depression. The scapula is depressed or pulled downward as when trying to close an overfilled suitcase.

Almost all of the motions of the arm and shoulder entail the scapula in one of the above ways or in a combination thereof. Reaching upward for a book on a high shelf, for example, requires protraction and elevation of the scapula. These movements place the glenoid fossa facing the area of activity, thus permitting the arm and hand to be used to best advantage.

Muscles Acting on the Scapula

In addition to the muscles of the rotator cuff and the deltoid, 11 other muscles are attached to the scapula:

Coracobrachialis. The muscle arises form the coracoid process and inserts to the shaft of the humerus. This muscle assists the deltoid in flexion of the arm.

Levator Scapulae. This muscle originates on the transverse processes of the first four cervical (neck) vertebrae and inserts on the medial border of the scapula. It assists in "hunching" the shoulder.

Long Head of the Biceps Brachii. The muscle originates on a tubercle superior to the glenoid fossa and inserts on a radial tuberosity of the radius (forearm). It assists in flexion of the arm at the shoulder.

Long Head of the Triceps Brachii. Like the long head of the biceps, this muscle originates on a tubercle; however, this tubercle is on the inferior aspect of the glenoid fossa. It inserts into the olecranon. It assists in extension of the arm at the shoulder.

Pectoralis Minor. This muscle originates on the chest wall and inserts onto the coracoid process. It helps depress the scapula as well as protract it.

Rhomboideus Major. This muscle originates on the spines of thoracic vertebrae and inserts onto the medial border of the scapula. It retracts the scapula or "squares" the shoulders.

Rhomboideus Minor. It has the same general origins and insertions as the major except it is superior to the major. It retracts the scapula.

Serratus Anterior. This muscle arises from the first eight or nine ribs and then reaches posteriorly under the scapula and the subscapularis to insert on the medial border deep to the rhomboids. It is a powerful protractor of the scapula and is known as the "fencer's" muscle.

Short Head of the Biceps Brachii. Like the pectoralis minor and the coracobrachialis, the short head of the biceps originates on the coracoid process. It shares the insertion of the long biceps. It also helps flex the shoulder and provides some adduction.

Teres Major. Arising form the inferior angle and the lateral border of the scapula (Fig. 6.8, A and C), the teres major inserts onto the humerus at the medial lip of the bicipital groove. It acts to adduct the humerus.

Figure 6.8C Relationship of the teres major and minor. Note the major nerves and arteries of the posterior aspect of the arm.

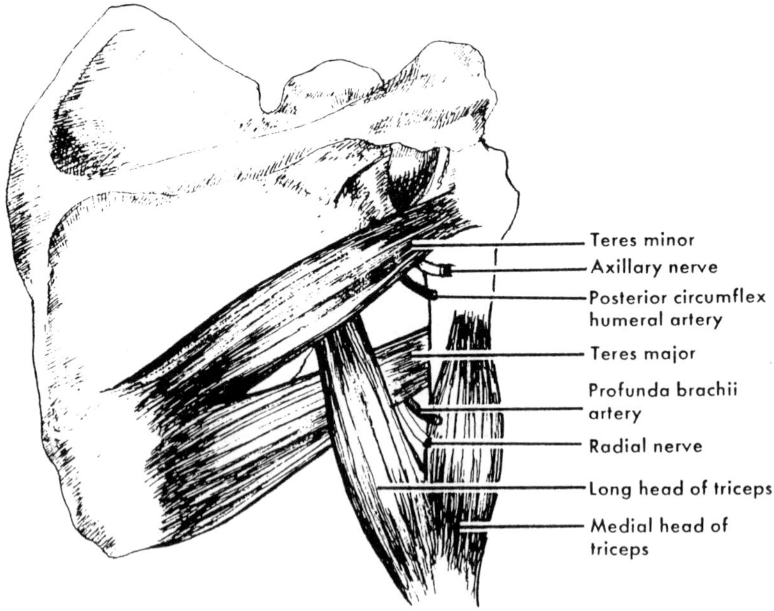

Trapezius. This muscle of the back is shaped like a trapezoid, hence its name. It attaches to the clavicle, acromion, and spine of the scapula, but it originates on the spinous processes of the seventh cervical and all twelve thoracic vertebrae as well as the ligament of the neck, the ligamentum nuchae. Like the deltoid the trapezius has three sets of fibres and each provides a different function. The upper fibres elevate the scapula, the middle retract, and the lower third depress the scapula.

Muscles of the Brachium

The brachium or arm is that area of the upper extremity from shoulder to elbow. It is divided into anterior and posterior compartments by tough fascia (septa) (Fig. 6.9). This division is based on the innervation as well as on the septa (walls) between the two. The anterior compartment muscles are innervated by the musculocutaneous nerve and the posterior by the radial nerve.

Figure 6.9 Compartments of the arm. Tough fascia septum separates the anterior from the posterior compartment. The coracobrachialis is not shown because the section was made below the point on the humerus where the short coracobrachialis inserts.

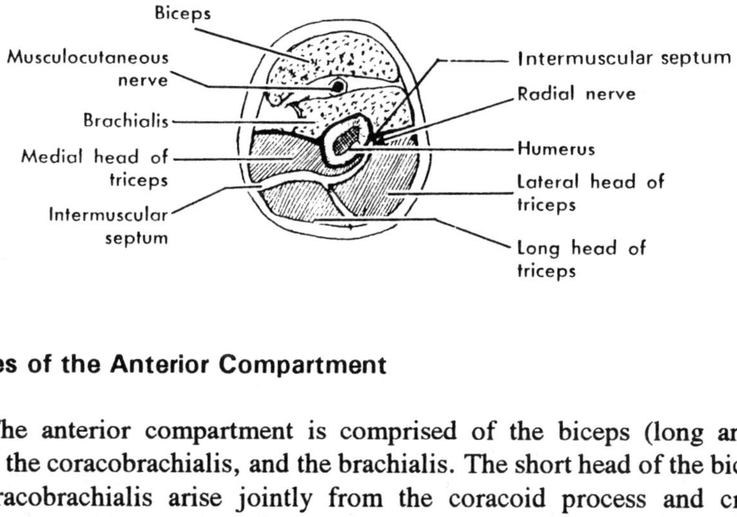

Muscles of the Anterior Compartment

The anterior compartment is comprised of the biceps (long and short heads), the coracobrachialis, and the brachialis. The short head of the biceps and the coracobrachialis arise jointly from the coracoid process and cross the shoulder. The coracobrachialis runs from the coracoid process to a point midway down the humerus on the medial side; the biceps inserts on the tuberosity of the radius. The brachialis originates on the lower third of the humerus and inserts on the tuberosity of the ulna.

The muscles of the anterior compartment provide mainly flexion of the elbow, as well as flexion of the shoulder. The workhorse is the brachialis, which may come into play only when the load being moved is very heavy.

The two heads of the biceps, having a common point of insertion on the radial tuberosity, also have a second function, to provide additional power for supination. Changing the hand from the normal anatomical position, i.e., thumb lateral, palm forward, to a position with the thumb touching the thigh, i.e., thumb medial, is *pronation*; returning the hand to the normal anatomical position is *supination*. When resistance is met during supination, as when one turns a balky doorknob or opens a screw-top jar, additional power is supplied by the biceps.

Muscles of the Posterior Compartment

The posterior compartment is comprised of the three heads of the triceps muscle—the long, lateral, and medial. They have different origins but a common insertion on the olecranon. The principal action of the triceps is extension of the elbow, although the long head crosses the shoulder joint and extends the shoulder as well.

The long head of the triceps arises from the infraglenoid tuberosity of the scapula; the lateral head originates about one third of the way down the humerus; and the deep (medial) head originates slightly lower and deep to the other two heads.

The Elbow

The elbow is the joint between the arm and the forearm, consisting of articulation between the humerus and the radius and ulna (Fig. 6.10). The articulations are covered with hyaline cartilage, and the joint is encased in a synovial capsule. The elbow joint has a hinge action; it may flex and extend. No other action is possible at the elbow joint because of the tight closure between the humerus and the ulna. The fitting of the proximal end of the ulna on the humerus is shaped much like the open jaws of a wrench. The articulation between the radius and humerus is minimal, but the head of the radius is solidly attached to the ulna (Fig. 6.10).

A second movement takes place in this region, although it is not of the elbow joint. It occurs at the radioulnar joint during pronation and supination. In these movements the ulna stays relatively stable while the radius rolls over across the ulna.

The ligaments of the elbow joint are strong, especially laterally where the articulation with the radius is so shallow. The ligaments are found only on the medial and lateral aspects and are called collateral ligaments. "Collateral" is a general term applied to the ligaments of hinge joints such as the elbow and knee. The ligaments of the elbow are the collateral radial and collateral ulnar ligaments; the ligament joining the head of the radius to the ulna is the annular (circular) ligament.

Figure 6.10 Elbow joint. In the frontal section note the prominence of the medial epicondyle (right elbow).

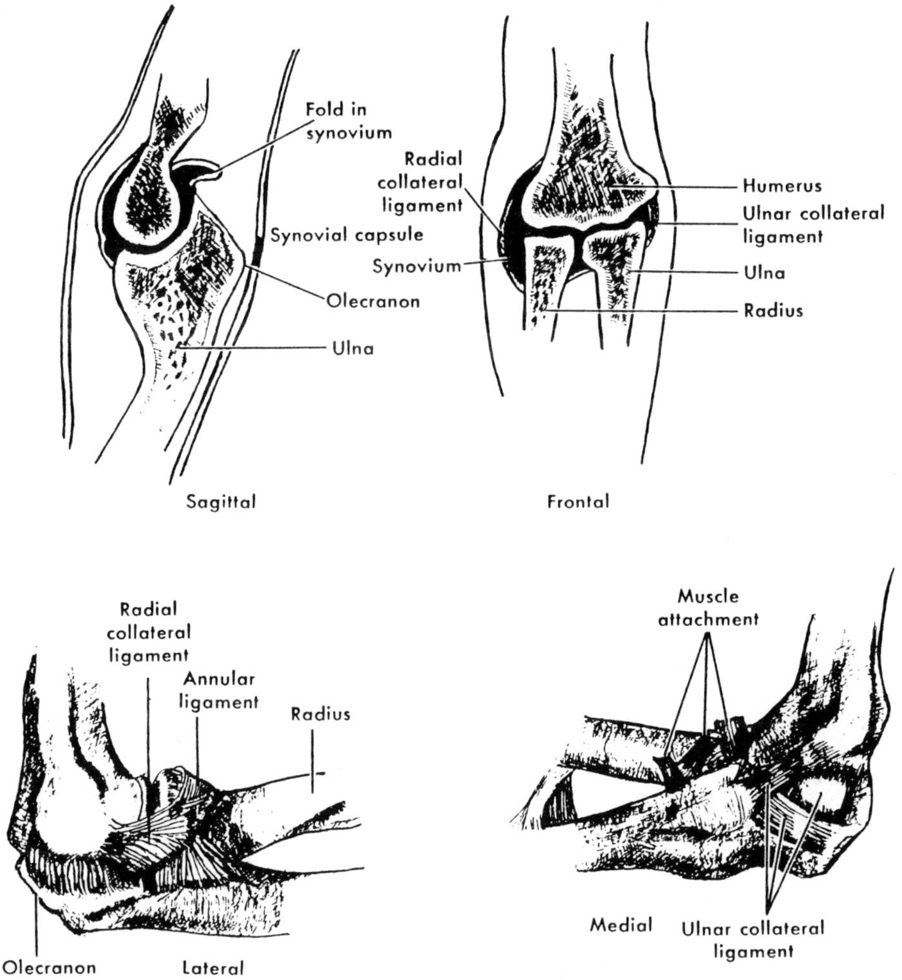

Muscles of the Forearm

The muscles of the forearm are divided into anterior and posterior compartments. The muscles of the anterior compartment are innervated by the median nerve, while those of the posterior compartment are stimulated by the radial nerve. The muscles in both groups are further subdivided into superficial and deep. Some of both groups are two-joint or multijoint muscles; that is, they originate above the elbow joint on the humerus and insert distal to the wrist joint. In such cases the muscles can act upon both joints.

The muscles of the anterior compartment can be termed (with certain exceptions) the flexor group, while those of the posterior compartment can be called the extensor group.

Muscles of the Anterior Compartment

The superficial muscles of the anterior compartment of the forearm include the pronator teres, flexor carpi ulnaris, flexor carpi radialis, flexor digitorum superficialis, and palmaris longus (Fig. 6.11).

Actions of the Superficial Muscles. The actions of the superficial muscles are diverse. The major function is flexion of the hand and fingers; however, the pronator teres serves to pronate the wrist. In addition, since the muscles originate above the elbow, they contribute to flexion of the elbow as well.

The principal wrist flexors are the two carpi (wrist) muscles, one on the radial side and one on the ulnar side. The palmaris longus is inserted into a broad sheet of fascia covering the palm, and it would seem to be an important wrist flexor, also; however, not only is the muscle very weak, it is absent altogether in some people. It is therefore not an important muscle.

The flexor digitorum superficialis is an important muscle of the hand. As its name implies, it flexes the digits. Since its major bulk is outside the hand, it is termed an extrinsic muscle of the hand. The principal characteristics of this group of muscles (i.e., the extrinsic muscles of the hand) is that they supply power and have long tendons (as opposed to the intrinsic group that provide precision of movement and have relatively short tendons).

Tendon Sheaths. Throughout the body there are muscles with the same characteristics as those of the flexor digitorum superficialis—long tendons. These tendons move with great frequency and can be likened to the transmission on a car. Like a transmission, they must be lubricated, and this function is carried out by the synovial sheaths that encase each tendon (or sometimes a set of tendons) much as a scabbard protects a sword. The inner lining of the sheath is similar to that in a synovial joint. The lining secretes synovial fluid so that the tendons sliding back and forth inside will not suffer from friction.

Occasionally athletes or laborers suffer form inflammation of the tendon. This condition known as tendinitis, can prevent function for several days or longer. It occurs most often in the tendons associated with the ankle joint, but it also occurs in the tendons of the wrist.

Figure 6.11 The origin of the superficial muscles of the anterior compartment of the forearm is the medial epicondyle, with the exception of the pronator teres.

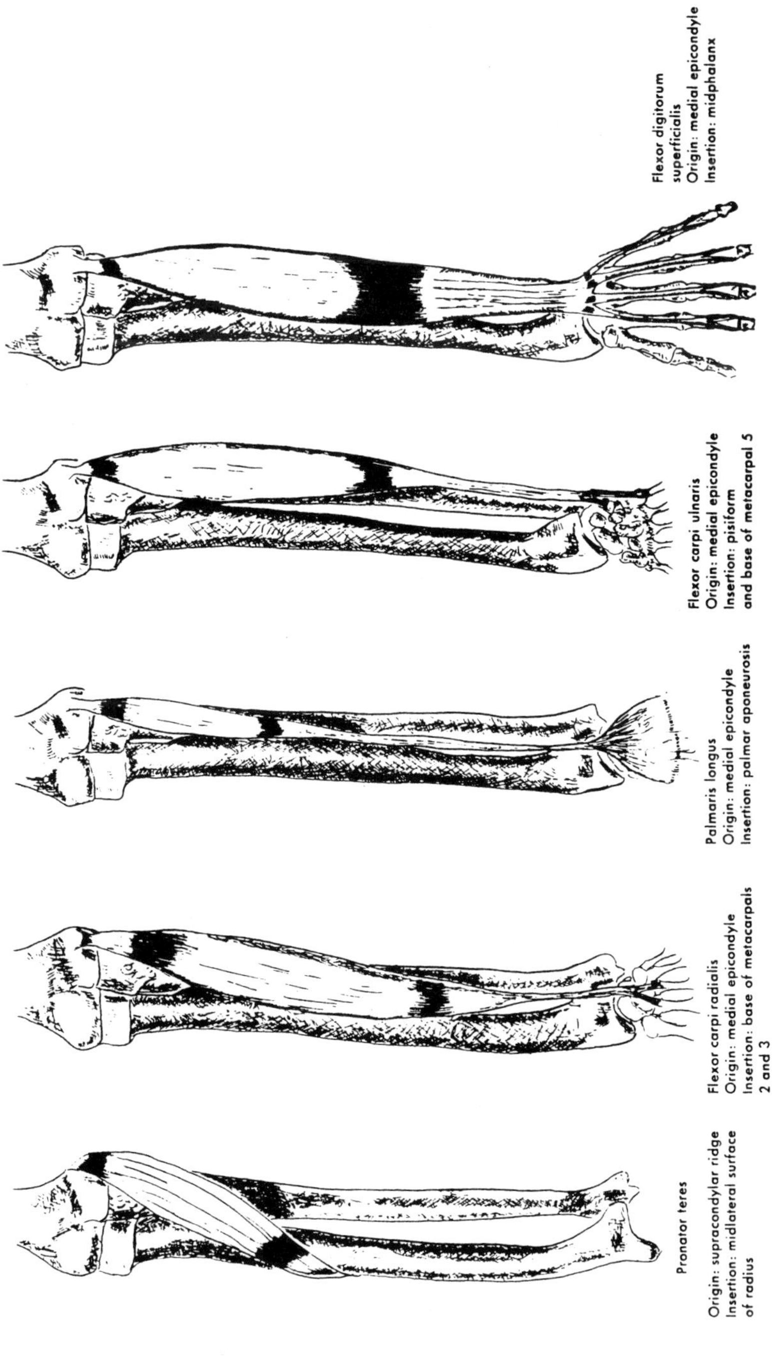

Action of the Deep Muscles. The deep muscles of the anterior compartment are the flexor digitorum profundus, flexor pollicis longus, and pronator quadratus (Fig. 6.12).

The flexor digitorum profundus (deep) is obviously a muscle similar to the superficialis. Both muscles run to the fingers (first, second, third, and fourth digits) and insert there. The profundus muscle inserts at the end of the finger or the distal phalanx, and its action is as its name suggests—flexion. The flexor pollicis (thumb) longus is analogous to the flexor digitorum but goes to the thumb. The pronator quadratus is the deepest of the group and is situated just above the wrist. Its function is to pronate the hand, i.e., turn it from a facing-forward position.

These extrinsic muscles of the hand provide power—power for gripping, which is essential. It is interesting that a champion weight lifter, lifting 1000 pounds, relies on his fingers to grip the bar while his arms, shoulders, back, etc., do the lifting. The fingers must withstand the 1000-pound pressure first.

The Retinaculum. The tendons of the extrinsic muscles would have tendency to "bowstring" during strong flexion were it not for the flexor and extensor retinacula. A retinaculum is a sheet of tough fascia found at the wrist (and ankle) that holds the tendons down to the bone beneath to keep them in place (Fig. 6.12).

Muscles of the Posterior Compartment

There are 12 muscles in posterior compartment. Like the anterior group, they are subdivided into superficial (seven) and deep (five) muscles. If the principal function of the anterior compartment is flexion, then the opposite action, extension, is the major responsibility of the posterior compartment. There are, of course, other actions that the muscles of the posterior compartment supply. The seven superficial extensors are the brachioradialis, extensor carpi radialis longus, extensor carpi radialis brevis, extensor carpi ulnaris, extensor digitorum, extensor digiti minimi, and anconeus (Fig. 6.13A).

Action of the Superficial Muscles. The action of the brachioradialis is flexion. The muscle may be considered an oddity, since it seem to be in the wrong group or compartment. It does not cross the wrist joint so its flexing action is exerted on the elbow joint. All the remaining muscles are extensors of the elbow and wrist, and in the case of the extensor digitorum and extensor digit minimi, of the fingers.

To note the action of the brachioradialis, hold the hand and forearm as though you were about to use a tennis racquet. Press downward on your wrist

Figure 6.12 Three deep muscles of the anterior compartment of the forearm. The pronator quadratus is the deepest muscle of the compartment.

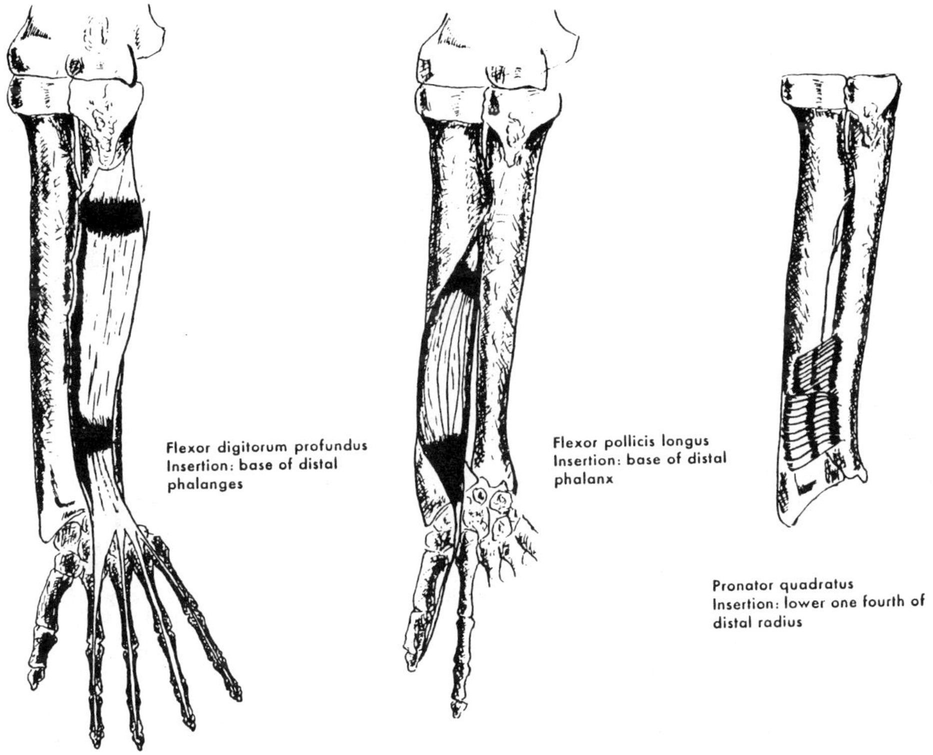

Figure 6.12 (con't) Three movements of the limb. From right to left, abduction, flexion, rotation.

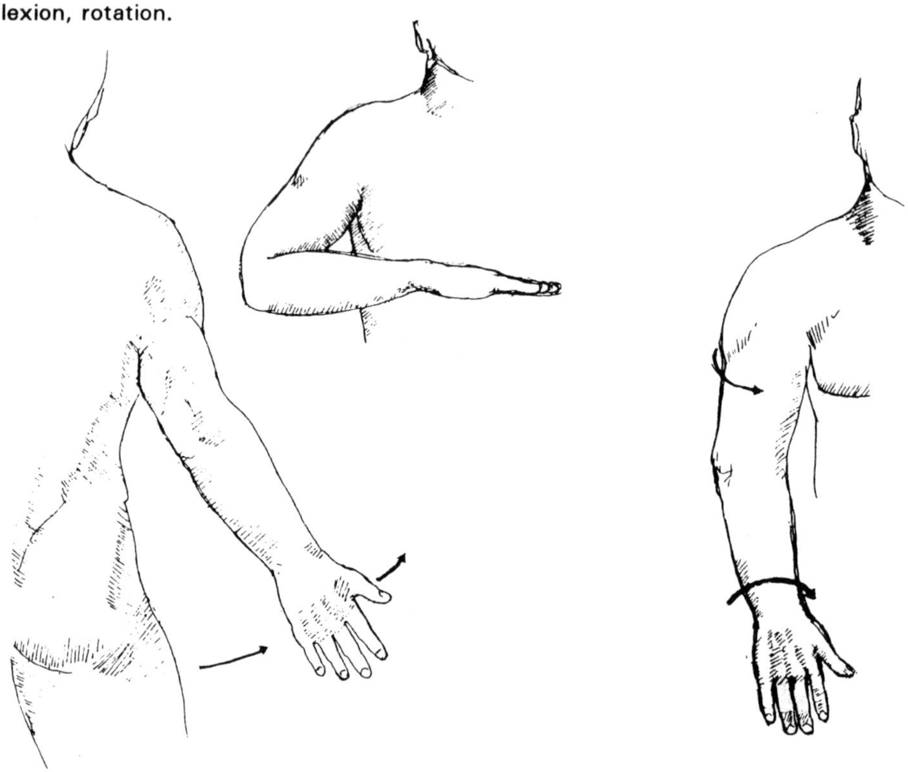

with the opposite hand and resist this pressure. The brachioradialis will contract and show as a ridge along the surface of the radius.

The two extensor carpi radialis muscles lie medial to the brachioradialis. Taking the same position of the forearm as indicted above, cock or extend the wrist back fully, and the extensor carpi muscles will be seen to contract at the lateral aspect of the elbow joint. In individuals with well-developed muscles the extensor carpi radialis longus will appear about the size of a golf ball under the skin when the wrist is extended. These extensor muscles are obviously important in gripping and in action of the hand and wrist such as playing tennis or other racquet sports and hockey.

The extensor carpi ulnaris acts, as do the two extensor carpi radialis muscles, to extend the wrist. If one thinks of the wrist as a square, there is a muscle or muscles, (two flexors and three extensors) attached at each of its four corners. If both ulnar muscles contract (the flexor carpi ulnaris and the extensor carpi ulnaris), a new movement is created—adduction. Similarly if the flexor carpi radialis and extensor carpi radialis longus and extensor carpi radialis brevis are contracted, abduction occurs. These two movements, abduction and adduction, provide the action in hammering or throwing a javelin.

Figure 6.13A Origin of the seven superficial muscles of the posterior compartment of the forearm. Note the common origin is the lateral epicondyle with a few exceptions.

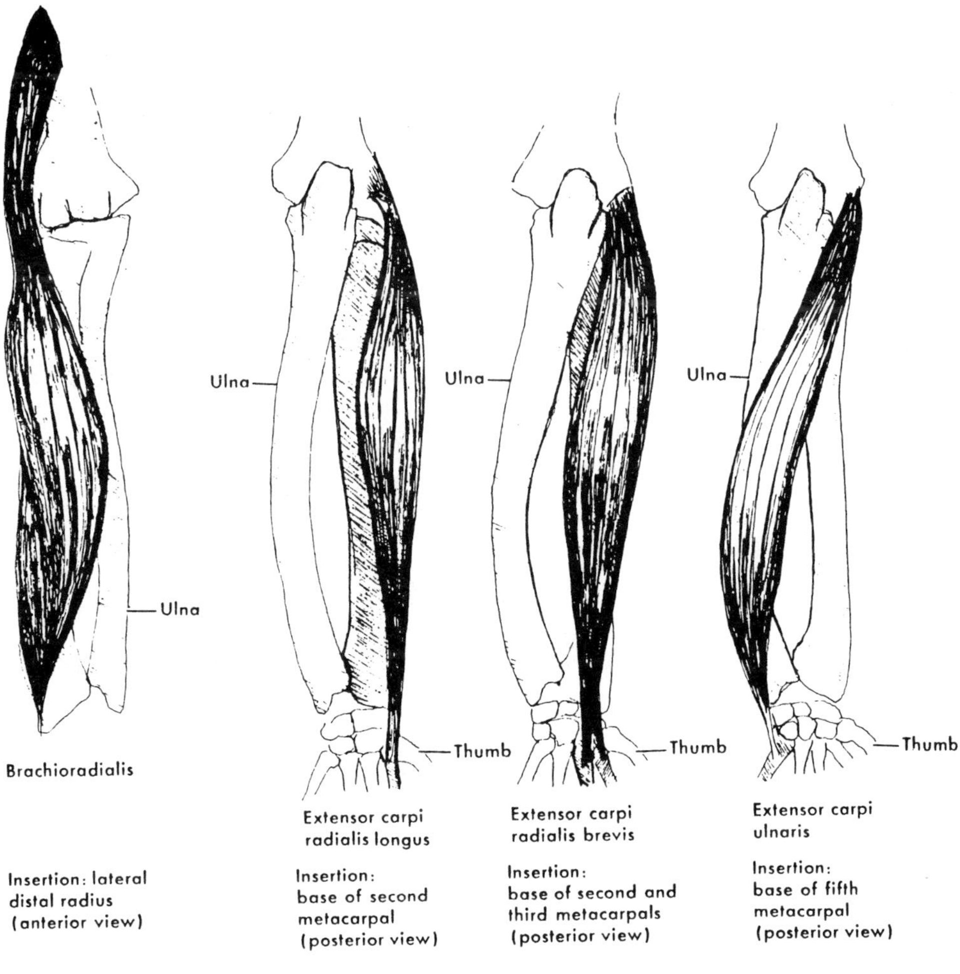

Figure 6.13B For legend see opposite page.

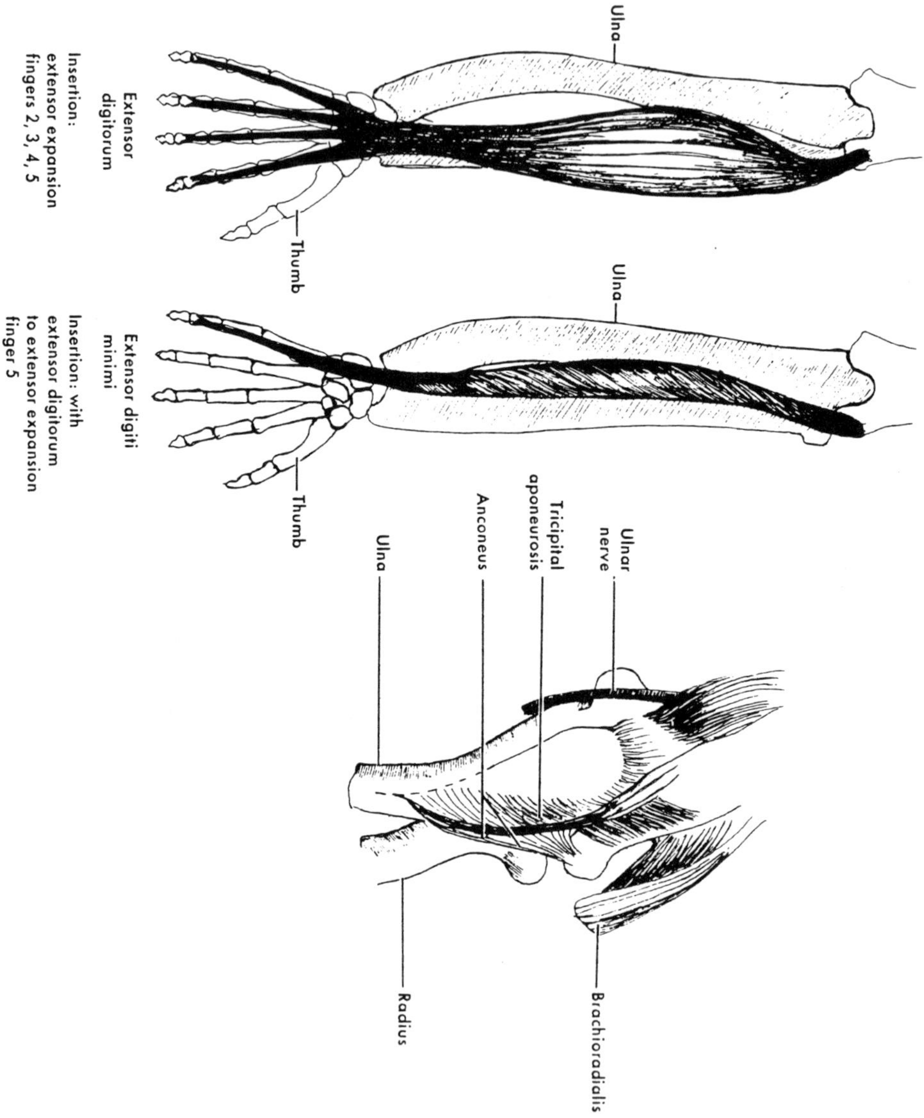

The extensor digitorum inserts into a special area of fascia covering the posterior surface of each finger. It is called the extensor expansion or hood. The most important action of the extensor digitorum is to extend the fingers at the knuckle or metacarpalphalangeal joint.

The extensor digiti minimi is simply a separate slip of muscle that sends a tendon to the fifth digit or little finger.

The deep muscles of the posterior compartment are the supinator, abductor pollicis longus, extensor pollicis longus, extensor pollicis brevis, and extensor indicis (Fig. 6.13B).

Actions of the Deep Muscles. The supinator takes its name from its action (Fig. 6.14). It supinates the hand. To do so, it must wrap around the radius as it proceeds from its origin on the ulna to its insertion on the radius. If supination is resisted (e.g., in using a screw driver), then the biceps brachii assists.

The three pollicis (thumb) muscles are sometimes termed "outcropping" muscles since they proceed downward toward the hand and then make a sharp turn over the carpal bones to attach to the thumb. The reason for this is found in evolution. As man developed, his thumb moved from its original alignment beside the fingers (where it still remains in nearly every mammal, including the ape and monkey) to a new position that placed it at a right angle to the fingers. This gave man an opposable thumb and thus the ability to use tools. The tendons followed the thumb in its migration; hence they outcrop from the other muscles of the posterior compartment. The three pollicis muscles also combine to form a landmark called the anatomical snuffbox (Fig. 6.14).

The extensor indicis is simply a second muscle going to the index finger.

The general action of the entire posterior compartment is extension, principally of the wrist. This action, paradoxically, is very important in gripping. To exert maximum grip pressure, one must not only flex the fingers but must cock back (extend) the wrist. Extending the wrist slightly allows the finger flexors to contract fully. (This can be tested by the following experiment: Flex the wrist as far as possible and clench the fingers. Then extend the wrist as far as possible and flex the fingers. Note the difference in the pressure exerted.)

Muscles of the Wrist and Hand

The bones of the wrist and hand are arranged to permit a wide variety of movements (Fig. 6.15). There are eight carpal (wrist) bones arranged roughly in two rows. They are held one to another by a web of interosseous ligaments that does, however, allow them some degree of movement. Only two of these bones, the scaphoid and lunate, articulate with the radius. That articulation represents the wrist joint proper. There is no bony articulation with the carpals and the ulna.

Figure 6.14 Origin of the five deep muscles of the posterior compartment. Note that the supinator has two portions; the deeper of the two wraps around the shaft of the radius from behind. The tendons of the three pollicis muscles form the anatomical snuffbox.

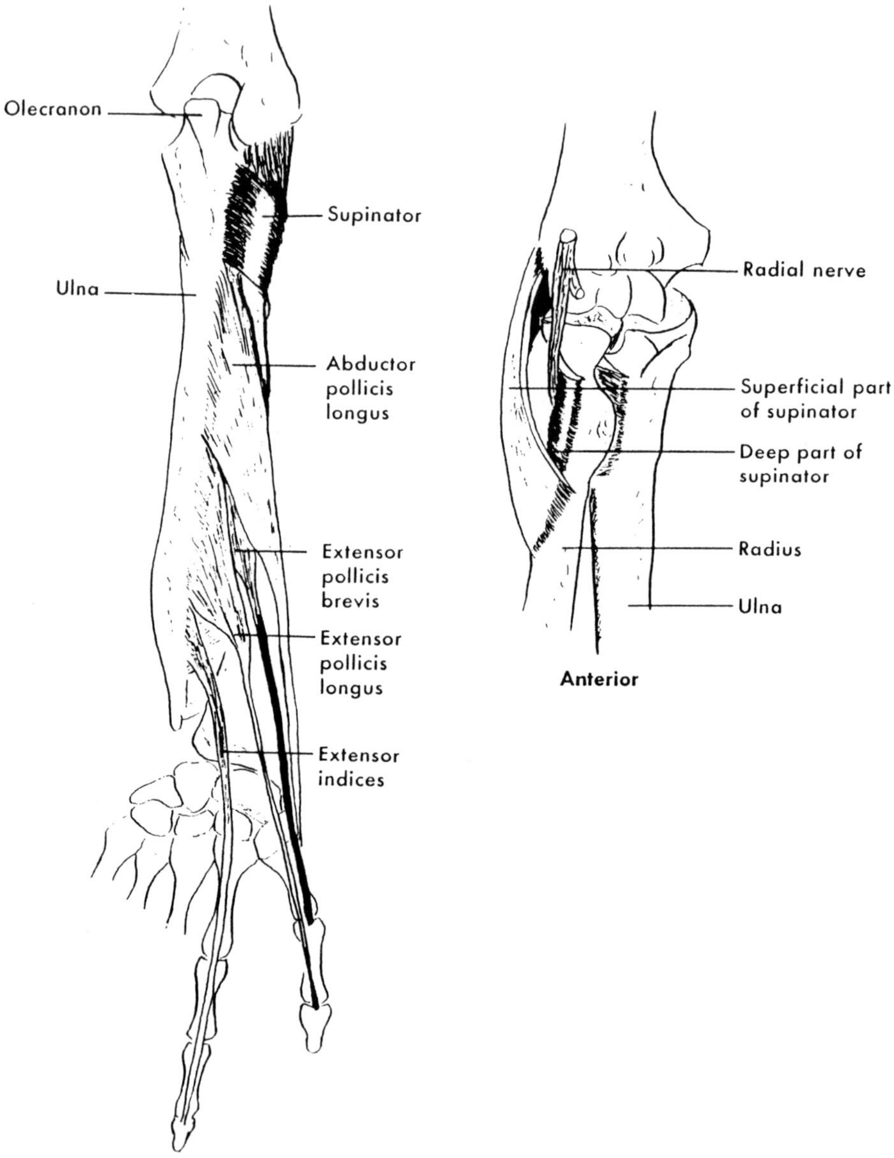

Figure 6.14 (con't) Anatomical snuffbox outlined by the tendons of the extrinsic muscles of the thumb in the posterior compartment.

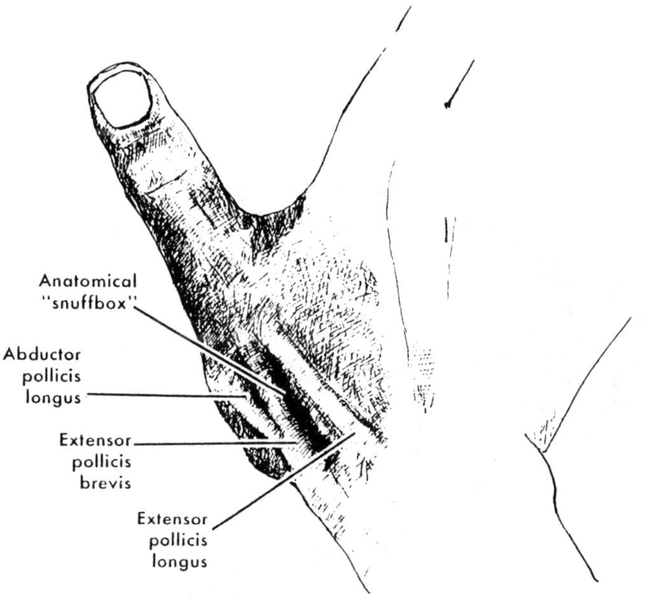

The five metacarpals form the palm of the hand. They have a limited degree of movement and serve as the origin of some of the intrinsic muscles of the hand.

The phalanges are highly mobile; there are three to each digit except the thumb, which has only two, a total of 14. The joint between two phalanges is the interphalangeal joint (often referred to as the IP joint), while the joint between the carpal bone and the proximal phalanx is the metacarpophalangeal joint (or the MP joint).

The Intrinsic Muscles of the Hand

The muscles of the hand proper are the precision muscles. They are divided into groups: the lumbricals, palmar interossei, dorsal interossei, muscles of the thenar eminence, adductor pollicis, and muscles of the hypothenar eminence.

Action of the Intrinsic Muscles. The four *lumbricals* (worm-like) are unique in that they originate from the tendons of the flexor digitorum profundus rather than from a bony structure (Fig. 6.16C). The insertion is also different from normal. Like several intrinsic muscles of the hand, the lumbricals insert

Figure 6.15 Palmar surface of the carpal bones of the right hand.

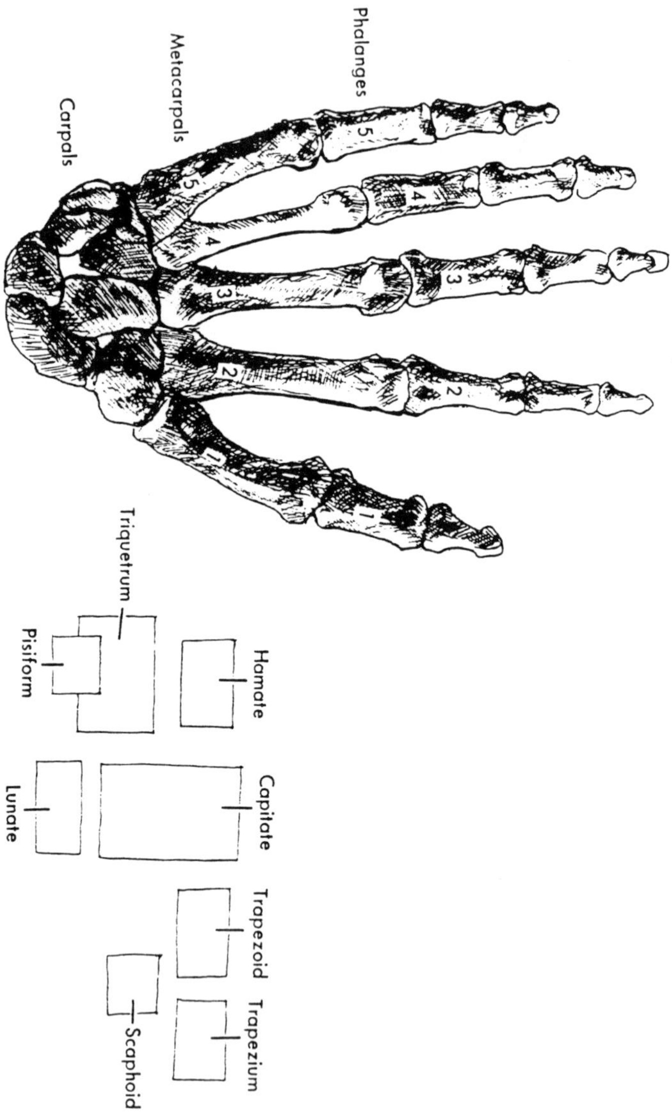

into the extensor expansion and thereby are able to produce two action—flexion of the metacarpophalangeal joint and extension of the interphalangeal joint. These actions are used in writing.

Figure 6.16C Lumbricals. All insert from the radial side.

The *dorsal and palmar interossei* originate on the inner-facing surface of the metacarpal bones and insert into the extensor expansion. Their actions are used in writing.

There are four dorsal and three palmar interossei muscles (Fig. 6.16 A and B). When abduction and adduction of the fingers take place, the movement is relative to a line down the length of the middle digit. Taking the fingers away from the midline or spreading them is abduction and returning them is adduction. The middle finger (third digit) may be abducted from this imaginary midline by its two abductors. Note that the third digit has no adductors.

The *thenar eminence* is the bulge of muscle at the base of the thumb. It is comprised of three muscles: the flexor pollicis brevis, abductor pollicis brevis, and opponens pollicis (Fig. 6.17).

Figure 6.16A and B *Left,* palmar interossei. *Right,* dorsal interossei. Note the direction the muscle runs in each case.

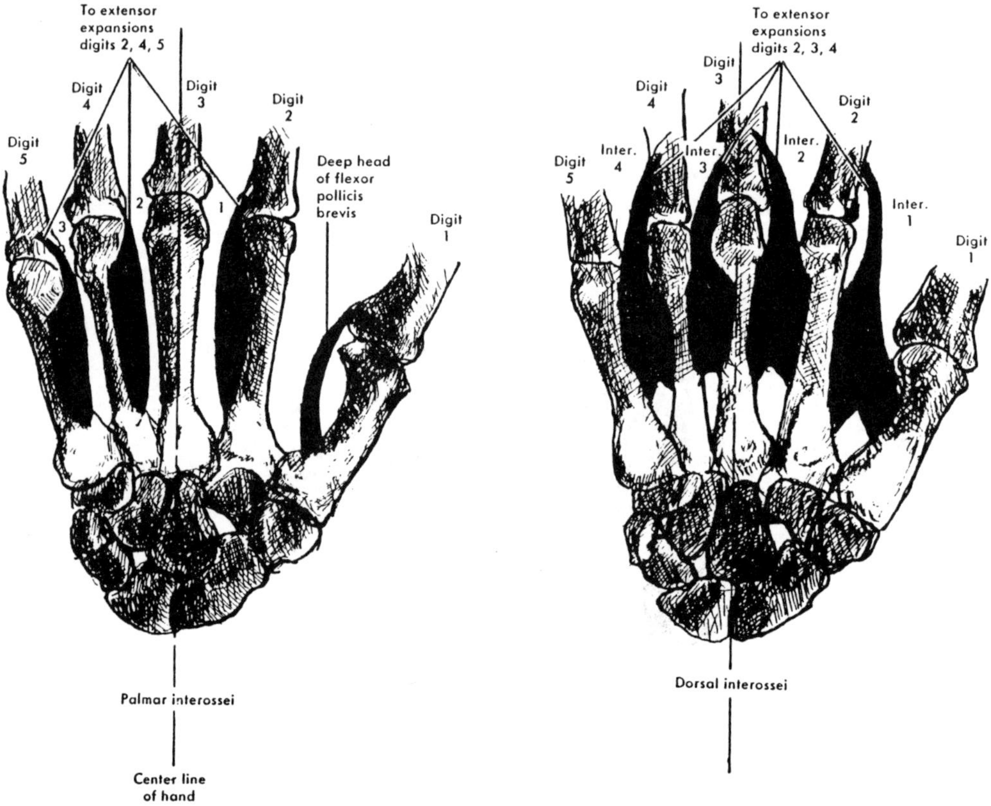

Figure 6.17 Muscles of the thenar eminence.

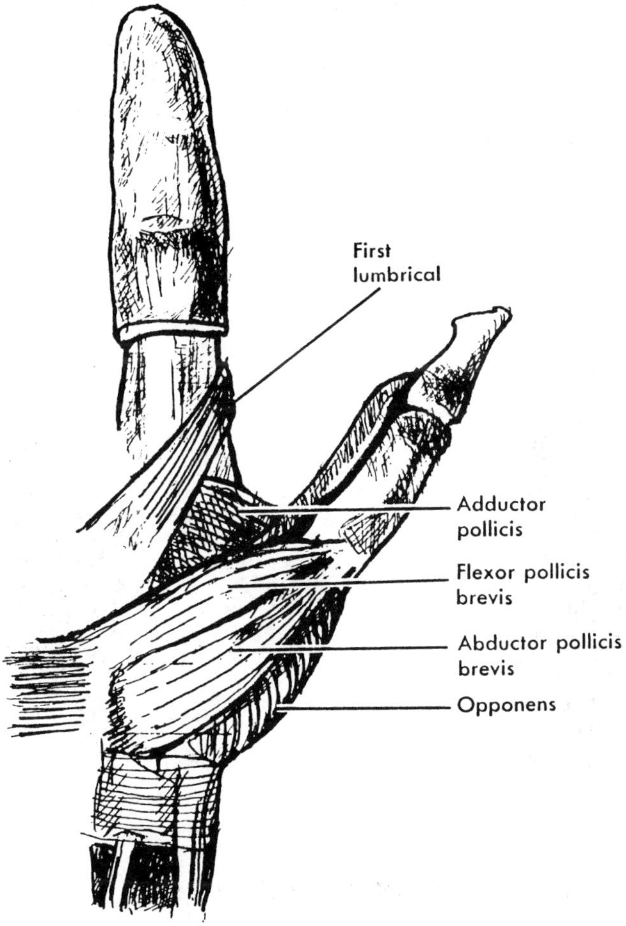

To understand the functions of these muscles it is first necessary to appreciate that the thumb operates on a plane at right angles to the fingers. If the hand is palm up on a desk and the thumb is moved to point to the ceiling, that movement is abduction. Returning the thumb to its normal anatomical position is adduction. Scraping the thumb nail down and across the palm is flexion, while holding it out as in hitchhiking is extension. Pressing the tip of the thumb to the tip of the little finger is opposition.

The muscles of the thumb in the thenar eminence act as their names suggest (i.e., the flexor pollicis brevis provides flexion, the abductor provides abduction, etc.). Another muscle of the thumb, the *adductor pollicis*, is not of the eminence. It is deep to the flexor pollicis in the web between the first and second digits. The adductor pollicis is important in gripping.

The *hypothenar eminence* is the bulge of muscle at the base of the little finger. The muscles are named like those of the thenar eminence and have a similar function. They are the flexor digiti minimi brevis, abductor digiti minimi, and opponens digiti minimi (Fig. 6.17). These act to flex, abduct, and oppose the fifth digit.

Figure 6.17 (con't) Muscles of the hypothenar eminence. Note that they are named in a fashion similar to the muscles of the thenar eminence.

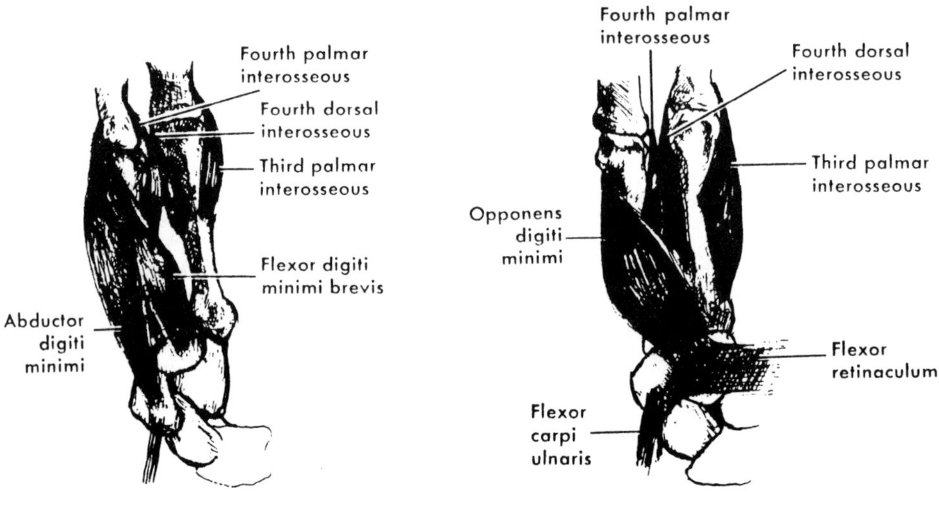

BASIC STRUCTURE OF THE LOWER LIMB

The structure of the lower limb is somewhat analogous to that of the upper limb; however, modifications have been made through evolution that sacrifice the mobility of the upper limb to give greater stability to the lower. The pelvic bones, and indeed all the bones of the lower limb, are more massive than the shoulder girdle and arm bones by virtue of the function of weight bearing.

The hip joint is extremely well supported by ligaments, and the basic bone structure of the pelvis is vaguely similar to that of the shoulder girdle except that the bones are fused to give greater stability. The hip bone consists of three bones, the ilium, ischium and pubis, that join in the acetabulum to form the deep socket that contains the head of the femur (Fig. 6.18A and B). This ball-and-socket joint, the hip joint, is reinforced by a capsule and three broad, strong

Figure 6.18 A, The pelvis distributes the body weight to the supporting columns of the legs. **B,** Lateral view of the pelvis. Note the fusion at the acetabulum of the three bones—the ilium, ischium, and pubis.

A

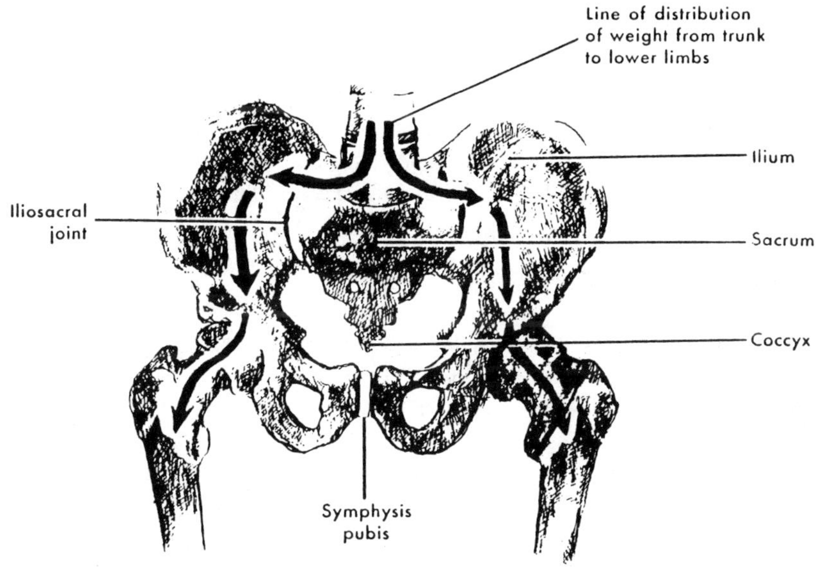

B

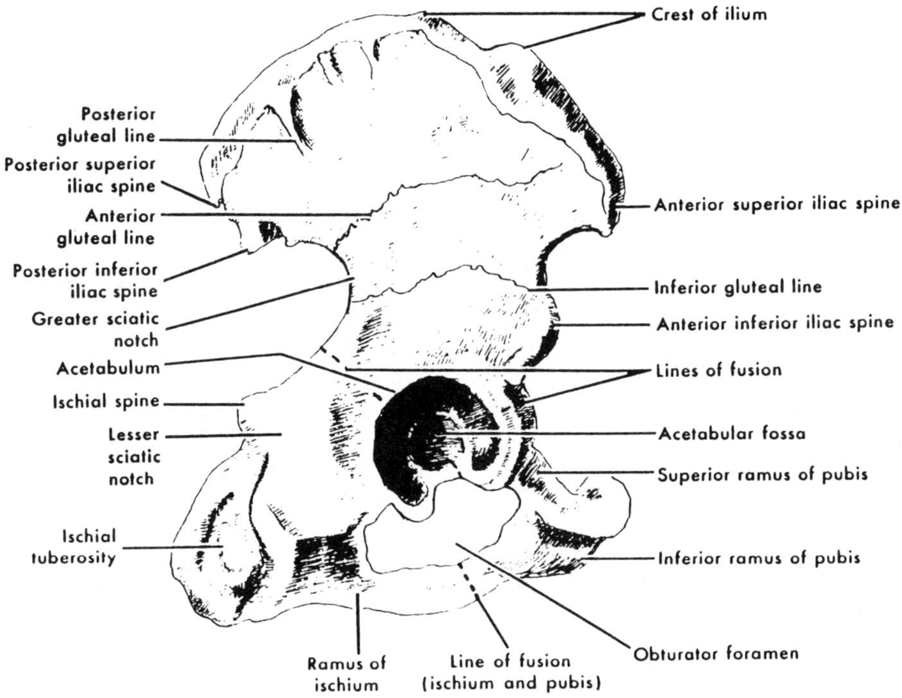

ligaments. Its movements are rather restricted in comparison to those of the shoulder joint.

Movement at the Hip Joint

The movements of the hip are flexion (bringing the knee to the chest), extension (taking the knee back as far as possible), abduction (raising the limb laterally), adduction (squeezing the legs together), lateral rotation (turning the foot outward), and medial rotation (turning the foot inward).

Ligaments of the Hip Joint

The three strong ligaments of the hip are the iliofemoral, pubofemoral, and ischiofemoral. The iliofemoral is the most important; it prevents overextension. The pubofemoral prevents overabduction, and the ischiofemoral prevents overadduction.

When a person is standing at rest, the centre of gravity pulls downward posterior to the hip joint. The joint is held in extension by the force of gravity, therefore, and the burden is taken by the iliofemoral ligament. Since ligaments have no contractile powers, holding the hip joint steady does not expend any caloric energy; yet this function is carried on for hours daily.

Musculature of the Hip

Gluteal Muscles

Study of the muscles of the hip and lower limb usually begins with the buttocks. There are three separate gluteal muscles, the gluteus maximus, gluteus medius, and gluteus minimus (Fig. 6.19). The gluteus maximus may be compared somewhat to the deltoid of the shoulder. The gluteus maximus is a large coarse-grained muscle (making it suitable for injections) originating on the crest of the ilium and the sacrum and inserting into a tuberosity on the femur as well as into the fascia of the lateral aspect of the leg, the fascia lata. Its major function is to extend the hip. This movement is normally that of stretching the leg posteriorly; however, if the legs are held fast, the trunk may be extended, at least in part, by the gluteus maximus. This is the position used for chest raises, an exercise. The gluteus maximus is not needed in the act of walking on level ground, but climbing stairs, jumping, sprinting, etc., all require strong contraction of the gluteus maximus. The final action of the gluteus maximus is external rotation of the femur. The muscle is innervated by the inferior gluteal nerve.

Figure 6.19 Muscles of the posterior compartment of the thigh, glutei, and lateral rotators.

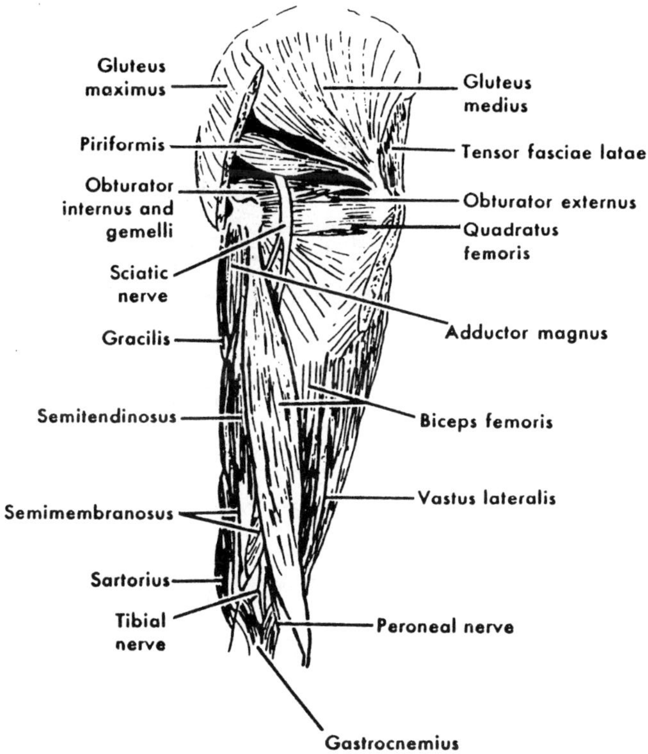

The two smaller gluteal muscles, the medius and minimus, underlie the maximus, sharing the winglike spread of the ilium as their origins. They insert into the greater trochanter of the femur. Their special function is concerned with walking. When a step is taken, one side of the body is unsupported for a short period. The smaller glutei in the *opposite* hip contract and thus prevent the unsupported side from falling or sagging. In a sense, the two smaller gluteal muscles abduct the trunk away from the unsupported side. In addition, the gluteus medius and minimus rotate the femur medially and abduct it. They are innervated by the superior gluteal nerve.

Lateral Rotators. While the gluteus medius and minimus medially rotate the thigh (because of the "offset" head of the femur and the forward-facing acetabulum), the maximus assists a group of very small muscles to laterally rotate the thigh. These muscles of lateral rotation, in descending order from superior to inferior, are the piriformis, gemellus superior, obturator internus, gemellus inferior, obturator externus, and quadratus femoris (Fig. 6.19 and 6.20).

Figure 6.20 Lateral rotators of the femur. Note that the obturator externus runs behind the head and neck of the femur to reach the greater trochanter.

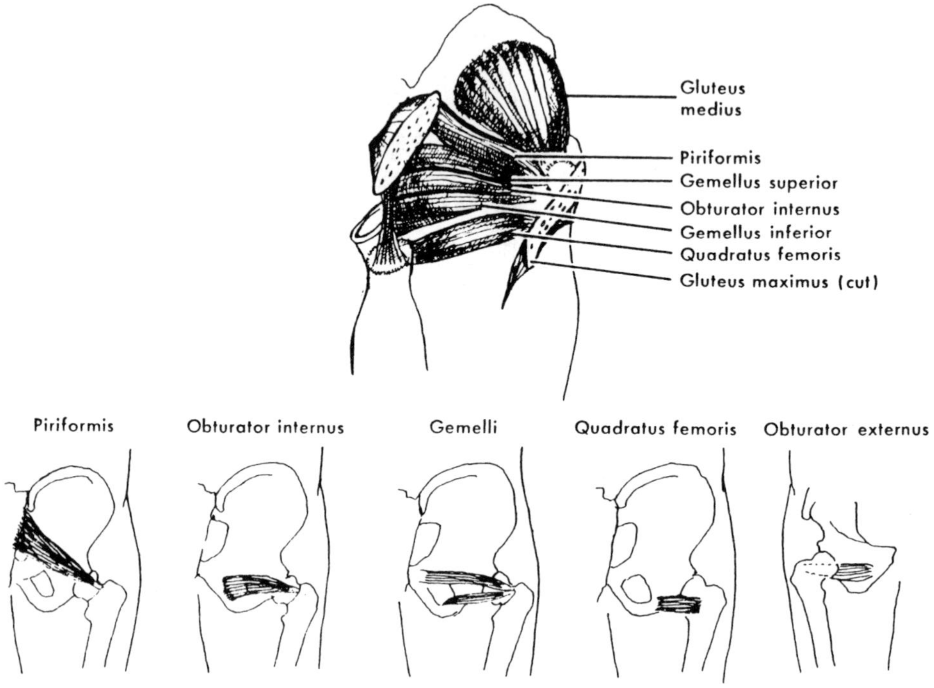

All originate somewhere on the ilium or ischium and insert on the greater trochanter deep under the two smaller glutei. The quadratus femoris inserts onto the shaft of the femur just inferior to the greater trochanter. They are innervated by nerves from L-4 to S-2.

The lateral rotators are quite small, relatively speaking, compared to the other muscles of the hip and so are of less significance than the rotator cuff muscles of the shoulder to which they distantly relate. To understand their relationship it is necessary to form a three-dimensional concept of their position. The obturator externus, for example, originates on the obturator membrane (*obturator* means "plug" or "stopper") on the outer surface and proceeds backward and laterally to its insertion on the inside of the greater trochanter.

The major hip flexor opposing the extension of the gluteus maximus is a compound muscle called the iliopsoas. The psoas major muscle originates on all five lumbar vertebrae and runs through the pelvis where it joins with the iliacus to form a common tendon that inserts on the lesser trochanter (Fig. 6.21). As it passes over the brim of the superior pubic ramus, the iliopsoas makes a sharp, nearly right-angled, turn backward to its destination. This gives the muscle a certain mechanical advantage much like a rope running over a pulley. The psoas is important in hip flexion. If the legs are held down, the trunk can be flexed by the action of the ilipsoas—but at risk to the lumbar vertebrae. It is worth noting that, for this reason, all sit-ups should be done with bent knees to prevent injury to the lumbar spine. The iliopsoas is innervated by nerves from L-1 to L-5.

Figure 6.21 The psoas and iliacus have a common tendon of insertion to the lesser trochanter. The pectineus arises from the superior ramus of the pubis, and the adductor magnus and gracilis arise from the inferior ramus.

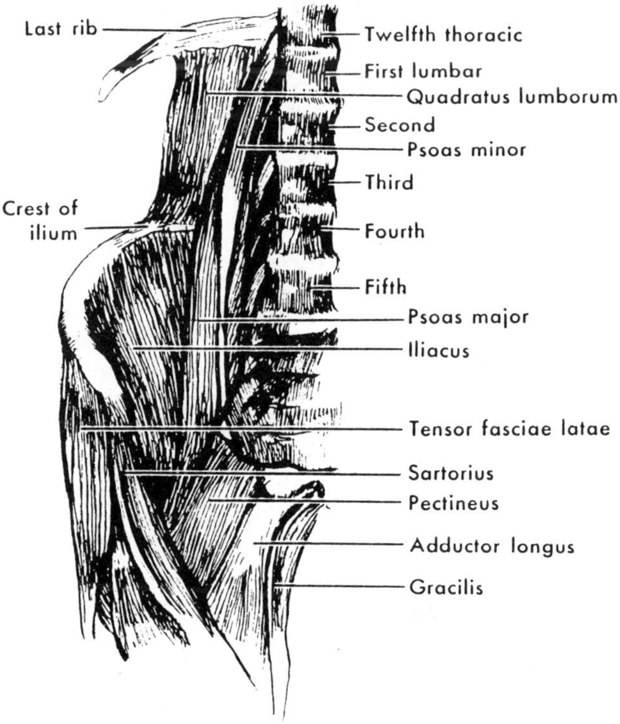

The tensor fascia latae is generally included with the gluteal muscles because it is innervated by the superior gluteal nerve. Arising from the anterior superior iliac spine, it inserts into the iliotibial tract, a broad sheet of tough fascia that attaches to the fascia below the knee.

Figure 6.21 (con't) The rectus femoris crosses two joints. The reflected, or posterior, head arises from the rim of the acetabulum.

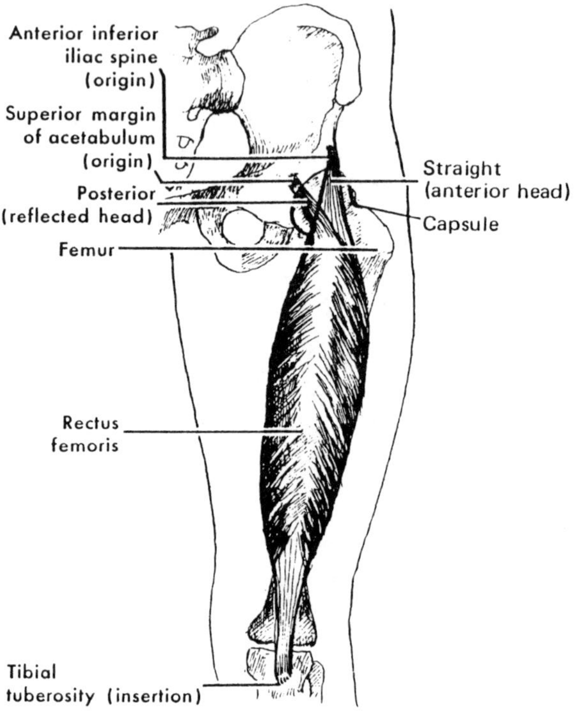

Muscles of the Anterior Compartment of the Thigh

The components of the quadriceps femoris are the bulkiest muscles in the body; as the name implies, there are four, the largest of which is the vastus lateralis. Accompanying this group in the anterior compartment is the sartorius, which is the longest muscle in the body. All the muscles of this compartment are innervated by the femoral nerve.

The muscles of the anterior compartment are, from lateral to medial, the vastus lateralis, vastus intermedius, rectus femoris, and vastus medialis, which comprise the quadriceps femoris, and the sartorius (Fig. 6.22 and 6.23). Only two of the group are two-jointed muscles—the rectus femoris and the sartorius. All the others originate on the femur and insert just below the knee joint on the tibia. The principal function of the quadriceps is to extend the knee. Thus, these muscles are very important in all forms of locomotion—e.g., walking, running, swimming,—as well as in jumping, lifting, etc. The rectus femoris, which

Figure 6.22 Quadriceps, anterior view. Note the sartorius running diagonally across the three visible muscles of the quadriceps: the vastus lateralis, rectus femoris, and vastus medialis.

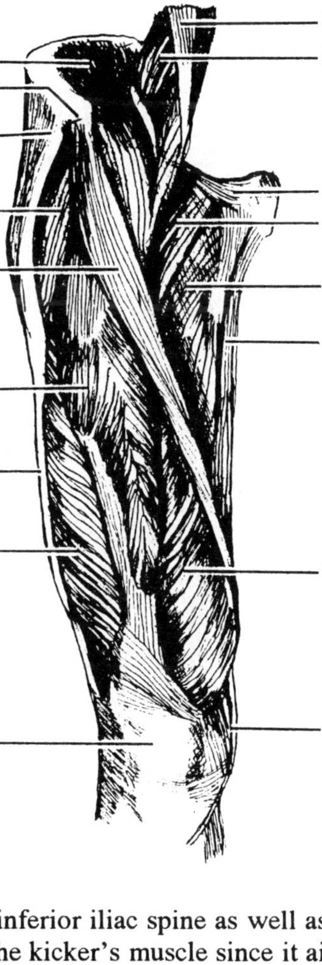

originates on the anterior inferior iliac spine as well as on the upper rim of the acetabulum, is known as the kicker's muscle since it aids in knee extension and hip flexion.

The components of the quadriceps have a common tendon that encases a sesamoid bone, the patella or knee cap. After passing the patella, the tendon is known as the patellar ligament, and it inserts at the tibial tuberosity.

Because of the size and strength of the quadriceps, it is not unusual, in adolescents who are very active in sports, for the muscles to pull loose a portion of the tibia to which they are attached. The tibial tuberosity is a growth centre and, until it becomes completely ossified or bony, it can be damaged by the strong contraction of the "quads," whose maturity may have outstripped that of the skeleton. This condition is known as Osgood-Schlatter's disease.

Figure 6.23 Horizontal section of the midthigh, showing the three compartments, their muscles, and one major nerve in the posterior compartment.

1–Vastus lateralis
2–Vastus intermedius
3–Vastus medialis
4–Rectus femoris
5–Biceps femoris
6–Semitendinosus
7–Semimembranosus
8–Sciatic nerve
9–Adductor magnus
10–Gracilis
11–Adductor longus
12–Sartorius

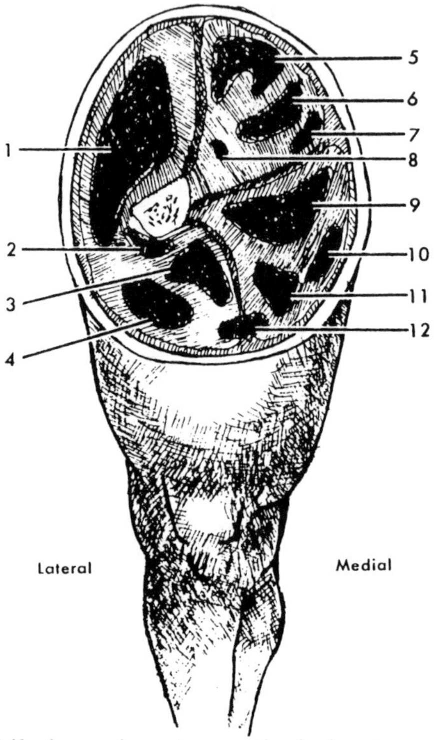

The sartorius, while long, is not a particularly strong muscle. It is used chiefly to flex the hip and knee as in assuming a cross-legged sitting position such as tailors once used (sartorius means "tailor").

The bulky vastus lateralis in well-developed individuals projects both laterally and anteriorly. The vastus medialis is the only one of the group with fibres pulling medially. A strong medialis is important for stability of the knee. It is used only in the last 15 degrees of extension; thus, if one walks with a limp, the medialis may not be used and it will atrophy. This atrophy and subsequent weakness will then affect the stability of knee joint.

The majority of the fibres of the quadriceps run upward and laterally following the 10° offset of the femur. They therefore tend to pull the patella somewhat laterally. As a result, most dislocations of the patella are in a lateral direction.

Muscles of the Posterior Compartment of the Thigh

The muscles of the posterior compartment are innervated by the sciatic nerve, of which there are two major motor branches—the common peroneal and the tibial. The latter is the more widespread.

The muscles of this compartment are also called hamstrings. They are important in flexing the knee and extending the hip. When the leg and thigh are held, they extend the trunk. Except for the short head of the biceps femoris, which originates on the femur, they have a common origin on the ischial tuberosity. If the knee is fully flexed, the hamstrings are so shortened that they cannot act on the hip to extend it. Similarly, if the hip is fully extended, the hamstrings cannot flex the knee.

The hamstrings comprise the long head and short head of the biceps femoris; the semitendinosus; and the semimembranosus (Fig. 6.22 and 6.23). The biceps inserts on the head of the fibula and makes up the lateral aspect of the popliteal (knee) space. The semitendinosus and semimembranosus are medial and can be felt on the medial side of the popliteal space. The tendons are easily palpable behind the knee joint in a person sitting with feet flat who rises the heel while pressing down with the toe of the same foot.

The semitendinosus sits atop the semimembranosus and inserts into the medial aspect of the tibia. It is rather undistinguished as a muscle. Its "cousin," the semimembranosus (as its name implies, it is approximately one-half membrane) has a rather novel insertion; a superficial portion is reflected upward and laterally to become the oblique popliteal ligament running from the posterior medial aspect of the tibia to the lateral condyle of the femur. The deep part of the tendon attaches to the medial condyle of the tibia, and a short slip attaches to the tubercle just below.

The short head of the biceps arises from the linea aspera and from the lateral intermuscular septum separating it from the vastus lateralis. The biceps femoris inserts on the head of the fibula.

Muscles of the Medial Compartment of the Thigh

The muscles of the medial compartment are innervated by the obturator nerve and comprise the pectineus, adductor longus, adductor brevis, adductor magnus, gracilis, and obturator externus (included with the gluteal group) (Figs. 6.22 and 6.23).

Essentially the action of the muscles of the medial compartment is to adduct or draw the legs together. Anatomists of old referred to the gracilis as the "guardian of virginity." It is a weak muscle. The obturator nerve exits from the trunk via the obturator foramen, divides into two branches (anterior and posterior), and supplies all the muscles of the medial compartment. In addition to the obturator, the sciatic nerve (tibial portion) supplies part of the adductor magnus. The pectineus, being "fickle," sometimes is supplied by the obturator and at other times by the femoral.

Generally the muscles of this compartment arise somewhere on the inferior aspect of the pelvis and insert on the medial or posterior shaft of the femur. The pectineus (comb-like) assists in crossing the legs, an action that is a combination of flexion and adduction.

The adductor magnus, the largest of the group, has two portions. The upper portion, whose fibres run obliquely adducts the thigh. The lower portion, whose fibres run more vertically, extends the thigh. Only the gracilis in this group is a two-joint muscle, arising as it does from the ramus of the pubis and inserting into the medial shaft of the tibia.

The gracilis, sartorius, and semitendinosus (one muscle from each compartment) have a special combined insertion called the pes anserinus ("goose's foot") on the medial-anterior aspect of the tibia. Athletes and others who suffer damage to the medial ligaments of the knee often have this common insertion lifted and moved surgically. The increased tension in the muscles gives the support of dynamic ligaments to the knee. Since they are from separate compartments, any imbalance is rather insignificant.

The Knee Joint

The knee joint (Fig. 6.24) is probably the most vulnerable of all the joints in the body. Despite having strong collateral ligaments, the joint is susceptible to injury because of its mechanical structure and the uses and strains to which it is subject.

Being for the most part a hinge joint, with only a limited amount of medial and lateral rotation possible, the knee suffers when rotational forces act on it. This occurs when a person changes direction quickly while running or simply slips on a patch of ice. Any such force is compounded, of course, by the fact that the knee joint supports the body weight. In addition, there are two semicircular wedges of cartilage called menisci inside the joint that can be damaged and that deteriorate with age. They, too, cause knee problems.

Movement at the Knee Joint

The basic movements are extension (provided by the quadriceps), flexion (provided by the hamstrings plus additional muscles of the leg), lateral rotation (provided by the biceps femoris), and medial rotation (provided by the semitendinosus and semimembranosus).

Figure 6.24 The knee joint is supported by several ligaments, a capsule, and several tendons. Note the position of the menisci.

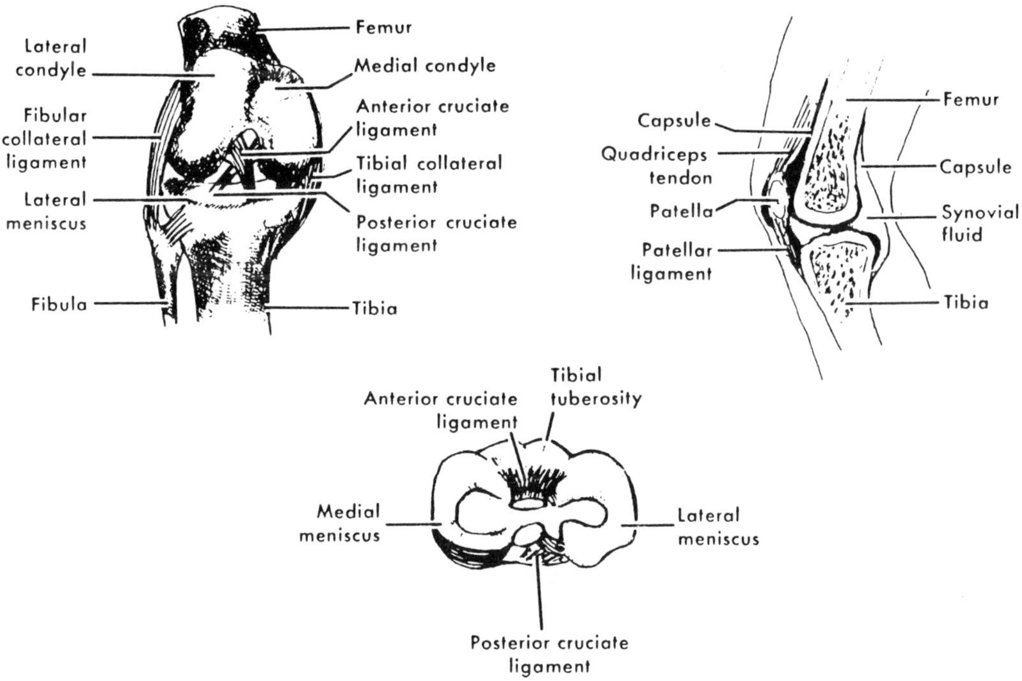

Ligaments of Knee Joint

The four strong ligaments of the knee joint are the lateral and the medial collateral, the cruciate (inside the knee joint), and the oblique popliteal (at the posterior aspect).

When a person is standing at rest, the centre of gravity pulls downward anterior to the knee joint, thus holding it in extension. In this position (knee locked) the ligaments provide most support. They provide least support when the knee is flexed. Because of incongruities between the surfaces of the tibia and femur, the femur normally rotates medially a few degrees when the knee is fully extended while a person is standing. (This does not occur in walking and running.) This action "locks" the knee, and there is a special muscle, the popliteus, that "unlocks" the knee by rotating the femur laterally before the knee is flexed. It is significant to note that, if the knee is extended while a person is sitting, the knee will lock; however, in a non-weight-bearing situation the tibia rotates laterally, instead of the femur rotating medially. This situation occurs during rehabilitative exercises.

Musculature of the Leg

The leg is the portion of the lower limb below the knee. It is divided into three compartments that are separated by septa of tough fascia and innervated by three distinct nerves (Fig. 6.25). The actions of the muscles provide movement at the knee, the ankle, and the foot.

Figure 6.25 Compartments of the leg. The fascial septa divide the leg into three compartments. This section is taken about midcalf and will not show the peroneus tertius.

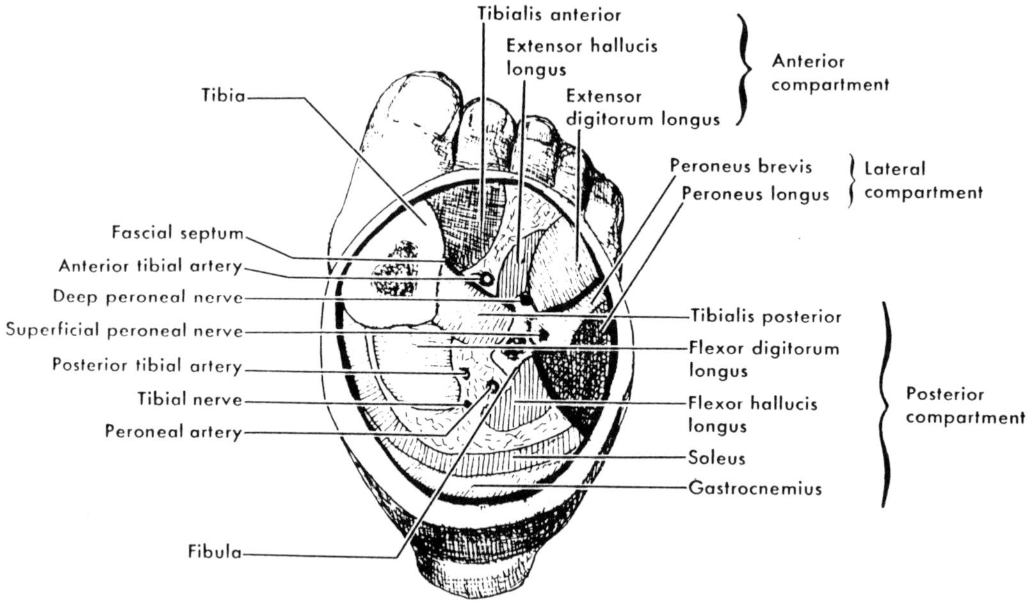

Muscles of the Anterior Compartment

The anterior compartment has three muscles that lie between the lateral aspect of the tibia and the fibula: the tibialis anterior, extensor hallucis longus, and extensor digitorum longus, part of which is the peroneus tertius (Fig. 6.26).

The muscles of this compartment are innervated by the deep peroneal (anterior tibial) nerve and act principally to dorsiflex the foot—that is, to pull the toes and foot toward the face. The tibialis anterior also helps invert the foot, while the extensor digitorum everts the foot.

Figure 6.26 A, Tibialis anterior. **B,** Extensor digitorum longus. The enlargement shows the tendons passing under the two portions of the extensor retinaculum.

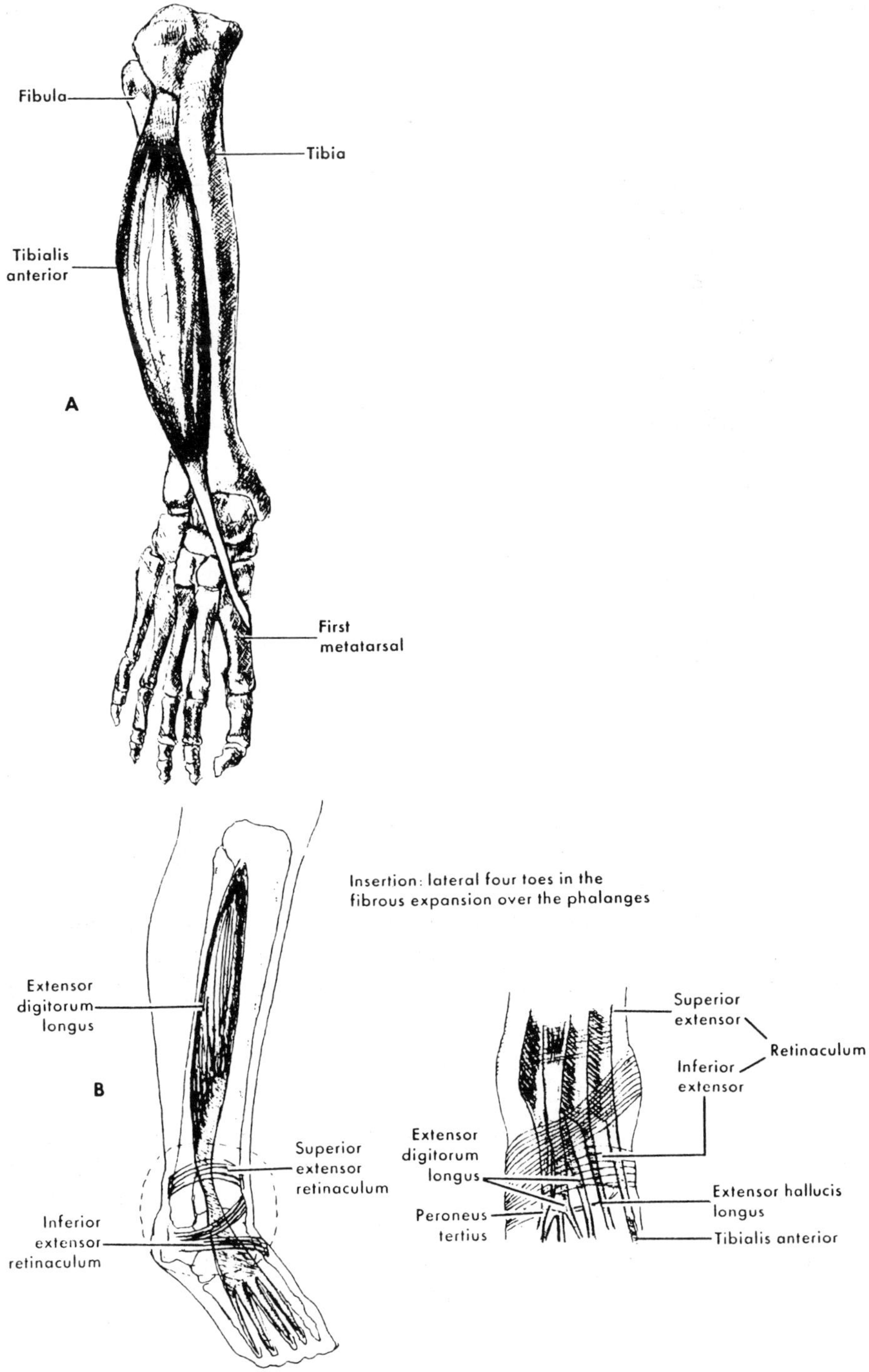

Figure 6.26 (con't) Triceps surae. The plantaris is not considered one of the triceps surae. The name triceps arises from the two heads of origin of the gastrocnemius and the deeper lying soleus. The muscles share a common tendon, the Achilles tendon.

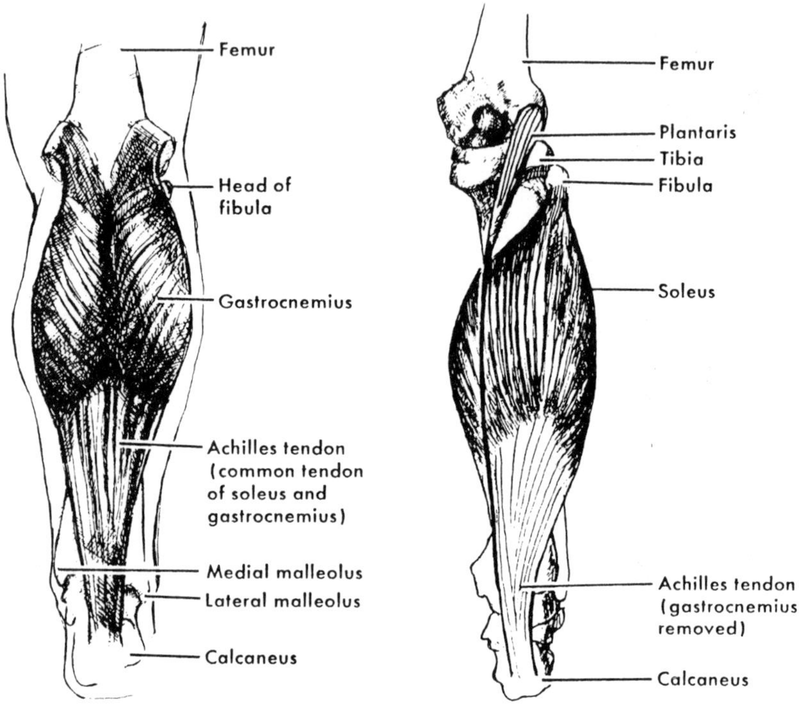

These muscles originate from the tibia and the interosseous membrane and insert well down on the foot. They are extrinsic muscles of the foot.

The tibia is triangular to provide a solid flat surface for muscle origin. The sharp edge of the shin bone can be palpated quite readily. It is vulnerable to damage such as "barking" and also to "splints." This condition occurs in association with hard running on a hard surface, especially after a long layoff.

Muscles of the Lateral Compartment

The lateral compartment contains only two muscles, the peroneus longus and peroneus brevis (Fig. 6.26), and is innervated by the superficial peroneal nerve. The muscles lie between the anterior and posterior septa lateral to the fibula.

The longus, as its name implies, is the longer of the two. It runs behind the lateral malleolus (little hammer) of the ankle, diagonally across the sole of the foot to the first metatarsal. It can thus act to plantar flex (point the toes) the foot and to evert it. The peroneus brevis inserts on the opposite side of the foot on the fifth metatarsal and does not cross the foot. It is responsible for eversion only. Eversion of the foot is important in walking as it helps the toes clear the ground when the foot is swung forward.

Figure 6.27 Ligaments of the ankle.

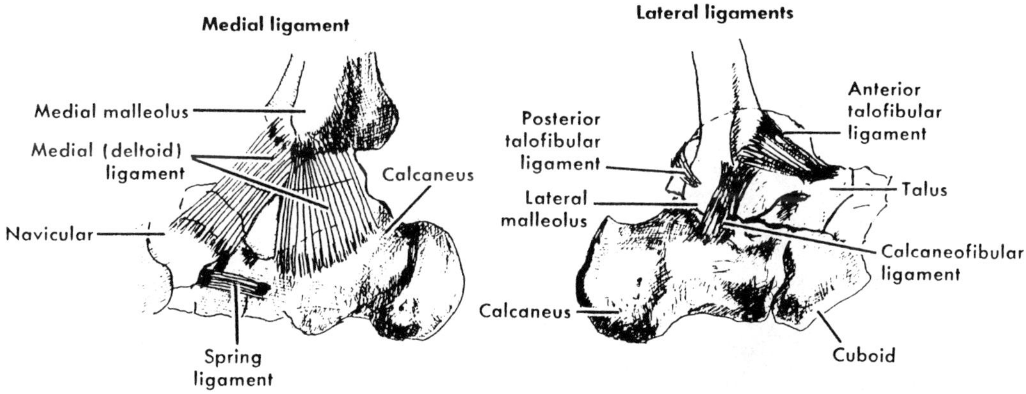

Figure 6.27 (con't) The fit of the tibia and fibula over the talus creates the ankle joint.

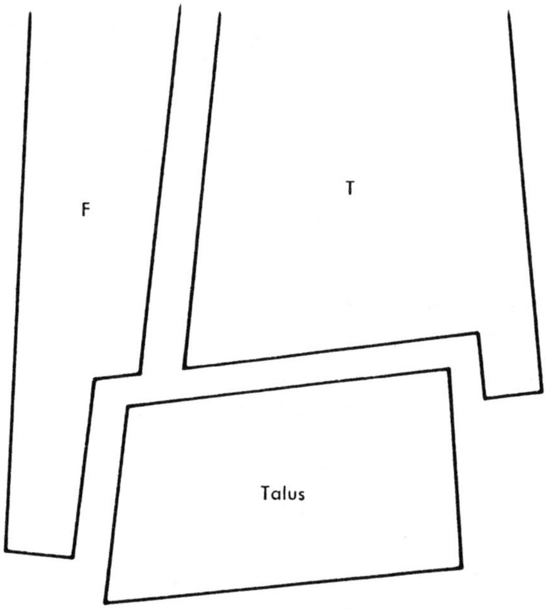

Figure 6.27 (con't) Sole of the right foot. The long plantar ligament should not be confused with the plantar aponeurosis (the latter does, however, offer some support to the arch). The three ligaments, long, short, and spring ligaments, are also supported by wide tendinous insertions of some muscles such as the tibialis posterior shown here on the plantar view of a right foot.

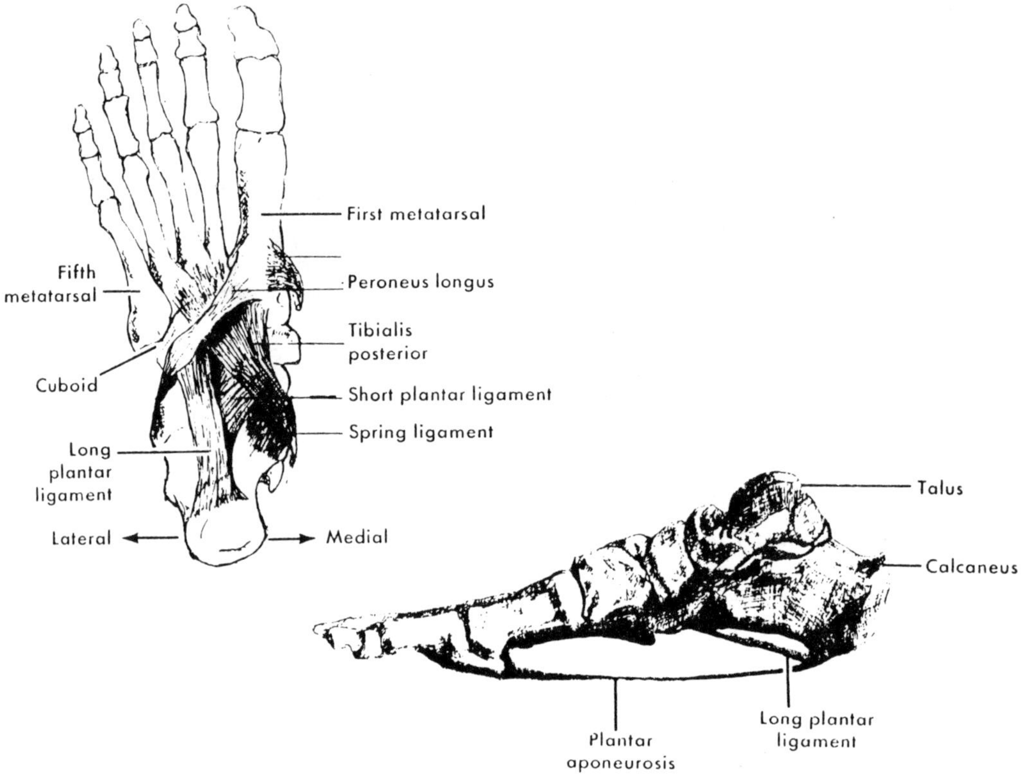

Muscles of the Posterior Compartment

The posterior compartment, innervated by the posterior tibial nerve, is the largest of the three groups. Since the primary function of this group is plantar flexion against the full body weight as a class 3 lever, it develops into a powerful group of muscles. The muscles in the compartment are the gastrocnemius, soleus (Fig. 6.26), plantaris, popliteus, flexor digitorum longus, flexor hallucis longus, and tibialis posterior (Fig. 6.26).

The two heads of the gastrocnemius and the soleus together form the triceps surae; its tendon of insertion, easily palpable at the posterior of the ankle, is the tendo calcaneus or Achilles tendon. The triceps surae is important in walking, dancing, running, etc.

Since the gastrocnemius is a two-joint muscle, it flexes the knee as well as plantar flexes the foot; however, it cannot do both simultaneously. If the knee is fully extended, the lengthened gastrocnemius tends to pull the foot into plantar flexion and vice versa.

The plantaris is analogous to the palmaris longus of the forearm. It has little function and is often used by plastic surgeons for replacement of material elsewhere in the body.

The popliteus, as its name implies, is a muscle of the knee. Its specific function is to unlock the extended knee. Since it is a knee flexor, it contracts at the start of flexion. At the same time it rotates the femur laterally at the start of the flexion movement.

The flexor digitorum longus, as its name implies, plantar flexes the toes and, since it crosses the ankle joint, plantar flexes the foot, also.

The flexor hallucis longus functions in a manner similar to the flexor digitorum longus, but, of course, it is inserted on the great toe.

The tibialis posterior is the deepest muscle of this compartment; it passes behind the medial malleolus to insert on eight of the bones of the foot. The tibialis posterior is the major inverter of the foot and also acts as a dynamic ligament for the arch of the foot.

The Ankle Joint

The ankle joint is a hinge joint involving the tibia, fibula, and talus. The major weight-bearing component is the talotibial joint. All the remaining movements of the foot are found in subtalar joints. The movements of inversion and eversion are very important in walking on uneven ground, since they permit the body to remain upright and steady while the subtalar joints make all the adjustments to the terrain.

The two malleoli (Fig. 6.28) clamp the talus between them and act as pulleys, giving mechanical advantage to the muscles of the posterior and lateral compartment passing behind them. The talus itself is wedge shaped, being wider in front than behind and convex from front to back. This shape facilitates the hinge action and also makes the joint solid in dorsiflexion and much looser in plantar flexion.

There is a vast web of ligaments holding the seven tarsal bones in position (Fig. 6.27). Among the more significant are the medial and lateral collateral ligaments of the ankle joint—the large deltoid ligament on the medial side joining the medial malleolus to the navicular, calcaneus, and talus—and the lateral series of ligaments—the calcaneofibular and the anterior and posterior talofibular ligaments. The majority of ankle injuries are to the lateral side, partly because of the weaker lateral structures of the joint.

Figure 6.28 First layer (superficial) of muscles of the sole of the foot.

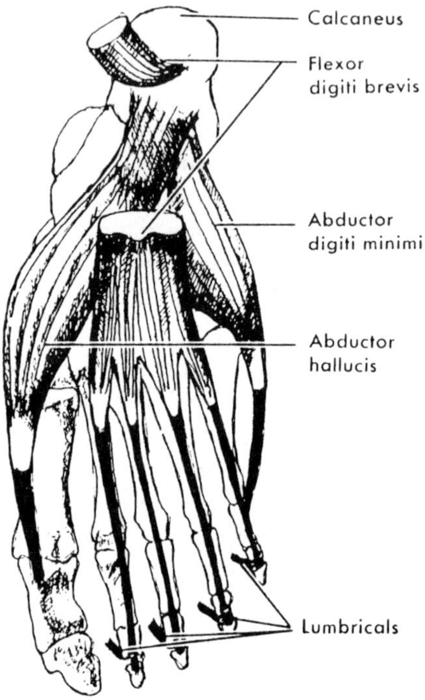

Musculature of the Foot

The foot, although analogous to the hand, does not have the mobility or dexterity of the hand. The muscles can be dealt with in less detail since they contribute as groups to locomotion rather than individually to discrete functions as do the muscles in the hand.

On the dorsal (extensor) surface there is only one muscle, the extensor digitorum brevis. It has little discrete function and assists the extensor digitorum longus. With a sprained ankle, the foot is often everted, causing the muscle to contract. This contraction is often mistakenly diagnosed as swelling of the ankle.

The muscles of the plantar surface are generally considered in four layers (Fig. 6.28). The unique feature of these muscles is that they act in close harmony with the heavy ligaments that hold the arch of the foot. In a normal foot the ligaments bear the load and preserve the arch in a quiet standing position. During activity the foot muscles, including some of the extrinsic muscles, especially the peroneus longus and tibialis posterior (the cross-strap

Figure 6.28 (con't) Second layer of muscles of the sole of the foot.

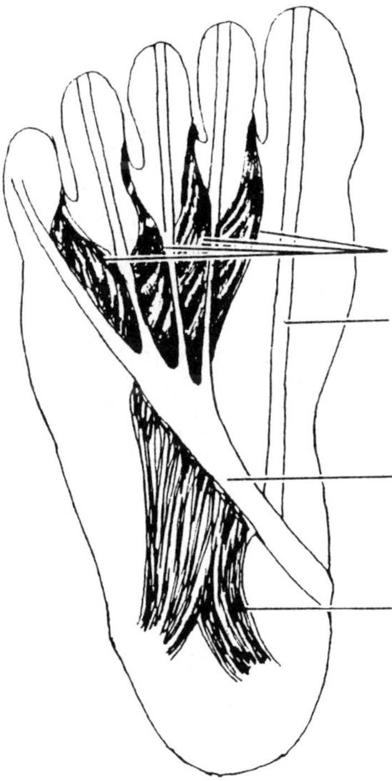

muscles, so called because they come from opposite direction and cross deep on the sole of the foot), contract not only to provide locomotion but to aid the ligaments in maintaining the arch of the foot.

The muscle groups or layers of the foot are considered from superficial to deep:

1. Abductor hallucis, flexor digitorum brevis, abductor digiti minimi
2. Quadratus plantae, lumbricales, and long tendons of extrinsic muscles
3. Flexor hallucis brevis, adductor hallucis, flexor digiti minimi brevis
4. Interossei and long tendons of extrinsic muscles

The muscles are innervated by the medial and lateral plantar nerves. The one unique muscle in the sole of the foot is the quadratus plantae, or flexor accessorius, which arises in the calcaneus and inserts into the tendon of the flexor digitorum longus. The quadratus plantae straightens the pull of the diagonally placed flexor digitorum longus.

Figure 6.28 (con't) Third layer of muscles of the sole of the foot.

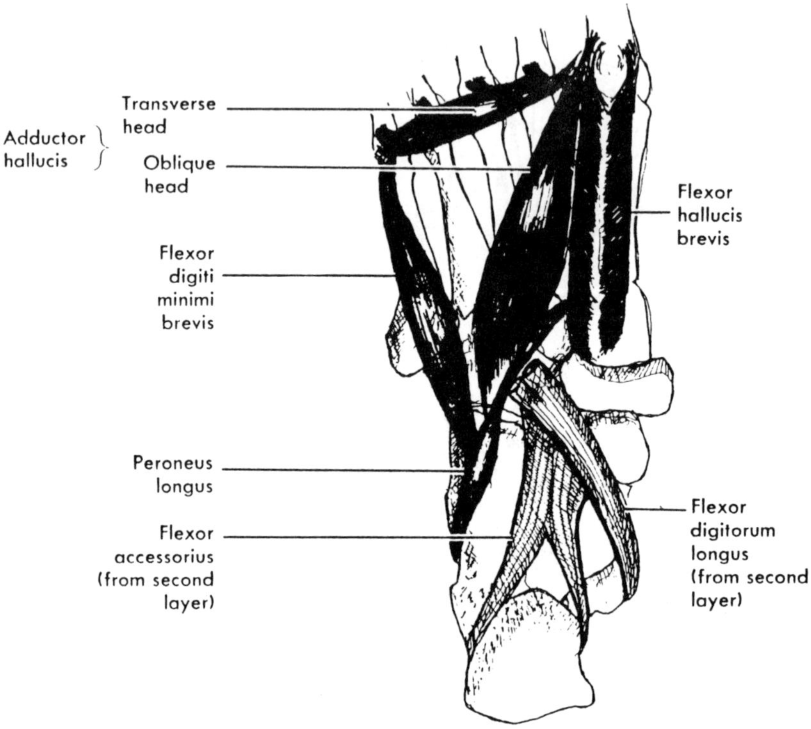

IMPLICATIONS FOR GENERAL EDUCATION

The study of the structure and function of the human body is central to a good general education, especially if one views that education as a means to enhance the quality of life. there is no doubt that an understanding of the body and its workings is a subject that each one lives with daily. Accurate knowledge of the body permits one to make decisions that are appropriate in regard to diet, dress, exercise, general health, etc. Additionally, a better grasp of many other subjects is held by those with a background in anatomy. In psychology, for example, one area of study is motor learning. A more complete understanding of that area of study is possible by those with a background in anatomy.

Figure 6.28 (con't) Fourth layer of muscles of the foot—the interossei. **A,** Plantar. **B,** Dorsal.

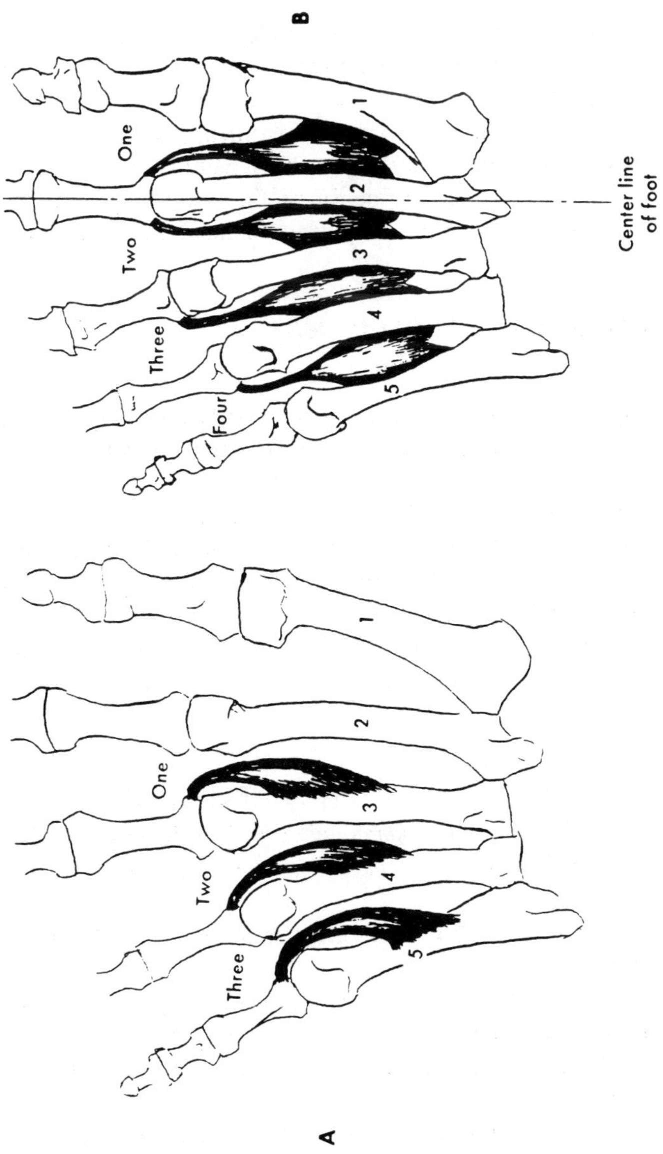

IMPLICATIONS FOR PROFESSIONAL PRACTICE

For anyone interested in a career in physical education and sport, a study of human mechanical and muscular function is mandatory. How could a study of *physical* education not include a study of how the human body works? Certainly, all biomechanical analysis, treatment and prevention of injuries, physiology, coaching, and other topics bear heavily on a basic knowledge of bodily function. In a sense, the study of the body is central to the study of virtually all other subdisciplines of physical education and sport.

PROFESSIONAL OPPORTUNITIES

The opportunities to pursue a career in physical education and sport in the subdiscipline involved with the functioning of the human body are on a par with other subdisciplines. There is great potential in the areas of physical education, coaching, biomechanics, athletic injuries treatment, and the like for those with a sound background in human mechanical and muscular function.

The study of the human body is a fascinating field for it is one in which every student provides his own study specimens. A knowledge of one's own physical capacities and liabilities and of one's own structures and their functioning can be a never-ending source of wonderment.

REFERENCES

BASMAJIAN, J. (1967). *Muscles alive.* (2nd Ed.). Baltimore: Williams & Wilkins.

CROUCH, J. E. (1982). *Essential human anatomy.* Philadelphia: Lea & Febiger.

CROUCH, J. E. (1979). *Functional human anatomy.* (3rd Ed.). Philadelphia: Lea & Febiger.

GARDNER, E., GRAY, D., & O'RAHILLY, R. (1966). *Anatomy.* (2nd Ed.). Philadelphia: Saunders.

GARDNER, W. D., & OSBURN, W. A. (1973). *Structure of the human body.* (2nd Ed.). Philadelphia: Saunders.

GOSS, C. M., ED. (1973). *Gray's anatomy of the human body.* (29th Ed.). Philadelphia: Lea & Febiger.

HOLLINSHEAD, W. H., & JENKINS, D. B. (1981). *Functional anatomy of the limbs and back.* Philadelphia: Saunders.

LEESON, C., & LEESON, T. (1972). *Human structure.* Philadelphia: Saunders.

LEYSHON, G. (1974). *Programmed functional anatomy.* St. Louis: Mosby.

LOCKHART, R., HAMILTON, G., & FIFE, F. (1969). *Anatomy of the human body.* Philadelphia: Lippincott.

SKINNER, H. (1949). *The origin of medical terms.* Baltimore: Williams & Wilkins.

Chapter Seven

Biomechanics: The Mechanics of Human Movement

Marion J. L. Alexander

How is Michael Jordan able to give the impression that he is suspended in the air for an extended period of time during a jump shot? How is Steffi Graf able to serve a tennis ball at a speed over 40 metres per second (145 km/hr)? How is Roger Clemens able to throw a curve ball which can curve downward over 55 cm on the way to the plate? How is Katarina Witt able to perform a triple-twisting jump in figure skating, and land with perfect control? These feats of athleticism can all be explained by the laws of physics and mechanics which govern the motion of athletes and all other objects on earth. These sport biomechanics questions will be answered in detail at the end of the chapter, using some of these laws of mechanics which comprise the discipline of biomechanics.

A key perspective which is essential in the understanding of human movement is the study of biomechanics, or the physics and mechanics which govern the motion of the body, the body parts, and any object projected by the body. When the anatomy of the body has been learned, and the physiology of muscle contraction and nervous system operation have been understood, the student may then study biomechanics (Robertson, 1992). An understanding of anatomy and the structure of the human body, and the mechanisms which produce movement from study of physiology are essential to an understanding of biomechanics. Biomechanics is the application of mechanical principles to the study of the living body in motion and interacting with the environment.

WHY STUDY BIOMECHANICS?

Biomechanical analysis will enable the teacher or coach to determine the sequence and timing of the major joint movements during the performance of a skill in sports or dance. Teachers and coaches are often concerned with the improvement of the technique of the athletes they are teaching, and an understanding of the biomechanical principles which govern all movements may assist in providing useful cues for improvement. Biomechanics is also important to engineers developing new athletic equipment for the prevention of athletic injuries, to health care professionals examining injury mechanics, and to rehabilitation specialists in designing assistive equipment for the disabled.

All skilled movements are produced by the contraction of skeletal muscles; so, the student must understand the mechanism by which muscle contractions combine to produce skilled movements. Since the muscles pull on the bones and act as simple lever systems in the process, a knowledge of the components of lever systems is important to understanding human movement. Since sports skills occur in very brief periods of time, special computerized filming and analysis equipment has been developed to record the details of these movements, the forces exerted, and the muscle actions as they occur (Hall, 1991). The knowledge of the bones, joints, and muscles which will be used in performing sport skills will enable the teacher or coach to more fully understand the techniques of these skills and to train the specific muscle groups used in the skill.

Most of the sports skills which are found being performed in the gymnasia and playing fields of today are developed from the basic skills of early man's survival: running, jumping, throwing, and swimming. Analysis of performance of sport skills, and correction of errors based on sound mechanical principles, are key skills which should be acquired by students of human movement. Scientists who work in biomechanics have studied many physical skills from a scientific perspective, and have produced research which suggests the optimal performance for athletes of a certain body size and strength in that skill (Torrey, 1984; Whieldon, 1979).

BIOMECHANICS AND KINESIOLOGY

The terms biomechanics and kinesiology are often used interchangeably in the description of this discipline within physical education which applies physics and mechanics to human motion analysis. The term kinesiology is the more general of the two, as it includes the study of the joints and muscles involved in movements, as well as the mechanical principles which govern the movement. Some first- and second-year courses in the scientific study of human movement in a physical education degree program may be described as kinesiology courses, since they cover more than pure mechanics. There are also a number of physical education departments in North America which are now called departments of kinesiology. The word kinesiology literally means the scientific study of human movement, or the science of motion (Gensemer, 1992). In this context, any program which includes the scientific study of human movement may be called a program of kinesiology.

The term biomechanics has a somewhat narrower definition, focusing on the principles of physics and mechanics which can be applied to movement analysis. The undergraduate course in biomechanics usually includes quantitative analysis of athletes and sports skills, in which calculation of quantities such as force, velocity, and acceleration are included. An attempt is made to explain why a movement happens and to describe the force-motion relationships.

TECHNOLOGY VS. VISUAL ANALYSIS OF SKILLS

The science of biomechanics has become a popular topic in the mass media. In recent years there have been many television programs and magazine articles describing the computerized analysis of human movements (Vizard, 1992). There are sophisticated computer systems which are used by biomechanists to analyze world-class athletes, and their performances can be simulated and altered by computerized analysis (Kluger, 1982; Torrey, 1984; Whieldon, 1979). The filmed performance of the athlete is analyzed frame by frame, by storing the location of each joint center in the computer. This process of storing video images as numbers, and the locations of the joints, is called digitizing (the process of changing images into digits). These computer systems are beyond the reach of most physical education professionals, but they can use the results of this research in their work. Knowledge of the results of research in the field of biomechanics can greatly assist the teacher or coach in improving the performance of their athletes or students.

The newest applications of computers to analyze athletes in motion are sophisticated computer programs to be used by coaches (Miller, Jones, & Pizzimenti, 1991; Sprigings, Watson, & Stilling, 1989). Computer programs are available which accept as input the video images from a video tape of an athlete, and these images can then be compared to digitized performances of these skills. These new athlete-analysis systems will be a useful addition to the tools used by coaches of elite athletes, as they do not require a biomechanics specialist to conduct the analysis. It may be that in the future this technology will reach the gymnasium, and then the physical education teacher will have the analysis programs available for regular class instruction.

The science of biomechanics has a substantial contribution to make to the training and subsequent effectiveness of physical education professionals, as well as for those in allied professions such as coaching, athletic therapy, fitness leadership, and physical therapy. Each of these fields requires biomechanics training and knowledge to be effective in understanding human movement, effective skill-learning, and athletic-injury mechanisms.

MECHANICS AND MOVEMENT

The science of biomechanics treats the human body as a machine, governed by the laws of physics and mechanics. The basic principles of mechanics are applied to the body as if it were an inanimate object, with motion produced by the actions of a series of simple machines (Kluger, 1982). The limb segments form a system of levers, the ends of the bones act as single fixed pulleys, and certain rotational movements of the head and trunk are produced by wheel and axle systems. The biomechanist views the athlete as a mechanical system, and the motion of the system is limited only by the length of the levers and the size of the muscles, as well as the timing and coordination of their firing patterns. Although physiological and psychological differences may affect performance, only the mechanical aspects of the movements are considered in a biomechanical analysis.

TYPES OF MUSCLE CONTRACTIONS

All human movement in physical education and athletics is produced by contraction of muscles, but all muscle contractions are not shortening contractions. The most familiar type of contraction is the shortening contraction, in which the active muscle group shortens to lift a weight or move a body part (Figure 7.1). Another very common type of muscle contraction is an eccentric contraction, in which the muscle lengthens while producing tension, so the weight is lowered with control. This type of contraction occurs during any downward or lowering movement of the body, as when landing from a jump, landing during a running stride, or sitting down in a chair. A third type of contraction is the isometric contraction, in which the muscle length does not change, but the muscle is producing tension. An example is during isometric exercises, in which the athlete pushes against an immovable object so the muscle length does not change, but the muscle is using energy and producing tension. Another type of contraction is one described on the basis of the speed of the contraction; this is a constant velocity contraction which can be either concentric or eccentric. This is the type of contraction seen in most modern strength-testing machines which are isokinetic dynamometers as they control the speed of the contraction being tested (Figure 7.2).

Figure 7.1 Types of muscle contractions which produce human movement: (1) isometric (no movement) contraction, (2) eccentric (lengthening) contraction and (3) concentric (shortening) contraction.

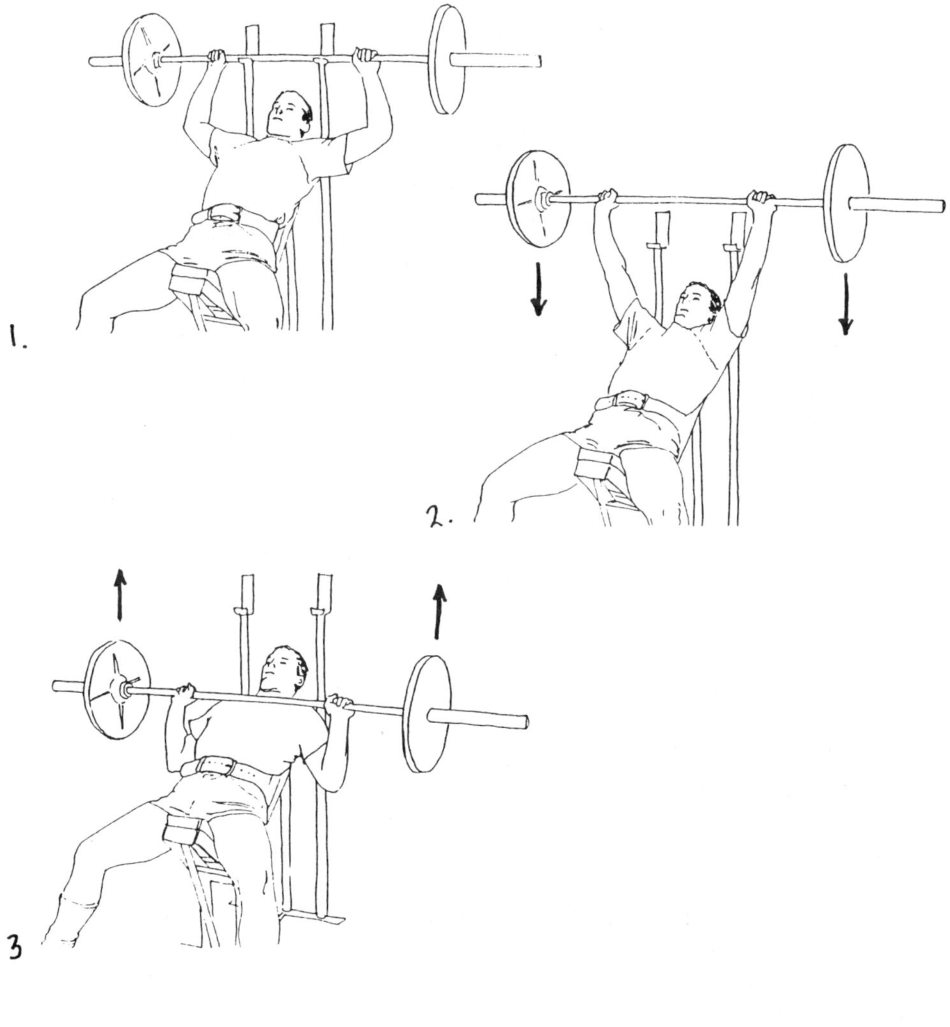

Figure 7.2 An isokinetic dynamometer used to test the strength of the knee extensors of an elite athlete.

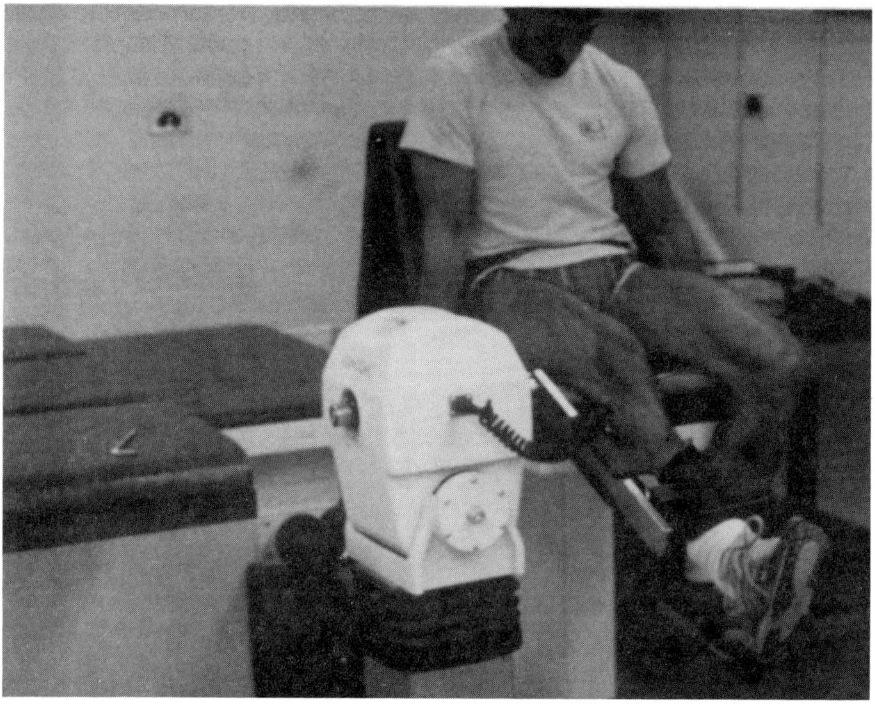

APPLICATION OF BIOMECHANICS TO MOTION ANALYSIS

Mass and Weight. The terms mass and weight are often used interchangeably, but they are quite different in mechanical terms. Mass is the quantity of matter in an object. It remains unchanged whether on the moon or on earth, as it does not change due to changes in gravity. An astronaut on the moon has the same mass as on the earth; so his or her mass would be 80 kg whether on the earth or on the moon (Hall, 1991) (Figure 7.3). The standard measure of mass is the mass of 1 litre of water, which is 1 kilogram. Mass is a measure of the resistance of an object to linear motion; so, the greater the mass is, the greater the resistance to movement.

Weight. Weight is a measure of the gravitational force acting on a mass; so, weight will change depending on the gravitational pull. The astronaut's weight is much less on the moon, because the force of gravity is much less (Figure 7.3). Weight is the mass in kilograms multiplied by the acceleration of

Figure 7.3 Although the body's mass remains unchanged on the moon, its weight is less due to the smaller acceleration of gravity, from (Hall, 1991).

gravity: **W = m g, where g = 9.81 m/s/s = 9.81 m/s²**. Weight is measured in Newtons force, where 1 Newton is the force required to accelerate a mass of 1 kilogram 9.81 m/sec². **Force (Newtons) = mass (kg) × g (9.81 m/sec²)** Weight is the force due to the attraction of gravity, and can be calculated as roughly the mass x 10 m/s² (actually 9.81 m/s²) to give Newtons force, e.g., an athlete with a mass of 120 kg, also has a weight of 120 kg × 10 m/s² = 1200 Newtons. When referring to the weight of an athlete, the more correct units to use are Newtons, which is the metric measure of weight. What is your weight in Newtons?

Mass. Mass is a measure of resistance to linear motion, and is measured in kilograms. The shot thrown by a male shot putter has a mass of almost 8 kg, a large resistance to linear motion. Moment of inertia is a measure of the resistance to angular movement, or resistance to movement in an angular pathway around an axis. The hammer has a great resistance to angular movement during the turns of the throw, due to both the mass of the hammer and the length of the wire handle and the arms of the thrower.

Moment of Inertia. Moment of inertia is slightly more complex to calculate than mass, since it includes both the mass of the object, and the distribution of the mass around the axis of rotation. The formula to calculate moment of inertia (I) is mass (m) times distance to axis squared (d^2): **($I = m\ d^2$)**. In the diagram of a golf club below (Figure 7.4), the moment of inertia is the sum of product of the mass of each of the segments of the golf club, times the distance of each from the axis through the hands. As the golf clubs increase in length (9-iron to driver), and the mass of each of the sections of the club increase, the moment of inertia increases. The resistance to angular motion also increases; so, it takes more force from the golfer to swing the longer club, or the one with a greater mass.

Figure 7.4 The moment of inertia of a golf club is determined by summing the mass × $radius^2$ of each section of the club: $\Sigma\ I = m\ r^2$.

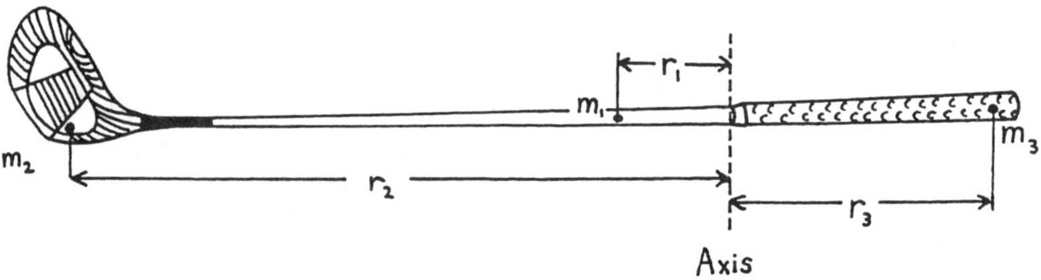

The concept of moment of inertia is of considerable importance in the skill of batting, since the standard wooden bat used in the major leagues is 91 cm (36 inches) long and weighs 992 g (35 ounces) (Brancazio, 1984). This mass and length gives the bat a very high moment of inertia, or a very great resistance to be swung at a high speed. A more ideal bat weight is 567 g (20 oz). A solid wooden bat of 91 cm length will always weigh more than the ideal, but a 20 oz bat of any reasonable thickness would be too short. The problem with most major league batters is that the standard bat is too heavy for most players to swing at the optimal speed, and the slower swing takes longer to complete. Some major league batters tried to solve the problem by hollowing out the center of their wooden bats and filling in the hollow core with cork. This would weigh much less and decrease the resistance to swinging (Brancazio, 1984). This alteration allowed batters to bring the lighter bat around to the ball much more quickly, but unfortunately it was an illegal alteration, and the batters were disqualified for their use.

The concept of moment of inertia also applies to athletes attempting to rotate around their own axes of rotation. A gymnast has less resistance to rotation around her longitudinal axis (twisting axis) than to rotation around her anterior posterior axis (cartwheeling axis). It is possible to quantify the moment of inertia by multiplying the mass of each body part times its distance to the axis of rotation, and it has been estimated that the moment of inertia is 12 times greater around the anterior posterior axis than the longitudinal axis (Hay, 1993). It is also notable that top female gymnasts are usually very short in stature, with a relatively small mass, as this will give them a lower moment of inertia and less resistance to rotation during their tumbling and bar skills. There are few tall, thin gymnasts, since their limb moments of inertia would produce too great a resistance to rotation, and they would not be successful in tumbling skills. The most important physical feature of skilled gymnasts is their shorter stature, as some have a relatively high mass for their height; so, it is clear that the length of the segments is a more important contributor to resistance than mass. Recall that moment of inertia is equal to mass times distance squared; so, length is weighted far more heavily than mass.

Force. What is force? We often talk about force, perhaps describing a forceful blow or a forceful slap shot. Force is defined as a push or a pull, which causes a change in linear motion of an object (or has a tendency to change linear motion). When your car is stuck in the snow, a friend pushing the car will either move the car and cause a change in linear motion of the car, or the car will almost move and this can be described as a tendency to move. Force is the product of mass (m) in kilograms times acceleration (a) in metres per second squared, and the magnitude of a force can be estimated by measuring the acceleration produced by that force. If your friend manages to push the car out of the snow and move it along the street, the car has accelerated from a velocity of zero to a velocity of 2–3 m/s. The amount of force applied to the car could be calculated as the product of the mass of the car times the rate of acceleration down the street (**F = m a**).

Torque: Torque is a measure of the tendency to rotate around an axis of rotation and produce a change in angular motion. If you push a friend on a swing in a playground, you are applying a force to the seat of the swing, which is some distance from the axis of rotation (the horizontal bar supporting the swing ropes). The harder you push on the swing, and the greater the distance from the axis to the seat, the greater the torque you are applying. Torque is the product of a force times the distance from the line of the force to the axis of rotation, and is a measure of the tendency of that force to produce angular motion (or rotation). When describing the causes of linear motion, forces are described; when describing the causes of angular motion, torques are described. It is important when describing human movement to use the correct term, and this is dependent on whether the resulting motion is linear or angular.

Most human motion consists of a combination of linear and angular motion, not just one simple type of motion. This combination of linear and angular motion is known as general motion. To accurately describe motion, it is necessary to describe both the linear and angular kinematics of the motion. In sprinting, for example, the center of gravity moves in an almost linear pathway down the track to the finish line, while the arms and legs undergo angular motion around axes through the shoulder, elbow, knee, and hip joints.

Joint Mechanics. For the purposes of biomechanical analysis, the human body can be divided into a number of individual segments that are separated by the joints or articulations between segments. These segments usually include the following: head, trunk, upper arm, forearm, hand, thigh, lower leg, and foot. The segments are free to move around the joints, and these angular movements at the joints will produce linear movements of the body and objects held by the body. Analysis of human motion is usually performed by viewing the body as a link-segment model, in which each segment is assumed to be a rigid link, joined by a frictionless and freely moveable joint. Although some of the segments, such as the trunk or hand, are not actually rigid, they are assumed to be rigid for the purposes of mechanical analysis. The joints are not actually frictionless, but the coefficient of friction is so low that they are assumed to be frictionless.

Axis of Rotation. An axis of rotation is defined as an imaginary line around which rotation occurs. Knowledge of the axis of rotation is necessary in order to describe angular motion accurately. The playground swing described earlier was free to rotate around its point of support, which was an imaginary horizontal line through the support. Human body limb segments are also free to rotate around axes through the joints. In fact, the whole body may rotate around an axis which passes through the center of gravity if the athlete is airborne and has some angular motion. A baseball batter will rotate his arms around vertical axes through the shoulder joints while swinging the bat. A diver performing a somersaulting dive is rotating her whole body around a left-right axis passing through the center of gravity. When the athlete is airborne, the three primary axes pass through the CG and are perpendicular to each other. The three axes are the left-right axis, anterior posterior axis, and the longitudinal axis (Figure 7.5):

Figure 7.5 The three primary axes of the human body intersect at the center of gravity.

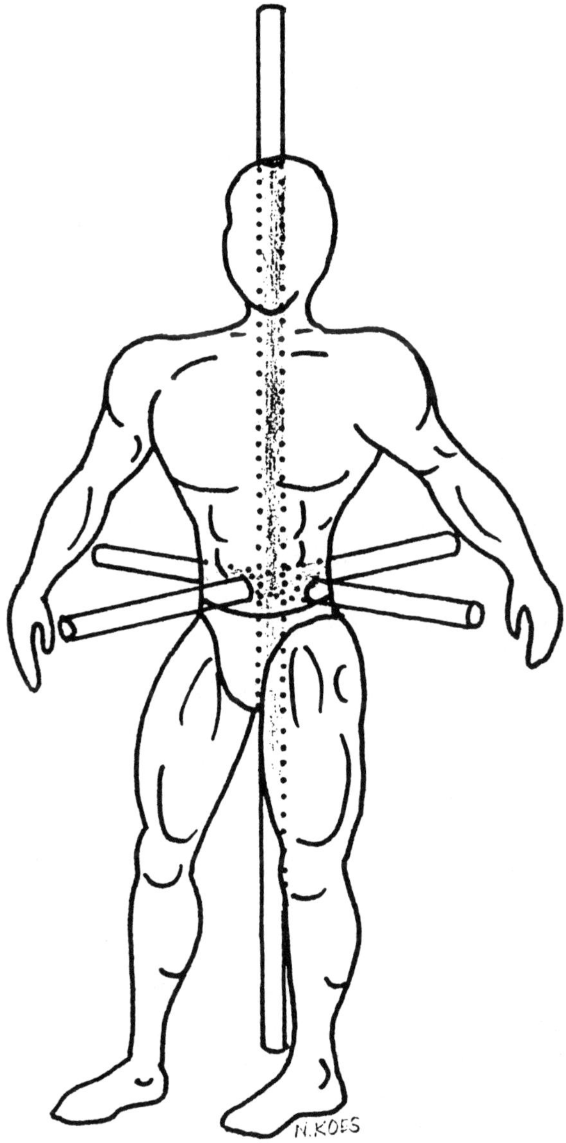

-e.g., action of the thigh in sprinting occurs around the left right through the hip joint axis, in the sagittal plane
-e.g., action of the arms in jumping jacks occurs in the frontal plane around the anterior-posterior axis passing through the shoulder joint
-e.g., rotation of the trunk in twisting dives occurs around the longitudinal axis passing through the center of gravity

Plane of Movement. A plane of movement is an imaginary two-dimensional surface through which movement occurs. Description of the plane through which movement occurs is necessary is describe angular motion accurately. There are three primary planes of movement, each of which corresponds to one of the three primary axes of motion (Figure 7.6). The sagittal plane passes from front to back through the body, and movements around the left right axis occur in this sagittal plane. An athlete performing a somersault is moving in the sagittal plane. The frontal plane passes from side to side through the body, and movements around the anterior posterior axis occur in this frontal plane. The cartwheel movement occurs in the frontal plane. The transverse plane passes horizontally through the body, and movements in the transverse plane occur around this longitudinal axis. A diver performing twisting movements is moving in the transverse plane around the longitudinal axis through the CG.

Anatomical Levers. A lever is a simple machine which either magnifies the effectiveness of a force, or increases the speed and range of motion at the end of the lever. The basic mechanical unit of the human body is the lever, which in mechanical terms consists (1) of an axis of rotation which passes through the joint, (2) some source of force in the body which is the contracting muscles, and (3) a lever, or rigid bony segment, to which the muscles are attached. A simple mechanical joint system consists of the bony lever, the attached muscles, and the axis through the joint around which the limb segment or body part is free to rotate (Figure 7.7).

A simple lever system is usually designed to perform a specific task, often to lift a weight, to move a load held in the hand, or to increase the speed at the end of a system of levers. The system illustrated in Figure 7.7 consists of the biceps muscle attached to the radial tuberosity, which will move the lower arm around the axis at the elbow joint, and cause the weight in the hand to be lifted or lowered (depending on the type of contraction occurring in the biceps muscle). The human body is made up of a number of simple lever systems, which together form a complex lever system consisting of several axes of rotation acting through several joints in a complex skill (such as a football pass).

The simple lever system can be altered in several different ways: (1) the attachment of the biceps muscle could be moved further down the forearm toward the hand, producing greater muscle torque at the elbow joint (Figure 7.8); (2) the location of the axis through the elbow joint could be altered due to

Figure 7.6 The three primary planes of the body intersect at the center of gravity.

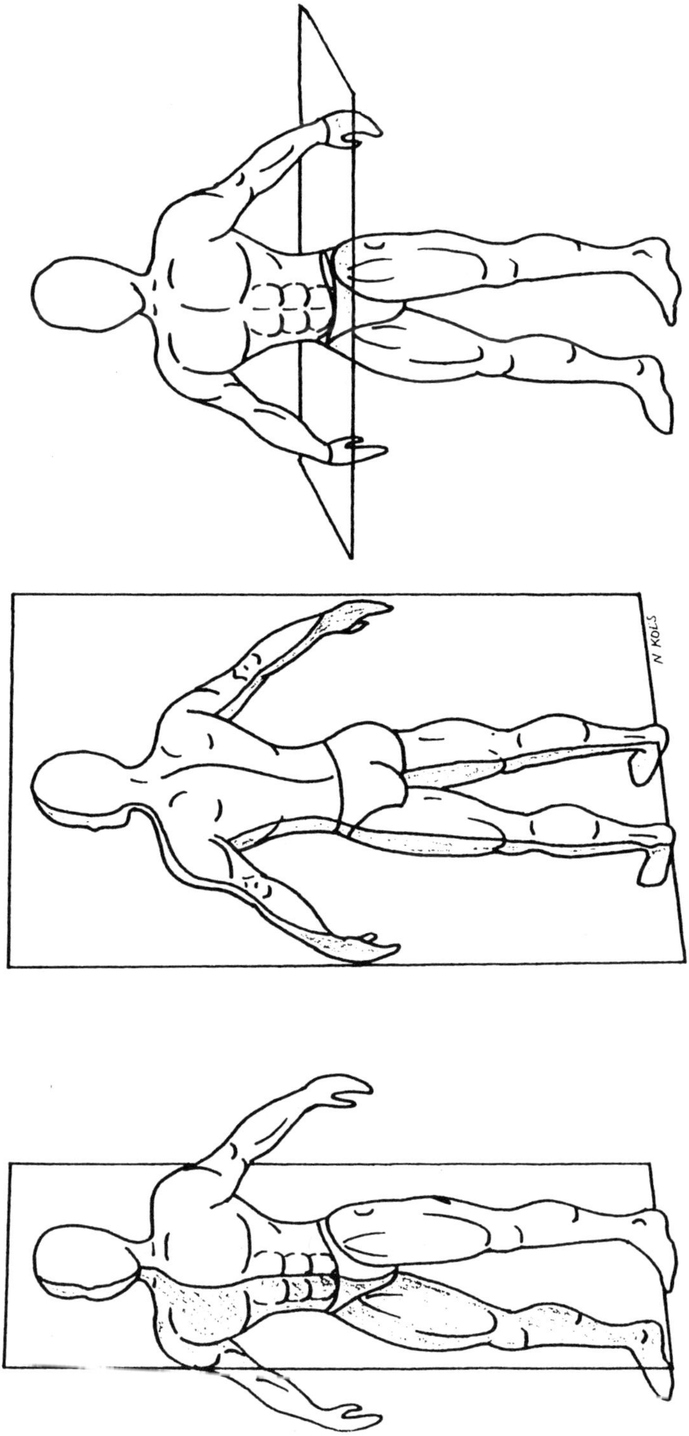

Figure 7.7 A simple anatomical lever system consists of an axis passing through a joint, a bony lever, and the muscle attached to the lever and providing force to move the lever.

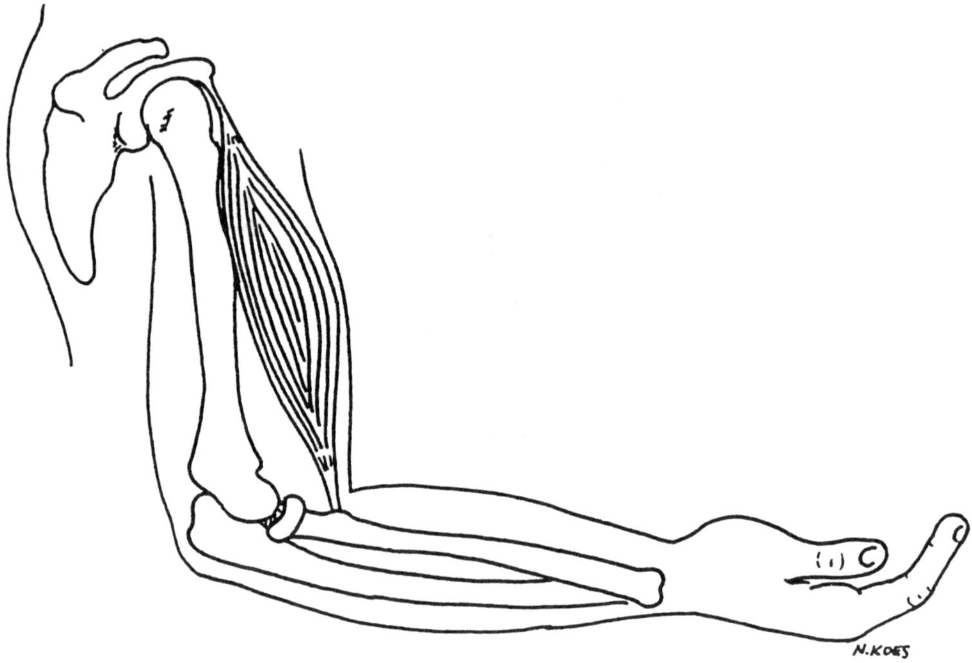

some injury at the joint; (3) the length of the forearm could be increased, as during the growth spurt; or (4) the load to be lifted by the lever system could be increased by increasing the size of the weight. Each of these changes would produce some alteration in the mechanical efficiency of the lever system, and can help to explain the differences in performance between athletes. An athlete whose muscle insertions were located further down the limb segment from the joint could produce greater force at the end of the lever.

Muscle Torque. Recall the earlier example of a person pushing the swing, and the applied torque was described as the product of the pushing force times the distance to the axis of rotation. A torque can also be produced around a joint by the action of muscle contraction. When the muscle contracts to move the limb segment, a torque (or moment) is produced; this is defined as the tendency of the body to rotate around the axis. It is possible to calculate the magnitude of the torque acting at a joint if the muscle force can be estimated from muscle

Figure 7.8 The biceps muscle at various points of elbow flexion, showing variations in the moment arm.

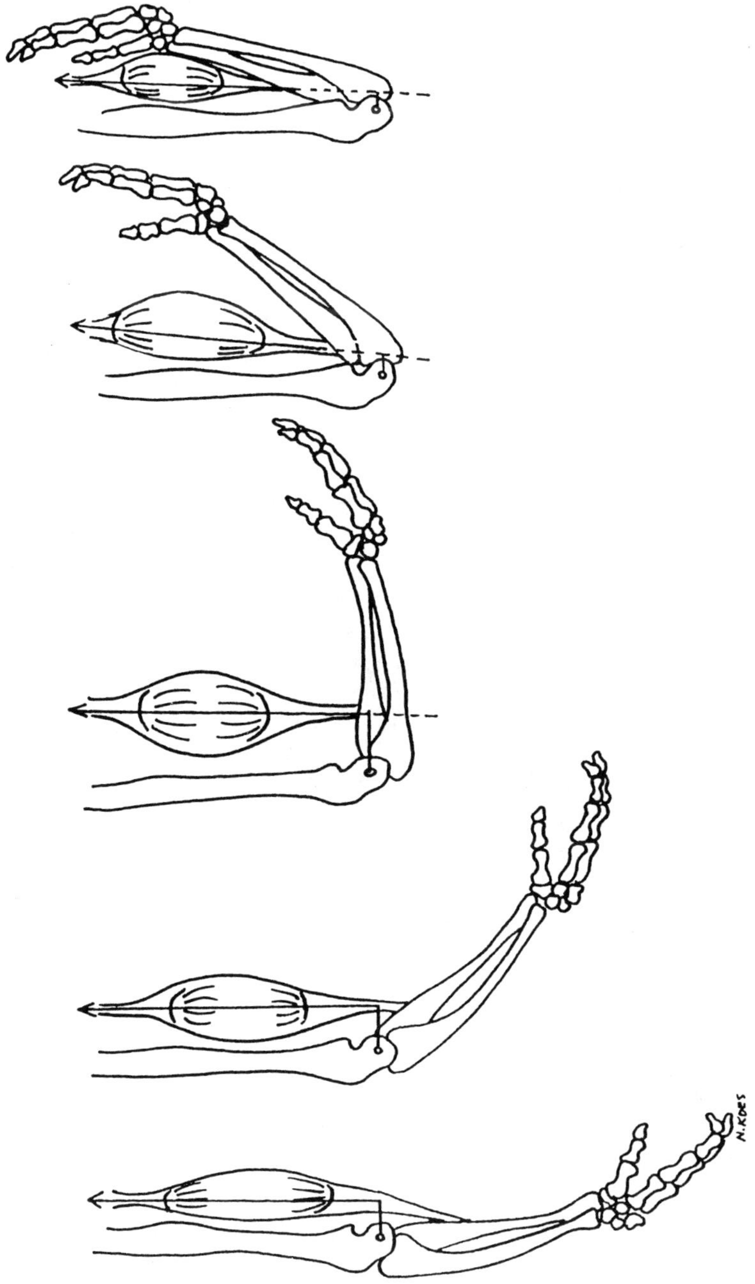

size. The torque (moment) produced by a muscle is the product of the force times the distance from the line of force to the axis (moment arm) (Figure 7.7). **Torque = force × distance (to axis of rotation); T= F × d.** The moment-arm for a muscle is the perpendicular distance from the axis of rotation at the joint to the line of pull of the muscle. This moment arm changes throughout the range of motion at a joint, so that it is often shorter at the beginning and end of the range of joint motion, and increases in length up to an angle of pull of 90° (usually the longest point). An example is the biceps muscle as it acts to produce elbow flexion; the line of pull is close the axis when the arm is fully extended or fully flexed, but moves away from the axis during the middle of the range of motion so that the distance increases, and then decreases during the range of flexion (Figure 7.8). As the moment-arm changes, the torque at the joint changes; so, the torque produced at a joint during the range of motion varies.

Angular Motion. Most of human movement consists of angular motion, or the movement of the body parts around axes of rotation at the joints. Angular motion is the movement of the body (or body parts) around an axis of rotation, so that the body part moves through a definite angular displacement In Figure 7.9, the arm is rotating around the shoulder-joint axis, and so is producing angular motion at this joint.

Figure 7.9 Angular motion is produced when the arm rotates around the shoulder joint axis, as in this skilled windmill pitcher.

Another example of angular motion is included in Figure 7.10 that depicts a soccer player kicking a soccer ball (Roberts, Zernicke, Youm, & Huang, 1974). There are two major lever systems in effect in this example, the thigh rotating around the hip joint and the lower leg rotating around the knee joint. In skilled movements of this type, the timing of the angular motions of each of the segments occurs in sequence, from larger to smaller, or from slower to faster movements. The thigh starts to rotate more slowly, then it speeds up to a peak angular velocity; then as it begins to decelerate, the lower leg begins to speed up. The timings of the speeds of the segments are closely related, since generally, when the larger segment reaches peak speed, it then decelerates as the smaller segment increases speed. The eventual speed of the foot at impact is closely related to the sequence and timing of the movements at each of the body joints involved in a skill. In Figure 7.10, the foot velocity at contact was 17.73 m/s, with resultant ball velocity reaching 24.09 m/s (Roberts, *et al.*, 1974).

Figure 7.10 Sequence and timing of the joint movements of the lower limb during a skilled soccer kick, from (Roberts, Zernicke, Youm, & Huang, 1974).

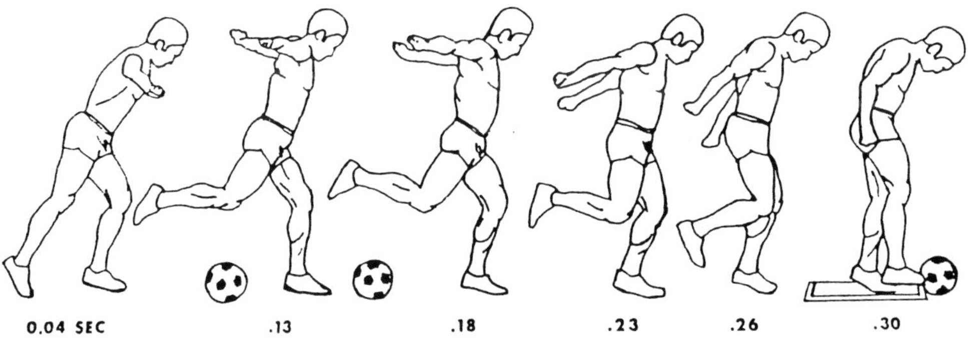

The soccer player does not attain foot speed only from the angular motions of the legs, but also from the angular motions of all the body parts that can contribute to the speed of the ball. The skilled soccer player will increase ball speed by using several other joints to produce velocity. The body is moving forward with a high linear velocity as the player approaches the ball (due to the run up), and this speed will add to the speed of the kicking foot. Rotation of the body as the player approaches the ball will also increase foot speed, since the player starts the kick with the body positioned at an angle to the ball and finishes in a position with the shoulders facing the kick. The arm swing may also aid in the increased velocity of the kicking leg due to increases in ground-reaction forces.

Center of Gravity (CG). When an athlete is running a 100 m race, or competing in an event such as the high jump, the motion of the athlete is best represented by a point which represents the total mass of the athlete. When the human body, or an implement such as a javelin are represented by a point, the body is said to be represented by a particle. This point is known as the center of gravity, or the center of mass, which is the balance point of the body. This is the point at which the athlete would balance if suspended from one single point. Thus the sum of the weights and distances of the body parts on all sides of this point is equal. This point can change position in the body as the positions of the limb segments change due to movements at the joints. In a normal standing position, the center of gravity is at the level of the navel (or just above the hip joints). If the athlete raises the arms above the head, the center of gravity will also rise up in the body, as the balance point will now be raised relative to the feet (Figure 7.11).

Figure 7.11 The alteration of the position of the center of gravity of an athlete by redistribution of body parts, from (Luttgens, Deutsch, & Hamilton, 1992).

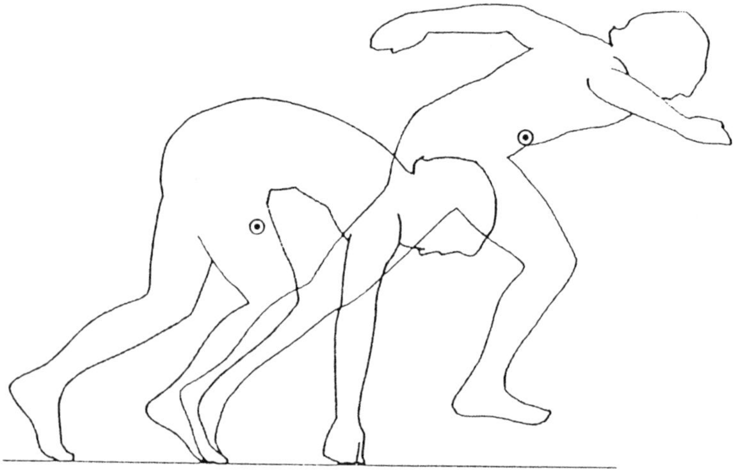

Male-Female Structural Differences. There are few significant structural differences between males and females, although there are a number of misconceptions regarding those differences. The average height of the center of mass is slightly higher for males than for females. This is due to the greater amount of muscle mass and wider shoulder girdle of males, along with the greater storage of adipose tissue in the thighs and buttocks of the average female. The average height of the male Cm is 56.2% of standing height, while that for females in 55.4% of standing height (Atwater, 1988; Atwater, 1990). This is less than a 1% difference in the average height of the CM, which is insignificant in its effect on the performance of most sport skills.

It has been suggested that females have a wider pelvis than males of similar height and weight, and that this may interfere with their performance in sports activities such as volleyball or basketball. It is true that a wide pelvis, especially if it is covered with a layer of adipose tissue, will have increased resistance to rotation as seen in throwing (high moment of inertia). However, the speed of the limb attached to the wider hip will also be greater, due to increased lever length; so wide hips are actually an asset in a sport such as soccer. This is assuming that the athlete with the wider hips can generate the same angular velocity in hip rotation. In any case, anthropometric measurements have determined that the absolute pelvic width is very similar in both males and females, whereas males do have wider shoulders than females (Atwater, 1990). The wider shoulders of the average male are also an advantage from a biomechanical viewpoint. Since wide shoulders will also produce a greater linear velocity at the shoulder joint, the same angular speed can be attained.

Another structural difference often cited between males and female athletes is the carrying angle of the forearm relative to the upper arm. Some authors have suggested that females are generally poor throwers due to their increased carrying angle. However, Atwater (1988) has suggested that there are no significant differences in carrying angle between males and females.

Linear motion. Athletes use angular motions of the limb segments and the trunk to produce linear motions of the body as a whole. The linear motion of a great 100m sprinter can best be described by describing the pathway of the center of gravity, which is a point. The position of the center of gravity of any athlete can be determined by mathematical calculations based on the weight of each segment and its distance from any arbitrary axes. These calculations can be performed by computers programmed to use joint centers and segment weights to calculate the center of gravity. Most biomechanics laboratories have such a program, so that CM locations can be determined easily and quickly from digitized film data.

The center of gravity can be tracked by viewing digitized video film of the race. When the displacement of the point has been determined from the film, the linear velocity and acceleration can also be determined. One of the key features in the examination of the technique of skilled athletes is the linear velocity and acceleration of the CG during the event. These can be calculated when comparing two athletes in the same event to determine the velocity and acceleration patterns that may have led to the winning performance.

Linear and Angular Kinematics. The science of mechanics can be divided into two parts: kinematics and kinetics. Kinematics is concerned with describing the *nature* of motion, and kinetics is concerned with the *causes* of motion and description of forces causing motion (Hay & Reid, 1982). Kinematics is, therefore, that branch of mechanics which describes the motion, including its distance and speed. The most common descriptive terms used to describe motion are: time, displacement, distance, speed, velocity, and acceleration, all of which are terms which describe how the athlete or object is moving in space. When these terms are used to describe linear motion, they are known as linear displacement, velocity, or acceleration. When they are used to describe angular motion, they are known as angular displacement, velocity, or acceleration.

The time (or temporal characteristics) of motion is important in several activities. In track and swimming events, for example, the performance of the athletes is determined by the time recorded for the event. The football player who has the shortest time for 40 yards is often highly regarded by coaches in the sport. The speed of an athlete is the distance covered over the time it takes to cover that distance, so that both the distance travelled and the time taken are required to determine the speed (Hay, 1993). Speed is an important determinant of performance in sports, since the faster athlete will often be an effective performer in team sports such as basketball, soccer, and football.

The terms speed and velocity are often used interchangeably, although they technically should not be used in the same context (Hay & Reid, 1982). Speed is a scalar quantity (has only magnitude), since the actual distance travelled is divided by the time taken. Velocity is a vector quantity (has both magnitude and direction); so only the displacement from the start to the finish is divided by the time taken. In a 400m race, where the start and the finish are at the same point, the velocity is zero. However, the terms speed and velocity will be used as synonyms in the present discussion, since this distinction is seldom made except by biomechanists or physicists.

The speed of take-off of a jumping athlete is another important aspect of performance, as the speed at take-off will determine how high or how far the athlete will jump. A top high-jumper requires a high vertical velocity at take-off to reach the highest possible height, while a top long-jumper requires a high horizontal velocity to produce longer jump distances. A great jumping athlete like Michael Jordan will have a very high vertical velocity at take-off, which will require a large impulse (force x time) to be produced during take-off. The angular speed of the motions of the limbs during skilled performances is also important in performances, since the angular speed of the limb of a windmill pitcher will determine the speed of the ball at release (Figure 7.9).

Acceleration, another important descriptor of performance, is the rate of change of velocity. An athlete who can change his velocity over a shorter time period has a higher rate of acceleration, or a faster rate of change of velocity. An athlete with a higher acceleration, such as former Canadian sprinter Ben Johnson, will increase velocity at a faster rate and reach maximum velocity sooner in the race. During his prime as a sprinter, Ben Johnson was usually the first sprinter out of the blocks and the first to reach the 10 m mark of the race (indicating a fast rate of acceleration). His top rival, Carl Lewis, had a slower rate of acceleration, but he was often able to maintain his top speed for a longer period during the race.

Examples of the use of the formulae for linear and angular accelerations follow:

1. *angular displacement* is the change in angular position of a limb segment, it occurs around an axis of rotation (e.g., the knee moves through 90 degrees of rotation)
2. *linear displacement* is the change in linear position (e.g., the 100m runner will cover 100m of displacement during the race)
3. *angular velocity* is the rate of change of angular position; so, if the knee moves through 90 degrees in 1 second, the angular velocity is 90 degrees per second (angular velocity [ω] = angular displacement/time)
4. *linear velocity* is the rate of change of linear position; so, if the 200m runner takes 20 sec to run 200m, his average velocity is 10 m/s (linear velocity = linear displacement/time; $v = d/t$)
5. *angular acceleration* is the rate of change of angular velocity; so, if the velocity increases from 0 deg/s to 90 deg/s in 1 sec, the angular acceleration is 90 deg/sec/sec (angular acceleration [α] = angular velocity/time)
6. *linear acceleration* is the rate of change of linear velocity; so, if the velocity increases from 0 m/s to 10 m/s in 1 sec, the rate of acceleration is 10 m/sec/sec (angular acceleration = angular velocity/time)

Linear and Angular Kinetics. Kinetic analysis is the branch of mechanics that describes the causes of motion, and describes the forces that produce motion. It is possible to measure forces directly by the use of force dynamometers such as the force platform or force transducers (Figure 7.12). However, these devices can usually only be used in the laboratory, so that an indirect method of measuring forces which does not interfere with the technique of the athlete is desirable. The most common method of indirect force measurement is the use of film analysis, in which the athlete is filmed while performing the sports skill. Then the various kinematic measures are calculated from the film. These measures of velocity or acceleration can be used to estimate the forces produced or absorbed by athletes during a contest.

The linear forces acting on the ground or on the joints of athletes can be calculated from film by the use of one of several techniques of biomechanical analysis: the impulse-momentum approach, the force-mass acceleration approach, or the work-energy approach. These three techniques are all methods used to estimate forces exerted by athletes during sports skills by use of kinematic quantities calculated from film data. Each of these three techniques can apply to either linear or angular motion, since the formulae are altered only slightly to apply to angular motion. The ability to estimate the forces produced by athletes during the competitive situation is important in the analysis of technique, as well as in the comparison of the techniques of different athletes in the same skill.

Stability and Balance. One of the most important mechanical principles which can be used by teachers and coaches in analysis of athletes performing skills is the principle that describes the stability and balance characteristics of the

Figure 7.12 Tracing of the force output recorded by a force platform during amputee running, from (Whieldon, 1979).

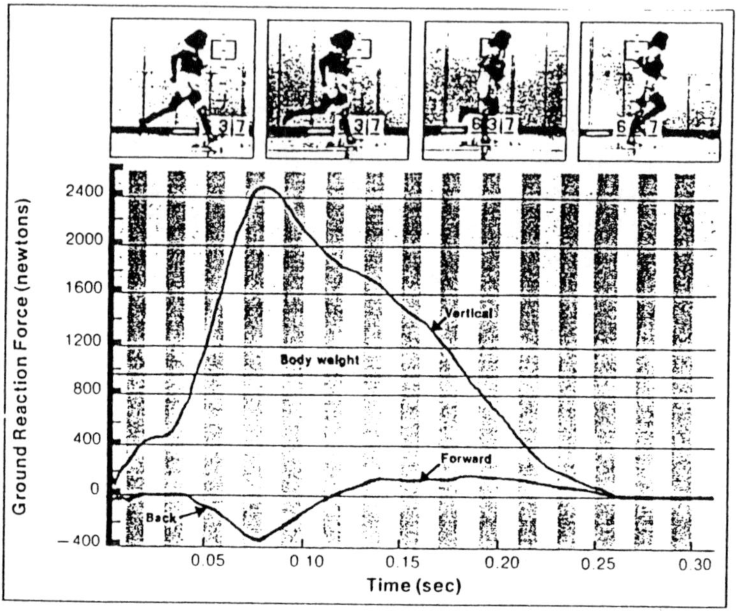

athlete. An athlete is stable when the center of mass or center of gravity (CG) is positioned directly over the base of support. The base of support includes the parts of the body which support the body weight (such as the feet in standing) and the area between the body parts (such as the area between the feet in standing). The base of support can therefore be widened by moving the feet further apart, thus increasing the area of the base. Stability is also affected by the height of the center of gravity, since increased height of the CG will decrease the stability of the athlete (Adams, 1991) (Figure 7.13). A ballet dancer who is up on her toes during a dance movement is unstable due to the high CG and the very small base of support. When an athlete lowers the CG (e.g., a football lineman who moves down into a three-point stance), the CG is lowered closer to the base of support and the athlete becomes more stable due to both the lower CG and the increased area of the base.

Stability is also affected by the position of the line of gravity (a straight line drawn down from the CG to the center of the earth). This line is a vector representing the force of gravity acting on the mass of the athlete. The line of gravity will move relative to the base of support, since the position of the CG in the body is altered due to movements of the body parts. The closer the CG is to the edge of the base, the less stable the athlete, since the CG has to move a shorter distance before it lies outside the edge of the base. When the CG lies outside the edge of the base of support, the athlete is unstable. This is so,

Figure 7.13 Lowering the center of gravity increases stability, and moving the center of gravity toward the edge of the base decreases stability, from (Kreighbaum & Barthels, 1990).

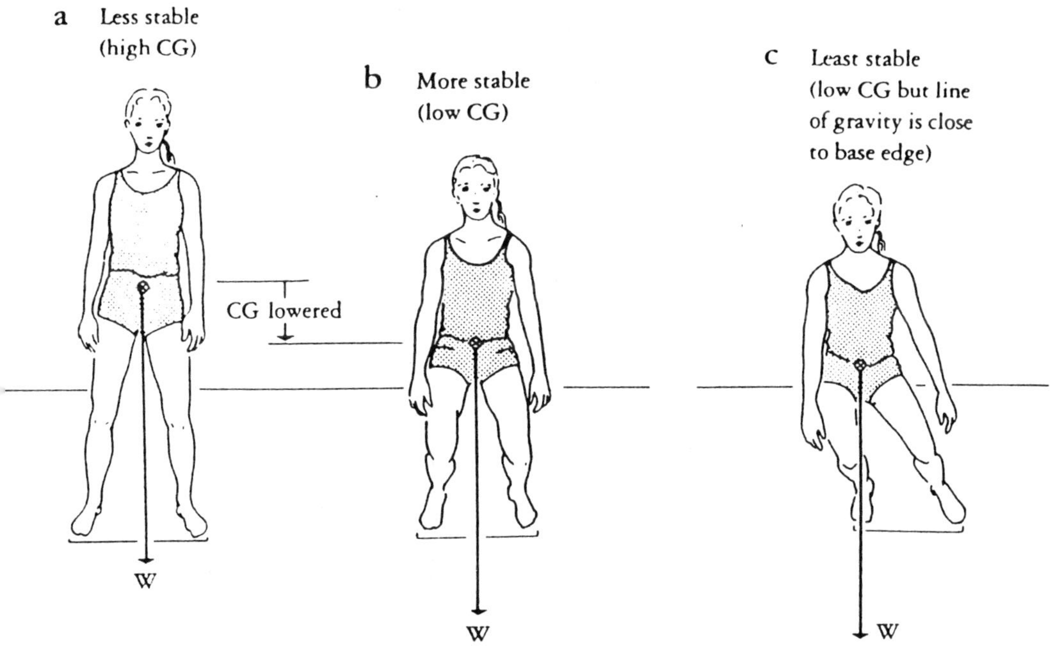

because the force of gravity acting on the body weight produces a torque which will cause the body to rotate over the edge of the base in the direction of the torque. Often in sports skills the athlete wants to assume an unstable position, such as in the sprint start or the swimming start; so, the athlete will move the line of gravity to the outside edge of the base to increase instability.

Summation of Joint Torques. There are a number of sport skills that require a high velocity at the end of the arm or leg, such as a tennis serve, a javelin throw, a soccer kick, or an ice-hockey shot. When the objective of a sports skill is to generate a high velocity at the end of a system of levers, the athlete will produce torques at several of the joints during the performance of the skill. These torques are summed as the athlete brings in each successive joint in sequence, so that the speed of the limb increases to a maximum at release or impact. Skilled athletes will use as many joints as possible to generate these high velocities, and each joint will move through the greatest range possible during the delivery. One of the key features of highly skilled athletes is the large range of motion which each active joint will undergo during the forward movements (having been preceded by a very large backswing) (Figure 7.14).

Figure 7.14 The skilled tennis server uses as many joints as possible to generate joint torques during the delivery, from (Plagenhoef, 1971).

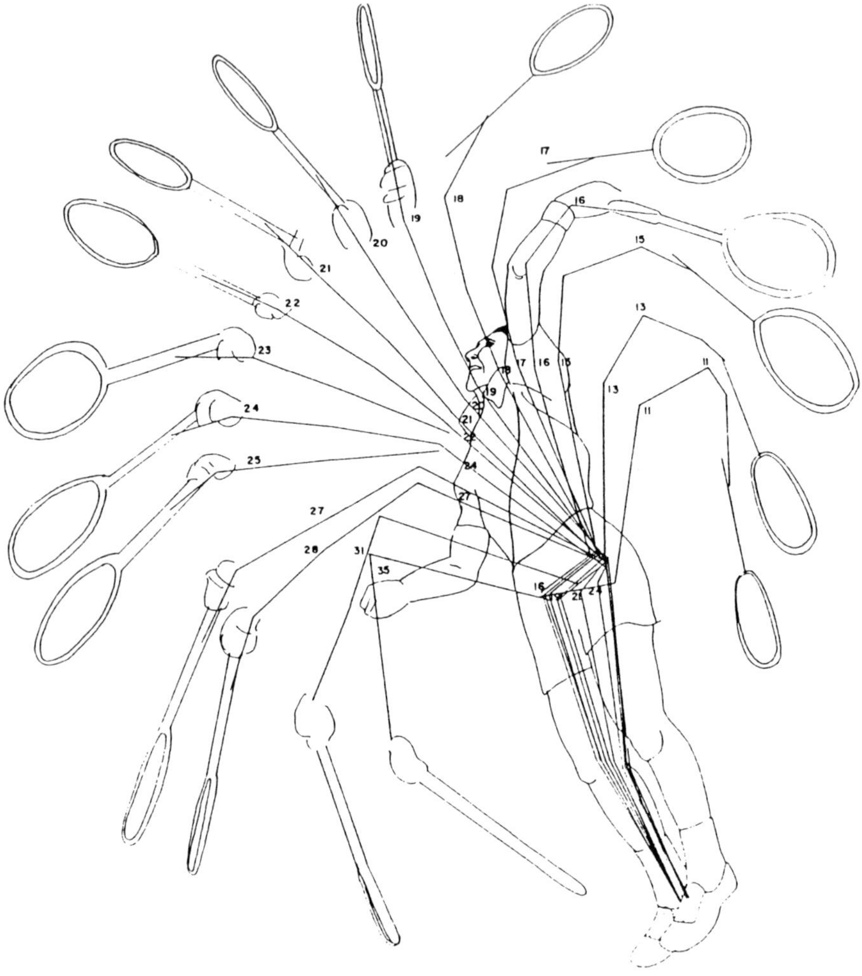

Examination of the skill performance of top athletes will indicate that top athletes will use the maximum number of joints to generate velocity in a skill, as well as moving each joint through the greatest range of motion possible. Since joint movements are produced by joint torques, or muscle forces acting over a certain range of motion of the joints, the skilled athlete will use a larger number of muscle groups to generate high velocities. The strength of each of the muscle groups, especially those of the trunk muscles, are the key to the skill of top athletes, since it is these which produce the movements for the skill. Another key aspect of the performance of top athletes is the timing of the firing of each of the muscle groups, so that the larger, slower muscle groups are contracted first, and the smaller, faster muscle groups are contracted later in the skill performance.

In the skill of baseball pitching, for example, the pitcher takes a very long step onto the foot opposite to the pitching arm, and drives forward onto this foot by extension of the joints of the rear limb. This is followed by rotation of the muscles at the hip joints, to bring the hips around to a position almost facing the pitcher. The trunk is then rotated to a position facing the pitcher, and this trunk rotation is followed by movements in the pitching arm. The movements in the pitching arm include rotation of the shoulder medially toward the plate, elbow extension, forearm pronation, and wrist flexion and adduction. The larger joints make their contribution first, as they are larger and slower, and the smaller joints continue to increase the velocity of the hand until the ball is released.

Linear Impulse-Momentum. The impulse-momentum relationship is of considerable importance in mechanical analysis, since it allows the biomechanist to estimate the forces required to produce a change in velocity in an athlete or object. An understanding of this concept will assist the student in seeing how athletes produce velocity changes of their bodies or objects they manipulate. The term momentum is in common use in sports; coaches often refer to their team gaining or losing momentum during the course of a game. The use of the term momentum here is different than that used in popular sports magazines, since in biomechanics the term can actually be quantified. The mechanical definition of momentum (M) is that it is the product of the mass(m) of the athlete or object, times the velocity (v) that the athlete (or object) has at that instant. **Momentum = mass × velocity.** If an athlete has a mass of 200 kg, and a linear velocity of 9.5 m/s, then his or her momentum is: Momentum = 200 kg × 9.5 m/s = 1900 kg m/s.

Impulse is the product of force × time; (Impulse = force × time) and the impulse-momentum relationship states that impulse will produce a change in momentum. **Impulse (F t) = change in momentum = mv_f - mv_i.** Since mass of any athlete or object is constant, impulse will produce an increase or decrease in velocity; so, in high jumping the athlete strives to maximize the impulse exerted against the ground, and impulse can be increased by either increasing the force exerted, the time of force application, or both. In the high jump, the athlete is interested in increasing the vertical velocity at take-off to a maximum, which requires maximal vertical forces exerted over a greater time period. Vertical forces are maximized by: (1) assuming a low position at touchdown, (2) using a full swing of the arms and free leg at take-off, and (3) full extension of the take-off leg. Time on the ground is maximized by: (1) leaning back at touchdown, (2) reaching forward with the take-off leg, and (3) contacting the ground in a heel-toe position.

Angular Impulse-Momentum. The impulse-momentum relationship can also be applied to angular motion, which consists of only slight changes from the linear form of the equation described in the previous section. The application of an angular impulse will produce a change in the angular momentum of an athlete or object. In the previous example of pushing someone on a swing, the pusher will apply a torque to the swing, over a certain period of time, and this angular impulse will produce angular momentum (or angular motion) in the swing. *Angular impulse* is the product of torque times the time of application of torque:

Angular impulse = torque × time

Angular momentum is the amount of angular motion that an athlete has acquired due to the application of a torque. Angular momentum (H) is the product of moment of inertia (I) and angular velocity (ω):

Angular momentum = moment of inertia × angular velocity

$$\mathbf{H = I\,\omega}$$

The Law of Conservation of Angular Momentum states that the angular momentum of an airborne body is constant (Hay, 1993), since the athlete is unable to apply torques to an airborne body to change the angular momentum. A diver has constant angular momentum after leaving the diving board, but can speed up or slow down her rate of rotation by altering the moment of inertia. If the diver changes her body position from an extended position to a tucked position while airborne, the angular velocity, or rate of rotation will increase due to the decreased moment of inertia. If the diver then moves from the tucked to the extended position, the rate of spinning will decrease.

The angular impulse-momentum relationship states that the angular momentum can be changed by the application of angular impulse, where angular impulse (J) is the product of the applied torque (T) times the time (t):

Angular-impulse (T t) = change in angular momentum = $\mathbf{I\,\omega_f - I\,\omega_i}$

A football quarterback, who wishes to apply spin (angular momentum) to the football at release, must apply a torque over some time period to change the angular momentum of the ball from zero to some positive value following release. The torque is applied by pronation and medial rotation of the arm during delivery of the ball, and the angular momentum changes from a value of zero ($I\omega_i$) to a positive value ($I\omega_f$), which is the product of the moment of inertia of the ball (I), times the angular velocity (ω) (or the rate of spin of the ball around its long axis). A good quarterback will impart a large amount of angular momentum to the ball, while a weaker quarterback will impart low values of angular momentum, and this low rate of spin will produce wobbly motion during flight through the air.

Isaac Newton. Newton's three laws of motion are the basic laws which govern the motion of all objects moving on the earth, including athletes and implements. These laws were formulated by the Englishman, Isaac Newton

(1642–1727) who was by far the single greatest contributor to present knowledge in the field of biomechanics (Hay & Reid, 1982). The original three laws were formulated to describe linear motion, but they have been expanded to include three analogous laws of angular motion. Only the linear form of the laws will be included here, but note that there are similar laws which govern angular motion and the relationship between angular motion and applied torque.

Newton's First Law. Newton's first law is the law of inertia, and it states that "every body at rest, or moving with constant velocity in a straight line, will continue in that state of motion unless acted on by an outside force." When a speed skater pushes off during a stride, that velocity would be maintained indefinitely if there were no forces acting on the skater (Figure 7.15) (Adrian & Cooper, 1989). The skater is acted upon by the outside forces of friction and air resistance that slow the skater down following the push-off until the next drive from the opposite skate. Similarly, discus thrower releases the discus with some initial velocity which will be constantly decreased following release due to the same forces of air resistance and gravity. Thus, no objects on earth will continue to move with constant velocity due to the forces of air resistance and gravity which join to slow the velocity during motion.

Figure 7.15 The speed skater will continue to move in a straight line during the glide phase of the stroke, until additional force is applied by other skate, from (Adrian & Cooper, 1989).

Keeping Newton's First Law in mind (i.e., a body will remain in motion, or at rest, unless acted upon by an outside force), all parts of a moving body, or system, have the same amount of motion or linear velocity. If you are a passenger on a bus that is moving down the street, you are part of the system that includes the bus and all the passengers on board. As the bus moves down the street, therefore, the bus and the passengers have a constant amount of motion or momentum. When the bus is stopped by the application of the brakes, this braking force (F) produces deceleration (a) of the bus ($F = ma$), including the seats of the bus and all other objects attached to the bus. The passengers are not attached to the bus, except by perhaps holding onto a handle; so, when the bus stops, the passengers will tend to continue moving forward with the same velocity as the bus had initially (since all parts of the system had the same velocity). The passengers may indeed continue to move with a high velocity in a forward direction, and they could easily become projectiles moving through the bus's windshield. Similarly, all objects which are part of the system will have all the motion characteristics of that system.

An athlete carrying an object also comprises a system with one set of motion characteristics. When a basketball player on a fast break lay-up leaves the ground to take the shot, she has a high horizontal velocity due to her high-speed run-up. The ball also has the same high horizontal velocity and, if it is released with the hand on the back of the ball, it is likely to rebound sharply from the basket and the shot may be missed. A more effective technique may be to use the underhanded lay-up, with the hand in front of the ball, so that the player can decrease the horizontal velocity of the ball by moving the ball backward at release (Hay, 1993) (Figure 7.16). This is known as "softening" the shot, and skilled basketball players have this ability to remove unwanted horizontal velocity from the ball at release.

Figure 7.16 The basketball player on a fast break will soften the shot by using an underhand layup, from Hay (1993).

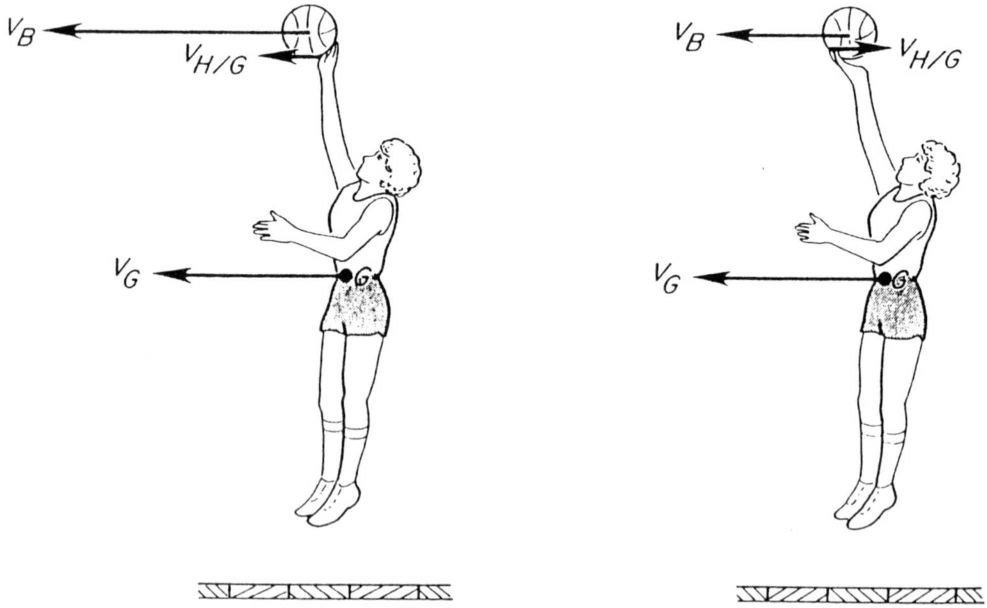

Newton's Second Law of Motion. Newton's second law is the law of acceleration, which states "that the acceleration of a body is proportional to the force causing it, and takes place in the direction in which the force acts." This can be stated in the following formula: **Force = mass × acceleration, or F = m × a.** This law is important to students of human movement, because it states the relationship between force and acceleration: the acceleration that an athlete or object experiences is directly proportional to the force applied. The greater the applied force, the greater the acceleration of the athlete. When the sprinter pushes off from the blocks, the acceleration produced is directly proportional to the forces applied by the sprinter. A stronger sprinter will produce higher muscle forces and will accordingly be able to produce higher acceleration values. The mass of any sprinter is constant, so that the acceleration experienced will be proportional to the applied forces. Sprinters include high volumes of strength training in their training programs to increase their force output, because they are concerned with producing the highest possible rates of acceleration. Football running backs are also concerned with the production of high forces to maximize their rates of acceleration while attempting to move the ball downfield. Athletes who must produce high rates of acceleration to be successful in their sport will usually be very muscular and include extensive weight-training in their training programs.

Newton's Third Law of Motion. Newton's third law is the law of action-reaction, which states "that for every action force that is exerted by one body on another, there is an equal and opposite reaction force exerted by the second body on the first." This law is especially applicable when an athlete is taking off for a jump or beginning a running stride, since the downward-backward forces exerted by the athlete will determine the forward-upward velocity which results from the takeoff (Figure 7.17). When the long-jumper exerts a downward-backward force against the board during take-off, the board exerts an equal and opposite reaction force against the jumper to drive her in a forward-upward direction. The athlete is accelerated upward and forward into the jump, and the earth is accelerated downward and backward due to the forces of the jumper. However, because the earth is so massive relative to the force of the jumper, the acceleration is very small (or negligible).

When the jumper jumps in the sand, the sand particles have a relatively small mass and, when a force is applied to them, they will be accelerated backwards. Some of the ground reaction forces are lost due to the movement of the ground (sand) backwards; so, the acceleration of the jumper is less for any give force of take-off. The jumper has to work harder to jump any given height from the sand due to the decreased ground reaction forces at take-off. Long-jumpers would lose most of their jumping distance if they were forced to take off from sand! Landing in the sand is less stressful than landing on the floor, because the sand gives at impact and increases the time of force application. The force is therefore applied over a longer period of time; so, the force-per-unit

Figure 7.17 The downward-backward forces exerted by this skilled long-jumper on the ground, will produce an equal and opposite forward-upward force on the jumper.

time is less, and there is less stress on the muscles and joints on landing. Note the application here of the Impulse-Momentum relationship in which the impulse (force × time) is applied to decrease the velocity to zero at landing.

Newton's third law also applies to throwing events in track and field, especially to the shot put event. When the thrower releases the shot, it has been suggested that the feet of the thrower should be firmly planted on the ground, so that the downward forces of the 7.26 kg shot do not move the shot putter backward during release. However, most world class throwers release the shot with the feet not in contact with the ground, since they want to release the shot with the maximum velocity, and some of this velocity is gained from driving the body up off the ground during release. It is likely that skilled throwers gain more distance from driving up off the ground into the throw, than they would be attempting to keep both feet on the ground through a release.

KINETICS OF MOTION

Force, Mass and Acceleration. Newton's Second law also provides students of human movement with a useful method of analysis of motion by providing the relationship between force and acceleration. High-speed film analysis will provide the biomechanist with the ability to calculate acceleration values. Recall in the process of film digitizing that the position of each body joint is recorded by the computer, and this position data can be used to calculate velocity by using the time between frames and the formula for velocity: velocity

= displacement/time. When velocity is known, it is possible to determine acceleration values since acceleration is the rate of change of velocity. These acceleration values can be placed into the equation $F = m \times a$ along with the mass, and estimates of the forces required to produce those accelerations can be produced. This equation is a useful tool in biomechanics, as it allows estimates of the forces produced by athletes during running and jumping events (either forces against the ground, or forces at the joints).

Work and Energy. Mechanical work (w) can be quantified as the product of the forces (f) applied times the distance (d) over which the force is applied: Work = force × distance. The work-energy approach to biomechanical analysis is useful when the distance over which forces are applied can be calculated accurately (usually from film data). This approach is used in the analysis of speed skating, for example, as the distance of each propulsive phase of the stroke can be measured from video film of a race (Koning, de Boer, de Groot, & van Ingen Schenau, 1987).

The work-energy relationship states that the work done by any athlete is proportional to the change in the total mechanical energy of the athlete. The two major types of energy which undergo change in an athlete during a sport skill are kinetic energy and potential energy, where kinetic energy (KE) is the product of the mass (m) of the athlete times the velocity squared (v^2) or (**$KE = 1/2\ m\ v^2$**); and potential energy is weight (w) times height (h) above the ground (**$PE = w \times h$ or $PE = m \times g \times h$**). Since all of the variables in the energy equations can be calculated from video film or measured from the athlete (mass, velocity, height), these changing energy values can be used to calculate the work done. Since distance can also be measured from film, the forces exerted by the athlete to produce these changes in energy can be estimated.

Methods of Analysis of Motion. The most common method of movement-analysis is to film an athlete performing a skill with a video camera or a movie camera, and then analyze the film frame-by-frame using a computerized video analysis system. One of the most popular of these systems in sport biomechanics laboratories is the Peak Performance Video Analysis System (Peak Performance Technologies, 1990). The video film is played back one frame at a time on a VCR, and each frame is captured by the computer and appears on the computer screen as a computer-enhanced video picture. This picture is then digitized, a process by which the location of each of the joints is stored in the computer as a numerical position on the screen, and each successive frame of the skill performance is digitized in this manner. At the end of the skill, all the joint position data are stored in the computer, and this data can be used to calculate kinematic and kinetic data describing the skill and the athlete. This digitized data can be used to calculate the displacement, velocity, acceleration, joint forces, joint torques, and ground reaction forces produced by the athlete. The most time-consuming part of this process is the digitizing of the film data, but once the data is digitized a very large number of variables can be calculated from this original time-displacement data.

One negative feature of this data collection procedure is that there are some errors associated with it, primarily those which occur when attempting to locate the joint centers which are not in view of the camera, or which are covered by clothing or other objects in the frame. The data is smoothed by the computer using numerical smoothing programs stored in the computer, but often the error, or noise in the data, is difficult to separate from the actual data describing the athlete's performance.

Another common type of motion analysis is the estimation of forces using force transducers attached to various sports implements. A force transducer is an electrical device which measures strain across the transducer. This can be calibrated to estimate the forces applied to the device. The sport of rowing is often studied by instrumenting the oars with force transducers, to determine the force-time characteristics of the stroke or the total impulse that the rower can apply during the stroke (Zatsiorsky & Yakunin, 1991). The high bar in men's gymnastics is also often instrumented to determine the moments of peak force application to the bar by the gymnast, either to examine the technique of the gymnast or to determine the tolerances of the bar (Kopp & Reid, 1980). Force transducers have also been placed in the skate blades of elite speed skaters to determine the magnitude and direction of the push off forces (Jobse, Schuurhof, Cserep, Schreurs, & de Koning, 1990).

Muscle action can be studied by the use of electromyography or the measurement of the electrical activity in muscles. When the muscle is stimulated to contract, a wave of depolarization passes along the muscle cell membrane, and this electrical activity can be measured by sensitive electrodes placed on the skin surface over the contracting muscles (Stevenson, 1984). The electrical current measured by these electrodes is then amplified and recorded by computer or plotter. This technique enables biomechanists to determine the timing of the contraction of muscles providing force in a movement, and also to learn the relative amounts of contraction in various muscle groups. This information is useful in determining which muscles are the most important contributors to force in a particular movement.

Another useful tool in the analysis of athletes is the force platform, an electromechanical device which measures and records the ground reaction forces exerted by athletes against the ground during sports activities (Gagnon, Robertson, & Norman, 1987). The pattern of forces applied to the ground in running has been extensively studied, and there are definite patterns which are common among most runners. Runners with exceptionally high force impacts against the ground have been found to suffer higher incidences of running injuries. The pressure patterns of the footstrike of runners has also been used to assist in the design and testing of running shoes to determine which shoes may have the most effective impact attenuation. The pressure patterns of throwers and weightlifters have also been extensively reported, and some patterns have been associated with success in these activities.

ANSWERS TO BIOMECHANICS QUESTIONS

1. How is Michael Jordan able to give the impression that he is suspended in the air for an extended period of time during a jump shot? Is it possible for an athlete to 'hang in the air'?

It is ***not possible*** for athletes to increase the actual time that they are in the air during a jump, as they become a projectile at takeoff, and are acted upon by the constant acceleration of gravity. Once the body loses contact with the floor, the center of gravity will follow a parabolic trajectory that is totally determined by the magnitude and direction of the velocity at take-off, and the athlete is unable to alter this pathway (Laws, 1984). The CG of all athletes follows a perfect parabolic pathway, as it is constantly decelerated on the way up to peak height, then constantly accelerated back down to the floor. One of the explanations for the illusion that athletes are suspended at or near the peak of the jump, is that their velocity at peak height is very slow, as they are decelerated to 0 m/s vertical velocity at the peak of the jump, then accelerated back to take-off velocity at landing (Brancazio, 1984). Since the vertical velocity reaches 0 m/s at peak height, the athlete slows down, and the time taken to drop 15 cm near peak height is much slower than to drop 15 cm just before landing. An athlete jumping vertically for height has his highest velocity at takeoff, which is then decelerated at a rate of 9.81 m/s every second he is in the air until it reaches 0 m/s. He is then accelerated downward by gravity until he again reaches take-off velocity at the time of touchdown with the floor.

The other explanation for the illusion of being suspended is that the athlete can stop the upward movement of the head by moving the arms and legs upward relative to the trunk to alter the position of the CG in the body (Bishop & Hay, 1979). The CG moves upwards in the trunk, while the head remains in the same position; this gives the illusion that the athlete is hanging in the air, but the CG is actually following a parabolic pathway while moving within the trunk (Figure 7.18). The head of the athlete is actually stationary for an extended period of time, which will likely improve accuracy in skills such as basketball shooting or volleyball spiking, and the athlete does appear to "hang in the air" due to the level position of the head, but the CG continues to move within the trunk. This action can also occur on the way down (i.e., the athlete can move the arms and legs downward, and the CG will move downward in the trunk, while the head remains at the same level).

Figure 7.18 The skilled basketball player will move the limbs upward to give the illusion of hanging in the air (Bishop & Hay, 1979).

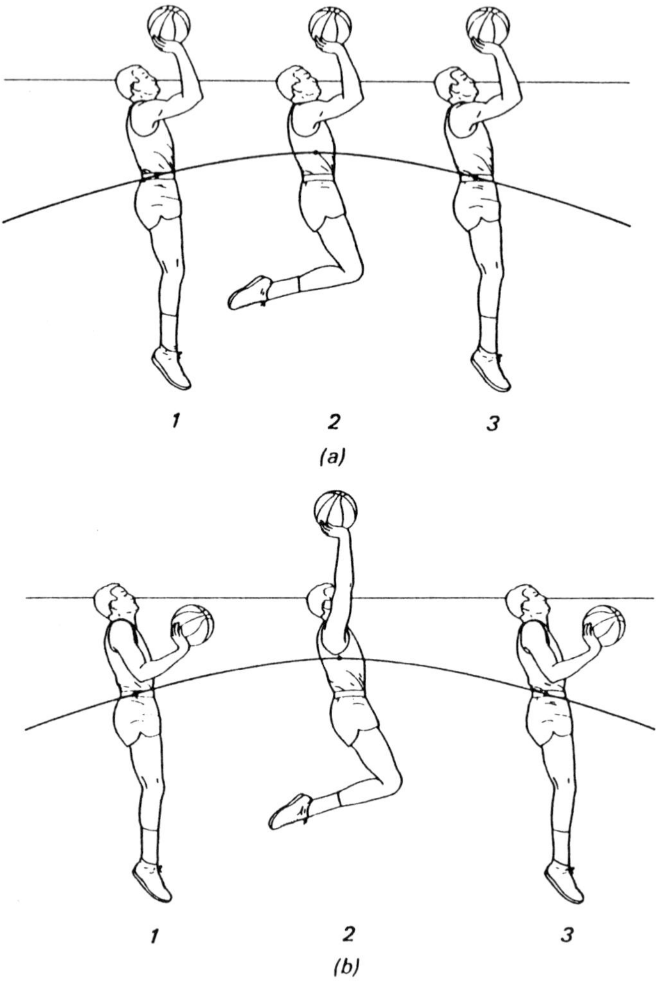

Another group of athletes who give the illusion that they are hanging in the air are ballet dancers, especially during a high horizontal jump known as the grand jeté (Laws, 1984). Dancers performing the grand jeté give an illusion of floating, in which the center of gravity follows a parabolic trajectory but moves its position in the body as the configuration of the body changes. The head appears to stay at the same level, but the center of gravity is moving up within the trunk due to the raising of the arms and legs as the peak of the jump approaches, and then down due to lowering of the arms and legs following the peak of the jump (Laws, 1984). A skilled dancer will raise the legs to a position of the split at the peak of the leap, and this increases the effect of "flying," or keeping the head level for an extended period (Figure 7.19).

2. How is Steffi Graf able to serve a tennis ball at a speed over 40 metres per second (145 km/hr)?

First, it must be noted that this great athlete is assisted by her tall stature, broad shoulders, and long arms. Recall that the speed at the end of a longer lever system is always greater; so, athletes trying to generate high velocity at the end of a system of levers will benefit by longer limbs. A taller female player, with longer arms, will usually be able to generate higher ball velocities than her shorter opponents. As well, her broad shoulders will also potentially increase the speed of the racquet, as they also increase the length of the lever arm from the spine. Finally, her broad shoulders will allow her to attain a higher reach at ball contact with a lower angle of projection that will increase the downward ball velocity, thus making the ball harder to return.

Skilled athletes are able to generate very high velocities at the end of the limb segments. This is due to the timing of the contributions made by each of the joints in the skill and the summation of joint torques. The joints move in a specific sequence and timing, so that the larger, slower joints move first, and the faster joints make their contribution later in the sequence. The major contribution to racquet velocity is made by the rotation of the hips and trunk (Reed, 1991) followed by the movements of the joints of the upper limb.

During the backswing, the trunk is rotated backwards so that the body is facing sideways relative to the direction of motion of the ball. As the trunk is rotated sideways, the front (left) arm is normally elevated to a position above the head, often with the front shoulder as the highest point on the trunk (i.e., the hitter pointing the front arm at the ball). At this point, the rear shoulder (the right shoulder) is often much lower, with the hitting arm flexed well behind the body. From this position, the shoulders are rapidly rotated forward, and as they are rotated, the front shoulder drops downward as the front arm is adducted in towards the trunk (See Fig. 14). As the front arm drops down, the elbow is brought in to the trunk to assist with deceleration of the trunk rotation (Alexander, 1983). At the same time the trunk is decelerating, the hitting arm is moving from a position of maximal lateral rotation, to one of medial rotation and extension As the hitting arm is medially rotating, it is also extending at the elbow. As this elbow extension is occurring, the arm is extended as high as possible above the athlete causing the front shoulder to assume a very high position. At the instant of impact, the hitting shoulder is at its highest point, while the front shoulder is at its lowest point, producing a "change in elevation of the shoulders." The dropping of the front shoulder has the effect of speeding up trunk rotation, as well as increasing the height of reach of the hitting/throwing arm.

Figure 7.19 A dancer performing the grand jeté gives the illusion of being suspended in the air during the leap.

One of the major contributors to the speed of the racquet in tennis is the medial rotation of the shoulder joint prior to the hit. In the skill of serving in tennis, the position of maximal shoulder lateral rotation is very important. This position is seen at the end of trunk rotation forward, when the trunk has been forcefully rotated forward, and then has been rapidly decelerated in a position facing the net. The serving arm is in a position of over 90° of abduction, the elbow is flexed to 90°, and the forearm is in a position pointing to the floor. This position is produced by the inertia of the lower arm and hand, and their tendency to stay in a motionless position behind the trunk of the server (Atwater, 1979). The trunk has literally "rotated out from under" the serving arm, which remains in position behind the server (this position placing the medial rotators on a stretch, which will facilitate their subsequent contraction).

The medial rotators must initially remain relaxed during the trunk rotation, so as not to provide resistance to the laterally rotating arm. At the end of the range of trunk rotation, there will be strong eccentric contraction of the medial rotators to decelerate the lateral rotation of the throwing arm. This will be followed by a powerful concentric contraction of the medial rotators, to produce the high velocity medial rotation and extension of the serving arm. Movement is best taught by emphasis on rapid and powerful trunk rotation, by driving from the back leg, and pulling through by the front hip. If the trunk rotation is done correctly, and the serving shoulder remains relaxed to allow the arm to remain behind the trunk, the lateral rotation will occur without conscious effort by the server.

Another major contributor to the speed of the serving arm is the deceleration of the trunk following the rapid rotation forward into the serve. The trunk abruptly stops rotating forward, and will remain stationary during the arm movement forward (Alexander, 1983). This deceleration refers to the abrupt stopping of trunk rotation which occurs in skilled throwing and striking movements. The skilled server will accelerate the trunk from a sideways position to a position facing the direction of motion. As the trunk approaches this forward-facing position, the rotation is rapidly and abruptly stopped by the eccentric contraction of the trunk muscles (serratus anterior, internal and external obliques). This rapid deceleration of the trunk will cause some of the angular momentum of the trunk to transfer to the throwing arm, and the throwing arm will speed up. The throwing arm will speed up at a much greater rate than the trunk slows down due to the differences in moments of inertia (mass times distance) between these two body parts. The throwing arm does not start to accelerate forward rapidly until the trunk has almost stopped, as this is the point of most dramatic transfer of momentum from trunk to arm.

3. How is Roger Clemens able to throw a curve ball which can curve over 55 cm on the way to the plate?

The ball curves for several reasons: (1) the pitcher imparts spin to the ball by rotation of the wrist and lower arm at release, (2) the seams on the ball trap a boundary layer of air which is carried along by the ball to the plate and (3) the oncoming air interacts with the boundary layer around the ball, producing an area of low pressure on one side of the ball. A ball curves due to the action of the oncoming air on the boundary layer of air which is carried by a ball with spin. Spin is imparted to the baseball by the action of the lower arm, wrist, and fingers at release, and the application of spin by the pitcher is aided by the friction with the seams on the ball. As the ball spins, the seams pick up a boundary layer of air which is carried around the ball in the direction of the spin (Allman, 1982; Shadewald, 1979). As the ball moves forward through the air on the way to the plate, the oncoming air interacts with the boundary layer of air causing an increase or decrease in the airflow around the ball. The ball will move toward the direction of the spin which will determine the direction of the curve. Studies of the curve ball have found that a major league curve ball is thrown with topspin; so, it is the topspin which produces the rapid drop of the ball (Allman, 1982).

Assume a curve ball is thrown with topspin, and the boundary layer of air is moving around the ball from top to bottom. On the bottom of the ball, the boundary layer of air is moving in the same direction as the oncoming air, so the airflow around the ball has relative high velocity. According to the Bernoulli principle, high velocity air flow produces an area of relative low pressure, so there is a low pressure area formed below the ball (Figure 7.20). Since objects tend to move toward areas of relative low pressure, the ball will tend to drop more rapidly than it normally drops due to gravity, giving the batter the illusion that the ball drops straight down as it approaches the plate. This illusion is partly due to the rapid drop of the ball due to its spin, as well as to the acceleration of gravity which has been accelerating the ball downward for up to .5 second en route to the plate (Shadewald, 1979).

On the top of the ball, the boundary layer of air is moving in the opposite direction to the oncoming air, so there is slowing of the air flow near the top edge of the ball thus forming an area of relative low velocity and high pressure. This high pressure area will cause the ball to drop more rapidly downward toward the low pressure area on the bottom of the ball. The amount of deviation from a normal pathway that a curve ball will take is dependent on the amount of spin imparted to the ball and also to the velocity of the ball en route to the plate. The greater the rate of spin is, and the greater the horizontal velocity, the greater the deviation will be.

4. How is Katarina Witt able to perform a triple-twisting jump in figure skating, and still land with perfect control?

Only the most skilled of figure skaters are able to perform a triple-twisting jump, since it requires time in the air to perform the three spins. Time in the air

Figure 7.20 The air flow around a spinning baseball will produce a deviation in the direction of the spin (Luttgens, *et al.,* 1992).

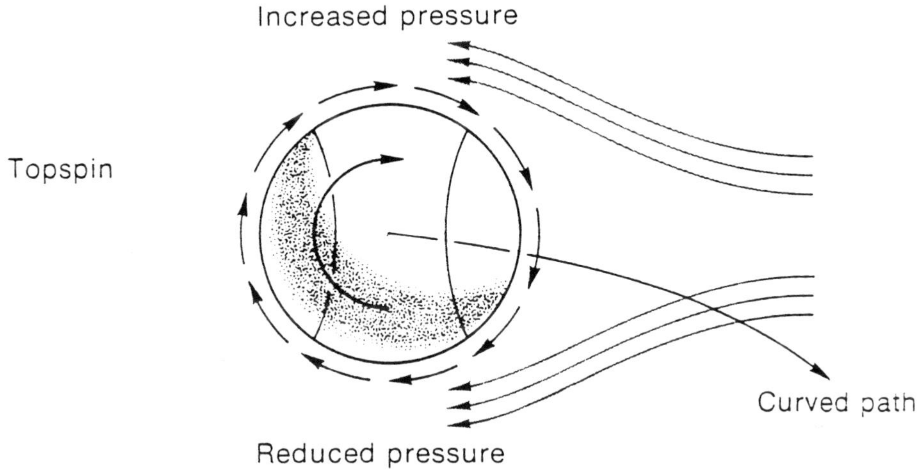

is generated only by vertical velocity at take-off, which is a measure of the ability of the skater to apply high vertical forces at take-off. If the athlete requires more time in the air, and a higher jump, the athlete also will have much higher forces to absorb and control at landing.

Skilled figure skaters can perform very difficult spinning skills. They are able control the rate of spinning by exerting high muscle forces at landing, as well as by applying the Law of Conservation of Angular Momentum. The skater applies an angular impulse at take-off to generate a high value of angular momentum which will allow her to rotate three times around her longitudinal axis while airborne. While she is airborne, she will bring her limbs in close to the longitudinal axis, to minimize the moment of inertia and decrease the resistance to rotation. This decrease in moment of inertia will produce an increase in angular velocity, since her angular momentum is constant while airborne. Just prior to landing, she will extend the limbs out sideways from the body, and this will increase the moment of inertia and decrease the rate of spinning.

At the landing, her rate of spinning has been reduced, and she applies torques from eccentric contraction of the leg and trunk muscles to take up the angular momentum she had while airborne. She uses the angular impulse-momentum relationship in the opposite sense to that at take-off, in that angular impulse is now applied to decrease the angular momentum back to zero in preparation for the next skill in the routine. As the skate contacts the ice at initial contact on landing, the leg extensor muscles are strongly contracted to absorb the vertical forces and the rotational torques generated during the airborne phase. The ability to control this large amount of angular momentum is a result of many years of practice, as well as high levels of strength which must be applied both at takeoff and at landing.

SUMMARY

The science of biomechanics is exciting and dynamic. It enables the student to understand and explain the mechanics of human movement. The basic principles of physics and mechanics, along with the universal laws of motion, can be used to explain all athletic activities, as well as other human movements such as driving a bus or playing a cello. Future study in the discipline of biomechanics is an exciting challenge for all students of human movement.

REFERENCES

ADAMS, W. C. (1991). Biomechanics of human movement. In *Foundations of physical education, exercise and sport sciences* (pp. 42–79). Philadelphia: Lea and Febiger.

ADRIAN, M. J., & COOPER, J. M. (1989). *Biomechanics of human movement.* Indianapolis, IN: Benchmark.

ALEXANDER, M. J. L. (1983). The pattern of body segment movement in high speed sport skills. *Coaching Science Update,* 15–19.

ALLMAN, W. F. (October 1982). Pitching rainbows: The untold physics of the curve ball. *Science, 82:* 32–38.

ATWATER, A. E. (1979). Biomechanics of overarm throwing and of throwing injuries. In Hutton, R. S. & Miller, D. I. (Eds.), *Exercise and Sport Sciences Reviews* (pp. 43–85). Philadelphia: The Franklin Institute.

ATWATER, A. E. (1988). Biomechanics and the female athlete. In Puhl, J., Brown, C., & Voy, R. O. (Eds.), *Sport science perspectives for women* (pp. 1–12). Champaign, IL: Human Kinetics.

ATWATER, A. E. (1990). Gender differences in distance running. In Cavanaugh, P. R. (Ed.), *Biomechanics of distance running* (pp. 321–362). Champaign, IL: Human Kinetics.

BISHOP, R. D., & HAY, J. G. (1979). Basketball: The mechanics of hanging in the air. *Medicine and Science in Sports, 11*(3): 274–277.

BRANCAZIO, P. J. (1984). *Sport science: Physical laws and optimum performance.* NY: Simon and Schuster.

GAGNON, M., ROBERTSON, G., & NORMAN, R. (1987). Kinetics. In Dainty, D. A. & Norman, R. W. (Eds.), *Standardizing biomechanical testing in sport.* Champaign, IL: Human Kinetics.

GENSEMER, R. E. (1992). Biomechanics: The science of human motion. In Gensemer, R. E. (Eds.), *Physical education: Perspectives/inquiry/applications* (pp. 97–112). Dubuque, IA: Wm. C. Brown.

HALL, S. (1991). *Basic biomechanics.* St. Louis: Mosby Year Book.

HAY, J. G. (1993). *The biomechanics of sports techniques, 4th ed.* Englewood Cliffs, N.J.: Prentice-Hall.

HAY, J. G., & REID, J. G. (1982). *Anatomy, mechanics and human motion, 2nd ed.* Englewood Cliffs, N.J.: Prentice-Hall.

JOBSE, H., SCHUURHOF, R., CSEREP, F., SCHREURS, A. W., & DE KONING, J. J. (1990). Measurement of push-off force and ice friction during speed skating. *International Journal of Sport Biomechanics, 6*(1): 92–100.

KLUGER, J. (June 1982). The human machine. *Science Digest,* 64–71.

KONING, J. J., DE BOER, R. W., DE GROOT, G., & VAN INGEN SCHENAU, G. J. (1987). Push off force in speed skating. *International Journal of Sport Biomechanics, 3*:103–107.

KOPP, P. M., & REID, J. G. (1980). A force and torque analysis of giant swings on the horizontal bar. *Canadian Journal of Applied Sport Sciences, 2*:98–102.

LAWS, K. (1984). *The physics of dance.* NY: Schirmer.

MILLER, D. I., JONES, I. C., & PIZZIMENTI, M. A. (1991). *Biomechanical feedback system for Canada's high performance divers.* Unpublished report to Sport Canada, The University of Western Ontario.

PEAK PERFORMANCE TECHNOLOGIES, I. (1990). *Peak Performance Technologies Instructional Manual.*

REED, A. T. (1991). A quantal approach to movement. *Science Periodical on Research and Technology and Sport, 12*(1).

ROBERTS, E. M., ZERNICKE, R. F., YOUM, Y., & HUANG, H. (Eds.). (1974). *Kinetic parameters of kicking.* Baltimore: University Park Press.

ROBERTSON, D. G. E. (1992). Human anatomy. In Anderson, D. (Ed.), *Foundations of Canadian physical education, recreation and sport studies* (pp. 11–35). Dubuque, IA: Wm C. Brown.

SHADEWALD, R. (September 1979). It's 1-2-3 strikes and yer out at the old ballistics game! *Science Digest,* 56–61.

SPRIGINGS, E. J., WATSON, L. G., & STILLING, D. S. D. (1989). *Development of a knowledge-based expert system for skill analysis of forward non-twisting dives.* Unpublished report to Sport Canada, University of Saskatchewan.

STEVENSON, J. (1984). Electromyographic analysis techniques. In Alexander, M. J. L. (Ed.), *Technology for the biomechanical analysis of athletes.* Ottawa: CAHPER.

TORREY, L. (August 1984). Science goes to the Olympics. *Science Digest,* 33–37.

VIZARD, F. (February 1992). The technology of the Olympics. *Popular Mechanics,* 26–29.

WHIELDON, D. (1979). Biomechanics: Space-age sportsmedicine. *Physician and Sportsmedicine, 7*(5): 106–117.

ZATSIORSKY, V. M., & YAKUNIN, N. (1991). Mechanics and biomechanics of rowing: A review. *International Journal of Sport Biomechanics, 7*(3): 229–281.

Chapter Eight
Management Theory and Practice

Daniel G. Soucie

In North America, as well as in many countries around the world, sport management is the last born child of the large physical education and kinesiology family. Over the years the field of physical education and kinesiology has expanded into many related areas. As research developed and the knowledge base broadened, the curriculum in institutions of higher education has become more and more specialized and discipline-oriented. As such, many subdisciplinary fields developed, and today, for example, courses in the following cognate areas are required for program recognition or even for accreditation: physical growth and development, exercise physiology, biomechanics, motor learning and control, anthropometry, adapted and remedial physical activity, sport sociology, sport psychology, sport history and philosophy, curriculum and instruction, and (more recently) sport management theory.

Parallel to the development of these related subdisciplines, several subprofessional fields of practice emerged as viable careers in physical education and kinesiology. In fact, in many instances, it was the involvement on the part of university graduates in innovative fields of practice which more or less forced academics to develop professional preparation programs and to conduct research to address their concerns and problems. The area of sport management theory and practice is a good example of such concomitant development of the discipline and the profession.

Academic programs in sport management have developed not only as a result of the explosion of knowledge and as a result of felt needs by practitioners in the field, but also due to the saturation of the job market in the area of teaching (Soucie, 1993). Teaching physical education in schools had been and still remained, until approximately the late 1970s, the dominant career choice for graduates in the field. As the 1980s progressed, one of the more popular program areas with students became sport management because jobs were becoming available in this field of practice.

THE UNIVERSAL NECESSITY OF MANAGEMENT

Management exists everywhere: at the plant, at the hospital, in the government, in business, as well as at the tennis club. Whenever people get together within an informal group or a more formal organization to accomplish common objectives, it becomes necessary that the efforts of members be coordinated so that, together, they can work as a team and be more effective. One must recognize that in society as a whole, as well as in the world of sport, organizations abound. Everywhere groups of people join forces and form associations, societies, and clubs of all kinds to achieve objects of mutual concern or interest. Furthermore, the same individuals relate to many different groups and organizations, whether they are associations, societies, church organizations, social clubs, or sport clubs.

Our North American society is indeed characterized by the many bureaucratic organizations that constantly affect our very own lives. Some time ago, folk singer Peter Seeger, in a song entitled "Little boxes on the hillside," referred to the word "boxes" to depict the many bureaucratic structures and institutions within which people are slotted over the course of their lives. In fact, is it not true that we spend the vast majority of our lives in one or another "box"? After we are born in a *hospital,* we spend our childhood years in a *nursery,* in *kindergarten,* and finally in *primary school.* Then we go to *high school, college,* and *university.* After spending a considerable amount of time in *courses, classes,* or *labs,* we are awarded a degree which grants us the privilege to enter yet another institution, that of the *workplace.* We then spend the rest of our life going from one employment to another to eventually end it all, likely back at the *hospital,* and then to be buried in a "box" for our final rest at the *cemetery.* What a structured life!

In the world of sport, amateur as well as professional, and in the field of institutional physical education and athletics, the situation is no different. Sport clubs, national or provincial sport organizations, professional sport teams, minor sport leagues, interscholastic and interuniversity athletics, etc., are all examples of organizations or "boxes" which possess the same basic bureaucratic characteristics. In all such organizations, there are rules, procedures, policies, tasks, and functions which are designed to rationally and systematically guide human interaction. Such organizations have purposes, and for these to be accomplished a minimum of coordination is required. This coordination is essential in order to determine who does what and when, and how things are to be handled. Coordination means to harmonize or to act together in a concerted way so that the collective efforts of people are all oriented in the same general direction (i.e., towards the realization of the organization's goals and objectives). That's what management is all about. Simply stated, management or administration therefore consists of coordinating the efficient use of available resources in order that objectives of the organization and of its members can be accomplished. Those who, within the organization, are charged with this coordinating responsibility, are referred to as managers or administrators.

Titles of managers and administrators vary considerably. They may be called directors, department heads, supervisors, coaches, coordinators, presidents, or simply "responsible for." Moreover, managers may be elected by their peers or formally appointed by the organization. Also, the formal power held by these individuals varies considerably from one situation to another. Hence, some managers are responsible for larger amounts of resources (human, material, or financial) than others. Furthermore, the larger the organization becomes, the more managerial levels are required. Typically, as managers get promoted through the hierarchy, they are given more power—and also more responsibility. However, as will be explained later in this chapter, regardless of their official title and their level of power and responsibility, all managers essentially do the same thing—that is, they must plan and organize the work to be done in their unit, and then direct workers or subordinates in the execution of that work.

In sport as well as everywhere else, more and more individuals are called upon to take over such managerial responsibilities. The fact is that there are vast resources in the world of sport which require efficient management. Whether it is at the professional or the amateur and recreational level, there are thousands of organizations, associations, and clubs requiring efficient and sound management. And the numbers are growing! Sport management is the main source of income, and a full-time job for many. Individual careers therefore do exist in sport management. This occupation has emerged over the last quarter of a century because many individuals got involved on a full-time basis working towards the solution to specific problems related to recreational and/or competitive sport in society. Members of this occupational group have begun to claim the territory, and stake out a jurisdiction, and there currently exists an implicit attempt by university graduates in the field at controlling this "social space" (Soucie, 1993). The recent publication and promotion of standards in the United States for university curricula in sport management is evidence of that phenomenon. These norms, which reflect a set of values shared by those responsible for the programs, more or less constitute an attempt at defining the basic and essential traits which sport managers ought to possess, and determining what the functional contribution of sport management to society ought to be.

NEW IMPERATIVES FOR MANAGERS

As we head for the 21st century, the role of managers will become more and more complex and difficult. The fact is that people have changed considerably since the industrial revolution when workers were considered like cogs that had to fit into the production assembly line. Management through rigid rules and threats of punishment is no longer possible or desirable. A bit later, scientific management and overrationality destroyed the individuality and the creativity of workers. Thus, whereas effectiveness and efficiency in producing goods and services were the only objectives of yesterday's industrial organizations, both the wise use of available resources *and* the satisfaction of human interests are at the top of today's manager's agenda.

Our society has indeed shifted toward more people-oriented organizations where objectives, policies, and procedures cannot be decided upon unless the individuals who make up the organization have some say in the matter. Recent democratic trends have brought about a new set of definitions for organizational concepts such as chain of command, delegation of authority, control, performance evaluation, communication, and decision-making. Participative management and decision-making today require that each member of the organization plays a role and contributes to the optimization of decisions. However, the task of empowering subordinates to establish goals and of motivating them toward achieving these goals, is not an easy one. Individuals making up organizations differ in many ways, and they consequently think and react differently under various circumstances. People are better educated, better informed, and more assertive about what they want. People differ in personality, character, and previous exposure to organizational environments. People have different needs, interests, and levels of aspiration, and consequently assign often radically different priorities to the many goals and objectives put forth in organizations. Such individual differences inevitably lead to organizational goal displacement, often opposing role-expectations, and give rise to various situations of conflict. People will often disagree over means and ends, because they hold opposing views about what is good and desirable for them *and* for the organization of which they are an integral part.

Furthermore, largely because of the increasing democratization and bureaucratization in North American society, new functions and interrelations have emerged in the social structure of organizations. Accordingly, specialization and professionalization have then resulted. In bureaucratic structures, specialization is required for organizations to attain their objectives in the most rational manner. Resultantly, responsibilities are delegated to persons holding competence (specialists, professionals) in the respective areas of specialization that are a part of an organization's mission.

This has spilled over into the field of sport management where new leadership roles and responsibilities are emerging, particularly in areas such as strategic planning and organizational development. Sport managers must now approach change in a pro-active manner, and they must lead in the introduction of change if they wish to avoid being left behind by change. In the current economic context where service cut-backs and accountability are at the top of the political agenda, sport managers are being asked to refocus, to integrate, and to revisit their values. As will be explained later in this chapter, if management is the art of getting things done through others, it also cannot be truly effective unless resources are used to accomplish the things that are most important. Is there anything so useless as doing with great efficiency those things that are not important?!?

LACK OF ADEQUATE MANAGEMENT TRAINING

Even though jobs are becoming available in sport management, not all incumbents have graduated from college or university and have received proper training in kinesiology and physical education. University degrees in sport management attest to the acquisition of required competencies. They should serve as a quality-control mechanism for the recruitment of practicing professionals.

It is indeed sad to realize that the myth still exists that seniority and past membership within a particular sport organization often constitute the (major if not the only!) criteria for selecting sport managers. In many cases in sport, managers are appointed not on the basis of their sport management training, but solely because of their long association with that particular sport organization, either as a coach or as an athlete. One must agree with Parkhouse (1978) when she writes that "one of the incongruencies in the multi-billion dollar business of athletics is the willingness to turn over the administration of this enterprise to these individuals who have had little, if any, formal preparation for the job" (p. 22).

According to the now very well-known Peter principle, many individuals reach their level of incompetence when they get promoted to a management position. Indeed, it does happen quite often in our field that someone, because he or she is the best worker, the best teacher, or the best coach, etc., will be elevated to the rank of manager or administrator. From one day to the next, these individuals are asked to do something at which they are usually quite inexperienced and for which they have often never been prepared—that is, to plan, organize, direct, and control the work of their peers. There is, in fact, a whole world of difference between doing things well as a worker or subordinate, and getting things done through others as a manager or superior.

Management requires knowledge of, and experience with, effective planning strategies and organizational techniques, as well as proper communication skills, decision-making capability, and know-how. As stated by McCleary (cited by Zeigler, 1987, p. 17), "to be competent is to possess sufficient knowledge and ability to meet specified requirements in the sense of being able, adequate, suitable, capable." Management is an art as well as a science, and sport managers must be properly trained and carefully selected if our sport organizations are to be effective. Competencies which are essential for practicing sport managers will be discussed later in this chapter. But first let us look at the basic terminology of the field of management.

A FEW BASIC DEFINITIONS

For a better appreciation of the material presented in this chapter, the reader should have a clear understanding of several key concepts basic to the field of administration.

Management and Administration. The act of coordinating the efforts of workers toward the attainment of objectives in an organization has been called many different things over the years. Basically, however, two verbs of action have endured: to administer and to manage. Hence the words administration and administrator, and the words management and manager. To avoid becoming a prisoner of any one of these two terms, it is possible and acceptable to equate them, and to use them interchangeably. Some people may disagree with this equation. However, even though subtle differences do exist, they are more useful in theory than in practice. Therefore, in this chapter, management and administration are considered synonymous. The two concepts carry the same fundamental connotations of coordinating the efforts of people and of activating, directing, or leading the group or the organization toward its goals.

For those who insist on making a distinction, it would appear that the term *administrator* is reserved for those individuals at the top of the organizational hierarchy. As explained by Soucie (1989, p. 29), an administrator, for example someone who is a member of a Board of Administrators (or Board of Governors or Board of Directors) of a national sport organization, is more preoccupied with formulating policy and with the strategic direction of the organization. Typically, administrators are charged with the more important decisions such as defining the mission and strategic goals of the organization, hiring the executive director, approving budgets, etc. In the business world, these people are often the owners or shareholders of the enterprise. On the other hand, *managers* do not have shares in the company, in the sense that they "manage" the affairs of the company *for* the owners. Moreover, as we go down the echelon of the organization's hierarchy, the more concrete, specific, and routine duties are the responsibility of managers. Generally speaking, the following parallels illustrate some of the subtle differences between the roles of administrators and managers: administrators are involved with goals and strategic planning, whereas managers are charged with tactics and operational planning; administrators deal with values, managers with facts; administrators spell out policies, managers execute them; administrators are persons of reflection, managers are persons of action; and the work of administrators is more qualitative as opposed to the work of managers which is more quantitative.

As stated earlier, regardless of the title, the hierarchical position, or the level of power and responsibility of the incumbent, management or administration involves the responsibility of orienting human, material, and financial resources in dynamic and structured units for the purpose of greater effectiveness and efficiency. Managerial effectiveness generally refers to the accomplishment of specific objectives, whereas managerial efficiency generally refers to the successful attainment of objectives with the available resources (people, money, materials, and time).

Supervision and Leadership. Supervision is also often used interchangeably with management. However, the concept of supervision is more restrictive, and generally applies to the management of human resources in organizations (e.g., supervision of personnel). Borrowed from military and industrial settings, the term supervision is generally restricted to the functions of directing, controlling, and appraising human performance in organizations. The function of supervision prevails in the larger organizations; it involves proposing objectives to aim for, developing programs and procedures conducive to the accomplishment of those objectives, and evaluating the adequacy of people, programs, and procedures in relationship to organizational performance.

Leadership is another concept which is prevailing in the management literature. Management cannot be viewed as absolutely equivalent to leadership, but it inevitably involves the leadership qualities, skills, and style of the manager.

Taxonomies of managerial tasks reveal that the work of managers involves many varied and fragmented activities including constant interactions with different people inside as well as outside the organization (Kotter, 1982), and then making decisions related to more problems generated by these people than the manager can handle (McCall, Kaplan & Gerlach, 1982). Furthermore, it is well known that such managerial decisions are typically characterized more by emotionality than rationality (Simon, 1987), and are often highly political (Mintzberg, Raisinghani & Theoret, 1976). Managing is therefore largely about people, and this constitutes the manager's most important responsibility because most everything else depends on it. Hence, the importance of one's leadership skills as a manager in influencing people and outcomes is paramount.

Of course, leadership and management are different. Obviously we all know that one can be a leader without being a manager. The reverse is not impossible, but it is certainly more difficult to imagine. Leadership involves an influence process. Bergeron (1979) defines it as "the sum of activities through which a hierarchical superior influences the behaviour of subordinates toward the voluntary and more effective pursuit of organizational objectives" (p. 24). For their part, Katz & Kahn (1978) stipulate that leadership is "the influential increment over and above mechanical compliance with the routine directives of the organization" (p. 528). The extent of the manager's leadership skills will indeed have a considerable impact on the outcome of his or her directives. Outcomes may include behaviors by subordinates such as enthusiastic commitment, indifferent compliance, reluctant obedience, or full resistance!

It can readily be observed that even though they may be qualitatively different, management and leadership go hand in hand, and are certainly complementary. Zaleznik (1977) has suggested that managers are concerned with how things get done while leaders are more concerned with what things mean to people. More recently, Bennis and Nanus (1985) have proposed that "managers are people who do things right and leaders are people who do the right things." Certainly, in human service organizations in which sport organizations are classified, effective managerial leadership has to be concerned with both.

Managerial leadership is complex, and it may involve many different and distinct activities and actions by the leader-manager. It is not always easy to place one's finger on the specific intervention, attitude, or trait which causes the manager to have influence over subordinates. Leadership is indeed complicated. It is partly inherited and partly acquired. It is a subtle mixture of skills, knowledge, and information; formal authority; intelligence; courage; tenacity; instinct; and hard work (Soucie, 1994, p. 3).

Power and Authority. Basic to an understanding of the complexity of relationships within organizations, particularly those between managers and subordinates, as well as understanding how roles and functions are shared, are the concepts of authority and power.

In order to make things happen in an orderly fashion in formal organizations, it is necessary to have power or the capacity to control decisions. Moreover, things do not just happen on their own. There needs to be a motor, a cause, an agent, a leader who initiates action. Power must be exercised. Power is more or less equivalent to the influence exercised by someone within a given situation. It is the ability to get people to do what you want them to do. Power is the affecting of the situation by human action. It is often difficult to measure the amount of power held by someone. The fact is that power can only be considered and understood in the specific social context where it takes place. Moreover, the sources of power are varied and complex.

On the other hand, authority has a narrower scope than power. Authority is a source or a form of power. Authority is the accepted right to engage in certain actions. It is more explicit than power which is not so clear. Over the years, several authors (Weber, 1947; Blau & Scott, 1962; Peabody, 1962; French & Raven, 1968; Etzioni, 1975; and Mintzberg, 1983). have each presented their own classification of the sources of power and authority. Figure 8.1 summarises the different sources of power and authority identified in this literature.

Power stems from formal or institutional authority and from personal competence. Institutional authority could stem from tradition, from the legal system, or from the status or position occupied in the formal organization. Traditional authority rests on the established status of people who have exercised authority in the past. Whoever inherits the position also inherits the authority established by custom. Legal authority is anchored in laws. It corresponds to a recognized and accepted right for someone to act in a certain way or to make certain decisions. Status authority is related to the position held by someone in the formal organization. Authority of status is established in rules and regulations edicted by the organization. Such formal authority stems from a legally established agreement between the organization and the workers. Rights and privileges rest with the position established in the structural hierarchy of the organization. Such status allows the incumbent to control the allocation of resources and to make decisions including the remuneration of workers and determining who gets rewarded or punished. It also allows the holder of the position to access and control important information.

Power also stems from the personal competence of the individual. Competence derives from several factors, notably from traits, skills, knowledge, and experience. Personal traits are numerous and include such characteristics as self-confidence, emotional stability, energy level, initiative, stress tolerance, empathy, tact, charm, etc. Such traits are particularly relevant in the development and maintenance of good interpersonal relations and effective communication. Skills are also numerous and include technical skills, interpersonal skills, and conceptual skills. Technical skills, which mainly have to do with "things," relate to knowledge about methods, processes, procedures, and techniques for doing the work. Interpersonal skills, which mainly deal with "people," relate to knowledge about human behaviour, ability to understand the feelings, attitudes and motives of others, oral and written communication ability, and ability to establish cooperation relationships. Conceptual skills, which mostly relate to "ideas and concepts," are concerned with general analytical ability, logical thinking, deductive and inductive reasoning, problem solving ability, creativity, anticipating, visioning and strategic-thinking ability.

Figure 8.1 Difference sources of power in organizations

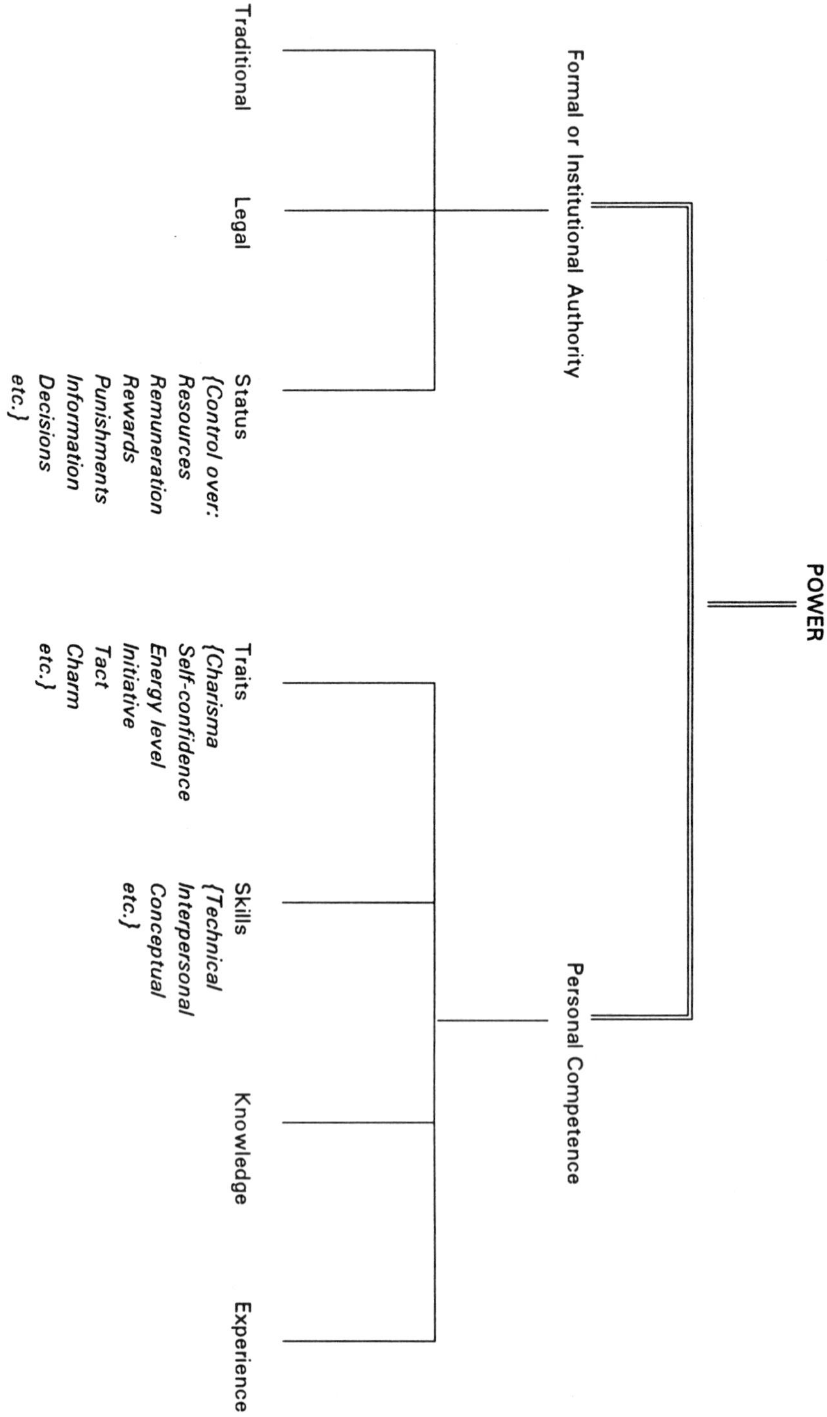

It is well known that, in many sport organizations, certain managers hold status authority by virtue of their position and title but lack personal competence. It is usually this type of manager who must rely on his or her formal authority to obtain obedience and compliance with directives. Managers who lack the personal traits or skills eventually lose the respect and support of subordinates. On the other hand in the absence of formal authority, other individuals, in the same organization, be it because of their charisma, skills, knowledge, expertise or otherwise, often exercise a strong influence over decisions. This typically results in serious conflicts between the formal manager and the informal leaders. As stated earlier, it is essential to understand how power is shared and exercised, and how the interplay between formal and informal leaders in organizations affect the overall effectiveness of any unit. It is indeed the subtle mixture of formal and informal power within any group or organization which determines how decisions are reached, and which direction is taken. Finally, it must be understood that such overlap of formal and informal decision-making structures are inevitable in any kind of bureaucratic organization where responsibilities must be shared between people, between managers and workers, between superiors and subordinates.

ROLES AND FUNCTIONS OF SPORT MANAGERS

What is a sport manager? What does that person do? Where do we find such individuals? How can we define sport management?

De Sensi, Kelley, Blanton, and Beitel (1990) have suggested that sport management includes "any combination of skills related to planning, organizing, directing, controlling, budgeting, leading, and evaluating within the context of an organization or department whose primary product or service is related to sport and/or physical activity." Sport managers are persons who act in managerial leadership roles in the field of sport. As such, they are involved in various and quite diversified tasks, and the organizations where they work may be quite different from one another.

We find sport managers working within recreation and parks departments; in schools; in sports or recreation centers; in regional, provincial or national sport associations; in sports-event organizing committees, etc. They work within sports clubs, with teachers, coaches, fitness instructors, and with sports participants of all ages. Their tasks mainly consist of planning and directing various activities and services designed for specific clienteles in the field of sport. Sport managers are therefore involved in facilitating the access to sports programs for people whose objectives may range from simple recreational participation to performance excellence. Their goals are "to enhance sport performance and/or competition and/or to enhance efficient supervision and governance of sport" (Harris, 1993, p. 392).

Characteristics, roles, and functions of sport managers are no different from those of managers or administrators in other fields of practice. As suggested in the definition of sport management at the beginning of this section, sport managers exercise the same general functions of planning, organizing, directing, etc., as do all managers. Let us then turn to these general characteristics, roles, and processes of management.

Basic Characteristics of Managerial Work. Everybody knows that administrators are always busy, that they work long hours in the office, and that they have little free time for themselves. From empirical observations conducted by Henry Mintzberg (1973) and John Kotter (1982), we know that the work of managers is typically feverish and consuming. Their work is varied and fragmented in the sense that managers literally hop from one problem to another and work in a very disjointed fashion. Also, their work is often very superficial in that it touches upon a lot of subjects but does not necessarily treat them in depth. Managers are action-oriented and are called upon to resolve problems that require their immediate attention. Managers often move from one meeting to another with totally different agendas. As explained by Hoy and Miskel (1991), "decisions are not based on a rational consideration of the existing data by a studious manager, but evolve from a fluid and often confusing series of short, disjointed conversations, meetings, and memos" (p. 256). Moreover managers are in touch with a lot of people, formally as well as informally, at planned as well as at impromptu meetings. Finally, it has been observed that managers work mostly through verbal media—i.e., they rely on the spoken word during brief face-to-face conversations or on the telephone.

General Roles of Managers. The empirical data collected by Mintzberg (1973) allowed him to define three sets of interrelated roles for managers (p. 95–96):

Interpersonal Roles. These are related to the status and the formal authority level of managers. There are three kinds of interpersonal roles:

1. *Role of Figurehead*

   Because of their status and the importance of their position, managers are required to be present at various events, to speak on behalf of the group, and to officially represent the organization.

2. *Role of Liaison Officer*

   Managers are at the heart of the networks between people in the organization, and must serve as liaison among workers, colleagues, and superiors, as well as with people outside the organization.

3. *Role of Leader*

   In that capacity, managers contribute to shaping the work atmosphere or the climate of the organization. Managers must assume the proper leadership to reconcile the members' expectations with those of the organization.

Information Roles. These are related to communication and include three sub-roles:

4. *Role of Monitor*

   Managers often constitute the nervous system of the organization and continuously receive information from within as well as from outside the organization. This information may relate to internal operations or external events.
5. *Role of Disseminator*

   Managers are often charged with circulating information to members. This information may be a fact, a simple opinion, an idea, an instruction or directive, or simply an advice.
6. *Role of Spokesperson*

   Managers become spokesperson when they intervene, on behalf of the group, with the higher authorities within the organization or with the general public or people outside.

Decision Roles. These are important for the organization since managers are often the only ones authorized to engage the group in new directions. There are four roles which relate to decision-making:

7. *Role of entrepreneur*

   Managers are change-agents within their organization. Because of their role of monitor and disseminator, they have opportunities to effect change and decide on new directions for the organization.
8. *Role of Disturbance Handler*

   All sorts of problems arise in organizations, and managers are there to solve them. It is often them who are called upon to resolve conflicts between members.
9. *Role of Negotiator*

   Because of their status and authority, managers are also called upon to negotiate agreements either with individuals, groups, or their representatives, inside the group or with other outside organizations.
10. *Role of Resource Allocator*

    Managers must decide how money and equipment are to be spent, and determine to whom resources are to be allocated within the organization.

The presence of managers is indispensable. It is essential that responsible people ensure that the organization does what it is suppose to do. Managers are there to ensure the stability of operations, and to create a working environment within which the group may operate orderly and cohesively. Managers are those who are charged with orienting and developing the organization so that it evolves, progresses, and adapts to changes in the environment. Managers are essential to ensure that the organization pursues its mission and does not defer from its charted course.

Classic Management Processes. All managers and administrators rely on the same general processes. Regardless of their hierarchical level in the organization and their specific assignments, they are all more or less involved in planning, organizing, staffing, directing (leading, motivating), and evaluating (or controlling) resources and the work to be done. In doing so, managers also make use of two other general management processes, that of decision-making and communicating.

Figure 8.2 illustrate the relationship between these universal management processes which, together, operate as a cycle. Simply stated, management consists of *determining direction* or what you want to do (planning) and how you plan to do it (organizing), and then making sure that you do in fact *get there* (by directing, leading, and motivating workers towards your plan). Decision-making and communicating are essential organizational processes that will allow you to do that. Evaluating is the final management phase which keeps the cycle going and allows you to monitor *how successful* you are at it.

Planning consists of establishing a line of action or a plan in order to reach the desired objective. It's the thinking process which precedes any action. Strategic planning deals with mission and vision and answers the questions "why and what." It is required to determine "what to do" with the resources. Structural planning deals with the assignment of tasks and responsibilities to people in the organization and answers the questions "what and who." Structural planning is useful to ensure that we "do the right things" with the resources. Operational planning relates to policies and procedures, finances, equipment, priorities, and deadlines. It addresses the questions "how, how much, where, and when." It is necessary to ensure that we "do things right" with the resources at our disposal. Planning is essential since it allows the manager to identify needs, but also to establish limitations. In sport management, for example, planning is clearly required in order to determine the needs of participants, to establish objectives and content of programs, schedules, budgets, required equipment and facilities, procedures, etc.

Organizing is the process of establishing a framework required to implement the plan. It is synonymous with structural planning, and it is concerned with the division of labour (who does what), the coordination of functions and tasks, and the establishment of a structure where functions and responsibilities are clearly identified, where relationships between functions are spelled out, and where the lines of communication and flow of authority (chain of command) are clearly identified. The purpose of the process of organizing is absolutely essential for a smooth operation and unity of direction. It is the blueprint for teamwork.

Figure 8.2 Basic and universal management processes

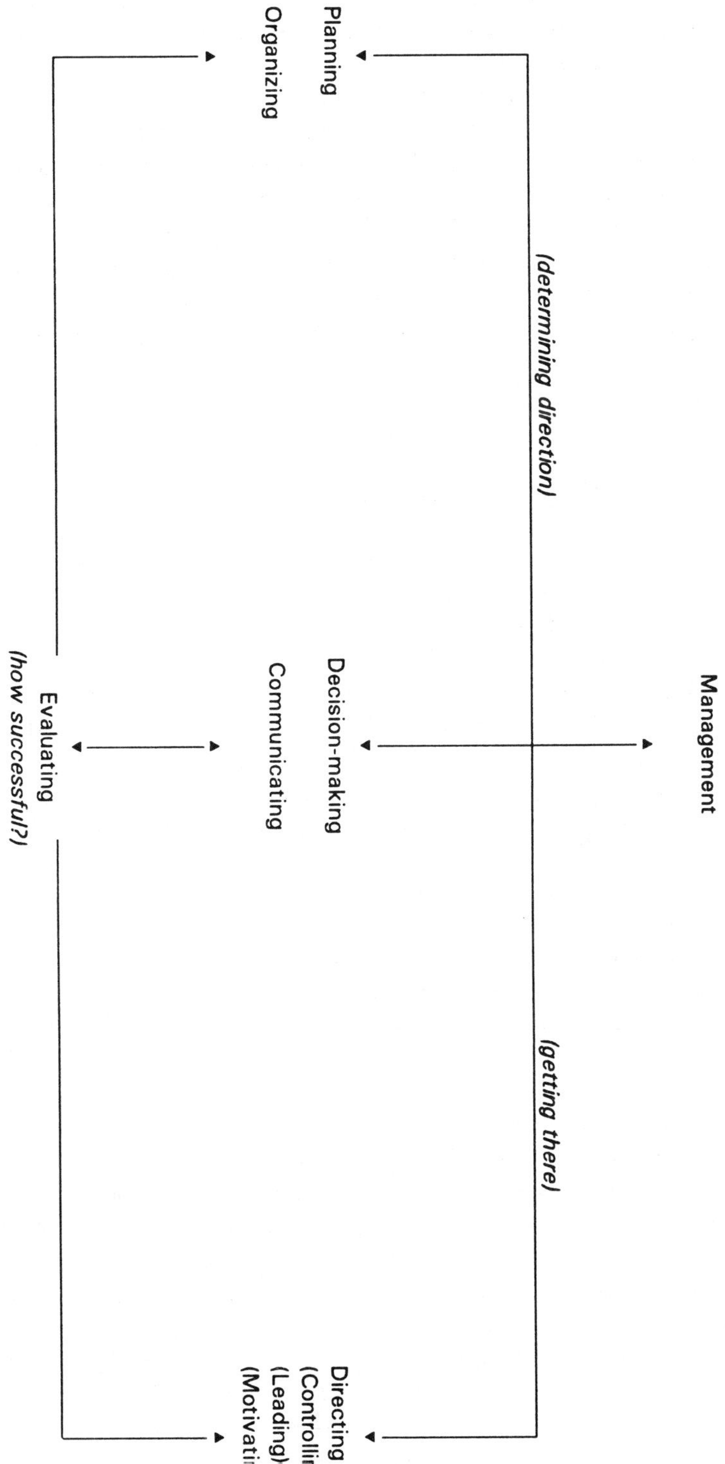

Directing consists of giving directives to members, and controlling or evaluating the direction of work and the execution of the plans. Directing involves an element of control, leadership, and motivation. Controlling is a technique or method used to gather and evaluate information to find out if the accomplished action (the actual performance) corresponds to the planned action (what ought to be or the ideal performance) in the organization. For various reasons, the control function has traditionally carried a negative connotation in the minds of subordinates. However, as a management function, the concept of control does not mean "to hold in check" or "to regulate," but rather it refers to the setting of standards and the evaluation of performance. Two forms of control are available to managers: preventive or permanent control, and corrective or occasional control. Preventive controls aim at forechecking problems and making sure that everyone does what is expected of him or her. Preventive controls take two forms: *standards of performance,* which are established criteria (usually quantity, quality, cost, and time) against which actual results are measured, and clearly defined and written *task descriptions.* Corrective controls consist of occasional (systematic or random) spot checks or visits to determine or identify discrepancies between work completed and objectives planned. In the final analysis, however, self-control on the part of subordinates is the best form of control, and managers ought to concentrate on problem employees and exercise "management by exception." That is precisely why directing is more than controlling. It also requires the proper exercise of leadership and the use of appropriate work motivation so that workers contribute efforts towards the pursuit of the organization' objectives. Directing is in essence the equivalent of acting as the conductor of an orchestra.

Giving orders and providing directives is not necessarily an easy task given the diverse personalities and characters of people who make up the organization. People have different needs and role expectations, different levels of experience, skills, and knowledge, hence the vital importance of one's ability as a leader, and the necessity of understanding human psychology and work motivation.

Managers are people of action, and are constantly confronted with decisions to be made. *Decision-making* is a process allowing managers to examine alternative solutions to problems. It is the essence of the art of management. Good decisions are the trademark of efficient managers. The process is used in planning, organizing, directing, and evaluating. It involves defining problems, determining decision criteria, listing options or possible solutions, examining pros and cons of each alternative solution, choosing the best alternative, planning appropriate action to implement the solution, and evaluating, afterwards (if the decision has or hasn't resolved the problem). Finally, it should be noted that not all managerial decisions are easy and routine decisions. In many instances, managers are confronted with important and more complex decisions where consensus is not easily reached. Typically, many such decisions rest more on abstract values than concrete facts, and are not always rational but rather based on sentiments and emotions. Deciding is evaluating or stating that one thing is more important or more urgent than another. That is why decisions are often the source of tension and conflict between members and may affect the whole climate of the organization.

Communication is another universal management process which is essential for efficient administration. Better decisions result from a sharing of information and more frequent exchanges between members. A good and effective communication system leads to a better organizational climate, open discussions, and group cohesiveness. It is the simple fact of talking to each other that allows interactions and reciprocal influences to take place in organizations. As a management process, communication can be defined as an exchange or information from one person to another for the purpose of encouraging a climate of trust and cooperation within a team of workers, and encouraging them to offer their skills, knowledge, and experience for the benefit of the entire organization. Communication is essential for the manager who has to plan, organize, direct, and evaluate organizational performance. It is essential for informing members about plans and objectives, and in motivating them toward the attainment of goals. It is also required for proper feedback from workers and clients.

Communication is all-encompassing in organizations. It follows formal as well as informal networks. It is vertical and horizontal; it is one-way or two-way; it takes place in dyads, triads, small groups, or large assemblies. It is verbal and non-verbal. It is written and comes in different forms (e.g., memos, letters, reports, books, and manuals). It is oral or visual, and it comes through the telephone, the intercom, the TV monitor, the computer screen, or the fax machine. It pervades every aspect of the manager's roles.

Evaluation relates closely to the control phase of management. It is complementary to all other management processes, and it allows managers to verify if they are on the right track and to question the effectiveness of their strategies and interventions. It allows managers to diagnose strengths and weaknesses and errors committed. It also allows them to establish a prognostic of changes to implement in order to effect the desired future performance. Coming at the end of the cycle of management, and when applied to all other management processes, evaluation allows managers to question every aspect of their job.

As general processes, planning, organizing, directing, communicating, decision-making, and controlling or evaluating apply to all managerial functions and all types of organization. They become operative and meaningful when applied to specific tasks, and are essential tools to the actualization of tasks. Furthermore management processes are cyclical. One process leads to another. The act of planning, for example, will spin the wheel and engage the manager into more actions. This cyclical aspect of management is characteristic of open and dynamic systems where goals constantly evolve as the organizational environment dictates. It should finally be understood that different management cycles take place simultaneously; they are initiated at different levels of the organizational structure; they are concerned with various administrative matters; and they may vary in duration.

PROFESSIONAL PREPARATION OF SPORT MANAGERS

Most colleges and universities in North America offering professional preparation programs in physical education and kinesiology have traditionally offered courses in administration. Courses in organization and administration of physical education and sport have been offered as for back as 1890 and, starting in 1927 such courses were generally included in all academic physical education curricula in the United States (Zeigler, 1975, p. 22). In Canada, a survey conducted by Soucie and Bedecki (1980) revealed that 88% of the universities offering curricula in physical education offered at least one course in the area of physical education/sport/athletic administration. The survey also revealed that such a course was mandatory in 30% of cases.

Today many institutions of higher education in the United States and Canada offer structured undergraduate and graduate programs of study in sport management. In 1967, Ohio University began offering a master's degree in sports administration. In 1973, St. Thomas University (Florida), then Biscane College, offered the first baccalaureate program, and introduced a master's degree program in 1977. In Canada, the University of Ottawa initiated a master's degree program in physical education administration in 1969. At the undergraduate level, Laurentian University launched its baccalaureate degree program in sport administration in 1975. Several inventories (see, for example, Parkhouse, 1978 & 1987, and Soucie & Bedecki, 1980) of sport management programs in North America have been conducted in the past fifteen years, and the most recent one (NASPE/NASSM, 1993) reveals that no fewer than 207 such programs currently exist in the United States and Canada. Similar programs in other continents around the world have also emerged recently (see, for example, Gouws, 1993). From data recently collected, Thoma (1993) was able to delineate 23 programs in Europe, eight in Asia, three in Africa, and one in Oceania.

Academic programs in sport management have been promoted (Soucie, 1988) when institutions were competing with leading universities where such programs had been developed, and academics were adopting sport management ideas and concepts from professional and/or scholarly conferences and publications in the field. Furthermore, it was clear that the academic and administrative responsibility for such innovative programs rested with physical education and kinesiology departments in the United States (Parkhouse and Brassie, 1993) and in Canada (Soucie and Bedecki, 1980).

True professionals have usually completed university studies in their discipline, often at the graduate level, and have received professional training such that they have acquired specialized and unique knowledge and developed competencies which are essential for professional practice. Required competencies for sport managers have been identified and classified (NASPE/NASS, 1993). These normative statements have resulted from academics detailing proficiencies needed by practitioners, and through surveys conducted with employers in the field, with graduates from sport management programs, from current sport management practitioners, and from current faculty teaching courses in the discipline (Brassie, 1989; Chouinard & Soucie, 1988; De Sensi, Kelley, Blanton, & Beitel, 1990; Fielding, Pitts & Miller, 1991; Hardy, 1987; Hatfield, Wrenn & Bretting, 1987; Jamieson, 1987; Lambrecht, 1987 & 1991; Mullin, 1984; Parkhouse, 1987; Parkhouse & Ulrich, 1979; Parks & Quain, 1986; Quain & Parks, 1986; Slack, 1991; Ulrich & Parkhouse, 1982; Williams & Miller, 1983; Zanger, 1984; and Zeigler, 1987).

At the undergraduate level, the guidelines prepared by a joint task force of NASPE/NASSM (1993) propose the following program content areas to provide students with the essential common body of knowledge in sport management: (1) behavioral dimensions in sport; (2) management and organizational skills in sport; (3) ethics in sport management; (4) marketing in sport; (5) communication in sport; (6) finance in sport; (7) economics in sport; (8) legal aspects of sport; (9) governance in sport; and (10) field experience in sport management. At the master's level, the task force suggests eight program areas as follows: (1) management leadership and organization in sport; (2) research in sport; (3) legal aspects of sport; (4) marketing in sport; (5) sport business in the social context; (6) financial management in sport; (7) ethics in sport management; and (8) field experience in sport management.

The establishment of standards will undoubtedly assist in achieving greater homogeneity of academic programs in this field of study. However, there currently exist marked differences in the conception and design of such programs. Moreover, most programs do not currently meet the above standards. A recent study by Eden, Baker, and Judd (1993) revealed that "none of the 10 highest-ranked programs met the eight curriculum areas proposed by NASPE/NASSM standards . . ." The authors add further, "Only four programs required the completion of an internship, and three others offered it as an elective."

Most programs prepare "generalists" in sport management. The preoccupation with the preparation of "generalists" concurs with the conclusion arrived at by Chason (1984) who believes that programs of study in sport management should focus on required competencies and on interdisciplinary studies preparing future sport managers for a variety of managerial and administrative positions. As stated earlier in this chapter, sport managers are indeed called upon to play a wide variety of roles and perform diversified tasks in sport settings.

Certainly the practicum and the internship are critical components of such academic programs. A practicum is related to work experience obtained concurrently with coursework, while an internship is a full-time work experience in an organizational setting usually after all other program requirements have been fulfilled. There is general consensus among experts in this field on the value of internships (Chouinard, 1993). Internships ought to be the cornerstone of the students' academic experience. As expressed by Bell and Countiss (1993), "While the actual tasks performed may be menial, the observations that can be made and the interaction with professionals in the field can be invaluable for ongoing professional development" (p. 45). These clinical experiences help students to develop professional attitudes, behaviors, and values. They also help students to understand and grasp early the hard realities of organizations. Finally, these experiences help students to develop knowledge as to how to implement some of their own ideas and effect change in sport organizations.

Another important component of professional preparation in sport management, particularly at the graduate level, is the development of research skills. As stated by DiBrezzo (1993), "Being a professional is more than associating with a specific activity, career, or group. Professionals must understand their craft—the attributes, techniques and ethics of that career" (p. 48). That is why sport managers should develop skills in research methodology and techniques.

Finally, it is essential that professional programs develop critical and reflective skills to allow sport managers to look at problems from new and innovative perspectives. Emphasis should be on preparing sport managers "who can engage in activities such as thoughtful reflection and evaluation of technical competencies, creative reformulation and repackaging of major problems needing attention, development of empathy with clients, empowerment of clients, and promotion of changes in society" (Harris, 1993, p. 391). That is why courses in philosophy and ethics of sport, and in history and sociology of sport, are essential so that future sport managers gain an understanding of the broader social context of sport. What society needs are politically astute and change-conscious professional sport managers.

RESEARCH IN SPORT MANAGEMENT

Research is inextricaly related to theory. According to Kerlinger (1986, p. 10), "Scientific research is systematic, controlled, empirical, and critical investigation of hypothetical propositions about the presumed relations among natural phenomena." The purpose of scientific research is to assist us in understanding the world we live in. In the field of management, scientific research seeks to understand the structure and dynamics of organizational life. The basic aim of management research is to find general explanations called theories.

Theory and Practice. If sport management practice is oriented toward the solution of immediate, specific, and concrete problems in the real world of sport organizations, sport management theory focuses on an understanding of administrative phenomena in general. Theory related to management suggests hypotheses to be confirmed or rejected about the functioning of organizations. It attempts to explain why sport organizations are the way they are, and to determine what to do to change them if necessary. There are many hypotheses regarding organizational phenomena, and the most effective and efficient approaches to managing and changing organizations. Many of these have not yet been tested scientifically, and that is why further research is so critical for practising sport administrators.

Theories are general and abstract. They are neither true nor false. They are useful, or they are not, in assisting managers to be more effective and efficient in their job. Theory is related to practice in that it provides a frame of reference for the practitioner. It can guide sport managers in decision-making, and it can also provide a general mode of analysis for practical situations. All practice is based on some theory. If underlying theory is rational, so must practice be rational as well. Additionally, theory puts order in the already existing body of knowledge concerning practice. Theory guides research and generates new knowledge which then serves as a guide to enhanced action. As stated by Hoy and Miskel (1991, p. 26), "When theory, in the light of research, is applied to individual action, theory is transformed into practice". Furthermore, as stated earlier in this chapter, management is an art; Blumberg (1989) calls it a "craft." Management is the art of applying scientific knowledge to managerial problems.

Need for a Scientific Basis. The importance of a foundations base and a theoretical framework for the field of sport management has been made abundantly clear by Parkhouse and Ulrich (1979). They argue that what the field needs is a mid-range theory. "A mid-range theory is to a discipline what a coach's strategy or "play book" is to the actual game. The coach's strategies are not the play itself, but a conceptualization of it. The mid-range theory of sport management is not the discipline but its conceptual foundation" (p. 272).

Managerial practice in sport is in desperate need of a scientific basis. Research that leads to management theory can have two fundamental applications. First it may, as is the case for all other fields of research, aim at satisfying our curiosity. Fundamentally, the researcher in management science wants to know and understand. He or she wants to know the consequences of the application of different managerial approaches and styles (i.e., how to plan, organize, direct, and evaluate organizational performance. He or she seeks to understand the environment within which organizations perform effectively and efficiently. Secondly, as stated in the preceding section, management research can be of great service to practising sport administrators confronted with "everyday" management difficulties and problems. If there is one sector in physical education and kinesiology where it is vital to link theory and practice, to bridge to gap between researchers and practitioners, it is indeed in the field of sport management.

Many sport managers describe themselves as practitioners more than theoreticians. They claim to be more preoccupied with the here-and-now, the concrete stuff, the practical. They maintain that an ounce of theory is equal to a ton of practice. Such people too often take for granted that theory and practice are opposed. The truth is that they are complementary. Theory will always precede practice for one simple reason: practice is static. It works, and it works well when it knows what it is doing. But practice doesn't dispose of principles to confront what it does not know. Theory, on the other hand, is dynamic. It can adapt to change, examine alternate ways and possibilities, and envision the future.

Numerous and Unique Research Opportunities. Opportunities and avenues for conducting research in sport management are exceptional. Parkhouse and Ulrich (1979) have stated that sport management is a unique cross-discipline that is "constituted of portions of such related disciplines as journalism, business administration, educational administration, physical education, public administration and law" (p. 269). Indeed the avenues for research in sport are tremendous in that the field offers a unique opportunity for analyzing the organizational behavior of sport administrators, of coaches, and of athletes and sport participants of all kinds. Research can be conducted in areas such as facilities and equipment, public relations, budgeting, marketing, curriculum and programming, legal liability, human resources management, etc, covering the entire gamut of specific tasks that are the responsibility of managers and administrators in our field. There exist as many research topics as one can imagine hypotheses relating to the relationships between variables in the management of sport organizations. Some of these have been enumerated by Parkhouse, Ulrich, and Soucie (1982, p. 180), and may include conflict resolution; goal-setting; work motivation and job satisfaction; role expectations and role differentiation; planned change; organizational development; leadership; organizational climate; organizational culture; organization structures; use of power and authority; etc. Research topics of this nature are particularly interesting since they are founded in other research fields such as organizational theory and organizational behavior. Research on such organizational variables in the world of sport is complementary to research conducted in other settings, and may contribute to an enhancement of overall knowledge in management science.

Nature of Current Research in Sport Management. From a study by Spirduso (cited in Paton, 1987), we know that administration corresponds to the most frequently declared areas of graduate programs, faculty interests, and conferred doctorates granted in physical education and kinesiology. This observation concurs with Knight's (1974) finding that the subdisciplines of exercise physiology and administration constituted the two most popular areas of study at the doctoral level in our profession. If the subdiscipline of administration has not flourished and developed within the broader field of physical education and kinesiology in higher education, it is in my opinion largely due to the fact that the vast majority of doctoral graduates in this particular area have pursued a management career rather than a research career following graduation. It is also my belief that many who have graduated from these doctoral programs lacked the required knowledge in research methodology in the behavioral and social sciences, hence the lack of interest and motivation in conducting research following graduation. This phenomenon is currently being reversed, and the future of research in sport management is much more promising today.

Following a pattern similar to business and educational administration, earlier research made use of status surveys and job analysis techniques for the main purpose of proposing general principles and policies and procedures that presumably helped to solve immediate problems confronting administrators in our field.

Table 8.1 *Classification of Doctoral Dissertation Topics in Administration From the Field of Physical Education and Kinesiology: 1949 to 1993**

	Cluster	n	%
1.	Survey and appraisal of administrative practices, policies, and procedures; prescriptive principles:	94	16.3
2.	Analysis of administrative tasks and job descriptions; analyses of qualifications and required competencies of administrators; prescriptions for academic professional preparation programs; career patterns and job market:	81	14.0
3.	Survey and description of programs; current content and future projections for these programs:	75	13.0

Table 8.1 (Continued)

	Cluster	n	%
4.	Analysis of leadership traits, styles, and behaviors; management systems; organizational climate, environment, and culture; power; communication:	75	13.0
5.	Financial aspects; budgets; accounting; booster clubs; fund-raising:	39	6.8
6.	Survey of facilities; construction and design; management of facilities and equipment:	31	5.4
7.	Equity; discrimination; Title IX:	31	5.4
8.	Legal aspects; negligence; tort; liability:	29	5.0
9.	Job satisfaction; stress and burnout; work motivation:	28	4.8
10.	Public relations; public attitudes toward the field; publicity and promotion; advertising; marketing; sponsorships:	26	4.5
11.	Analysis and comparative analysis of organizational structures; government and sport; sport and politics:	25	4.3
12.	Role expectations between administrators and subordinates; attitudes toward roles:	18	3.0
13.	Personnel management: recruitment and selection; assignment of tasks; workloads; staff development; performance appraisal:	13	2.2
14.	Philosophy and values of administration; ethics; issues in administration; governance and goal-setting:	13	2.2
15.	Use of computers in administration; applications:	3	0.1
	TOTAL:	575	100.0%

*As reported in *Dissertation Abstracts International*

Table 8.1 represents an attempt at classifying the topics of doctoral dissertations in physical education and kinesiology from the specific subdiscipline of administration. It is estimated that between 1949 and 1993, a period of almost 45 years of reporting in *Dissertation Abstracts International*, a total of 575 doctoral studies have been completed on an administration topic in physical education and kinesiology. This number does not include topics in pedagogy, curriculum, and teaching which were frequently reported, particularly in the 1950, 1960, and 1970 decades. Only topics which were clearly related to administration were included in this review. If nothing else, the data presented in Table 8.1 give some sort of indication of management research concerns and interests in physical education and kinesiology in higher education in the United States (doctoral dissertations from Canada and Europe have only recently been incorporated into the same project).

Table 8.1 shows that the largest number of dissertations have dealt with existing administrative practices, policies, and procedures in physical education and athletics, along with prescribed principles for enhanced administration in the field. Analysis of tasks and jobs of administrators in our field, qualifications, required competencies, and prescriptions for the design of professional preparation programs constitute the second most important cluster. Descriptive surveys of current physical education and athletics programs with suggestions for future improvements represent 13 per cent of doctoral studies. Finally, also corresponding to 13 per cent of reported dissertations is the cluster which includes the following organizational behavior topics: leadership, organizational climate, organizational environment, power, communication, and organizational culture. Other clusters include financial aspects, sports facilities and equipment, equity, legal aspects, job satisfaction and stress, public relations and marketing, and comparative analyses of structures, government and politics.

Table 8.2 *Classification of Titles of Articles Published in the Journal of Sport Management: 1987 to 1993*

	Cluster	n	%
1.	Analysis of tasks and job content in sport management; required competencies; guidelines for academic programs; program accreditation; careers; career development; employability of graduates; mentoring of students:	18	18.59
2.	Description of the current state of the field of sport management; state of research; history and issues in the field; prescriptions for improvement:	17	17.51
3.	Marketing; advertising; spectator attendance; customer relations:	10	10.30
4.	Job satisfaction; stress and burnout; work motivation; attitudes toward jobs:	7	7.20
5.	Leadership; administrative behavior; participative management; organizational climate:	5	5.20
6.	Legal aspects; liability; lawsuits; arbitration:	5	5.20
7.	Gender equity; discrimination; affirmative action:	5	5.20
8.	Commitment to exercise and fitness programs; motivation for sport and fitness participants:	4	4.09
9.	Organizational structure:	3	3.08
10.	Research methodology; analytical frameworks:	3	3.08

Table 8.2 (Continued)

	Cluster	n	%
11.	Organizational change; conflict; strategic planning:	3	3.08
12.	Influence; decision-making; goal setting:	2	2.06
13.	Control; information systems; program evaluation:	2	2.06
14.	Program delivery:	2	2.06
15.	Organizational effectiveness:	2	2.06
16.	Financial aspects; economics:	2	2.06
17.	Computers; computer applications:	2	2.06
18.	Professional ethics:	2	2.06
19.	Analysis of policies and procedures:	1	1.02
20.	Government and sport:	1	1.02
	TOTAL:	97	100.0%

For the purpose of presenting a different view of published research in sport management, Table 8.2 constitutes a similar classification, but with topics of recent sport management articles published in the *Journal of Sport Management.* Administrative tasks and job analyses for the purpose of recommending curricular guidelines for academic programs in sport management account for the greatest number of articles. Articles describing the field and the status of theory and research rank second. Marketing appears to be a growing area. Job satisfaction and stress, leadership, and legal aspects are still popular themes. Gender equity is a more recent topic of investigation. It should be pointed out that several articles recently published have resulted from data collected as part of requirements for a doctoral degree in the field.

The research content of doctoral and master's theses in our field has been analyzed and criticized by several authors. Spaeth (1967) reviewed a sample of doctoral dissertations written between 1940 and 1966, and stressed the following weaknesses of the doctoral research surveyed: lack of theoretical orientation; inadequate sampling; subjective measurement in data collection; inadequate control variables; and inappropriate use of statistical procedures. The need for greater attention to the development of meaningful concepts and models in sport and physical education administration research was further demonstrated in another study by Penny (1968). A third study (Paton, 1970) showed that there was a significant lack of theoretical orientation in graduate administration courses and doctoral dissertations in the field. The author recommended that the emphasis be redirected from the existing focus on principles of management to a focus on organization theory, management analysis, and human relations. Seventeen years later, the same researcher (Paton, 1987) reviewed recent doctoral and master's theses as well as textbooks in sport administration, and noted that theses and textbooks reflected a more theoretical orientation during the post-1965 period. However, the author observed that the research methods were still almost exclusively descriptive.

After a comparative review of published research in the sport management literature as opposed to the administrative science literature, Olafson (1990, p. 113) observed that the quality and depth of empirically based research had improved in sport management. Olafson (1990) remarked: ". . . it is clear that sport management research is more empirically based and is using more sophisticated methods for gathering and analysing data" (p. 116). The author further suggested that, in order to enhance the quality of research, researchers in sport management explore the use of the many different methodologies available for conducting research instead of relying almost exclusively on survey questionnaires.

If research is to be useful for practising administrators, the body of knowledge must be developed from management research and theory in *sport*. Slack (1991) insists the we must develop our own knowledge structures. If we want our field to be recognized by other academic disciplines, Slack (1991), believes that: "These knowledge structures must be of a higher order than practical how-to knowledge and they must have a theoretical foundation" (p. 95). Criticising the content of recent master's and doctoral theses for their lack of theoretical orientation, Slack (1991) observes: "Unfortunately, in most cases, the quality of this research has left something to be desired" (p. 97). Furthermore, as expressed by Zeigler (1987, p. 11), research in sport management should be anchored in the social sciences, particularly the behavioral sciences because professionals from our field work predominantly in human service organizations. Finally, Slack (1993) has recently suggested that research in our field explore alternate images of sport organizations. He argues that scholars in sport management have so far considered sport organizations strictly as either machines or organisms, resulting in a partial and limited view of our field. He suggests that alternate images, such as envisioning organizations as brains, cultures, political systems, and instruments of domination offer "considerable potential to increase our understanding of the structures and processes of sport organizations" (p. 189).

PROFESSIONAL OPPORTUNITIES IN SPORT MANAGEMENT

Specialized university programs, particularly at the graduate level, constitute an important phase in the recognition of a professional occupation.

Societal recognition of sport management as a profession will take time, but this process is being accelerated when professional sport managers with graduate degrees secure important management positions at the highest levels of competence within government and the private sector. Professionals with academic credentials in sport management will increasingly assume more demanding positions, thereby contributing to the autonomy of the occupation.

As stated earlier in this chapter, sport managers are everywhere. A close analysis of different forms of social and formal organizations or groups relating to sport, physical education, athletics, fitness, active living or recreation, reveals that, indeed, many professional opportunities do exist for people who wish to consider sport management as a career.

In the United States, Quain & Parks (1986) have identified six career areas in sport management:

1. Physical fitness industry, which may involve clinical or corporate settings or in YM/YWCAs, fitness centers, health clubs, and community exercise programs;
2. Sport promotion, which may involve advertising, public relations, and media operations;
3. Sport marketing, which may include advertising, merchandising, product planning, publicity, research and development, and sales;
4. Sport administration and management which may include public relations direction, corporate administration of sporting events, contract-advising, tournament management and promotion, college athletic direction, management in sports franchises, and fund-raising management;
5. Sport directing which involves leadership roles in intramurals, recreational sports, club sports, youth sports, and other similar activities; and
6. Aquatics management, which involves teaching, coaching, operating pools, and organization and supervision of aquatics programs and facilities.

In Canada, Soucie (cited in Haggerty & Chelladurai, 1990), has suggested the following taxonomy for job opportunities in sport management:

1. Amateur sport: As executive or general director, technical director, program supervisor, or coordinator within sport-governing bodies at the federal and/or provincial level:
2. Educational institutions: As director of intramural or inter-scholastic sports programs at the high school, college, or university level;
3. Municipal recreation and parks departments: As manager or supervisor of sports/recreational programs for children, youth, the elderly, etc.;
4. Governmental agencies: As managers of sports and fitness policy program units within Sport Canada, Active Living Canada or ParticipAction;
5. Private sports clubs: As manager in fitness, tennis, squash and racketball clubs or centers, as well as program manager in outdoor education centers, summer camps, camping and/or youth centers, etc.;

6. Private agencies: As manager of various sports and recreation programs in agencies such as Red Cross, Royal Life Saving, YMCA/YWCA, National Lifeguard Service, etc.;
7. Facility management: As director of operations in arenas, sports centers, and facilities at all levels;
8. Merchandise and equipment enterprises: As production or marketing manager of sports equipment and merchandise;
9. Professional sport: As program manager, publicity director, marketing and promotion agent, and negotiating agent for professional athletes; and
10. Professional associations: As manager of various programs for the membership of national or provincial associations in physical education, recreation, sport or coaching.

Sport management is unique, and clearly points to a definite "field of competence." Sport management requires certain specific knowledges and skills. Even though research is this field is only at an infancy stage, there is a beginning, at least, of a body of knowledge already available in the general field of administration, as well as some established principles to guide sport managers' basic activities.

Another important step toward recognition as a profession is the existence of a formal professional organization. In North America, the North American Society for Sport Management (NASSM) was established in 1985 and held its first conference at Kent State University in 1986. The European Association for Sport Management (EASM) was founded in 1993 and held its first conference at the University of Groningen in the Netherlands in October of the same year. These associations provide opportunities for collegiality and communication among members, essentially through annual conferences and publications.

As stated in its constitution (NASSM, 1991), the purpose of the North American Society for Sport Management is to promote, stimulate, and encourage study, research, scholarly writing, and professional development in the area of sport management. Members of the Society are concerned about the theoretical and applied aspects of management theory and practice specifically related to sport, exercise, dance, and play as these enterprises are pursued by all sectors of the population. The Society publishes the *Journal of Sport Management (JSM)* which focuses on the theoretical and applied aspects of management related to sport and physical activity. As stated in its editorial policy, *JSM* publishes research and scholarly review articles; short reports on publications, test development, and data analysis ("Research Notes"); reports related to sport management in countries other than Canada and the United States (beyond North America); editorials that focus on significant issues pertaining to sport management ("Sport Management Perspectives"); journal abstracts ("Sport Management Digest"); book reviews ("Off the Press"); and news items of interest to professionals in sport management ("Management Memos"). As suggested by DeSensi and Koehler (1989), students contemplating a career in sport management should carefully select the institution where they wish to complete their education and training. As they further their studies, they should accumulate as much experience as possible in sport management-related tasks, either through the practicum and internship program, or through volunteer work in the field. Finally, they should affiliate with existing professional organizations, such as NASSM, attend conferences, and develop contacts with professionals in the field.

SUMMARY AND CONCLUDING STATEMENT

The existence of a vast number of organizations and associations that relate to sport and physical activity in our society cannot be denied. Because quality of life is now considered by many as their prime objective, it can be speculated that the end of the twentieth century will witness further emergence of sport organizations, particularly in the area of recreation living and participative sports.

These organizations need to be managed by the best qualified individuals our profession can offer. So far, the field of physical education and kinesiology has not done too well in this area. Our best "qualified" managers have often been, and in many cases still are, the ones who have "come up through the ranks," the ones with experience and seniority. While these variables have great importance in the recruitment of managers in our field as well as in any other field of endeavor, specific professional training in sport management is essential. In today's increasingly more complex organizations, knowledge and understanding of organizational behavior and theory is indispensable. Scholars in physical education and kinesiology have a responsibility to develop the necessary scientific basis and theoretical framework for the management of our enterprises. Human behavior in sport and physical activity settings offers a unique and challenging research opportunity for scholars in physical education and kinesiology.

Zakrajsek (1993) is of the opinion that the area of sport management has recently developed in a remarkable fashion. She states: "What you have developed in a short period of time in terms of new courses, specialized knowledge and skills, and a network of public and private agencies, is not only remarkable, but is unmatchable among other specializations" (p. 4). Much progress has been made over the past two decades. But we must not rest on our laurels; we must continue to strive for further recognition. Sport management theory and practice is but one subdisciplinary segment of the broader profession of physical education and kinesiology. Together we must continue to pursue our collective mission which is to promote the values of living actively. In that context, sport management theory and practice have a vital role to play in improving the health of our nation and the quality of life of its citizens.

REFERENCES

BELL, J. A., & COUNTISS, J. R. (1993). Professional service through sport management internships. *Journal of Physical Education, Recreation & Dance,* **64** (7), 45–47, 52.

BENNIS, W. G., & NANUS, B. (1985). *Leaders: The strategies for taking charge.* New York: Harper & Row.

BERGERON, J.-L. (1979). Les dimensions conceptuelles du leadership et les styles qui en découlent [Conceptual dimensions of leadership and ensuing styles], *Relations industrielles,* **34** (1), 22–40.

BLAU, P. M., & SCOTT, W. R. (1962). *Formal organizations: A comparative approach.* San Francisco: Chandler.

BLUMBERG, A. (1989). *School administration as a craft: Foundations of practice.* Needham Heights, MA: Allyn and Bacon.

BRASSIE, P. S. (1989). Guidelines for programs preparing undergraduate and graduate students for careers in sport management. *Journal of Sport Management,* **3,** 158–164.

CHASON, R. F. (1984). *A survey of athletic directors, principals, and facility directors to determine the need and curriculum content of a sports administration program.* Unpublished doctoral dissertation, Middle Tennessee State University.

CHOUINARD, N. (1993). Some insights on meaningful internships in sport management: A cooperative education approach. *Journal of Sport Management,* **7,** 95–100.

CHOUINARD, N., & SOUCIE, D. (1988, June). *An analysis of management competencies as viewed by directors of sports and physical education programs, and by professors in sport administration in Québec colleges and universities.* Paper presented at the Third Annual Conference of the North American Society for Sport Management, University of Illinois, Urbana, IL.

DESENSI, J. T., KELLEY, D. R., BLANTON, M. D., & BEITEL, P. A. (1990). Sport management curricular evaluation and needs assessment: A multifaceted approach. *Journal of Sport Management,* **4,** 31–58.

DESENSI, J. T., & KOEHLER, L. S. (1989). Sport and fitness management: Opportunities for women. *JOPERD,* **60** (3), 55–57.

DIBREZZO, D. (1993). Being professional - How does research fit? *Journal of Physical Education, Recreation & Dance,* **64** (7), 48–49.

EDEN, R. A., BAKER, J. A. W., & JUDD, M. R. (1993, June). *Determination of the characteristics of outstanding graduate programs in sport management in North America.* Paper presented at the Eight Annual Conference of the North American Society for Sport Management, Edmonton, Alberta.

ETZIONI, A. (1975). *A comparative analysis of complex organizations.* New York: Free Press.

FIELDING, L. W., PITTS, B. G., & MILLER, L. K. (1991). Defining quality: Should educators in sport management programs be concerned about accreditation? *Journal of Sport Management,* **5,** 1–17.

FRENCH, J. R. P., & RAVEN, B. H. (1968). Bases of social power. In D. Cartwright & A. Zander (Eds.), *Group dynamics: Research and theory* (pp. 259–270). New York: Harper & Row.

GOUWS, J. (1993). Sport management curricula in Rand Afrikaans University, South Africa. *Journal of Sport Management,* **7,** 243–248.

HAGGERTY, T., & CHELLADURAI, P. (1991). Physical activity program management. In C. Bouchard, B. D. McPherson, & A. W. Taylor (Eds). *Physical activity sciences* (pp. 207–212). Champaign, IL: Human Kinetics.

HARDY, S. (1987). Graduate curriculums in sport management: The need for a business orientation. *Quest,* **39,** 207–216.

HARRIS, J. D. (1993). Using kinesiology: A comparison of applied veins in the subdisciplines. *Quest,* **45,** 389–412.

HATFIELD, B. D., WRENN, J. P., & BRETTING, M. M. (1987). Comparison of job responsibilities of intercollegiate athletic directors and professional sport managers. *Journal of Sport Management,* **1,** 129–145.

HOY, W. K., & MISKEL, C. G. (1991). *Educational administration: Theory, research, and practice* (4th ed.). New York: McGraw-Hill.

JAMIESON, L. M. (1987). Competency-based approaches to sport management. *Journal of Sport Management,* **1,** 48–56.

KATZ, D., & KAHN, R. L. (1978). *The social psychology of organizations.* New York: John Wiley.

KERLINGER, F. N. (1986). *Foundation of behavioral research* (3rd ed.). New York: Holt, Rinehart & Winston.

KNIGHT, W. J. (1974). *Specialization in physical education doctoral programs as it relates to the eventual professional/vocational responsibilities of doctoral graduates.* Unpublished doctoral dissertation, Ohio State University.

KOTTER, J. P. (1982). *The general managers.* New York: Free Press.

LAMBRECHT, K. W. (1987). An analysis of the competencies of sports and athletic club managers. *Journal of Sport Management,* **1,** 116–128.

LAMBRECHT, K. W. (1991). A study of curricular preparation needs for sport club managers. *Journal of Sport Management,* **5,** 47–57.

MCCALL, M. W., KAPLAN, R. E., & GERLACH, M. L. (1982). *Caught in the act: Decision-makers at work* (Technical Report No. 20), Greensboro, NC: Center for Creative Leadership.

MINTZBERG, H. (1973). *The nature of managerial work.* New York: Harper & Row.

MINTZBERG, H. (1983). *Power in around organizations.* Englewood Cliffs, NJ: Prentice-Hall.

MINTZBERG, H., RAISINGHANI, D., & THEORET, A. (1976). The structure of unstructured decision processes. *Administrative Science Quarterly,* **2,** 246–275.

MULLIN, B. (1984). A graduate curriculum in sport management: Considerations before taking the big plunge! In B. K. Zanger & J. B. Parks (Eds.). *Sport management curricula: The business and education nexus* (pp. 110–117). Bowling Green, OH: Bowling Green State University, School of Health, Physical Education and Recreation.

NASPE/NASSM. (1993). *Sport management - Directory of professional programs.* Unpublished manuscript.

NASSM. (1991). *Constitution of the North American Society for Sport Management.* Unpublished manuscript.

OLAFSON, G. (1990). Research design in sport management: What's missing, what's needed? *Journal of Sport Management,* **5,** 95–99.

PARKHOUSE, B. (1978). Professional preparation in athletic administration and sport management - Graduate programs in the United States. *Journal of Physical Education and Recreation,* **49** (5), 22–27.

PARKHOUSE, B. L. (1987). Sport management curricula: Current status and design implications for future development. *Journal of Sport Management,* **1,** 93–115.

PARKHOUSE, B. L., & BRASSIE, S. (1993, June). *The current state of sport management curricula: A descriptive assessment of undergraduate and graduate preparation programs.* Paper presented at the Eight Annual Conference of the North American Society for Sport Management, Edmonton, Alberta.

PARKHOUSE, B. L., & ULRICH, D. O. (1979). Sport management as a potential cross-discipline: A paradigm for theoretical development, scientific inquiry, and professional application. *Quest,* **31,** 264–276.

PARKHOUSE, B. L., ULRICH, D. O., & SOUCIE, D. (1982). Research in sport management. A vital rung of this new corporate ladder. *Quest,* **34,** 176–186.

PARKS, J. B., & QUAIN, R. J. (1986). Curriculum perspectives. *Journal of Physical Education, Recreation and Dance,* **57** (4), 22–26.

PATON, G. A. (1970). *An analysis of administrative theory in selected graduate administration courses in physical education.* Unpublished doctoral dissertation, University of Illinois, C-U.

PATON, G. (1987). Sport management research - What progress has been made? *Journal of Sport Management,* **1,** 25–31.

PEABODY, R. L. (1962). Perceptions of organizational authority: A comparative analysis. *Administrative Science Quarterly,* **6,** 463–482.

PENNY, W. (1968). *An analysis of the meanings attached to selected concepts in administrative theory.* Unpublished doctoral dissertation, University of Illinois, C-U.

QUAIN, R. J., & PARKS, J. B. (1986). Sport management survey: Employment perspectives. *Journal of Physical Education, Recreation and Dance,* **57** (4), 18–21.

SIMON, H. (1987). Making managerial decisions: The role of intuition and emotion. *Academy of Management Executive,* **1,** 57–64.

SLACK, T. (1991). Sport management: Some thoughts on future directions. *Journal of Sport Management,* **5,** 95–99.

SLACK, T. (1993). Morgan and the metaphors: Implications for sport management research. *Journal of Sport Management,* **7,** 189–193.

SOUCIE, D. (1988, June). *Promotion of sport management programs in Canada.* Paper presented at the Third Annual Conference of the North American Society for Sport Management, University of Illinois, Urbana-Champaign.

SOUCIE, D. (1989). *Fondements théoriques de l'administration du sport* [Theoretical foundations of sport administration]. Boucherville, Qué.: Gaëtan Morin Éditeur.

SOUCIE, D. (1993, September). *The emergence of sport management as a professional occupation.* Paper presented at the First European Conference on Sport Management, University of Groningen, The Netherlands.

SOUCIE, D. (1994). Effective managerial leadership in sport organisations. *Journal of Sport Management,* **8,** 1–12.

SOUCIE, D., & BEDECKI, T. (1980). Trends in physical education, sport, and athletic administration in Canadian universities and colleges. *Journal of the Canadian Association for Health, Physical Education, and Recreation,* **47** (2), 30–36.

SPAETH, M. J. (1967). *An analysis of administrative research in physical education and athletics in relation to a research paradigm.* Unpublished doctoral dissertation, University of Illinois, C-U.

THOMA, J. E. (1993). *Sport management education: A world view.* Paper presented at the Eight Annual Conference of the North American Society for Sport Management Edmonton, Alberta.

ULRICH, D., & PARKHOUSE, B. L. (1982). An alumni-oriented approach to sport management curriculum design using performance ratings and a regression model. *Research Quarterly for Exercise and Sport,* **53,** 64–72.

WEBER, M. (1947). *The theory of social and economic organizations.* A. M. Henderson & T. Parsons (Trans.). New York: Free Press.

WILLIAMS, J. M., & MILLER, D. M. (1983). Intercollegiate athletic administration: Preparation patterns. *Research Quarterly for Exercise and Sport,* **54,** 398–406.

ZAKRAJSEK, D. B. (1993). Sport management: Random thoughts of one administrator. *Journal of Sport Management,* **7,** 1–6.

ZALEZNIK, A. (1977). Managers and leaders: Are they different? *Harvard Business Review,* **55** (2), 67–78.

ZANGER, B. K. (1984). Sport management curriculum model. In B. K. Zanger & J. B. Parks (Eds.). *Sport management curricula: The business and education nexus* (pp. 97–109). Bowling Green, OH: Bowling Green State University, School of Health, Physical Education and Recreation.

ZEIGLER, E. F. (1975). Theoretical propositions for the administration of physical education and athletics. In E. F. Zeigler & M. J. Spaeth (Eds.). *Administrative theory and practice in physical education and athletics* (pp. 22–34). Englewood Cliffs, NJ: Prentice-Hall.

ZEIGLER, E. F. (1987). Sport Management: Past, present, future. *Journal of Sport Management,* **1,** 4–24.

SELECTED READINGS

CHELLADURAI, P. (1985). *Sport management: Macro perspectives.* London, ON: Sport Dynamics.

PARKS, J. B., & ZANGER, B. L. K. (Eds.). (1990). *Sport and fitness management - Career strategies and professional content.* Champaign, IL: Human Kinetics.

Chapter Nine

Curriculum Theory and Program Development

Ann E. Jewett

A taxonomical table of scholarly and professional dimensions of developmental physical activity in exercise, sport, play, and related movement provided the organization for this text. This table, developed by Zeigler and Huelster, identifies eight dimensions or components, five subdisciplinary components and three subprofessional components. As one of the three subprofessional components, the area of curriculum theory and program development has both disciplinary and professional aspects, but carries a particularly clear responsibility for relating its ordered generalizations directly to educational practice. A key goal of curriculum studies in exercise, sport, physical recreation, and expressive movement is to synthesize curriculum theorizing with scientific findings of the subdisciplinary components in application to educational practice. This effort will be directed toward the search for answers to four broad questions:

1. What is curriculum? (How is it defined? What does it include? How are key terms used?)
2. Why physical education? (What are the primary goals or purposes? What philosophical perspectives or value orientations influence curriculum development in our field? How do these perspectives differ from each other in desired program outcomes? What is the role of physical education in the school curriculum?)
3. How is the program developed? (What curriculum models are used to plan and implement programs in different local educational settings? How do these models differ in such characteristics as program goals, conceptual framework, selected content, instructional strategies, and evaluation procedures?)
4. Where shall we go from here? (What problems most urgently need attention now? What potential avenues for improvement of programs in developmental physical activity are open to us? Can we create alternative long-range approaches for

providing better quality life experiences through exercise, sport, physical recreation, and expressive movement?)

WHAT IS CURRICULUM?

Definitions of curriculum vary widely. Macdonald's 1977 definition of curriculum as a purposefully selected cultural environment has stood the test of time and is this author's definition of preference. Curriculum is the study of "what should constitute a world of learning and how to go about making this world" (Macdonald, 1977, p. 11). A broad concept of curriculum studies includes curriculum (in the narrower sense), instruction, teaching, and learning. Macdonald's definitions are useful in distinguishing among these four interrelated systems. "Thus, teaching is defined as the behavior of the teacher, learning as the change in learner behavior, instruction as the pupil-teacher interaction situation, and curriculum as those planning endeavors which take place prior to interaction" (Macdonald, 1965, p. 6).

Currently, the term curriculum development is frequently used by curriculum scholars because it places the emphasis on curriculum as a process, rather than on the product of that process. Curriculum development is an ongoing continuous cycle of planning a curriculum; implementing the plans through instruction; and evaluating both the product and the process in terms of the learnings experienced by the participants, in order to begin a new cycle of planning for program improvement. When a distinction is drawn between curriculum and instruction, curriculum is defined as an educative agency's plan for facilitating learning, and instruction is defined as the delivery system or teaching-learning process for implementing the plan. The major focus of curriculum is on ends, or the "why" and "what" questions; instruction tends to emphasize the means or the "how" questions. Curriculum is used in this chapter as a broad generic term, including instruction.

An increasing number of curriculum scholars, frequently referred to as "critical theorists," are now defining curriculum as praxis. These scholars emphasize the interrelatedness of action and reflection and the interdependence of theory and practice. Content, instruction, and social context are all viewed as interactive elements of curriculum (Kirk, 1988, p. 9). An important implication of this definition is that it emphasizes the need for continual examination and refinement of basic beliefs and goals as well as practical procedures. The study of curriculum as praxis requires analyzing the interaction of ideology, discourse, and action.

(A related term that needs clarification is sport pedagogy. This designation for the field that has long been called physical education and sport in North America and Great Britain has become the preferred name in some European countries <notably Germany>. The interests of the sport pedagogists embrace both curriculum and instruction, although instructional specialists appear to be more influential and more numerous at the present time.)

WHY PHYSICAL EDUCATION?

Answers to the question of what is of most value in a good physical education differ. The importance of making values explicit in curriculum work is now generally acknowledged. Any subject-matter field gains and/or holds its place in the curriculum only if the community supporting the schools believes that the program goals represent worthy educational ends, and is convinced that the instruction offered can lead to the desired outcomes. If physical education and sport programs are to survive in the schools, the educational goals must be well articulated. Educators are expected to clarify their own ideologies, to justify their proposed program goals, and to design curricula through which the goals can be attained.

Educational philosophy is translated into desired student learning experiences through planning curriculum activities consistent with particular value orientations. The sources of the curriculum have been viewed traditionally as the subject-matter content, the nature of the individual learner by whom the content will be utilized, and the goals of the society whose purposes the school is intended to serve. Curriculum approaches differ according to the relative and absolute values accorded to each of these three concerns. Varying curriculum perspectives or value orientations have been elaborated to clarify the implementation of contrasting philosophies by Eisner and Vallance (1974); Orlosky and Smith (1978); Giroux, Penna, and Pinar (1981); Macdonald (1981); McNeil (1985); Schubert (1986); and Ornstein and Hunkins (1988). Different terms are used by various authors and classification schemes vary. The classification scheme most frequently used in physical education includes five value orientations: disciplinary mastery, self-actualization, social reconstruction, learning process, and ecological integration (Jewett, Bain, & Ennis, 2nd ed. in press, chapter 2). Each of these value orientations is described briefly below.

Disciplinary-Mastery Perspective. The most traditional orientation to curriculum development places top priority on mastery of the subject matter and acquisition of the important knowledge. It stresses the integrity and primacy of the academic discipline. The role of the school is viewed as the transmittal of the cultural heritage from one generation to the next. Educators are concerned with guiding young people in acquiring the tools they need to participate in their cultural heritage and in attaining access to the wisdom of the ages. Those who place high value on disciplinary mastery assert that mastery of the most important subject-matter is the key to the best in schooling.

Disciplinary mastery curricula emphasize the importance of basic movement skills, both in elementary school movement education and in secondary school sport education. Elementary school children are expected to master basic disciplinary or motor performance tasks, variously designated as locomotor and non-locomotor movements; fundamental throwing, kicking, and striking patterns; body, space, and effort relationships; or gymnastics, dance, and games progressions. In most secondary school programs throughout the United States and Canada, the content is determined on the basis of those movement forms that constitute our popular sports, physical recreation, and athletic activities. Mastery of the discipline is sought through a quest for achieving higher levels of individual fitness or performance skill in selected sport activities.

Physical educators who structure lessons based on a disciplinary mastery value orientation place a strong emphasis on mastery of skills, sport, movement, and fitness content. There is a strong emphasis on the "correct" or most "efficient" way to perform. Practice is focused and concentrated, with a maximum opportunity presented to perform the movement or to extend participation time in fitness activities. Specific feedback is offered by the teacher to correct the performance. Effective disciplinary-mastery teachers use a wide range of teaching styles from command and practice to problem solving and free exploration. Evaluation is typically based on a narrow definition of effective performance, often within a specific skill test or drill.

Self-Actualization Perspective. In curricula with a self-actualization orientation, individual excellence takes top priority over both subject matter and broader social concerns. Curricular experiences are designed to challenge the individual to extend self, to cross boundaries, to exceed previous limitations, and to gain new perceptions of self. "Be all you can be" is a predominant theme.

From a self-actualization perspective, the curriculum should be directed toward the individual learner's growth in self-direction, and the development of self-management abilities. The function of the curriculum is viewed as a process of self-discovery, synthesis, and personal integration. Each person is responsible for identifying his or her own goals, for developing personal uniqueness, and for guiding individual learning. Process skills for individual development and personal learning are of major importance.

Many teachers with a self-actualization orientation use traditional sport content to provide opportunities for students to develop their self-confidence and a positive self-concept. They often emphasize the growth and maturity of the students by placing them in activities where they are challenged to perform a difficult skill, control their social behaviors, be responsible to self and others, and work effectively on their own or with others. Effective self-actualization teachers are skillful in framing movement sport and fitness tasks to encourage increased student self-understanding, goal setting, and personal decision making.

They encourage students to think, reflect on their performance, set realistic personal goals, and gradually develop their own plan to reach their goals. Evaluation stresses self-understanding and growth.

Social Reconstruction Perspective. The social-reconstruction value orientation places the highest priority on the third source of the curriculum, the society. While subject matter mastery is the top priority of the disciplinary mastery orientation, and the learner is accorded first priority in designing self-actualization curricula, the social reconstruction perspective's top priority is the society that provides and gives direction to the schooling of each younger generation. Curricula based on a social-reconstruction value orientation are planned to include instruction and practice in the skills of participation in a democracy, in leadership skills, and in group cooperation and problem solving.

From a social reconstruction perspective, societal needs take precedence over individual needs. If the nation needs more economic analysts, public health workers, environmental ecologists, or genetics scientists, curricula are modified to strengthen education in the appropriate subject matter areas. Vocational programs are provided to develop occupational skills for jobs created by new technology. When decision-makers aim to raise the level of appreciation and participation in the fine arts, government subsidies are made available to support educational programs in music, graphic arts, drama, and dance.

Since the 1950s social reconstruction has been a popular term with American educators who attribute high value to social reform. In this view, cultural change is an important goal. The school has a responsibility to the future, and educators are expected to accept a role in making school curricula the vehicle for creating a better society. Effective social reconstruction teachers must possess knowledge and skill in group dynamics, social modeling, communication, and values clarification. They encourage students to think reflectively about their own behaviors, compare their behaviors to class/social expectations, and develop strategies for change. Evaluation focuses on the extent to which students protect the rights and opportunities of others within the educational environment, and their success in working cooperatively within the classroom and the school.

Learning Process Perspective. For curriculum designers holding the learning process perspective, how we learn becomes as important as what we learn. The learning process approach places priority on the learner as well as the subject-matter, but takes a narrower view of each. Its focus on the learner is more limited than that of the self-actualization perspective; its perception of the appropriate subject content is narrower than that of the disciplinary-mastery orientation. The focus is on the individual as a learner and on the processes for mastering subject content rather than a wide range of product knowledge.

From the learning process perspective, the processes by which knowledge is generated in each subject field are an important curriculum concern. A major point in the rationale is that the knowledge explosion has made it impossible for the school curriculum to cover all important product knowledge. Consequently, learning the process skills for continuing learning has taken on increased importance.

The emphasis on high technology in recent decades has highlighted the need for curriculum focus on learning process in order to develop individual abilities to cope with rapid change. The communications revolution is changing the school and its curriculum, just as it is changing everything else in modern life. Education must be concerned with developing process skills that can be applied to learning whatever becomes important to the individual to learn. Problem-solving skills continue to be important. Higher level conceptual abilities are increasingly needed. Skills are needed for computer learning as it is applied in different fields. Effective learning process teachers have a clear understanding of appropriate progressions and learning processes specifically relevant to their own subject fields. They encourage development of aesthetic processes as well as scientific processes. Students are evaluated within the process of learning.

Ecological Integration Perspective. The ecological integration perspective is based on the assumption that each individual is a unique, holistic being, continuously in the process of becoming, seeking full personal integration in a changing environment. It emphasizes the personal search for meaning. This perspective incorporates the concept of fulfillment of individual potential which characterizes the self-actualization orientation. But it goes beyond that to a view of the holistic person integrated within the total natural and social environment in his or her particular place and time. The individual is viewed as responding to the environment, and at the same time determining, to some degree, the nature of his or her universe.

This perspective advocates balanced priorities between individual and global societal concerns. The world is viewed with a new appreciation of global interdependence. Value orientation is toward the development of a unique human person whose individual validity can be established only in a globally interdependent society. The school is responsible for the development of individuals who function effectively as citizens of a single world and whose commitment to human futures goes beyond personal competence, local achievement, and national pride.

The ecological integration orientation overlaps that of the social reconstructionist in that planned social change is a necessary strategy. Individual education is designed to assist in creating the future. The curriculum is concerned with learning to ask and examine critical questions. Students develop skills for writing alternative scenarios for desired human futures. The curriculum is designed with the perspective that we can create, to some extent, the nature of the world in which all of us will live. Its ideal is a future human condition dependent upon the incorporation of both biological and sociological balances within a total ecosystem. Ecological integration differs from all four of the other curriculum approaches in its broader, more encompassing worldview.

Teachers who advocate an ecological integration perspective envision the school system as a large ecological system where each event influences every other. They attempt to balance the social, individual student, and subject matter emphases within their curriculum. Effective ecological integration teachers are skillful in selecting content to meet the needs of students within specific developmental and social contexts. Their curriculum planning focuses on matching the "right" content to the "right" student at the "right" time. Evaluation techniques are chosen to ensure that students develop a holistic perspective on the role of learning within both personal and social settings.

Why physical education in the school curriculum? The response differs according to the prevailing curriculum value orientation. In disciplinary mastery curricula, the value of physical education is defined primarily by the importance of useful movement skills, sport participation competencies, and health-related fitness. In self-actualization curricula, the value of physical education is defined by its unique contributions to the holistic development of self-directed, self-responsible persons who seek to realize fully their individual potentials; the development of physical fitness and movement competence are emphasized only in the physical education curriculum. Social reconstruction curricula can use the different content and the physical activity setting of physical education as a laboratory for better understanding of the goals of social responsibility and social reform. In learning process curricula, the processes most appropriate to the domain of motor learning, underemphasized in other curriculum areas, receive major attention, thus promoting integrated learning across all three domains (cognitive, affective, and motor learning). In ecological-integration curricula, the unique value of physical education lies in its integrative approach to human development and learning, and its holistic approach to coping with the natural environment and to the development of critical thinking and creativity. Advocates for physical education can make the best case for its importance in the school curriculum based on its perceived value in terms of the relevant curriculum ideology.

How Is the Program Developed?

During most of its school history, the typical United States physical education program has been developed according to a *multiactivity* model. In a multiactivity model, the common building blocks are specific movement forms, fitness exercise units, organized games, recreational sports, gymnastics, dance, and aquatics activities. In practice, a well-articulated educational philosophy for the selection and organization of activities is not evident. The goals are usually a combination of fitness, movement performance skill, and social responsibility. The conceptual framework, if one is delineated, does not clarify the relative emphasis to be given to each goal, or provide an overall rationale for the sequencing of instruction or evaluation of outcomes.

An important project of the National Association for Sport and Physical Education was completed by the NASPE Outcomes Committee in 1992 (NASPE, 1992). The Committee produced a five-part definition of "the physically educated student," and stated 20 attendant outcomes that clarify and amplify the definition. The Committee wisely chose to identify "benchmarks" rather than "grade-specific competencies." This is an important document because it probably represents the greatest consensus the U.S. physical education profession is likely to achieve on the desired outcomes of quality physical education programs. It is worthy of note that the definition reflects a holistic view of the nature of education; that the outcomes represent important learning related to the major learning domains, stated as broad general goals; and that the committee chose *not* to recommend "a national curriculum."

Outcomes of Quality Physical Education Programs is already being used by many teachers and curriculum planners in the U.S.A. It is expected to have a major impact on strengthening multiactivity programs. It is hoped that it will also be the stimulus in many school districts to review and clarify the dominant local value orientation. Such review and analysis could lead to a commitment to a particular philosophical orientation appropriate in the community. A community's commitment could be implemented through effective use of the resources so well developed by the Outcomes Committee for stating program goals, selecting activities, and evaluating programs. Quality physical education programs throughout the United States depend upon delineation of a strong theoretical base for each program and the articulation of alternative value orientations as needed.

Five philosophical perspectives or value orientations on which program planning can be based have been identified and described above. A particular value orientation includes a set of beliefs concerning the important subject-matter content, the nature of the individual learner, and the goals of society. The curriculum development process varies in accordance with the dominant value orientation. The discussion following describes the curriculum development process as it can be implemented from each of the philosophical perspectives.

Translating a particular value orientation into a school physical education program design requires the selection or creation of a curriculum model appropriate to the dominant value orientation in a particular educational setting. Several common models have been developed in practice; others have been proposed by educators seeking major curriculum reform or specific program improvements. The theoretical or value base of the model chosen plays a key role in determining the content or learning activities selected for inclusion, the instructional strategies most likely to be effective, and the plan for program evaluation and improvement.

Disciplinary Mastery Curricula. From a disciplinary mastery perspective, the subject content is considered the first priority in curriculum planning. The primary educational goal is subject-matter mastery by all individual students. This decision automatically raises the age-old question, "what knowledge is of most worth?" The potential subject content is much broader than can be utilized to structure a single physical education curriculum design. There are three popular answers to the question, "what is the proper content of physical education."

Many physical educators take the perspective that the concept of *sport* as a cultural universal, or the broader concept of *play* as an essential human activity, is the theoretical base for the curriculum. Those who opt for *health-related fitness* establish their objectives in terms of the components of fitness, and develop programs designed to achieve specific fitness goals. Those who believe that *human movement* is the most appropriate subject matter for physical education place their focus on the development of effective, efficient, and versatile movement. The orientation is toward subject matter, whichever definition of the subject matter is valued most highly. Each of these three positions concerning the most important subject matter has led to the development of a generic model for building a physical education curriculum.

Sport education model. The primary goals of the sport education model are to achieve levels of skill development that will permit satisfying participation in appropriate lifetime sports, and to develop attitudes that will support voluntary participation in physical recreation activities. Siedentop, a leading advocate of the sport education model, defines the overall goal as follows:

> A physically educated person is one who has learned to play and appreciate sports more completely, to coordinate and manage their own sport experience, and to [accept] individual responsibility, and [demonstrate] group membership skills (Siedentop, in press).

The conceptual framework presently used for sport education is the body of knowledge about sport, although Siedentop's earlier writings acknowledged a framework based on a typology of play (Caillois, 1961). The content emphasizes a wide variety of popular sports and includes the development of motor skills, strategies, and attitudes important to successful participation. Knowledges fundamental to understanding the sport, rules, rituals, traditions, guidelines for competition, and expectations of desirable sporting behavior are all included. Scope and sequence are usually based on a developmental approach, modifying the rules, boundaries, and equipment of particular sports to accommodate the maturity, skill, and fitness levels of the participants.

The central "Sport for All" concept is based on the assumption that every student can participate in a sport activity at a level consistent with their physical, intellectual, and social abilities. Instructional strategies are designed to assist all students to be more successful in sport. Sport units must be long enough to permit individual students to reach satisfying levels of achievement and feel comfortable about continuing voluntary participation. Modified sports provide opportunities for low-ability students to focus on critical aspects of skill development and allow for concentrated practice on specific skills. Modified games and ample opportunity for full game participation are characteristic in order to ensure that all students experience the real fun of participation in competitive games. Successful sport education programs can contribute to the process of socializing participants into cohesive social groups. Team affiliation within a fair and equal competitive structure stimulates interest in activity and helps to develop skills for working together. Opportunities for team affiliation can be provided both through the planning of physical education classes and the organization of intramural tournaments to encourage maximum participation.

Evaluation in sport education programs typically focuses on performance of sport skills assessed by standardized or teacher-made skills tests; game-playing ability and sports-management skills such as officiating or serving as team captain, usually judged through teacher observation during game play; and knowledge tests covering rules, strategies, principles of movement, and sport terminology and selection of equipment. If there is genuine commitment to the primary goals of the sport education model, however, evaluation activities will also be directed toward assessing increased enthusiasm for sporting activities, more favorable attitudes toward sport, greater motivation toward voluntary participation, improved teamwork skills, more positive student interaction, and actual increases in participation in local organized sport and physical recreation programs. The most frequently used tools for such evaluation are surveys, questionnaires, self-reports, attitude inventories, records of community agencies sponsoring physical activity programs, and attention to informal student conversation and choice of leisure activities.

The sport education curriculum model can be expanded beyond the school to the larger community. Very successful coordinated programs are currently in operation in both Australia and New Zealand. The Australian Sports Commission began the AUSSIE SPORTS program in 1986. New Zealand's KiwiSports program was initiated in 1987 with the sponsorship of the Hillary Commission for Recreation and Sport (1991). Both programs are directed toward increasing nationwide participation in sport and encouraging positive attitudes toward sport among children. Both have been highly successful and receive large amounts of government funding because they are believed to enhance the quality of life for all citizens.

AUSSIE SPORTS sponsors programs for school children of all ages, training for teachers and coaches, and participation opportunities in 22 different sports (Clough & Traill, 1991). KiwiSports includes 22 different sports and involves students and physical educators in 95 percent of New Zealand's elementary and secondary schools. In addition to KiwiSport, the Hillary Commission funds additional sports programs for the disabled, women, older adults, and the native Maori population. The Commission is also operating playground safety programs and programs to address violence in sports.

Evaluations of the first five years of operation of both AUSSIE SPORTS (Robertson, 1992) and KiwiSport (Grant & Sharp, 1992) have documented their success. The results indicated increases in participation, more favorable attitudes toward sport, and gains in acceptance of values such as fair play. Although the Sport for All concept is growing in influence in a number of other countries, including Canada, most school sports programs in the United States are traditional multiactivity programs. Not many appear to exemplify the sport-for-all philosophy of the Siedentop sport education model. This situation is attributed to the preoccupation of Americans with elite sport.

Fitness education model. The educational philosophy supporting the use of the fitness education model identifies as our first priority physical education's potential contribution toward improving the quality and quantity of life through the development of individual physical activity skills, fitness knowledge, and attitudes of commitment to an active lifestyle. The value orientation underlying this model is disciplinary mastery. The subject-matter content priority is health-related fitness. The fitness education curriculum model has become increasingly popular in the U.S.A. as health care has become a central social issue, and the importance of health prevention is being promoted. The majority of the health objectives for the Year 2000 stated by the U.S. Department of Health and Human Services (1991) target school children and adolescents in the national effort to reduce preventable death, disease,and disability. Physical fitness is listed among the priority areas for health promotion.

For the most part, goals of physical education curricula based on fitness education models relate to the improvement of student fitness status. Although all fitness programs are designed to develop knowledge about fitness, skills in activities with health benefits, and habits of regular exercise, definitions of fitness are constantly changing. Most school fitness programs today place top priority on building commitment to active adult lifestyles. The primary outcomes sought relate to the adoption and maintenance of personal exercise programs beyond school years.

The conceptual framework for the fitness education model is based on the body of knowledge about fitness. A curriculum focus on fitness has usually emphasized the physiological components of health-related fitness: cardiorespiratory function, body composition, flexibility, and muscular strength and endurance. This leads to curriculum content that includes knowledge about how these components are affected by exercise and physical activity skills that contribute to one or more of the stated components. Aerobic activities, combined with strength training and flexibility exercises, dominate the program. As the goal has shifted beyond individual student fitness status toward commitment to regular exercise participation, the conceptual framework of the curriculum has broadened. The components of fitness are now perceived to include psychological components: positive attitudes toward exercise, exercise self-efficacy, self-motivation, and self-reinforcement. With increasing research on common barriers to exercise program participation, the conceptual framework has also come to include knowledge about environmental factors influencing exercise adoption and maintenance.

In the early 1990s, curriculum specialists began to envision a school core subject of health and physical education, perhaps called something like wellness or health enhancement, requiring a comprehensive K–12 curriculum. A fitness curriculum model for this core subject would demand a broader and more sophisticated conceptual framework. The physiological components of health-related fitness and the psychological processes of exercise behavior change would still be important elements, but others would be needed for a holistic approach to education for healthy lifestyle management.

Instruction in fitness-education programs is usually a combination of group instruction in vigorous aerobic activities, and a program for individual fitness needs assessment and planning of personal exercise programs directed toward individual improvement. These programs need to be supported with classroom activities focusing on understanding how fitness is developed and maintained. Class activities for stimulating self-motivation can include exploring the characteristics of physical activity that make regular exercise attractive and enjoyable, planning for supportive environments for desired exercise behavior, and developing personal attributes that lead to self-motivation. "Laboratory" activities that provide students opportunities to be directly involved in planning and managing their own activities can be effectively used in the development of self-management skills. "Behavioral fitness" programs emphasize learning goal-setting and decision-making skills, techniques for self-direction, self-monitoring and self-reinforcement, and strategies for preventing and dealing with lapses in one's personal exercise program. In comprehensive programs, students also receive instruction in related areas of personal health such as safety, accident prevention, and daily life tasks (Heitmann, 1993), nutrition, smoking, substance abuse, and stress management.

Programs based on the fitness education model tend to rely heavily on standardized fitness test batteries for evaluation purposes. If commitment to an active adult lifestyle is an important goal, students are taught both formal and informal assessment procedures to plan and monitor their personal exercise programs. Greater emphasis on student self-assessment and formative evaluation is more likely to build individual commitment to regular exercise.

Movement analysis model. In contrast to the two disciplinary mastery models described above, the third subject-oriented model, the movement analysis model, defines the content of the physical education curriculum as human movement. Movement analysis curricula reflect a disciplinary mastery value orientation. They are directed toward the understanding of human movement and the development of effective, efficient, and versatile movement performance. During the post World War II era, physical education programs were designed with this model in a number of British Commonwealth and European countries. Among the most influential writings in the English language professional literature were Laban (1960), Diem (1962), and Stanley (1969). Laban's (1963) framework of 16 movement themes was especially popular for designing elementary school physical education curricula in the United States in the 60s and 70s.

The major goals of physical education based on movement analysis models are the development of skillful movement, knowledge and understanding of movement, and the ability to solve movement problems. The conceptual framework is the structure of the discipline of human movement (major aspects of body, space, effort, and relationships). Varied labels including movement exploration, movement education, basic movement, and kinesiological studies are applied to these programs. A number of frameworks for operationalizing the movement analysis model are used, e.g. Logsdon, *et al.* (1984), Nichols (1990), Graham, Holt-Hale, & Parker (1992).

Scope and sequence are based on movement themes or concepts. Self-directed learning and problem-solving are preferred instructional strategies. Students are guided to analyze particular movement skills and to understand and apply scientific principles related to movement and exercise. Teachers focus on the major concepts that facilitate skillful performance, including concepts of force production, object manipulation, and offensive and defensive strategies relevant to many different sports. Students are also assisted in understanding the principles of safe performance of "life survival" skills, in order to avoid injury in performing movements of daily life tasks such as lifting, pushing, pulling, carrying, climbing, and rescuing (Heitmann, 1993).

Sequentially structured movement-analysis curricula use a lot of formative evaluation throughout the instructional program. Checklists of different movement sequences can be used by both teacher and student to determine current levels of skill attainment and to set goals and plan for further instruction. Problem-solving abilities can be tested by presenting students with enjoyable and increasingly advanced movement challenges. When practical, the achievement of targeted movement skills is evaluated in a broad context in which the desired skills are intended to be used. Program evaluation uses some standardized skills tests, but also requires assessment of individual competence on teacher-devised movement tasks, and judgments based on observations of student ability to apply movement principles to the solution of new problems. Informal evaluation of student involvement, self-confidence, and enjoyment of movement activities also plays a role.

It is not unusual to find in operation, at least in the United States, other disciplinary-mastery curricula that do not truly represent either the sport education, fitness education, or movement analysis models. Such programs are directed primarily toward disciplinary mastery, but do not reflect any clear conceptual framework for defining the body of knowledge of the discipline of physical education, or for selecting and organizing the curriculum content. This is often the case in local programs developed directly from a state curriculum guide that offers some combination of fitness, sport skills, and social development goals, without providing any guidelines for making curricular decisions concerning the determination of educational philosophy, selection of local program goals, and development of appropriate scope and sequence plans. Many of these guides are useful documents, but require knowledgeable curriculum specialists to assist the local program designers in using them effectively.

Self-Actualization Curricula. The self-actualization value orientation places the focus of physical education directly on the individual learner. The learner takes top priority over both subject-matter and broader societal concerns. The personal growth and development of each student is viewed as the primary focus of the curriculum. School programs are designed to assist each individual to reach his or her full developmental potential. The *developmental* curriculum model has been structured to reflect the self-actualization perspective.

Developmental model. The generic developmental model is designed to organize learning activities and experiences primarily for the holistic development of individual students. The enhancement of the development process is acknowledged as the aim of education and of physical education. Human beings are assumed to have common developmental patterns as well as unique characteristics that influence the development process. A nurturing environment is essential for individuals to reach their fullest potentials. It is the responsibility of educators to create such an environment and to guide the development process, giving attention to physical, intellectual, social, and emotional aspects of holistic development. Teachers are expected to assist their students in the search for personal identity, in developing self-esteem and self-understanding, and in creating satisfying interpersonal relationships.

The conceptual framework for a developmental education program is derived from the research on human development. The organizing themes are based on developmental characteristics, patterns, or stages. The curriculum planners may rely upon general developmental theories and hierarchies of objectives, or they may use a classification scheme designed specifically for physical education. For example, Thompson and Mann (1977) developed a taxonomy of objectives in six areas of development for which the physical education program is responsible: mental development, social-emotional development, physical development, body-handling development, object-handling development, and coordinated object and body handling development.

A number of other curriculum frameworks based on the developmental model are being used, primarily in elementary school physical education. Hoffman, Young and Klesius (1985) designed a holistic elementary curriculum using developmental themes, presented as generic goals for elementary education and specific goals for physical education. The themes identified are: becoming aware, becoming independent, accepting and expressing feelings and ideas, accepting responsibilities and acting cooperatively, improving quality of response, and drawing relationships. Gallahue's (1993) developmental model for elementary school physical education places the curricular focus on the development of movement skills, building cognitive and affective development into skill (e.g., stability, locomotor, manipulative) and sport (e.g., basketball, soccer, volleyball) units, arranged in strands to integrate diverse areas of knowledge.

Zakrajsek and Carnes (1986) describe a developmental task model for individualizing physical education using sequenced tasks encompassing a wide range of skill levels and sport interests. Teachers are encouraged to diagnose each student's entry level in order to assist them in selecting and practicing appropriate tasks. The model provides the instructor with content or actual problems for guiding the student's learning through each task. Another developmental model that focuses on personal diagnosis and individualization of learning activities and challenges has been provided by Heitmann and Kneer (1976).

Developmental models vary in the emphasis given to different aspects of development, in the degree of student autonomy encouraged, and in other specifics. A well-regarded developmental model is Hellison's responsibility model (Hellison & Templin, 1991). The Hellison model is a social development model that uses a five-level framework designed to encourage students to gain control of themselves and their behavior. The levels are identified as: irresponsibility, self-control and respect for the rights and feelings of others, participation and effort, self-direction, and caring and helping.

To achieve the goals of physical education supported by the developmental model, teachers work to facilitate the personal growth of each student within a nurturing class environment. Instructional strategies focus on self-esteem, self-responsibility, and lesson objectives that integrate cognitive, affective, and motor development.

> Teachers . . . give individual students the care, encouragement, discipline and attention they need, when they need it. The teacher guides the student to reflect about personal choices in class, school, and in life. Students learn to try new experiences to determine those that are useful. (Jewett, Bain, & Ennis, in press)

Teachers are responsible for selecting individually appropriate tasks that are consistent with individual levels of motor development and movement skill-learning. Several levels of performance are built into each task; children are encouraged to strive for higher levels of success.

Curricula built upon the developmental model incorporate diversity in goals, themes, and teaching strategies. The evaluation process must focus on progress in reaching individually appropriate goals. Student self-assessment plays a large role in the planning of daily instruction. Program evaluation and improvement necessarily includes procedures for building upon current student interests, increasing the scope of student choice and decision making, and maintaining and increasing the range of developmental-level challenges built into available learning opportunities.

Ecological Integration Curricula. The ecological integration value orientation incorporates concepts of holistic development and self-actualization, but it goes beyond the self-actualization perspective to a view of the holistic person integrated within the total environment in his or her particular place in time. This perspective seeks to build a curriculum that emphasizes the personal search for meaning, that balances individual and societal needs, and that reflects the importance of the total natural and social environmental context in integrative growth and development. The *personal meaning* curriculum model is the generic model developed to reflect the ecological integration perspective.

Personal meaning model. The educational goals of the personal meaning model are broad, general, and future-oriented. The focus is on holistic individual development and the personal search for meaning. The personal-meaning model is concerned with the development of the individual in a particular social context. It emphasizes growth in social responsibility and the development of cooperative skills for participation in planned social change.

The conceptual framework for a personal meaning model is some network of concepts identifying the nature of personal meanings sought through participation in movement activities. The most completely delineated conceptual framework for a personal meaning model is the Purpose Process Curriculum Framework (Jewett & Mullan, 1977; Jewett & Bain <Eds.>, 1987), informally identified as the PPCF. The PPCF conceptual framework has two major components, a series of 23 participant purposes for moving, and a seven-process, movement process category system.

The content for the personal-meaning curriculum is structured in terms of potential meanings for participants. Personal meaning can be approached either intrinsically or instrumentally, and the source of meaning in movement varies widely, both within and among individuals. The focus may be upon the feelings of joy, pleasure, and satisfaction inherent in the movement experience itself, or upon the use of movement activities to accomplish some extrinsic goal important to the participant.

Instruction is usually organized around specific purpose concepts, either by developing theme units (e.g., aerobic fitness, adventure sport, cultural diversity in movement traditions), or by teaching sport or dance activity units with an emphasis upon particular purposes or goals (e.g., object projection, teamwork, movement appreciation). The specific content within the unit is based upon an analysis of the sub-elements of the purpose category and upon the process dimension of the framework. The process dimension is used to select content designed to guide students in the processes of learning to move and moving to learn: perceiving, patterning, adapting, refining, varying, improvising, and composing. Students not only need to experience each of the processes, but also need to understand how to utilize processes to achieve their purposes. Processes also provide a basis for sequencing instructional activities.

Teachers using the personal meaning model need to analyze multiple potential sources of meaning. For every potential source of meaning, a wide variety of learning activities must be identified in order to provide access for individual students whose needs and interests vary widely. Teachers need to learn unique skills for responding supportively to each individual's personal search for meaning within a group of persons engaging in movement activities. These skills include highly refined skills of observation, listening, interpreting students' responses to class activities and events, offering positive comments to support self-esteem, giving suggestions for alternative activities to help students meet their goals, and many others. Class instruction should include experiences in goal-setting, evaluating personal progress, and re-setting new goals.

Personal meaning models also focus on helping students learn how to learn. The teacher is an enabler who encourages students to explore new physical activity challenges; who teaches them to apply movement learning processes to the solution of their individual skill-acquisition problems; who reflects with them about their progress; who teaches them to be critical thinkers and independent problem-solvers; and who helps them to develop the skills of cooperative learning. Instructional strategies also focus on the development of self-management, self-direction, self-monitoring, self-evaluation, and self-reinforcement.

The teacher with an ecological integration value orientation believes in the future and in the potential of the individual to be a participant in working toward social change. The physical education class has some unique possibilities for assisting in eliminating gender role stereotypes, as well as to support schoolwide efforts in multicultural education. Many of today's schools reflect social conflicts characterizing the larger community, particularly racial and ethnic tensions. The teacher working within a personal meaning curriculum model helps students learn to respect themselves and each other, to understand different cultural customs and values, and to appreciate diversity. Each person can learn how to improve conditions for all by working together. The process starts with small groups such as a single school class. The attitudes developed and the skills learned in small groups can be applied to broader communities as individuals mature and experience the right kinds of learning activities. Educators are challenged as never before to find useful strategies for increasing understanding and appreciation of cultural diversity, for breaking down gender and ethnic stereotypes, for resolving racial and religious tensions, for opening up opportunities for young persons to learn to contribute to positive social change.

Evaluating a curriculum designed with an ecological-integration orientation requires some combination of the usual relatively objective measures and other more creative approaches. An examination of the process of education is just as important as an evaluation of the products or outcomes. It is important to determine that the educational experience is involving, exciting, and meaningful to students. It is equally relevant to evaluate instruction in terms of the basic values of justice, equality, and human dignity reflected in the day-to-day interactions between teachers and students.

Figure 9.1 has been designed to illustrate the relationships between curriculum sources and the five value orientations, and to emphasize the dominant value orientation underlying each of the generic curriculum models. Table 9.1 provides a summary description of the five models.

Learning Process Curricula. With the learning process perspective, how individual persons learn in a physical activity environment becomes as important as what they learn. The curriculum focus is on the individual as a learner and on the processes for mastering the subject content. As pointed out earlier, this is a more narrow focus than that of any of the other four curriculum value orientations. It is believed that this aspect accounts for the fact that no models generated from the learning process perspective have been widely accepted for designing school physical education programs.

The learning process value orientation was conceptualized from the "technology" approach described by Eisner and Vallance (1974). Their five "conflicting conceptions" of curriculum became highly visible in the professional literature at the height of enthusiasm for expanding the role of instructional technology in curriculum development. The learning process orientation resulted from an effort to broaden the technology perspective to provide a more holistic focus on learning processes that included movement learning processes as well as more restrictively cognitive learning processes. Two decades later, Eisner (1992) discusses six ideologies that guide education. The earlier conceptions, except for the technology approach, can be seen to have evolved into broader conceptualizations; technology appears to have dropped out in that evolution.

While the learning process perspective is still held by a significant number of teachers, its focus is probably too narrow to provide sound models for designing today's K–12 physical education curricula. It is suggested that it may be more relevant as a conceptual framework for methodology or instructional design. This suggestion should not be interpreted to imply a lack of appreciation and concern for this perspective, however. On the contrary, a case can be made for building a learning-process orientation into almost any curriculum model in combination with its dominant value orientation.

Figure 9.1 Dominant Value Orientations of the Generic Curriculum Models

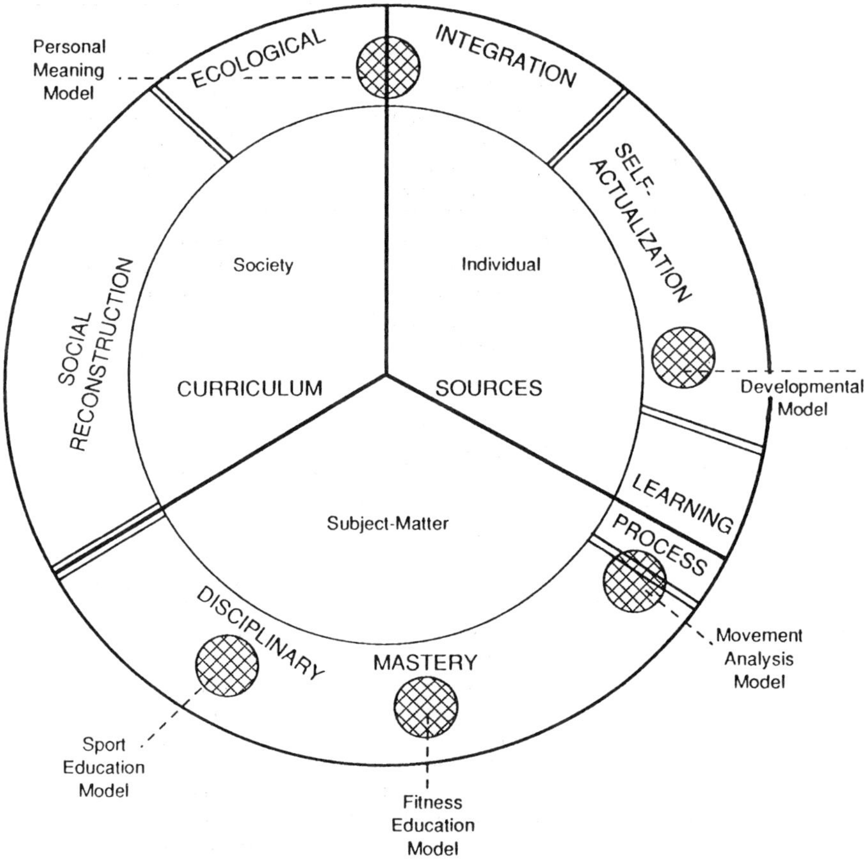

Whatever the subject-matter focus of a disciplinary mastery curriculum, the teacher who wants to foster self-directed learning can guide the student to reflect upon the process of learning and to understand and develop skill in movement-learning processes. The use of task contracts or mastery learning approaches in developing specific sports skills in a sport education curriculum promotes the attention of individual learners to their own skill learning processes. A teacher working within a fitness education curriculum to guide exercise behavior change might teach students about such change processes as reinforcement management and counter-conditioning to help them learn to prevent relapse of desired exercise behavior. Attention to the development of problem-solving skills is almost inherent in effective use of movement analysis models. A learning process orientation can help a teacher working with a developmental curriculum to assist students in developing their creative abilities or their skills for accommodating to varying movement-learning environments through guided experiences with the appropriate learning-process skills. Personal

Table 9.1 Summary Description of Curriculum Models

	Sport Education	Fitness Education
Dominant Value Orientation Perspective on: Individual Development Social-Cultural Goals Subject Matter	Disciplinary Mastery Expert diagnosis Preparation for existing society Sport (and dance)	Disciplinary Mastery Expert diagnosis Preparation for existing society Fitness
Goals	Increase interest in voluntary sport participation Develop sports skills, strategies, and understandings Socialize into sport environment Ethical sporting behavior	Knowledge about fitness skills in activities with health benefits Commitment to regular exercise and active lifestyle
Conceptual Framework	Structure of sport and expressive movement activities	Components of health-related fitness and processes of exercise behavior change
Program Characteristics	Focus on learning to participate in sport and play activities Instruction in a positive environment Opportunities for intra-school competitive sport experiences for all students	Focus on lifelong health-related fitness Emphasis on knowledge, attitudes, and behavioral change Vigorous activity program Regular testing and individual assessment

meaning curricula are usually designed to help students find meaning in movement process learning as well as in the activity content and the social context in which their learning occurs.

Social Reconstruction Curricula. A key belief in the social reconstruction value orientation is that the school has a responsibility to the future and educators should accept a role in making school curricula the vehicle for creating a better society. In this view, cultural change is an important goal. No social reconstruction models for human movement curricula, for which successful implementation has been demonstrated, have been reported in the professional literature. The probable reason for this lack of available models is that a single subject area curriculum plan directed toward social reconstruction would stand very little chance of success unless it is conceptualized as an

Table 9.1 (Continued)

Movement Analysis	Developmental	Personal Meaning
Disciplinary Mastery Expert diagnosis Preparation for existing society Movement	Self-Actualization Self-directed Preparation for existing society Movement	Ecological Integration Personal meaning Preparation for existing society and social change Movement, fitness, sport and dance
Move skillfully Knowledge about movement Problem-solving ability	Self-esteem Competence in movement activities Individual appropriateness Socialization and responsible choice Integration of experience	Individual development Environmental coping Social interaction
Structure of the discipline of human movement	Developmental characteristics, patterns, stages	Potential meaning for participants
Knowledge and performance integrated in the understanding and mastery of movement skills Scope and sequence based on movement themes or concepts Emphasis on problem-solving	Holistic approach to search for personal identity Varied opportunities for maximum development Nurturing environment supportive of individual differences	Focus on personal search for meaning Process skills essential content Learning in a social context Emphasis on individual talents, creative abilities, and long-term goals and satisfactions

integral part of a schoolwide curriculum reform plan designed for use in a supportive community context.

The social reconstruction value orientation appears to be well represented among U.S. physical educators, however. Ennis and her colleagues constructed a teacher value orientation inventory and have conducted several significant research studies in this area. This body of research suggests that teachers placing high priority on different value orientations may differ in their receptivity to using particular curriculum models, and in their willingness to incorporate certain strategies in their lesson planning. It appears common for individual teachers to hold multiple orientations. Of particular interest in the present context is a report comparing findings in separate studies of value orientations of midwestern physical educators and of urban physical educators (Ennis, 1992). The percentage of the midwest group placing high priority on social reconstruction was 25.6; percentages of high priorities on each of the other four value orientations ranged from 14.4 to 31.1. Among the urban physical educators, 56.8 percent placed high priority on social reconstruction, while the high priorities on the other value orientations were each scored at less than 25 percent (Ennis, 1992, pp. 122–123).

These findings seem to suggest that urban educators working in situations with high rates of crime and violence in their neighborhoods and schools are more concerned about the need for social change than those in less-threatening social environments. Another recent research study (Ennis, in press) examined the value orientations of teachers who valued social curriculum goals to determine the extent to which their curriculum decision-making represented the social justice and reform goals of social reconstruction, or goals of citizenship and positive interaction more consistent with social responsibility. Results suggested that teachers' content decisions were consistent with the goals of cooperation, teamwork, and involvement within a social responsibility orientation. It is likely that this work will lead to a proposed social responsibility curriculum model that could be viewed as an intermediate step toward development of a genuine social-reconstruction model.

Physical education curriculum specialists need to give serious attention to the need for developing social-reconstruction models for designing school programs based in developmental physical activity. The goals of such programs will continue to be social change to achieve basic human rights, equality of educational and economic opportunity, environmental sustainability, and world peace. These ambitious goals are clearly out of present reach. But many first steps are possible in seeking improvements in today's programs.

Emphasis on the development of greater social responsibility could be a good beginning. It requires almost no change in the formal curriculum, just procedural and attitude changes that help individual students learn to take personal responsibility for their own behavior within the group, to respect the rights of others, to seek positive interaction with their classmates, to try to understand differences in cultural values, and to work with classmates toward group goals. Teachers who value social reconstruction encourage students to reflect upon particular class situations and events, and guide their discussions of inequities observed in the school environment with a focus on "what can we do as concerned citizens to correct this situation?" and "what can you do as an individual?" Students can develop their own modifications of the sport rules and the class activities to ensure that everyone has a chance to play in the most desirable positions, that each participant can be involved in ways that make it enjoyable to be a member of the team, and that activities are conducted so that they learn to understand principles of group dynamics and develop the critical skills of working together effectively.

Problems identified in the school environment that demonstrate need for local social changes can become the focus for learning to identify and become a part of the solution of social problems and issues in the broader local community. Projects undertaken by a class, a school club, or the entire school population might focus on such problems as cleaning up the school environment, safety on the playground, spectator behavior at school sporting events, sponsoring a fun run, organizing a Special Olympics, or celebrating customs of various subgroups in the local community. The school should also seek opportunities for students to work with community service organizations in special events and volunteer drives or campaigns to provide needed services for persons who need help or in times of public emergencies. In such projects the students need to be involved in identifying an area of need in which they might play a meaningful role (e.g., planning the organization of responsibilities, publicity, and public relations; conducting the actual events; and evaluating the impact on their own learning as well as the contribution to building a better community).

A social reconstruction curriculum model provides a framework for educating learners to be agents of social change. This is probably the most difficult aspect to conceptualize clearly. At the very least, the characteristics of a social change agent would include the following: individual responsibility for maintaining personal health and total fitness; respect for the worth and dignity of every other individual; appreciation of the values of cultural diversity; and skills for understanding others, resolving conflicts, and avoiding violence in negotiating a new world order and creating a better future for all.

WHERE SHALL WE GO FROM HERE?

Physical education program development as a professional area of scholarly study and research is a relatively new scholarly specialization. It has been a focus for subdisciplinary concern for only about three decades; to date, advanced study in the area has not drawn a large proportion of the scholars of human movement. Not surprisingly, progress in defining, describing, and researching the various aspects of the field has been uneven. The work of general curricularists has provided a solid foundation for sketching out different sets of educational beliefs and value orientations, and guidelines for clarifying our own systems for inquiring into questions about curriculum ends and means. Usable classification systems for describing and examining physical education curriculum value orientations are now available. These provide for choice among frameworks for proposing curriculum designs. In the 80s and 90s, progress in the area of instructional research to support effective implementation has been excellent.

Current status in these areas has already been described. Appropriate applications of present knowledge in these areas suggest that it is time to refocus and move on. Scholarly study is especially needed to provide insights into several key areas for future progress in curriculum studies and program development. Recommendations for addressing four contemporary professional challenges are discussed briefly: (1) improving personal health and quality of life, (2) achieving equality for all, (3) creating global awareness and cooperation, and (4) stimulating and guiding curriculum change.

Personal Health and Enhanced Quality of Life. Almost unbelievable advances in medical diagnosis and treatment procedures have been made in recent years. Unfortunately, these advances have been accompanied by rapidly escalating costs of health care. It is clearly in everyone's best interests that more attention be given to prevention of disease, reduction of known health risks, and positive approaches to promoting healthful behavior. The U.S. Department of Health and Human Services (1991) has stated national objectives for the Year 2000, providing a "prevention agenda" that emphasizes reducing preventable death, disease, and disability, and focuses on improving the quality and quantity of life. Since education is obviously the best approach to prevention and to changing individual behavior, the school curriculum must carry a major responsibility for addressing the need for positive, more effective health education programs.

The goal is a holistic concept of "wellness." It is a positive concept of health enhancement, not just treatment, not prevention alone, but high level "quality living." Achieving this goal will require the support of a comprehensive health program, based in a broad subject-field. The subject-field might be called wellness or health enhancement. It should evolve into one of five or six core subjects in the K–12 school curriculum.

None of the physical education curriculum models currently in use is an adequate framework to plan for meeting this goal. The developmental model and the personal meaning model each have a strong focus on individual development; but neither provides for enough depth or breadth in health knowledge or a strong enough commitment to the total wellness concept. The fitness education model has similar goals, but its delineation of the subject content is much too narrow. A new model needs to be created to design curricula directed toward holistic health enhancement for all persons through successive life phases.

Health education and physical education as we know these school subjects now need to be reconceptualized as a single field of study. Physical activity should be a large component because sport skills increase enjoyment of physical recreation, and because the habit of regular exercise takes significant curriculum time to facilitate. Other movement skills are needed for daily life tasks and for regular exercise participation. Comprehensive health instruction will address a wide range of topics including, but not limited to, nutrition, oral health, physical activity, substance abuse, sexual behavior, violent and abusive behavior, environmental health, safety and first aid, immunization and infectious diseases, mental and behavioral disorders, vitality in older people, high blood cholesterol and high blood pressure, cancer, and other chronic disorders. Students need to develop decision-making skills, self-management skills, skills for organizing and managing sports and other group activities, and leadership and cooperative participation skills. The program will be focused on the development of a wide variety of knowledges, understandings, skills, and positive attitudes.

The instructional program in wellness will require the availability of gymnasia and other activity facilities, physical education equipment, classrooms, computers, and other types of instructional technology support. It will need to be supplemented by school health services, a healthful school environment, school food services, counseling programs, and school/community health promotion efforts. The potential for a new health enhancement curriculum model can perhaps best be summarized by quoting the goals of the 1989 state-mandated Montana Health Enhancement Program:

> (1) In general, a basic health enhancement program shall: (a) Integrate lifestyle management throughout the curriculum. (b) Focus on the total self and the development of responsibility, values, attitudes, and behaviors. (c) Give students decision-making tools for personal health. (d) Address intellectual, social, emotional, and physical dimensions of healthy lifestyles. (Montana School Accreditation Standards and Resources Manual, 7/11/89, Sub Chapter 13. Rule 10.55.1301. Health Enhancement Program)

Equality for All. Equality is a high priority in the value system espoused by a democratic society. Yet schools in many countries around the world which aspire toward democracy are operating in social contexts in which all people do not, in fact, have equal opportunity to enjoy "the good things in life." Equality for all cannot be legislated; laws can only provide the basic framework within which personal interactions can stimulate the development of respect for the rights of others and encourage appreciation of diversity and caring for others. A key challenge to educators is to help create a school environment which provides greater equality for all students and prepares them to participate in increasing equal opportunity in the larger community.

Many nations are attempting to initiate school reforms designed to increase equality of opportunity. There are historical conflicts in all parts of the world that have led to continuing biases, prejudices, and unequal treatment based on differences in religion, ethnicity, or race. Each country has its own patterns of inequality and discrimination. A number have initiated multicultural education programs in the public school systems, in higher education institutions, and in teacher preparation curricula. Generally speaking, success has been limited; but we have learned some things from these efforts.

We know that we can group children for learning activities in ways that encourage positive student interaction. We have found a variety of ways to select content that is more inclusive than the curriculum guide has typically provided.

A key focus in choosing instructional strategies should be concern for developing self-esteem. Each child should be allowed to develop pride in his or her own heritage. Teachers should be sensitive to specific cultural traditions and sanctions that may be challenged in the physical activity setting (e.g., approved dress, hairstyles, participation in dance activities). Children of minority subgroups often need help in learning how to respond to the dominant world in terms of their own culture.

Teachers and students need to learn to focus on the positive aspects of all cultures. Teacher education programs should prepare teachers to create strategies to capitalize on cultural differences. Teacher preparation should include accurate knowledge about the value conflicts between cultures; this aspect of multicultural education should include understanding of particular cultures represented in the populations with whom they anticipate working, and skills for learning to understand the value system of an unfamiliar culture. The classroom or gymnasium can be a positive setting for learning to challenge stereotypes. All of us need to develop skills for acceptable approaches to racial or ethnic conflict resolution.

In most democratic societies today, women are still subject to inequities when their opportunities are compared to those of men. School physical education programs have unique potential for addressing sexist stereotypes and gender inequities. Increased public interest in exercise and fitness has sometimes resulted in overemphasis on personal appearance as the desired outcome. A healthy body is sometimes equated with skillful performance or idealized appearance. Some "body-building" approaches actually have negative effects on a healthy body. A significant number of young women are at risk for such conditions as anorexia or bulimia as a result of obsessive concern for staying thin. It is important that programs provide factual information and guidance in planning personal exercise programs to eliminate such stereotypes. Attitudes designating some "feminine" physical activities for girls and other "macho" activities for boys, without reasonable foundation, should be replaced through instruction offering criteria for individual selection of activities for personal physical recreation. Class activities should provide experiences that help both male and female students to understand the importance of opening up and expanding sport programs to provide equal opportunities for girls and women. Equal opportunities for leadership roles and employment also need to be extended to females in coaching, athletic training, officiating, sports journalism, and sports business.

Equality of opportunity in physical education instruction and sports programs is often not a reality for the handicapped, especially those with physical disabilities. U.S. law requires equal access to all public educational programs and services in "the least restrictive environment." Teachers need to make special efforts to modify activities, to create roles in new activities, and to guide these students in developing skills and techniques to permit their active, satisfying participation in group activities.

The physical activity environment offers genuine potential for challenging ethnic, racial, gender, and disability stereotypes; for building self-esteem of all students and empowering disadvantaged students; and for appreciating diversity and developing commitment to accord equal opportunity to all. But equality for all cannot be achieved through the developmental physical activity curriculum alone. Significant progress in this direction requires a schoolwide curriculum committed to this goal. If equality is to be a top priority educational goal, curriculum designers will need to create viable social reconstruction models for the curriculum.

Global Awareness and Cooperation. Education in the post Cold War era requires a new orientation. We need to recognize that all nations are interdependent, that we cannot realize our goals for quality of life within our country without the cooperation of many others. "There is a growing need for global education, which studies problems that cut across national boundaries, cultivates cross-cultural understanding, and considers the earth as humankind's ecological home" (Coates & Jarrett, 1993). Understanding our world in transition requires us to consider how we can fulfil our role in building world peace, and to realize that issues such as human rights, environmental sustainability, and economic growth are global concerns that need to be resolved through international cooperation.

Nations need to plan together for the kind of future world we want. At the local school level, we can try to educate individuals in new ways of thinking. Gelatt (1993, p. 13) recommends that we recognize that the future is unknown without fearing it, acknowledge the importance of information without idolizing it, maintain openness for paradigm shifts, and develop attitudes of "positive uncertainty . . . (1) accepting the past, present, and future as uncertain, and (2) being positive about the uncertainty." Many things important for global cooperation can be learned in developing our own learning community. Protecting human rights; sharing, resources, technology, and communications networks; understanding other subcultures; reducing inequities among community subgroups; helping the disadvantaged to be part of the solution to their own problems; substituting win-win strategies for one-winner competition; and preserving the environment are among the most important.

Special challenges for futures education in exercise, sport, physical recreation, and expressive movement, include helping students learn to help and care for others, understand how a team "works," develop creativity, and become capable of problem-solving and critical thinking. The physical activity environment offers unique opportunities for developing global awareness and cooperative behavior. However, global education and futures education, like achieving equality, will require the creation of new social reconstruction models for schoolwide curricula.

Curriculum Change. Curriculum change is an essential aspect of social change. The pace of change has been accelerating at a dizzying rate in recent decades. Our world of the 90s looks very little like the world of the 80s. If education is to be a factor in seeking solutions to our current social problems or exploring new directions for the future, the curriculum must be directed toward meaningful goals and be relevant to today's concerns and tomorrow's hopes. The curriculum in any one subject-field must be perceived and reconstructed within its broader educational environment and its total sociocultural context. As human movement professionals we need to confront current problems in the larger context, rather than maintaining our isolation focused on a single disciplinary perspective.

Perceptions of future needs change; educational goals and directions change. The characteristics of our students are changing constantly. Teachers are not changing as much, but probably need to change more rapidly to maintain their relevance to the educational enterprise. Our field is changing with the continuing fluctuations in our social and economic setting. The curriculum certainly needs to change, but curriculum change is constrained by its very nature. Curriculum change is multidimensional, extremely complex, and highly political.

Three perspectives on the change process influence the approach used. The technical perspective is typically used for large scale innovations designed by external experts. The teachers who are charged with carrying out the changes are seldom involved in their development. In contrast, the teacher is an integral part of the process of curricular change guided by the ecological perspective. From this perspective, the teacher plays a key role in implementing the innovation according to the intricacies of the classroom context. The cultural perspective is based on a broader conceptualization of the role of the common beliefs and values of the school culture which must be gradually transformed to accept the innovation and implement it effectively.

From a technical perspective, top-down change strategies are usually selected; success is dependent upon persuading teachers of the superiority of the innovative content or teaching strategy proposed. Bottom-up change strategies, which reflect the ecological perspective, typically lack the funding and publicity for innovations to spread beyond a few classrooms. Fullan and colleagues (Fullan, *et al.*, 1990) have proposed a framework built on a cultural perspective of change that encourages teachers to become directly involved. The plan is responsive to the needs and concerns of both teachers and administrators and provides for negotiation and compromise on issues of scheduling, essential resources, and classroom decision-making.

Teacher involvement is central to the success of significant curriculum change. Positive rapport among the total faculty is needed. Administrative support is essential. Substantial parent involvement is necessary to effect any large scale change. Curricular change is probably effected most successfully in developmental or personal meaning curricula, because it is easier for educators and parents to agree on changes that are expected to serve the children better than on changes specifically tied to particular subject matter emphases.

CONCLUDING STATEMENT

This discussion of curriculum theory and program development in the field of human motor performance or developmental physical activity in exercise, sport, physical recreation, and expressive movement has highlighted questions of both educational ends and means. Considerable attention has been given to five alternative philosophical perspectives (disciplinary mastery, self-actualization, social reconstruction, learning process, and ecological integration). The curriculum development process has been described as it can be implemented within each of these perspectives. Generic models in operation include three developed from the disciplinary mastery perspective (sport education, fitness education, and movement analysis), the developmental model used to implement the self-actualization perspective, and the personal meaning model based on the ecological integration perspective.

Curricula based on each of the five value orientations have been described, giving emphasis to differing program goals, and to varying answers to the "how" questions or the instructional aspects (conceptual framework, selected content, instructional strategies, and evaluation procedures). It has been pointed out that scholars in this field need to give particular attention to the development of social reconstruction models and to new personal meaning models. More emphasis on learning processes, whichever curriculum model is used, is recommended. A serious professional effort to disseminate information concerning available curriculum models and the need for basing curriculum practice on a sound theoretical foundation is vitally important.

The primary recommendations for curriculum scholarship in the immediate future are restated briefly:

1. Physical educators should work with health educators and others interested in major curriculum reform to reconceptualize a broad core subject field of human wellness, giving thorough consideration to developmental physical activity and total health enhancement.
2. Major attention should be given to further research on inequities in our society, to seeking imaginative solutions to problems existing in our school settings, and to exploration of possible educational strategies for achieving greater equality of opportunity for all.

3. Global awareness and the need for developing cooperative behaviors should be acknowledged as important concerns of the educational experience. Physical educators need to work as members of school teams to find ways to move toward this goal.
4. We need to focus our best efforts on developing and refining better models for effecting curriculum change in our field. At the same time, we must help teachers to become social change agents. Hopefully, this will lead to the creation of instructional strategies for guiding students in becoming participants in positive social change.

REFERENCES

CAILLOIS, R. (1961). *Man, play and games.* New York: Free Press.

CLOUGH, J., & TRAILL, R. D. (1992). The 1991 report on AUSSIE SPORT, and sports for kids research. Belconnen, ACT, Australia: Australian Sports Commission.

COATES, J. F., & JARRETT, J. (1993). The future: Trends into the twenty-first century. As summarized in Marien, M. (Ed.), (1993), *Future survey annual 1993* (p. 137). Bethesda, MD: World Future Society.

DIEM, L. (1962). *Who can?* Frankfurt, Germany: Wilhelm Limpert.

EISNER, E. W. (1992). Curriculum ideologies. In Jackson, P. W., (Ed.), *Handbook of research on curriculum* (pp. 302–326). New York: Macmillan.

EISNER, E. W., & VALLANCE, E. (Eds.). (1974). *Conflicting conceptions of curriculum.* Berkeley, CA: McCutchan.

ENNIS, C. D. (1992). The influence of value orientations in curriculum decision making. *Quest, 44,* 317–329.

ENNIS, C. D. (In press). Urban secondary teachers' value orientations: Delineating curricular goals for social responsibility. *Journal of Teaching in physical Education.*

FULLAN, M. G., BENNETT, B., & ROLHEISER-BENNETT, C. (1990). Linking classroom and school improvement. *Educational Leadership, 47*(8), 13–19.

GALLAHUE, D. L. (1993). *Developmental physical education for today's children.* Madison, WI: Brown and Benchmark.

GELATT, H. B. (1993). Future sense: Creating the future. *The Futurist, 27*(55), 9–13.

GIROUX, H. A., PENNA, A. W., & PINAR, W. F. (Eds.). 1981. *Curriculum and instruction: Alternatives in education.* Berkeley, CA: McCutchan.

GRAHAM, G. F., HOLT-HALE, S. A., & PARKER, M. (1992). *Children moving: A reflective approach to teaching physical education* (3rd ed.). Mountain View, CA: Mayfield.

GRANT, B., & SHARP, P. (1992). Sports education research project: A collaborative research project in form 5 physical education. Wellington, New Zealand: Hillary Commission for Recreation and Sport.

HEITMANN, H. M., & KNEER, M. E. (1976). *Physical education instructional techniques: An individualized humanistic approach.* Englewood Cliffs, NJ: Prentice-Hall.

HEITMANN, H. M. (1993). *Fit for daily life tasks: A manual to provide activities to prepare students to safely perform daily life tasks requiring strength, balance, and coordination.* 5731 Woodland Dr., Western Springs, IL, 60558: Author.

HELLISON, D. R., & TEMPLIN, T. J. (1991). *A reflective approach to teaching physical education.* Champaign, IL: Human Kinetics.

HILLARY COMMISSION FOR RECREATION AND SPORT. (1991). Annual report. Wellington, New Zealand: Author.

HOFFMAN, H. A., YOUNG, J., & KLESIUS, S. E. (1985). *Meaningful movement for children: A developmental theme approach to physical education.* Dubuque, IA: Kendall/Hunt.

JEWETT, A. E., BAIN, L. L., & ENNIS, C. D. (in press). *The Curriculum Process in Physical Education* (2nd ed.). Madison, WI: Brown & Benchmark.

JEWETT, A. E., & MULLAN, M. R. (1977). *Curriculum design: Purposes and processes in physical education teaching-learning.* Washington, D.C.: AAHPER.

JEWETT, A. E., & BAIN, L. L. (Eds.). (1987). The purpose process curriculum framework: A personal meaning model for physical education. [Special Monograph]. *Journal of Teaching in Physical Education, 6*(3), 193–366.

KIRK, D. (1988). *Physical education and curriculum study.* New York: Croon Helm.

LABAN, R. (1960). *The mastery of movement.* London: MacDonald and Evans.

LABAN, R. (1963). *Modern educational dance* (2nd ed.). Rev. by L. Ullman. New York: Frederick A. Praeger.

LOGSDON, B. J., BARRETT, K. R., AMMONS, M., BROER, M. R., HALVERSON, L. E., MCGEE, R., & ROBERTON, M. A. (1984). *Physical education for children* (2nd ed). Philadelphia: Lea & Febiger.

MACDONALD, J. B. (1981). Theory-practice and the hermeneutic circle. *Journal of Curriculum Theorizing, 3*(2), 130–138.

MACDONALD, J. B. (1977). Values bases and issues for curriculum. In Molnar, A., & Zahorik, J. A. (Eds.), *Curriculum Theory* (pp. 10–21). Washington, D.C.: Association for Supervision and Curriculum Development.

MACDONALD, J. B. (1965). Educational models for instruction. In *Theories of instruction* (pp. 1–7). Washington, D.C.: National Education Association.

MCNEIL, J. D. (1985). *Curriculum: A comprehensive introduction* (3rd ed.). Boston: Little & Brown.

NATIONAL ASSOCIATION FOR SPORT AND PHYSICAL EDUCATION. (1992). *Outcomes of quality physical education programs.* Reston, VA: AAHPERD.

NICHOLS, B. (1990). Moving and learning: *The elementary school physical education experience.* St. Louis: Times Mirror/Mosby.

ORLOSKY, D. E., & SMITH, B. O. (1978). *Curriculum development: Issues and insights.* Chicago: Rand McNally.

ORNSTEIN, A. C., & HUNKINS, F. P. (1988). *Curriculum: Foundations, principles, and issues.* Boston: Allyn and Bacon.

ROBERTSON, I. (1992). Children, AUSSIE SPORTS and organized junior sport. Executive summary. Belconnen, ACT, Australia: Australian Sports Commission.

SAGE, G. H. (1993). Sport and physical education and the new world order: Dare we be agents of social change? *Quest, 45*(2), 151–164.

SCHUBERT, W. H. (1986). *Curriculum: Perspective, paradigm, possibility.* New York: Macmillan.

SIEDENTOP, D. F. (Ed.). (in press). *Sport education: Teaching sport in physical education.* Champaign, IL: Human Kinetics.

STANLEY, S. (1969). Physical education: A movement orientation. Montreal: McGraw-Hill of Canada.

THOMPSON, M. M., & MANN, B. A. (1977). *An holistic approach to physical education curricula: Objectives classification system for elementary schools.* Champaign, IL: Stipes.

U.S. DEPARTMENT OF HEALTH AND HUMAN SERVICES. (1991). Health people 2000: National health promotion and disease prevention objectives. Washington, D.C.: U.S. Government Printing Office.

ZAKRAJSEK, D., & CARNES, L. A. (1986). *Individualizing physical education.* Champaign, IL: Human Kinetics.

Chapter Ten

Measurement and Evaluation

Don Franks

Physical activity professionals (physical education teacher, fitness instructors, coaches, kinesiology scholars) are often asked their opinion about the fitness, skill, knowledge, and movement form of other persons.[1] These opinions are used for evaluation of self, teachers, programs, professional players, and students. The worth of the opinions depends on an understanding of both the activity being analyzed and the procedures used for the evaluation.

Other professional and disciplinary areas included in this book help sport and physical activity students learn the factors that are important for skill, fitness, movement forms, and the knowledge desired for different levels of activity. Testing, measuring, and evaluating are the focus of this chapter. The goal of this chapter is to provide information about the **process** by which an appropriate test is selected, administered, scored, and analyzed to allow assessment of the characteristic(s) being tested.

DEFINITIONS

Table 10.1 *Definitions*

Test	=	Instrument used to assess a variable
Measurement	=	Score assigned to a response to a test item
Evaluation	=	Value judgment placed on the test score

Table 10.1 defines test, measurement, and evaluation. For example, the vertical jump *test* is scored (*measurement*) by the distance (in inches or cm) between the height that the student could reach while standing and the chalk mark made during the vertical jump. *Evaluation* includes terms, such as, "good," "within the normal range," or "indicated a weakness." Each evaluative statement compares the person's score with some standard.

EVALUATIVE PROCESSES

The early approach to testing in sport and physical education often resembled the first part of this old native American saying: "Give me a fish and I will eat today; teach me how to fish and I will eat for a lifetime." Physical educators were taught about certain tests of fitness, sport skill, and knowledge. The professionals could do well as long as they needed tests solely in those areas covered in their test and measurement class. The more recent approach is to teach the basic evaluation procedures that can be utilized in any situation in which evaluation is desired. The major components of evaluation are listed in Table 10.2.

Table 10.2 *Components of Evaluation*

Knowledge:
- Goals
- Variables to be tested
- Factors that affect test scores

Ability:
- Select/construct a suitable test
- Administer test(s) efficiently and accurately

Basis for:
- Current status
- Realistic goals
- Next steps for improvement

Determine:
- Description of group
- Relationship between variables
- Difference between groups

These components are listed in sequence. The goals are derived from disciplinary and professional aspects of our field. The variables and factors that affect them are based on the goals. Specific tests are selected, administered, and interpreted. These activities are the process of evaluation.

OBJECTIVES

One cannot evaluate anything unless it is clear what the activity/professional/program is trying to accomplish. These goals are translated into specific objectives that can be clearly described. This information plus an understanding of the nature of the characteristics to be tested is provided by the bodies of knowledge in the other disciplinary and professional aspects of our field.

TEST SELECTION AND CONSTRUCTION

After the objectives are clearly perceived, the testing/measuring/evaluating processes are used. The first task is to find appropriate tests for all of the objectives of the person or program. A good test is defined by the extent to which it meets the criteria listed in Table 10.3.

Table 10.3 *Criteria for Test Selection/Construction*

Criterion	Purpose
Validity	Relevance to purpose of test
Reliability	Consistency of test
Objectivity	Consistency of testers
Accuracy	True absolute score
Feasibility	
Appropriateness	Differentiation of abilities
Cost	Time, personnel, facilities, and equipment

Validity. Does the test give us information we want about the person being tested? Does the test measure what it is supposed to? A valid test will have a yes answer to these questions. There are essentially three ways that one can determine the degree to which a test is valid.

The first way to explore validity is to ask, Does the test seem to be a good way to measure this characteristic of a person? Is it a logical test? Do experts in this area use it? Does the test appear to give the information that is desired? This approach to validity is called *content* or *face* validity. For concrete variables, content validity is the only type of validity that is needed. For example, measuring the number of centimeters from the bottom of a person's feet to the top of the head when standing straight would seem to be a logical way to test standing height. It is also the way used by experts in height testing. There is no need to provide additional evidence of validity for this test of height.

Table 10.4 *Validity*

Content	
	Logical
	Used by experts
Concurrent	
	Related to valid test
	Differentiates between groups
Construct	
	Relates appropriately to other variables
	Responds as expected theoretically

However, more abstract variables, such as cardiorespiratory function or attitude toward physical activity, require additional checks on validity before accepting the validity of a particular test. The tester starts with something that seems logical and is utilized by experts, but additional evidence of validity is needed before selection of a test. The quality of content validity depends on the initial logic in selecting appropriate test items. The extent of validity based on expert opinion obviously is as good as the experts involved.

A second way to determine the degree of validity is to compare the proposed test with an accepted (valid) test. *Concurrent* validity is established if the new test has a high positive relationship (correlation) with the test that is known to be valid (criterion test). For example, it would appear logical that a person's ability to continue to run (hop, swim, jump, step, cycle) for 9 minutes would depend, in part, on cardiorespiratory function. Endurance runs have been used to test cardiorespiratory fitness in several published fitness tests. Thus there is some content validity for the endurance run as a test of cardiorespiratory function. To establish concurrent validity, the endurance run needs to be compared with an established test of cardiorespiratory function. It is generally agreed among exercise scientists that maximal aerobic capacity (highest ability to utilize oxygen during increasingly strenuous work) is a valid test of cardiorespiratory function. The high, positive relationship between the distance one can run in 9 minutes and the maximal oxygen intake provides concurrent validity for the use of the run as a test of cardiorespiratory function. Another example of concurrent validity is the use of underwater weighing (criterion variable) to validate skinfold estimates of body density and percent fat.

Concurrent validity depends on the validity of the criterion test. If test A is valid because it correlates with test B, which is valid because it is related to test C, etc., eventually one has to accept validity of the original criterion test based on content and construct validity. A common, but questionable, method of establishing concurrent validity is to validate a single test item by comparing it with the whole test. Thus, question 16 on a 50-item written test might receive a validity rating based on how well that test item was related to the entire test.

A specific skill, performance, or fitness test is sometimes validated by comparison with the entire test battery of which it is a part. This approach to concurrent validity assumes that the entire test is valid. It may be that a single item measures an important objective that is not covered by any other test. In this case, it is a good test item even though it has a low correlation with the other test items. At the other extreme, a test item might have a high "validity" coefficient simply because it was one of several items testing the same concept. Thus one must critically evaluate the criterion test in interpreting the concurrent validity value.

Another way to establish concurrent validity is to show that the test differentiates among groups who are known to be different on the variable being tested. A valid test of golf ability would produce higher test scores for par golfers than for bogey golfers, who in turn do better than "weekend hackers." Although this is a recommended procedure for establishing concurrent validity, it is difficult to find groups that are known to be different on a particular variable without also being different in other ways. For example, persons who are clinically judged to be in separate categories on anxiety might score differently on an anxiety test, but they might also have other psychological distinctions.

A third way to determine test validity is to decide if the test reacts to varying situations the same way the characteristic being tested should respond to those situations. This *construct* validity is based on theoretical understanding of the characteristic of interest. One aspect of construct validity involves the relationship between the variables being tested and other variables. We know that a particular variable should be positively related to some variables, negatively related to some variables, and not related at all to some variables. For example, a valid test of cardiorespiratory function has a positive association with the components of cardiorespiratory function, such as stroke volume, oxygen transport, and ability of the muscle to use oxygen. A valid cardiorespiratory test has a negative relationship with low-density cholesterol, amount of obstruction in the blood vessels, and hypertension. At the same time, it has no relationship to variables such as arm strength, height, weight, IQ, and a host of other non-cardiorespiratory variables. Thus there would be evidence for construct validity if the distance run in 9 minutes had a high positive correlation with stroke volume and other components of cardiorespiratory function; a high negative correlation with cholesterol and other cardiorespiratory problems, and a close-to-zero relationship with non-cardiorespiratory variables such as strength and intelligence.

Another way to demonstrate construct validity is to show that the test changes in the same way the characteristic being tested would change. Again with cardiorespiratory function as an example, it is well known that cardiorespiratory function is decreased by prolonged bed rest and increased by appropriate endurance-running conditioning. Therefore, if the subject's 9-minute run distance improves after several weeks of a conditioning program and deteriorates after a few weeks of bed rest, then these results would provide additional construct validity for the endurance run of a mile as a test for cardiorespiratory function.

The person establishing construct validity must have a thorough knowledge of the characteristic being tested, statistical techniques, and research design. A theoretical understanding of the variable, its relationship to other variables, and how it should respond to various situations, is necessary to determine construct validity. In addition, the evaluation specialist must be able to design studies in such a way that the research will show to what degree the test being validated is related appropriately to other tests and the effects of various experimental conditions on the test. Either lack of knowledge about the variable being tested or faulty research design lessens the evidence for the test's validity.

A valid test is one that logically tests the variable of interest. It compares favorably with good tests of the same variable. It has positive, negative and near-zero relationships to the same things that the variable would or would not be associated with. It changes in response to different stimuli and situations in the same ways that we would predict the characteristic being tested would change. It can differentiate among persons who have different levels of the variable being tested. Every test used should have the highest degree of validity possible within the limitations imposed by the situation. The amount of validity evidence that is needed increases as the variable becomes more abstract and less concrete.

Consistency. Another aspect of a good test is its consistency. This has three elements relating to getting the same results from the test, compared to a known standard, and using different scorers.

Table 10.5 *Consistency*

Reliability
- Consistency in absolute score and relative rank with others
  - Two or more administrations of same test
  - Comparison of two versions of same test

Accuracy
- Does test score reflect true value?
  - Calibration with known standard

Objectivity
- Consistency between two (or more) testers
  - Comparison of testers' scoring of same performance

Reliability. Does the test give consistent results? Would I get the same score for this person today, tomorrow, and next week? A reliable test would provide a yes answer to these questions. A reliable scale for the body weight would indicate time after time the same weight for a person whose weight had not changed.

Reliability is determined by testing the same group of persons two (or more) different times under the same conditions. A reliable test will give similar absolute scores for each person and will rank the persons in the same relative order both times. Thus the persons who score in the 80s on the test battery will continue to score in the 80s. They will continue to score better than those who scored in the 70s, and worse than those who scored in the 90s. The reliability of using skinfold calipers to measure the amount of fat at the triceps and subscapular sites (used in the AAHPERD Physical Best Test) could be determined by having the same person measure the millimeters of fat at these two sites on the same group of students on two different days. It would be important that both days be within a short time so that the actual amount of fat is the same. In this way, any differences in score reflect either the unreliability of the instrument or the tester. To the degree that the same amount of fat is measured on the two separate days, the test is reliable.

Although giving the test twice is used in the examples for simplicity, one may want to estimate reliability by giving the test a number of times to determine if consistent results are obtained across a series of administrations (using intraclass correlation).

There are some situations in which a person's score changes simply by retaking the test. In these cases, obviously the same test cannot be given a second time for reliability. The reliability of this sort of test is estimated by having the individual take two versions of the same test of equal difficulty, style, and length. Reliability is determined by the degree of correlation between the two versions of the test. This is sometimes done by comparing one half of a test with the other half (odd vs even test items). For example, students might do better on a written test of soccer rules if it were given a second time (i.e., they would have a chance to think about answers, read the rule book again, and discuss the test with friends). The reliability of the written test is determined by dividing the test into halves for analysis. It is important for the halves to be as equal as possible in content, style, and difficulty. The students' scores on each half are compared and, the more nearly the two halves differentiate among the students in the same way on both halves, the more reliable the test.

Accuracy. Reliability does not indicate the absolute accuracy of the test score. For example, a scale for body weight could be a highly reliable scale (giving consistent results), but everyone's weight might be too high. The purpose of *calibration* of equipment is to ensure its accuracy. Calibration is accomplished by comparing a known standard with the reading of the testing instrument. Thus, known weights of 20, 40, 60, 80, and 100 kg are placed on the scale, the scales are adjusted (if necessary) to these known amounts, or a correction factor is computed to adjust the observed score to the actual score.

In some cases there is no known standard. For example, we don't have a test standard for many tests in our field. The accuracy of the score is also less important when looking in changes over time. For example, one could determine if a person gained or lost weight over six months with reliable scales, even if they had not been calibrated. In those instances in which a known standard is available, however, careful calibration of the equipment is essential for an accurate score. For example, drivers hope the radar used to determine speeding tickets are both reliable and accurate.

Objectivity. Do different testers give the same score for the same performance? The degree to which the same score is given by different scorers reflects the objectivity of the test. Whether the basketball went through the basket would be completely objective (all would agree); however, there would be less agreement whether the player used good form on the shot (a less objective measure). For those tests that are completely objective (e.g., multiple choice questions with only one correct answer, number of baskets made, number of strokes to play nine holes of golf), there is no need to provide evidence for objectivity. However, for those tests in which different scorers might rate the same performance differently (such as overall ability, form, ethical behavior), then one should know how objective the test can be with trained testers.

Objectivity is determined by having two testers measure the same test performance independently of each other. The degree to which their scores are the same indicates the degree of objectivity. An obvious example is judging a gymnastics or diving meet. The judges observe the same performance and then rate it independently on a predetermined scale. Although all the judges do not rate all performances exactly the same, there is a high degree of objectivity among well-trained judges. In the earlier example of skinfold fat measurement, the reliability is established by comparing the same tester's results of administering the test twice to the same group. The objectivity is determined by having two testers test the same group. The degree to which different testers measure the same amount of fat on the same individuals reflects the objectivity of that test.

Feasibility. Is this test appropriate for this group of persons? Can the cost of the test be supported? Is there enough time, personnel, facilities, and equipment for the test? "Yes" answers to these questions indicate feasibility. Test decisions are made within external restraints. Often, the question is, what is the most valid test that can be administered to 60 students in 20 minutes with no testing assistants, limited equipment, and in one half of a small gymnasium? The cost of tests in terms of money, time, personnel, facilities, and equipment severely restricts the choices for many physical activity professionals. The

Table 10.6 *Feasibility*

Appropriateness	
	Verbal level
	Skill level
	Developmental level
Cost	
	Time
	Personnel
	Facilities
	Equipment

importance of establishing concurrent validity for shorter, simpler tests that can be used for large groups in small spaces in a short time is a contribution that measurement specialists make to our field. The other aspect of the feasibility component of testing deals with abilities and differentiation. For example, even if a pull-up test were valid, reliable, objective, and feasible in terms of cost, it is not a good test for young children because it does not differentiate among them—almost all the children have a score of **0**—thus, the differences that exist in muscular endurance cannot be measured with this inappropriate test. A written test of self-concept constructed for educated adults is not appropriate for young children or mentally retarded persons because of the vocabulary. It is not a feasible test if the individual cannot understand the instructions, terms, or concepts being tested. At the other extreme, a skill test designed for beginning golfers would be inappropriate for advanced golfers who would score the maximum number of points on the test. Tests give the most information when they measure the variability among individuals—i.e., nearly everyone can make some score on the test and almost no one can make a perfect score.

Reliability, Objectivity, and Feasibility Related to Validity. One additional point relates to the relationship of validity to other components of test selection and construction. A test **cannot be valid** unless it includes the other desirable criteria for a test (reliability, objectivity, feasibility). This point is routinely made regarding reliability, but is true of objectivity and feasibility as well. How can a test give information about a person's ability if it yields inconsistent results? Unless the test provides the same results for the same level of ability time after time, it is not giving reliable information, and it cannot be valid if is not reliable. In a similar way, unless the same person is going to score all tests for all individuals forever, then the test cannot be valid without a high degree of objectivity. If qualified persons with training and practice cannot provide similar scores for a person's performance, the test lacks objectivity. It cannot be valid if the score depends on the tester rather than the level of performance.

If a test is not appropriate for a specific group in terms of instructions, ability level, development level, personnel, facilities, or equipment, then the test for is not valid.

At the same time, evidence for reliability, objectivity, and feasibility does not prove validity. Validity requires these attributes plus additional information that it measures what it is supposed to measure. *Thus reliability, objectivity, and feasibility are pre-requisites (essential ingredients) for validity, but they alone do not establish validity.* To use an absurd example, standing height is reliable, objective, and feasible, but it is valid only for testing height–*not* cardiorespiratory function. Thus valid tests must have high levels of reliability, objectivity, feasibility and direct evidence of its validity.

LOCATING TESTS

Table 10.7 *Locating Tests*

Test reviews	
	Mental Measurement Yearbook
	Kirby's Guide to Fitness and Motor Performance Tests
Research Indices	
	Completed Research in HPERD
	Current Contents
Reviews	
	Exercise and Sport Sciences Reviews
	Medicine and Science in Exercise and Sport
	Research Quarterly in Exercise and Sport
Measurement and Evaluation Texts	
	Johnson & Nelson
	See reference list

After deciding what variables are to be tested and the qualities desired in a test, it is helpful to find tests that have been used for the same purposes. There are several sources that can be used to locate tests.

The most comprehensive review of tests in many areas is the *Mental Measurement Yearbook,* which was initiated in 1938. Additional volumes are published intermittently. This source includes a listing of different tests designed to measure a particular characteristic with a critical review of the qualities of each test. Individual volumes are not comprehensive; so, one might need to search several volumes to find a review on a particular area. A similar approach directly related to physical activity has been taken in *Kirby's Guide to Fitness and Motor Performance Tests* (Kirby, 1991).

Textbooks in testing, measuring, and evaluating (see reference list) frequently include lists of tests that can be used. Johnson & Nelson (1986) includes a comprehensive description of tests.

Contacting experts in the area to be tested provides information about tests that can be used. Identifying tests that have been used in research studies is another source for locating tests. Many of these research studies can be located in AAHPERD *Completed Research in Health, Physical Education, Recreation, and Dance* (CRHPERD), which has been published annually since 1959. CRHPERD includes an extensive index for HPERD with references for published articles found in numerous research journals, and titles (with some abstracts) of theses and dissertations completed in major universities.

Review articles that synthesize the literature in a selected area often include a section on testing methods. The ACSM *Exercise and Sport Sciences Research Review,* published annually since 1973, provides excellent review in some areas of our field. In addition, the *Research Quarterly for Exercise and Sport* includes review articles periodically. Other journals, review articles, and indices are available in related fields.

IMPROVING TESTING

The use of criteria for improved test construction and selection will enhance the accuracy of assessment in sport and physical education. Providing concurrent validation for practical tests that can be used in mass testing is a continuing contribution that can be made by evaluation specialists working with persons in the disciplinary and other professional areas, as well as by practitioners in the field.

There are additional ways physical activity professionals can more accurately and more efficiently use the tests selected. A well-conceived testing plan is an integral part of teaching, coaching, fitness programs, and other professional plans. The testing is tied directly to the goals, learning experiences, and evaluation of the program. Effective professionals include testing and learning experiences throughout the program. Although there will be times when more time is spent on testing, it is not necessary to do all the testing, then all the learning, then all the testing in that order. Some testing is done initially to provide a baseline to evaluate individual improvement and to place persons in more homogeneous groups.

Testing is an important part of the learning process itself, so that students are given immediate feedback as they learn (formative evaluation). Testing at the end of a unit provides overall assessment of the extent the objectives have been accomplished (summative evaluation). Pre-planning for testing is an obvious and important characteristic of good evaluators. Pre-test instructions include what persons should and should not do on the day of the test. These instructions are

Table 10.8 *Types of Evaluation*

Formative	
	Provides feedback during learning
Summative	
	Provides overall assessment

based on controlling factors that influence the test results. A realistic testing plan minimizes standing in line and waiting. The plan involves having the equipment, markings, and needed assistants all in place in advance. The amount of time for each test is used to set up more stations for the longer test items. Instructions for the students are clear and provide the best way for them to move from one testing station to the next.

In addition to the aspects of the testing plan that provide for the maximum use of the time spent in testing, it is important that accuracy not be sacrificed for efficiency. All students are given enough practice on test items so that their scores reflect their true ability on the test, rather than how well they can "learn to take the test." Many performance test scores can be improved by practice on the test itself.

Test instructions normally indicate the number of trials that are optimal for the most reliable score. In general, two or three trials give a better estimate of the student's ability than a single trial. In most cases, more than three trials is not necessary. The average of the trials is more consistent than taking the best trial, but it increases the amount of teacher time in scoring, and the best of two or three trials is preferred to the score on a single trial.

SCORING

Two aspects of scoring deal with how each item will be scored and the relative weight of different test items.

Individual Test Items. The scoring of each test item depends on the nature of the test. In written essay test items, the answers are scored **correct, incorrect, or partially correct,** with a set number of points for each item. Objective skill tests are normally scored with a certain number of points for each skill. Often there are gradients so that more nearly accurate results are scored higher, with relatively less accurate performance receiving a smaller score. For example, more points are given for a clear badminton service if it hits within a certain number of centimeters of the back line, with fewer points for shorter serves.

Table 10.9 *Scoring Tests*

Test Scores
- Objective
  - One right answer
- Subjective
  - Requires tester judgement

Relative Weight
- More points for more important objectives

The more difficult test items to score are the subjective ratings. Subjective rating is essential for certain objectives (e.g., correct form in a skill), and it is time consuming when done well. Clear definition of each point on the rating scale, setting up game-like situations for the rating, and observing every student in a similar situation for the same amount of time, all increase the accuracy, objectivity, fairness, and efficiency of this necessary aspect of an overall evaluation plan. Video-taping can be a useful aid in subjective ratings.

Each thing being rated should have clearly defined components to differentiate between the ratings. Many beginning teachers try to include too many classifications for rating. Whereas a teacher or coach can distinguish among a 3, 2, or 1 on form for a jump shot, it is difficult to clearly differentiate on a 5- or 10-point scale. Sometimes the rating is based on how many elements are included in the movement. Other ratings are based on quality or how well each element is done. One might simply include whether a tennis swing is in the correct plane (yes or no) or its degree of smoothness (very smooth, a little rough, or very jerky).

Relative Weight. Within any single test the relative weight of each test item is determined by setting an arbitrary score. A particular component can be emphasized by including more test items on that one aspect or by having higher scores for the test items on that aspect. In the overall evaluation of any objective it is necessary to determine which things are more important, and then this relative importance should be reflected in the scoring. The same point can be made about an entire program—i.e., the test(s) of the more important objectives should receive proportionally more points than the test(s) of less important objectives. For example, having a class research paper in on time and written in proper form normally brings fewer points to the student than the quality of its content.

ANALYZING SCORES

Table 10.10 *Interpretation of Scores*

Improvement	
	Change from beginning to end of program or unit
Population Norm	
	Comparison with others of same age and gender
Criterion-referenced Norm	
	Comparison with a standard

Once the test items have been accurately scored, with appropriate weight given to both individual test items and various tests, then the score has to be interpreted. This interpretation includes breaking down the total score into its component parts and providing the basis for a value judgment concerning the scores in the various aspects of the total. To tell Sue or her parents that she had a total of 1486 points in physical education, with 182 in tennis, including 94 on tennis knowledge, 35 on the serve, 28 on the forehand, 16 on the backhand, 4 on volleying, and 5 on agility related to tennis would be meaningless without some additional information.

Improvement. One way that meaning is attributed to the score is to indicate how much improvement (or deterioration) has occurred over a time. Thus, to know what Sue scored at the beginning of the tennis unit would give some basis to judge her scores.

Comparison with Others. Another way to begin to understand an individual's test score is to describe some reference group in the population. One could describe Sue's class or a larger group of similar persons (same age, same beginning skill level). Whether Sue scored above or below the "typical" student of her age, and how she compared with most of these students, could then be decided. This comparison would normally be done with some sort of norm table from which the percentage of students who did better and worse than she did on each of the test items could be determined.

Comparison with a Standard. The score might be interpreted with a particular standard (criterion) that is established for that test. Sometimes this standard is based on comparison with others who are similar or with persons who have achieved high levels of achievement. In other cases there is some other reason to establish a standard. For example, based on information about health related to obesity, it would be reasonable to indicate that all persons should have less than 10% excess fat. Thus, one would take the essential fat (about 5% for males and 15% for females) and set a standard that mature males and females should have less than 15% and 25% fat respectively. Thus, the goal would be for everyone to at least reach that standard regardless of what percentages of persons were above or below the standard.

GRADING

Table 10.11 *Grading*

Objectives
Tests
Relative weight
Grading system
Final performance or improvement?
What standards?
Provision for atypical students
Plan to have grading understood and accepted

Another way to interpret scores is to assign a grade. It must be emphasized that grading is only one aspect of evaluation. Testing and evaluation have numerous uses besides their traditional use as a basis for assigning grades in educational institutions. The following issues have to be addressed before a grade can be assigned to individual students.

Objectives. Everyone agrees that the first step in setting up a grading plan is to clearly establish the relative importance of the objectives for the class. The implication is that taking showers, being dressed for participation, and attendance are not used for grading unless they are including as objectives for the class.

Tests for the Objectives. The second step in grading is to select or construct a test for each objective. Each objective should be tested with the best test available.

Tests for the Grade. In theory, all the tests used to evaluate the objectives should be used in the grading plan. However, there are some objectives that are important in the program that cannot be tested accurately enough to be included in the grade. For example, let us assume that the student's attitude toward physical activity is an important objective for a physical education class. Let us further assume that the best test available is a self-report, pencil-and-paper test asking the student to indicate preferences among a number of activities, combined with a questionnaire concerning the individual's leisure time activities. The test might have evidence for validity and reliability when given to students who have no incentive to give false information, but if the results are going to become a part of the student's grade, it would be quite simple for students to provide dishonest answers simply to make it appear that they had a very positive attitude toward physical activity. Other objectives may not have valid tests available at this time. Thus, the physical educator has to decide which objectives will be included in the grading plan based on the availability of valid tests. These tests that are chosen are weighted with relative importance.

Grading System. There are numerous grading systems. They are different in terms of how many categories are included. Some include two categories such as pass/fail, satisfactory/unsatisfactory, or credit/no credit. Others add a third category such as honors/pass/fail. A common system has five categories, A, B, C, D, F. At the other extreme there is the system with 100 categories in which the grade is reported from 0 to 100. In any case, there needs to be a clear description of what must be done to qualify for each category. Those supporting fewer categories argue that it puts less pressure on the student, and the learning atmosphere can be more positive with evaluation becoming less important. Those supporting more categories suggest that more precise and accurate evaluation information is given with more differentiation among students. Some physical educators have indicated that physical education should use the same grading system as other educational areas since all are attempting to set objectives, provide learning experiences, and determine to what extent the objectives have been achieved. Others indicate that physical education has unique objectives that are different in kind from other subjects and therefore should not use the same grading system that others use.

Another issue related to grading systems is the place of behavior, effort, and attendance. Many schools solve this issue by assigning separate grades for the content of an area, behavior, effort, and record of attendance. There might be some school-wide objectives with behavior, effort, and attendance, but the specific content grades are related to specific objectives of math, English, and physical education.

Final Performance or Improvement. This issue does not appear to be raised anywhere in the educational system except in physical education activity courses. Most people appear to agree that the reading grade should be based on the final performance (i.e., at what level this student is reading). Final performance is also used in physical education theory classes. To use final performance in these situations is "unfair" to the students who have a poor background or who learn more slowly—i.e., they can try harder and still make poorer grades. Some physical educators argue that physical education activity classes should be graded on the same basis; thus, the grade would reflect how nearly the objectives have been accomplished—not how much effort one had to expend in a particular class. Others suggest that the grade should be based on the amount of improvement that the student makes during a certain time.

What Standards. Regardless of whether one grades on final performance or improvement, certain standards have to be established for each grade category. One method that is inappropriate except for very large classes is to simply allocate a certain percentage of students to each grade category, such as 10%—A, 20%—B, 40%—C, 20%—D, and 10%—F. On the other hand, one could take such a percentage and apply it to scores that have been gathered over a number of years or based on some larger group. Some establish certain levels to be achieved based on their understanding of the activity, knowledge, fitness, and group.

Handicapped. Normally the same objectives will be appropriate for handicapped students. Some of the objectives, learning experiences, and tests will not have to be modified at all. However, when the handicap would cause the student to score differently on the test, modifications of the test and grading standards are needed. Until there is much more information available on all types of handicaps, this has to be done on an individual basis. Persons in adapted physical education and special education should be consulted to assist in setting realistic goals.

Acceptance. The many issues in grading in which there are legitimate differences of opinion make it impossible to establish a grading plan that will gain complete acceptance by colleagues, students, and parents. However, a well-planned grading scheme can be an asset for the program. It is essential that the plan be clearly outlined at the beginning of each course so that it is understood by the students, parents, and school administrators. A plan in which students know exactly what has to be done for a particular grade, with well-organized learning activities to assist them in achieving these levels along with valid tests carefully administered and fairly scored, will not only receive wide acceptance, but will also help educate persons about the important elements of sport and physical activity.

Feedback. Providing feedback concerning how well a student has accomplished certain goals can assist in additional learning and the setting of realistic future goals. The feedback should be provided not only with what has been accomplished, but also the next steps in this activity and what could be accomplished with additional effort. The improvement that has been made and the potential of further improvement should receive more emphasis than the status that will be reflected in the grade.

DESCRIPTION OF GROUPS

Table 10.12 *Description of Group(s)*

Typical score	=	**Central tendency**
Median		
Mean		
Normal fluctuation	=	**Variability**
Quartiles		
Standard deviation		
Norms		

One use of test scores is to describe various groups (e.g., tenth grade physical education students, college sophomores, athletes). Two characteristics of the test scores are needed to describe the groups—the typical score and the normal fluctuation.

Typical Score. If one score were chosen to represent the entire group on a particular characteristic, what score would be selected? Three different methods have been used to represent the group's central tendency: (1) the average score (mean), (2) the middle score, which divides the group into two equal halves (median); and (3) the score of the largest number in the group (mode). If the scores are normally distributed, all three of these typical scores would be the same. However, extreme scores in one direction affect the mean more than they do the other two indicators. Either the mean, which is more precise and has wider use mathematically, or the median, which is easier to determine, is appropriate in most educational situations. Either the mean or median would be preferable to the mode.

Normal Fluctuation. The variability of the group must be known along with the typical score to adequately describe the group. For example, two groups could have an average score of 75 on a 100-point test, but they would be quite different if one group had scores from 15 to 99 and the other group had scores between 65 and 80. Both the typical score and normal fluctuation would be needed to describe the group or interpret an individual's test score. The variability is sometimes described by the (1) range of scores (highest to lowest score); (2) the middle 50% of the scores (from the lowest quartile—25th percentile—to the highest quartile—75th percentile); or (3) the scores that one would expect to include two thirds of the population (one standard deviation above and below the mean).

The mean and standard deviation are used together, or the median and quartiles are combined for group description. The mean and standard deviation are slightly preferred from a mathematical sense, but the median and quartiles are easier to compute and are quite acceptable for most educational situations. When either of these methods is used, the range is also often reported.

Norms. The central tendency and variability scores from a large group that has been tested on a specific test are often used to construct a norm table that transforms the scores to a 0 to 100 table. When using the mean and standard deviation, one norm table (Standard Score Table) is to use the mean as 50 on the table, with 100 being the mean plus three standard deviations, and 0 equals the mean minus three standard deviations. For example, if 1000 students were tested after a beginning bowling class resulting in a mean of 120 and standard deviation of 15, then a norm table for beginning bowlers would extend from 100 = 165 (mean plus three standard deviations); 50 = 120 (mean); to 0 = 75 (mean - three standard deviations).

Another way to construct a norm table is to use the median/quartile approach by setting up a percentile table from 0 to 100. Again, a large group of persons is tested, then 100 = the score that is better than everyone tested, 50 = the median (50% of group above and 50% below), and 0 = the score that is worse than everyone who was tested. This type of norm table is often used in standardized testing (e.g., your score of 1100 on this test was at the 65 percentile, meaning that a score of 1100 was higher than 65% and lower than 35% of the people used to establish the norm).

RELATIONSHIP BETWEEN VARIABLES

Table 10.13 *Relationship Between Variables*

Direction
Strength of association
Relationship among more than two variables

Another area in which physical activity professionals are assisted by the evaluation processes is in determining the relationship between different characteristics. For example, what physical and psychological variables will be most highly related to a person's enjoyment of playing a particular sport? If our aim is to have all persons enjoy participation in a sport, the characteristics that are highly related to that aim might get some emphasis in our classes. It must be stressed that just because two variables are highly related does not mean that one caused or was caused by the other, but the high relationship allows certain hypotheses to be made that can be studied in experimental research. As an illustration, if it were found that persons who can hit a backhand off the back wall more accurately seem to enjoy racquetball more than persons who do not hit the backhand as accurately, then that skill could be emphasized in the racquetball class to determine if improving on that skill also increased enjoyment of the game.

The relationship between variables is normally determined by some form of correlation that quantifies the relationship between the variables into a number between 0 and 1. Thus, the more highly related the variables, the closer to 1 the correlation will be. The sign of the correlation indicates whether the relationship is positive (+) or negative (-). In the positive relationship, as persons tend to score higher on one variable, they also tend to score high on the related variable. For instance, one might find a correlation of +0.7 between height and weight, since as persons tend to be taller, they also tend to be heavier in total body weight. In a negative correlation, as persons tend to score higher on one variable, they tend to score lower on the related variables. For example, one might find a correlation of -0.8 between aerobic capacity and time in a mile run, that is, as the runner tended to have a higher maximal oxygen uptake, the tendency would be to run the mile in a faster (shorter) time.

The most common statistical technique used to determine the degree of relationship between two variables is the Pearson product moment correlation coefficient (represented by r). The correlation coefficient is computed when each person in a group has two scores. In addition to determining the relationship between two different variables, it is also used to determine concurrent validity, reliability, and objectivity. Concurrent validity is established by finding the correlation between the new test and a criterion test of the same variable. Thus, all persons in a group are tested on both the new and the established test, and those scores are correlated to find the degree of validity for the new test. In finding reliability, all the persons in a group are given the same test twice, and the two scores are correlated for the extent of reliability. Correlation is used to determine objectivity by finding the relationship between two scores given by two different scorers for the same performance for all members of the group.

Advanced correlation techniques are used to determine the relationship between two variables while holding a third variable constant (partial correlation); the relationship between several variables and one test (multiple correlation); between two groups of variables (canonical correlation); and to determine what tests tend to relate to each other in clusters (factor analysis). (In essence, factor analysis tells us what tests or measures "belong together," in that they tend to measure the same thing.)

DIFFERENCE BETWEEN GROUPS

Another question that is often asked is, "Are groups different on a particular variable?" This question may be asked of related (matched in some way) or independent groups. The groups may be two or more in number.

Table 10.14 *Difference Between Groups*

Independent or related groups
Two or more than two groups

Do athletes and nonathletes differ on certain physical or psychological traits? Does the group that has been running for the last 2 years differ from a similar group that has not participated in any physical activity? These two questions represent the two types of group-difference questions. In the first case, two identified groups are compared. One can determine to what extent the groups are different, but not why. To illustrate, boys continue to improve on certain physical performance items from age 12 to 17 years, whereas girls do not. There is no question that a difference can be demonstrated, but the reason for the difference is not known (i.e., to what extent it is biological, early socialization, peer pressure, or some other reason). On the other hand, one could take a group of 13 year-old girls and have half of them be active for a certain time, while the other half remained sedentary. If the subgroups (samples) taken from the same larger group (population) were significantly different after a certain amount of activity for the one group, then it could be concluded that it was the activity that caused the difference. In both cases, the same statistical analysis would determine to what extent the groups are different, but the conclusions drawn from differences (or lack of differences) between groups would depend on the type of research design.

Although there are a number of statistical techniques that can be used to determine group differences, the two most commonly noted in the literature are a t-test to determine difference between two groups and analysis of variance (ANOVA) to determine difference among more than two groups. There are different formulas of the t-test and ANOVA for related and independent groups.

Both of these analyses result in a probability statement ($p <$ some level less than 1), which should be interpreted that a difference this large between groups such as these on this variable would be expected to occur by chance less than the significance level. Thus, $p < .75$ would not show much difference between groups since a difference that large would be expected to occur by chance 75% of the time. However, $p < .01$ is such a large difference that it would occur by chance only 1% of the time, and most persons would conclude that it shows a real group difference. Many researchers use the .05 significance level to indicate whether they will conclude that these are "real differences" rather than chance differences. In those cases, if $p < .05$ the conclusion is that these are significant group differences. If $p > .05$ then the conclusion is that a significant difference is not shown in that study.

CURRENT STATUS OF EVALUATION

In this century there have always been persons in sport and physical activity who were making contributions in testing, measuring, and evaluation related to aspects of our field. We still refer to some of the tests developed by the name of the developer. In recent years the same thing has happened in evaluation in sport and physical activity that has happened in many of the disciplinary areas; namely our students have gained a new level of sophistication by studying the body of knowledge in measurement and evaluation and then applying that understanding in all aspects of the physical activity professions. The textbooks, special conferences (e.g., those sponsored by the AAHPERD Measurement and Evaluation Council), and research articles exhibit the basic issues and techniques found in measurement and evaluation per se. Evaluation is used to improve the disciplinary and professional components of our field. In addition, physical activity is used as a medium to further basic understanding in measurement and evaluation.

The continuing inclination to want to evaluate sport and physical activity that has historically permeated our field and the increasing understanding of basic evaluation processes are the bases for some optimism about the future. As bodies of knowledge are increased in the disciplinary, professional, and other aspects of movement themselves, these scholars will be seeking out evaluation experts to work with them to provide more valid tests and better evaluation standards.

IMPLICATIONS FOR GENERAL EDUCATION

The need for evaluative processes in the professional application of the various disciplinary aspects of sport and physical activity is apparent. The need for an understanding of the disciplinary foundations for all students in our field regardless of vocational goals is discussed in other chapters in this book. A legitimate question that is often raised in establishing our core curriculum is, "Do students who are studying sport and physical activity for its own sake need to understand the bodies of knowledge contained in the professional aspects of the field?" More specifically, is there a need for all persons in sport and physical activity to know evaluative processes?

A thorough understanding of evaluation is less important for those students who essentially want a "liberal arts" education in kinesiology with no professional application anticipated. However, the interrelationships between the disciplinary and professional aspects of the field make some understanding of the underlying discipline. The evaluative processes also contribute to the general education goals of ability to critically analyze literature and to make intelligent decisions about one's personal life style.

Table 10.15 *Implications for General Education*

Understanding body of knowledge
Analytic thinking
Lifestyle quality

Understanding the Discipline. The essential feature of a discipline is the body of knowledge that is known because of studies in that area. Thus the disciplinary aspects of our field provide many theories and concepts about human movement. One studies these truths as a foundation for one's education in a similar way one explores the disciplines in the humanities, natural or social sciences. The place of evaluation in the general study of a discipline is to assist the student in a better grasp of the fundamental knowledge of the discipline. One cannot dig very deeply into any aspect of sport and physical activity without having to think about how things that form the basis for our theoretical understandings were tested.

For example, one part of the disciplinary body of knowledge is the relationship between arousal and performance. In general, increased aroused up to an optimal point results in better physical performance. When aroused beyond the optimal point, performance decreases. The optimal point varies with the type of performance and perhaps with individuals. One cannot separate our knowledge of this relationship without dealing with how both arousal and performance are tested. Is arousal how people indicate their feelings? Is it the behavior patterns that best reflect arousal, or is it the physiological stress indicators? What about performance—is it a task performed in a laboratory, on an athletic field, with or without an audience? Is the performance tested in objective ways or with a subjective rating? Do the tests of performance include all important aspects of the ability in that activity? The point is that one cannot fully understand the relationship between arousal and performance, or critically evaluate the studies done in this area, without consideration of the testing processes. In fact, it may well be through improved testing that a more complete theory of arousal and performance will be developed. To ignore the evaluation procedures in studies in this area, or other aspects of the discipline, would be to acquire less than a complete understanding.

Analytic Thinking. The ability to critically analyze theories, textbooks, review articles, and research studies would appear to be an important outcome of general education. It would be impossible to adequately evaluate the quality of the oral and written literature without paying some attention to the testing and evaluation that were used. A position statement about exercise, nutrition, and obesity that was based solely on height/weight tables would be suspect because of inadequate testing. Persons familiar with sport and physical activity testing would recognize that more valid tests are available for determination of the amount of body fat.

Life Style. There are abundant examples of nonprofessional use of evaluation in a person's life. A physically educated person would make better judgments about the quality of evaluation seen in everyday life, whether in the judging of gymnastics seen on TV, the basis for support for a particular commercial item, the suggested benefits of a fitness program, or the adequacy of the device used to issue a speeding ticket. Persons understanding evaluation can assess levels of skill, fitness, knowledge, and other characteristics related to important areas of their lives for friends and themselves.

Processes of testing, measuring, and evaluating can therefore be helpful in the "pure" study of human movement to assist in understanding the disciplinary bodies of knowledge and in coping with survival within our society.

IMPLICATIONS FOR PROFESSIONAL PRACTICE

Many students of sport and physical activity will have vocational aspirations for the use of their program of study. These professional applications of our field may include working with persons of different ages, physical abilities, and levels of health in educational, governmental, health, business, or voluntary institutions. The comprehension of the disciplinary and professional bodies of knowledge is essential for career success. Part of one's accomplishments and the ability to determine the extent of the success will depend on a mastery of the processes by which one tests, measures, and evaluates the various aspects of the job.

Table 10.16 *Implications for Professional Practice*

Client
Staff
Program

Professional Evaluation. Several of the professional responsibilities will involve evaluation. These include evaluation of the individual's work, the program(s), and the clients (whether students, athletes, or post-cardiac patients). Any of the content areas of our field may be included as part of the evaluation.

The following are examples of questions that need to be evaluated by a teacher/coach:

Am I a good teacher?
Am I a good coach?
Do my students learn what I want them to learn?
Do my students feel good about what they learn and how they learn?
Do my students enjoy the activities used as learning experiences?
How much have individual students achieved?
How do these student achievements relate to realistic expectations?
Are the athletes learning what I want them to learn?
Which athletes should be played in which positions?
Am I accomplishing what the school and community expect in my teaching and coaching?
What fitness, performance, attitude, and knowledge aspects of sport and physical education need increased attention to this school?
What alternatives to my teaching and coaching would more nearly achieve what is desired within the limits of the situation?

Each of these broad questions would have many subdivisions that would require evaluation. For example, *Am I a good teacher?* would include defining the characteristics of a good teacher by using the body of knowledge from that professional area. Ways to test each characteristic of being a good teacher and assigning appropriate weights to the component parts would be the next step. Then one would need to measure oneself on the tests. These scores on teaching ability would need to be interpreted with comparison with other teachers and whether one's teaching is improving over time. Finally, the evaluation of the strength and weakness of one's teaching would provide a basis for recommendations of what could be done to improve teaching.

Regardless of the professional setting, physical activity professionals will be asked to determine to what extent their objectives are being met, and thus they will be expected to evaluate themselves, their programs, and their clients. The evaluation will include different aspects of the disciplinary and professional portions of sport and physical activity. Both a general understanding of evaluative processes and specific knowledge of the best tests available in each disciplinary and professional component of the position will be necessary for the dedicated professional. The general processes will help determine how to select (or construct) a good test. The specific knowledge will help decide the best way to test a specific performance skill whose evaluation is important.

RELATIONSHIP TO ALLIED PROFESSIONS

Persons in different professional settings and in fields related to sport and physical activity will be assessing different types of variables. However, the basic steps in evaluation are similar whether the test subject is volleyball serving ability, health behavior, or the safety characteristics of a work task. It is important for physical activity professionals to learn the underlying processes of testing, measuring, and evaluating rather than being trained only to utilize specific physical education tests. The person who knows evaluative processes can work with others in any field to assist in setting up appropriate programs, whereas the person who simply is familiar with a number of specific tests can function only in situations in which those tests are appropriate.

One of the aspects of our field that is somewhat frustrating for the beginning student in evaluation is the necessity of using many different types of testing (such as written, skill, fitness, subjective rating, attitude, or behavior). However, the application of evaluation processes through these diverse types of tests prepares a person to be a valuable consultant to a large number of related fields.

BASES OF COOPERATION

The main elements for cooperative efforts to achieve quality evaluation in related fields include:

Persons working together who understand evaluation and the specific characteristics to be evaluated.
Location of available information.
Decision to use or modify current tests or construct new ones.
Decision how the tests will be administered and by whom.
Decision on the basis for evaluation of test scores.
Decision how evaluation will be used.

Physical activity professionals are asked to assist with the physical fitness and performance of persons in a variety of professions (e.g., fire fighters, coal miners). It is necessary to establish what fitness and performance levels are desired, based on knowledge of work requirements and physical fitness. The next step is to determine how to test for these fitness and performance levels, based on knowledge of physical fitness and evaluation. In most cases there is concern for those who are below the desired standards, which leads to the establishment of an appropriate conditioning program based on test evaluation, exercise physiology, and exercise prescription information. The results of the testing and conditioning might be evaluated with better screening, in-service or on-the-job training improvements, and work productivity.

Benefits of Cooperation. Numerous professions have (and could) benefit from working together with persons in evaluation to set up testing, training, and evaluation programs. There has also been legal action asserting that certain requirements were not based on sound evaluation principles. For example, the absurd notion that females should not play baseball or full-court basketball or be employed in certain positions that require some muscular strength and endurance has been changed in some cases with the support of evaluation specialists.

PROFESSIONAL OPPORTUNITIES

There will be a few professional opportunities for evaluation specialists to conduct research in the area of measurement and evaluation and to teach and advise students solely in the body of knowledge in this area. Some major universities will select this as one of the areas in which to develop depth so that students may receive major emphasis in this area. In most cases persons will be asked to teach in the evaluation area as one of two or three areas of interest. Scholars in this area are invaluable to persons in all aspects of kinesiology, assisting with appropriate testing for research, program assessment, and accountability.

Evaluation experts will have opportunities to assist industrial, athletic, fitness, motor development, health, and community programs in setting up tests for screening and to assist with evaluation of the success of specific endeavors. There are also numerous internal and external programs evaluations at all levels of education that need assistance from those who understand evaluation processes.

At the current time there are not many openings for person with specialization in only measurement and evaluation. However, a good background in this area is often helpful in scoring a position. Once a person with abilities in evaluation is established in a professional position, there are numerous informal and formal opportunities to assist colleagues and allied professionals throughout the community and region.

CONCLUDING STATEMENT

The major thrust of this chapter is that the first step in evaluation is to understand the underlying processes used in testing, measuring, and evaluating persons and programs. These procedures are presented with practical examples of how they are used in our field. The importance of this area is supported in terms of understanding other areas as well as various aspects of one's personal and professional life.

After the basic concepts involved in evaluation and in each of the other areas of kinesiology are learned, the advanced learning involves cooperation between evaluation and these other areas of our field. As we learn more about evaluation, better ways to test variables can be devised that lead to better understanding of the disciplinary and professional concepts being studied. As better understanding of these other areas is developed, we can more clearly define what needs to be tested, and this can lead to better evaluation techniques. By working together we can assist each other in moving forward in both the extension of the body of knowledge and its professional application.

NOTES

1. Many of the concepts in this chapter were included in Franks and Deutsch (1973). My thanks to the late Dr. Helga Deutsch for her assistance in my education in evaluation.

SELECTED REFERENCES

AMERICAN ALLIANCE FOR HEALTH, PHYSICAL EDUCATION, RECREATION AND DANCE. (1993). *Completed research in health, physical education and recreation,* Vol. 35. (Vol. 1–34, 1959–1992).

AMERICAN ALLIANCE FOR HEALTH, PHYSICAL EDUCATION, RECREATION AND DANCE. (1990). *Physical best,* Reston, VA: Author.

AMERICAN COLLEGE OF SPORTS MEDICINE. (1993). *Exercise and Sport Sciences Reviews,* Vol 21. Baltimore: Williams & Wilkins. (Vol. 1–20, 1973–1993).

BAUMGARTNER, T. A., & JACKSON, A. S. (1987). *Measurement for evaluation in physical education,* 3rd edition. Boston: Houghton-Mifflin.

BUROS, O. K. (1978). *The eighth mental measurements yearbook,* Highland Park, NY: Cryphon Press.

FRANKS, B. D., & DEUTSCH, H. (1973). *Evaluating performance in physical education.* NY: Academic Press.

JOHNSON, B. L., & NELSON, J. K. (1986). *Practical measurements for evaluation in physical education,* 4th Ed., Minneapolis: Burgess.

SAFRIT, M. J. (1986). *Introduction to measurement in physical education and exercise science.* Englewood Cliffs, N.J.: Prentice-Hall.

Epilogue

Looking to the Future

Earle F. Zeigler

In this final section my objective will be to stimulate your thinking about the immediate present and to provide some incentive for you to move ahead with purpose into the open future in this interesting and challenging profession. There should be no doubt in your mind about the complexity of physical education and kinesiology now that you have read the subdisciplinary and subprofessional sections of this foundations text. I am anxious to reiterate here the unique role of exercise, sport, and related expressive movement in people's education throughout their lives. I also want to point out further the persistent professional concerns (or problems) that the profession still faces, as well as the ten "philosophical stances" that will have to be eliminated if we are to have the sort of future that can be envisioned. Here is truly a profession in which you can indeed develop a life purpose that will enable you to develop maximum energy for a truly worthwhile life.

EXERCISE, SPORT, AND RELATED EXPRESSIVE MOVEMENT WITHIN THE GOOD LIFE

Citizens of the United States and Canada are wont to say that they have the highest standard of living in the world. Someone from another continent might state that the Scandinavian countries or Japan or Germany have surpassed us both in several ways. This may thrust us immediately into debating what is meant by a high standard as opposed to a low standard—and how all of this may be measured. Any attempt to respond to this question with compete accuracy would be doomed to failure at present. Nevertheless, such statements about the quality of life should cause us all to take stock as we conjure the spirit and tone of life on this continent between now and the magic year 2001. Where ought we to be by then?

Obviously we will need to think very seriously about the character and traits for which Americans and Canadians will educate in the years immediately ahead. Although the availability and use of leisure and abundance by most people may have changed somewhat since Kateb wrote about "Utopia and the Good Life," his understanding of the opportunities available is still most pertinent (1965, pp. 454–473). Some of the dire predictions about overpopulation and possible ecological disaster were not clear to most of us at that point, but the progression of possibilities recommended are most interesting and provocative: (1) *laissez-faire* (doing what you want to do when you want to do it would presumably include becoming a professional person); (2) the greatest amount of pleasure possible (presumably following your own bent and inclination); (3) play (as opposed to work); (4) craft (pursuing an art or a skilled trade); (5) political action at some level of society; and (6) the life of the mind (following a scholarly pursuit that might involve basic research). His conclusion, not unexpected from a university scholar, is that the life of the mind offers the greatest potential in the world as we know it now or even may know it in the future.

Whatever conclusion you may have come to at this stage of your career regarding the good life and its various components, or how you will seek to improve the quality of life for yourself, your family, your friends, and your associates in the future, it may now be apparent to you that the level of future planning should be increased sharply. We simply must do better in preparing youth to learn how to adapt to change itself—an art that will not be acquired with the same facility that these words are written. Discussions about the future are entered into quite readily by many, but when an attempt is made to get people to do some concentrated and complex planning for the future, one soon learns that words are cheap. (See, also, Zeigler, 1989, Chap. 13.)

Admittedly, Kateb's recommendations concerning the six possible approaches to the good life have considerable merit. However, it occurs to me further that it should be possible in an evolving democratic society to strive for a very high quality of life through the correct blending, according to each person's choice, of these various approaches in such a way as to correspond most closely to the hierarchy of values that the individual determines for himself or herself in a world undoubtedly characterized by continuous change. If such change and novelty mean in the final analysis that there are no immutable and unchangeable values in the fabric of the universe—a debatable point, of course—we must all necessarily keep open minds to avoid rigidity, stultification, and eventual decay.

My considered response to Kateb's various alternatives for the good life would be that the individual in our society should be allowed the greatest amount of freedom consistent with that encroachment upon personal freedom that seemingly has to be made within the context of a evolving democracy. This would have to be the amount of *laissez-faire* that can be allowed to any one person in this type of political state. Second, we should understand that there are different kinds of *pleasure,* ranging from the purely sensual to the more refined and abiding types. Within this orientation the greatest amount of pleasure will probably result from active and creative participation in the various facets or categories of activity that life has to offer. Here we should understand that the concept of a "unified organism" implies that the human has the inherent capacity to explore successfully at least five types of interests—physical activity interests, as well as social, aesthetic and creative, communicative, and learning interests (e.g., educational hobbies).

Third, the idea that *play* might be chosen as one approach to the good life is momentarily appealing, but then one is faced with the prospect of determining what is meant by the concept "play." Some 40 years ago I recall stating, "Let play be for children, and let recreation be for adults." By that I was implying that recreation was some form of mature play in which intelligent adults engaged. Now a more analytical approach to this topic has shown that the word *play* has approximately 70 different meanings either as a noun or verb. Obviously this term merits careful analysis because of the confusion created by what appears to be a family resemblance term (philosophically speaking). In our society we speak of the play of kittens, and we use the word "play" to describe the contest that takes place each fall between the universities of Michigan and Ohio State (or Western Ontario and Toronto in Canada). I can argue, therefore, that all of us should seek to preserve some of the spirit of kittens' play in our daily lives to broaden the range of life's experiences and thereby to improve its quality. Conversely, it become apparent immediately that life and accident insurance rates would rise sharply if we sought to play games with our families and friends that employ the same spirit typically evident in "collision" sports between arch-rivals at either the university or professional levels where traditional grudges prevail.

Fourth, Kateb stated that *craft* represented a fourth approach to the good life. By this it is presumed that craft is defined as art or skill, and also that a person might use such talent as an occupation to make money. Keeping with the basic nature of the definition, then, I might argue that craft belongs in each person's life for the enrichment and satisfaction that it can bring.

Fifth, the concept of *political action* was presented. This proposal for achieving the good life may be the only one of the six offered by Kateb that bears little relationship to sport and physical activity (although even here politics and sport have been interwoven lately by language and other means in what seems to be an inextricable manner, and there are many who approach politics as a war game with strategy and goals and very few rules of conduct). Once again, however, I can argue that political action belongs in the life of each citizen in an evolving democratic state. This may should like a truism, but such must become the case if we hope to preserve and develop that form of political state with its ideal of individual freedom. Failing this, other forms of monarchy, oligarchy, or fascistic dictatorship seem to be the only alternatives left for the foreseeable future.

The sixth and final approach recommended, and that which Kateb asserted is the best one, was that titled *the life of the mind.* He felt that this approach offered the greatest potential in the world as it is presently known or as it may be known in the future. He concluded that "the man possessed of the higher faculties in their perfection is the model for utopia and already exists outside it. . . ." (p. 472). Once again, it seems that such an approach to life, that is, the pursuit of the life of the mind, should be part and parcel of the life of each man and woman in our society. To me it is amusing to witness the attitude taken by a not insignificant number of intellectuals in university circles as they go about their lives as presumably "disembodied spirits" in pursuit of the life of the mind. Such reasoning would seem to imply that the findings of psychology and closely related disciplines concerning the human being as a unified organism were never reasonably corroborated—that such theory is not tenable. Of course, it is possible to make a good case for the position that the so-called life of the mind can be improved in many ways—if such activity takes place within a healthy, physically fit body (to give such a state of well-being its minimum amount of credit).

PRESUMED "VIABILITY" OF A MULTIPLE TRANSCENDING APPROACH

What I am recommending to you, therefore, is that men and women now and in the future should combine all six of the approaches recommended for consideration into ne presumably "viable," multiple, all-encompassing approach. Further, I want to stress that at least five of these six approaches to the good life are either directly or indirectly related to the role that exercise, sport, and related expressive movement can fulfill within a society generally, as well as what it can mean *specifically* in the life of a mature person. Here is a way to truly "live in your body" (*vivre son corps,* as my French-speaking Canadian colleagues might say) as you truly begin to comprehend, and then seek to do full justice to the vital importance of human movement with purpose in these activities characterized by motor performance.

Fine educational experience is usually related to the mastery of various subject matters. Somewhat less do we expect it to encompass all of the changes that take place in individuals on the basis of their total life experience. Somehow the quality of the human motor performance experience aspect of education, of recreation, of all life has been slighted historically down to the present day. Huxley designated this as the "education of the non-verbal humanities"—the education of the "psycho-physical instrument of an evolving amphibian" (1964, p. 31). If the kinesthetic sense of humans were prepared more efficiently through the formal and/or informal educational process, the effects of such experience would inevitably influence subsequent behavior for better or for worse. Thinking, and who can deny that we "think with our entire body," has generally been characterized best as a symbolic experience, the assumption being that the formation of habits results from direct experience. An interesting finding, for example, is that thinking tends to be facilitated when there is a general increase in muscle tone. In addition, as thought becomes more concentrated, general muscle tone becomes even greater.

THE UNIQUE ROLE OF DEVELOPMENTAL PHYSICAL ACTIVITY IN THE EDUCATION OF "ECOLOGICAL MAN AND WOMAN"

No matter whether a person elects to follow primarily one of Kateb's approaches to the good life primarily or accepts my more balanced, multifaceted, transcending approach to the improvement of the quality of life, the field of physical education and kinesiology (as it is called in this book) must become fully aware as soon as possible of the environmental crisis facing humanity. The field of education must be its very nature play a vitally role in the development of what might be termed "ecological awareness."

Granting that this educational duty should fall to professional teachers at all educational levels who are specialists in all of the subject-matters taught in the curriculum, the physical educator/sport coach quite naturally has a general education responsibility. This is true, of course, in-as-much as this person is directly concerned with the human's relationship with self, fellows, other living creatures, the remainder of the biological environment, and finally the physical environment. Specifically, the physical educator/coach and the community recreation director are confronted daily with a population that has a very low level of what has been called *physical fitness* with a resultant decrease in overall *total* fitness.

In the next 25 years it will be increasingly imperative to affirm the priority of man and women over sport that is too highly competitive, as well as other types of physical activity that may be employed detrimentally. The late Arthur Steinhaus, M.D. (of George Williams College and Michigan State University) argued consistently that sport was created for the human's use, and not vice versa. This sound dictum has been forgotten far too often in the United States, and to a much lesser extent in Canada (except in hockey, in which there has been a significant overemphasis of violence). There is a very delicate balance that must be maintained between a program of healthful physical activity in sport, exercise, and physical recreation and a type of program that leads a select few to the heights of successful international competition. We can and should adapt reality to our own ends. Healthful physical activity can help to make life on this closed planet more pleasant, more vital, and more life-enriching—and even more "life-lengthening" (according to recent evidence)!

PERSISTENT HISTORICAL PROBLEMS THAT THE PROFESSION STILL FACES

We trust that you, the reader, have been at least somewhat convinced about the importance of the role that human motor performance as described here can (and should play) in people's lives now and in the future. It is on this basis that we feel young people can be challenged to make this profession their life work. Nevertheless, you have no doubt sensed the many difficulties that the profession has faced in the past, still faces in the present, and will undoubtedly have to overcome in the future. This should not trouble you unduly, because every profession has its problems to a greater or lesser extent. Granted that we seem to have a few more than most; nevertheless, the uniqueness of our field and its special problems has always been interesting and challenging to me.

During my professional career that began over 50 years ago, I have maintained a continuing concern for what I have called the persistent historical problems of physical education and sport, six of which were identified in the opening chapter as social forces of a pivotal or slightly lesser nature. The were designated as (1) values and norms, (2) the influence of politics (or *type* of political state), (3) the influence of nationalism, (4) the influence of economics, (5) the influence of religion, and (6) the influence of ecology. Science and technology was also mentioned as a seventh social forces, along with the possibility of a striving for world peace as an eighth influence. Of course, education and sport are also significant influences themselves. These persistent problems or social forces influence all of society, as well as the entire field of education. However, there are also other persistent problems with a strongly professional orientation confronting the profession of sport and physical education (NASPE), problems that have themselves been influenced by the various social forces listed above. The last of these problems, the concept of "progress," may be considered to be both a social force and a professional concern. All of these problems are shown Figure 11.1 below with the final one ("progress") indicated in an over arching manner. Those indicated as professional concerns are explained briefly below:

Figure 11.1 Persistent, Historical Problems of Physical Education & Sport

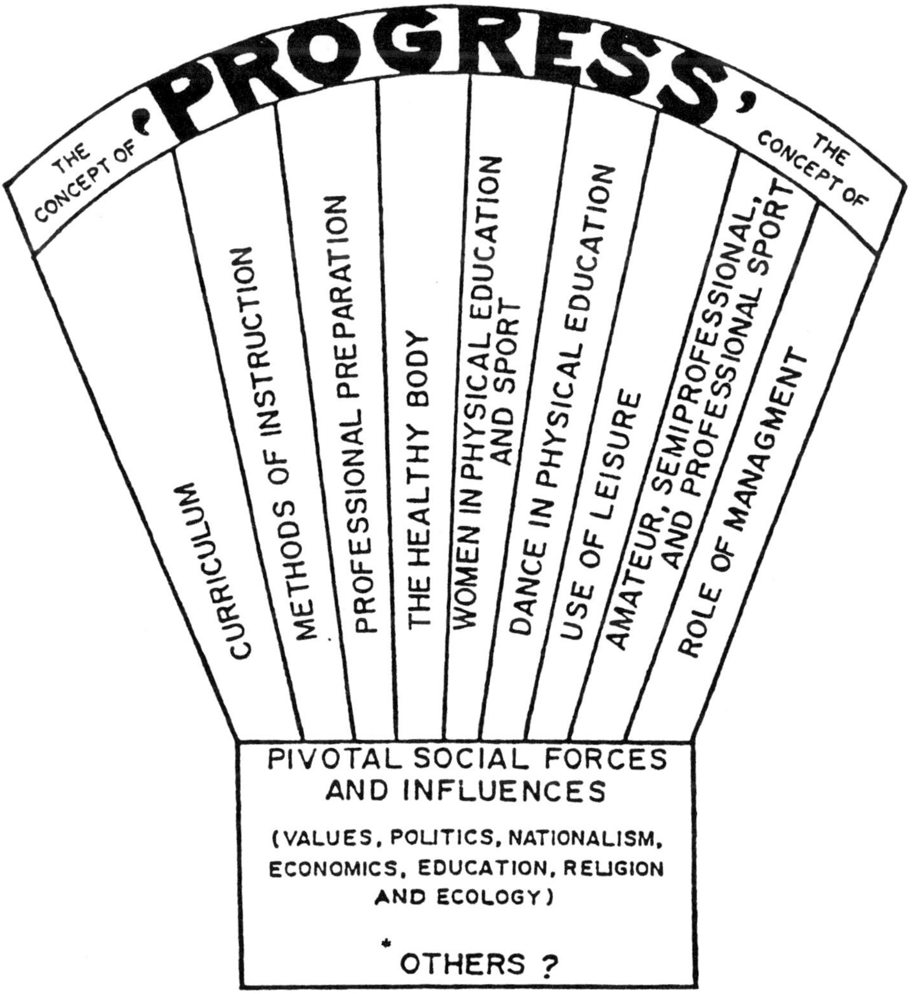

*OTHERS?

- Science & Technology
- Concern for World Peace
- Sport
- ?????

Earle F. Zeigler
(with design advice
from Glenda Dhillon)

Curriculum (Pers. Hist. Problem No. 7). Although this is the seventh persistent historical problem in my present overall listing, it is the first of the group that I have identified as professional concerns. A primary task in curriculum selection (or program development) is to determine which subjects should be included because of their recurring interest to the public and to educators. Decisions should be made regularly regarding the bases upon which a curriculum is selected. (Keep in mind, of course, that physical education has often been regarded formerly and presently as either "curricular," "co-curricular," or "extra-curricular.") The general curriculum in education has developed and expanded at a fantastic rate on this continent over the past few centuries, and many people now insist that this trend must be reversed so that the "essential" subjects can be taught adequately. The task of the physical educator/coach today is to ascertain the values and norms that are uppermost in the society, and then to attempt to implement them through the medium of developmental physical activity in exercise, sport, and related expressive movement.

Methods of Instruction (No. 8). We might argue that methods of instruction (or instructional methodology) and curriculum should go hand in hand if effective education is the desired end product. Initially we should appreciate that effective instructional methods involve more than merely what a teacher "does" to a subject matter. If we are talking about sport skills instruction in tennis, for example, the teacher needs to know how to teach tennis, what is taking place within the learner as he seeks to learn tennis from the instructor, and, finally, what the end result is (i.e., what a learner does when he or she has learned to play the sport).

Professional Preparation (No. 9). Professional preparation of teachers to any considerable extent began in the United States in the late nineteenth century. Starting with the normal school, this type of specialized professional preparation for teachers in the public schools progressed in the twentieth century to college and university status. Throughout much of the world, generally speaking, specialized professional training for physical education and sport has been included at the normal and technical school level. University recognition was achieved first in the United States at several universities before the turn of the twentieth century. Such status did not come to Canada until the 1940s, but progress has been steady since that time with the first Ph.D. in Physical Education being awarded in 1969. Although the first Ph.D. degrees in our field in the world were awarded in the United States and Germany in the 1920s, the systems of higher education function quite differently. (Subsequently the German Ph.D. in our field was dropped in the 1940s, but it was then reinstated in the early 1970s.) Progress has been made in countries such as England and the

Scandinavian nations in regard to the granting of university status. Japan now offers the Ph.D. degree in physical education in several universities as well.

The Health Body (No. 10). A study of past and present civilizations indicates that times of war and peace have produced quite different emphases on health. When a country has needed to win a war, freedom from disqualifying defects, strength, and endurance have been important qualifications. During periods of peace, which have been fewer than one would think from an overall global standpoint, the emphasis on health can be placed on the related questions of longevity and environmental health. Much of the disagreement over the role that school health education should play in the educational pattern stems from differing educational philosophies and from the various concepts of health that prevail.

Women in Physical Education and Sport (No. 11). (These statements apply also to what might be called "other minority and handicapped groups," although women certainly haven't been a minority group numerically.) Throughout recorded history, except for a few notable examples (e.g., Crete), women's physical education and sport has been hampered, not only by the place such activity has held in society, but also by the place that women themselves held in most societies. (See Eisler, R., *The chalice & the blade,* published by Harper San Francisco in 1987 for an interesting, highly thought-provoking discussion of the important role played by women in this society.) It had erroneously been concluded that women simply did not possess the intellectual capacity to profit from the higher types of education. Certainly one of the significant trends of the twentieth century—despite continuing efforts on the part of a significant number who for various reasons wanted to slow down such progress—has been the continuing and growing movement for women's emancipation. The ultimate goal in our field is, of course, an ideal program of developmental physical activity at all levels and on into later life for both men and women. The evidence gathered now indicates that men's and women's activity programs should much more nearly approximate each other in both scope and intensity.

Dance and Expressive Movement in Physical Education (No. 12). Throughout history people of all ages have moved expressively for personal pleasure, for religious purposes, for expression of the gamut of emotions, and for the pleasure of others. It has been stated authoritatively that an analysis of the dance forms of a civilization can tell a qualified observer much about the total life of that society. The twentieth century has witness truly remarkable development in the dance as it has moved to professional status. The body has been gradually rediscovered as a means of communication through the medium of dance. As both an art and a social function, dance will probably always be with us and will further reflect the dominant influence of the age in which it is taking place. In recent years on the North American continent there have been varied opinions as to where a division, department, or program of dance belongs on campus. The usual place for dance instruction at all educational levels has been within the field of education, but there has been a move in some quarters to transfer dance into the arts or humanities faculties.

Use of Leisure (No. 13). In primitive and preliterate societies there probably was not so sharp a division between work and play as in civilized societies. Early cultures developed certain folkways and ceremonials of a more controlled nature than were present previously. We were told in the 1960s that citizens in the industrialized and (now the) postindustrial world would soon have more leisure than ever before. Recently, however, these prognostications have become highly debatable because inflation and a desire for emancipation encouraged by the Women's Movement have brought a steadily increasing number of women into the workplace. Regardless, husbands have often been forced to take second jobs and part-time employment to keep up with the cost of living. The continuing promotion of the concept of "education for leisure" depends a great deal on whether the prevailing educational philosophy will allow sufficient support for the inclusion of such programs in the educational system. What we decide as professionals, and what the public will accept, will exert considerable influence on the place of physical education and sport in our educational systems and subsequently in the leisure patterns of our communities at large for our mature citizens.

Amateur, Semiprofessional, and Professional Sport (No. 14). Sport is viewed as a pleasurable diversion in part of the field of sport and physical education. However, when it describes athletics as a highly competitive sporting activity in educational circles in North America, such involvement usually brings some type of extrinsic reward along with the inherent intrinsic reward of a sound sporting experience. Despite the ever-present possibility of excess, sport is still thought by many to be a vital part of the lifeblood of our field and offers great benefits and satisfaction to participants and coach alike. Primitive and preliterate people undoubtedly felt the urge to play, and they often took part in contests and games (at times in connection with religious observances as well). There is no denying that what we today call sport gave early humans the opportunity to practice skills that they relied on for survival. Even then the aspect of over specialization because of the desire to win gradually tarnished the luster of the concept known as "the amateur ideal" that prevailed in Periclean Greece and then again as the twentieth century progressed. There is an urgent, unrecognized need today for the creation of a semiprofessional category in sport, as well as in other areas of endeavor. There is a further need for professional athletes who will recognize the need to devote their lives to a social ideal—to serve their fellow men through their wholesome contributions to the many phases of sports development.

Role of Management (No. 15). Social organizations of one type or another are inextricably related to the history of humans on earth. Superior-subordinate relationships evolved according to the very nature of human involvement. We are now facing a situation in which a steadily growing percentage of the person power available has been necessary to cope with the management of the efforts of the large majority of the people in our society, a development that has been called the administrative (or managerial) revolution. Within this development, education has become a vast public and private enterprise demanding wise management based upon tenable administrative theory. In many educational institutions the management of physical education nd athletics is not big business within big education. The same can be said to an even greater degree for the management of professional sport and professional exercise establishments conducted on a commercial basis. Unfortunately, although management science generally has been called on to some extent, there is very little theory that has been shown to be tenable or even ongoing research about the administrative task as it relates specifically to sport and physical education.

The Concept of "Progress" (No. 16). This final persistent problem can be viewed as either a social force (influence) or professional concern (or both). It relates closely to the values that society holds for itself. Any study of history inevitably forces a person to conjecture about human progress. Certainly there has been progression, but can this be called progress unless it is based on an acceptable criterion? Further, it is doubtful whether we as humans can be both judge and jury in this matter. In the field of physical education and sport we must search continually for further agreement, for the greatest consensus possible among the conflicting positions or philosophical stances extent today. There are undoubtedly some common denominators based on the field of physical education and sport than can be recommended at this time, as well as others that can be agreed upon through consultation with colleagues in our allied professions.

CONCEPTS OF "PROGRESS"

As we look ahead to the turn of the century, and to where physical education and kinesiology (now called the profession of sport and physical education by NASPE in the U.S.A.) might be by then, we should appreciate the difficulty of obtaining true historical perspective about our present status. In this highly personalized epilogue, we have considered first the possible relationship of developmental physical activity to the good life. Then, it was suggested that a "multiple transcending approach" might be applied to this dilemma that each of us faces in his or her life. After that I explained that exercise, sport, and related expressive movement can have a unique role in the education of "ecological man and woman." Finally, after presenting the complete set of 16 persistent historical problems facing our field (listing the six of the social forces only, but describing briefly the remaining 10 professional concerns), I will take a look at the concept of "progress," admittedly a difficult task. (Keep in mind that this concept can be considered as both a social force *and* a professional concern.)

To play with words a bit on the topic of progress, we might say, "Where in the world are we going?" This is really a good question, and I wish I could be truly definitive with an answer. "Futurology" (or "futuristics" as it is also called) can hardly qualify as a science, although few would deny that in many ways some progress has been made in regard to prediction in the world. The best answer I can give may not satisfy you. Our task, I believe, is to analyze the several meanings of the term "progress," and then to make our personal and professional determinations with the full understanding that our nonstatistical types of measurement are subject to errors of observation. To make matters even more difficult, we are not certain about the element to be measured, the motive force, the process of change, the route of change, the goals toward which the elements are moving, and how any goals can be measured. Except for these uncertainties we are in good shape. . . .

Almost 25 years ago, Schwartz, in an insightful but disturbing work *Overskill,* stated that:

> The twentieth-century version of progress turns out to be a blindly hurtling technology that has carried man to the moon, split the atom, created a cornucopia of commodities for a privileged few of the earth, and holds out a promise to carry with it the remainder of mankind. Whereas flaws and dangers inherent in progress were becoming more apparent, in the twentieth century the "laws" of progress were becoming ever more elusive. . . . In the past two hundred years many attempts have been made to complete the edifice of progress, and on numerus occasions claims have been made that the elusive, universal law of progress has been discovered. But the "law" of progress is still undiscovered. Nor is it likely to be discovered, for in fact progress is a state of mind based upon faith rather than an element of nature (1971, pp. 31–32).

I must confess that I find it disturbing to be told that progress *in fact* "is a state of mind based upon faith rather than an element of nature." It is not that I am opposed to acting on the basis of faith, although I recognize that this itself is a controversial subject. For example, I have faith in scientific method, and I have faith also that there will be eternal change—at least for the next few million years in our universe. Regardless of this uncertainty and keeping in mind that throughout much of our lives we "act on faith," I believe that there are several levels of progress that should be considered by us at this point.

DEFINITIONS OF PROGRESS

Keeping in mind that a concept is a general notion or idea, we realize almost at once that the word "progress" is used generally to explain two different concepts—that of "forward movement" and that of "proceeding to a higher state." Thus, when we turn our attention to the human's progress in evolution, it is immediately obvious that human development on this earth has exhibited progress—progress, that is, when it is defined as forward movement or progression. However, Simpson stated at the mid-century that he had rejected "the over simple and metaphysical concept of a pervasive perfection principle" (1949, pp. 240–262). We simply cannot assume that change is progress, unless we are prepared to reconsider a criterion by which our progress may be judged.

Next we are faced with the question whether men and women can dare to set their own criterion for human progress. Would we be exhibiting too much temerity to establish ourselves as both judge and jury in this regard? This question must be answered affirmatively, because to establish our own human criterion is to automatically assume that such is "the *only* criterion of progress and that it has a *general* validity in evolution. . . ." (Simpson, 1949, pp. 240–262). Throughout history (and prehistory, we must presume) there have been examples of progress and examples of retrogression. Presumably also, if it is a materialistic (in the philosophic sense) world, a particular species can progress and retrogress. Fortunately for us, human beings give every evidence of being the organism that is progressing most rapidly on earth at present.

Today many of us take the notion of human progress for granted. (What *did* happen to those dinosaurs?) Some think the idea of progress is of relatively recent origin, although it may have begun with the early Greeks. However it began, the idea of human progress gained some credence in the late seventeenth and early eighteenth centuries. It was Darwin's evolutionary theory that added a scientific base to the concept of "progress" for humans. However, we would need to make a careful analysis of each decade thereafter to understand whether the dominant social values and norms of a society were moving humans toward a better understanding of the idea of progress. Bury (1955), in his definitive work on this topic, argued generally that it was not until the late Renaissance that people realized their capacity to structure their own world as skillfully as the citizens of the Classical World had controlled their destiny earlier. Certainly the early Greeks gave some thought to the future, as evidenced by that phrase in the middle of the oath taken before the Council of Five Hundred by all young men at Athens: "I will transmit my native commonwealth not lessened but larger and better than I have received it" (Durant, 1939, p. 290).

Durant, in one of his earlier works before he started his monumental, multi-volume world history, asked, "Is progress a delusion?" Seeking to encompass the problem of progress in a total view, he assessed all of history as follows:

> It is unnecessary to refute the pessimist; it is only necessary to enclose his truth, if we can, in ours. When we look at history in the large we see it as a graph of rising and falling states—nations and cultures disappearing as on some gigantic film. But in that irregular movement of countries and that chaos of men, certain great moments stand out as the peaks and essences of human history, certain advances which, once made, were never lost. Step by step man has climbed from the savage to the scientist. . . . (1953, pp. 249–250).

Then he delineates the stages of human growth as (1) the invention of speech; (2) the discovery of fire; (3) the conquest of the animals; (4) the gradual development of agriculture; (5) the gradual introduction of social organization; (6) a perhaps dubious rise in the level of morality; (7) the development of tools (machines) to assist us; (8) the victory of man over matter that has not yet been matched with any kindred victory of man over himself; (9) the growth of education—"the development of the potential capacity for the comprehension, control, and *appreciation* of the world"; and (10) the power of writing to unite generations and of print to bind civilizations together (pp. 249–257).

PROGRESS IN EDUCATION

Durant's quite optimistic assessment of human progress was first written in the mid-1920s. Considering the events of the approximately seven intervening decades, it was revealing to read the Durants' (he and Ariel) analysis of the world situation published in the late 1960s in what was intended to be a brief volume summarizing the world history series they had struggled with for so many years. You may not wish to accept their definition of education as "the transmission of civilization" (p. 101), but keeping this phrase in mind, they asserted that "we are unquestionably progressing."

> Civilization is not inherited; it has to be learned and earned by each generation anew; if the transmission should be interrupted for one century, civilization would die, and we should be savages again. So our finest contemporary achievement is our unprecedented expenditure of wealth and toil in the provision of higher education for all. . . . Consider education not as the painful accumulation of facts and dates and reigns, nor merely the necessary preparation of the individual to earn his keep in the world, but as the transmission of our mental, moral, technical, and aesthetic heritage as fully

as possible to as many as possible, for the enlargement of man's understanding, control, embellishment, and enjoyment of life (p. 101).

Despite the Durants' cautious optimism, we are confronted with that fact the world's population, despite the death and destruction resulting from the ever-present wars and natural disasters, is mushrooming out of control and threatening the world's ability to cope with such an increase (not to mention the failure to recycle from an ecological standpoint). Thus, the threat of great strain and stress on the environment looms large in all of life's many aspects. We will undoubtedly have to devise better uses of leisure, especially if robots—not "foreign workers"—are gradually used more extensively in the hot, heavy, hazardous, and boring work that distinguishes much of the effort expended in our service occupations and our industry characterized by gradually advancing technology. Where does education fit into this picture?

Enormous sums of money—hundreds of billions of dollars—are being spent annually to finance the gigantic enterprise of education in the United States and Canada. And still the perennial question remains: What is a good education—that is, (1) what criteria shall we employ; (2) how should the prevailing educational practice be modified because of the current social and political scene; (3) what type of environment should be provided to guarantee the best educational outcome; and (4), specifically, what is the function of that educational institution known simply as the school, the college, or the university?

Durant's ideas stated above may have answered the question for most people. We cannot really find many who would not agree (along with progressivistic educators such as the great John Dewey) with the idea that the schools should serve a more creative function—to provide people of all ages with the knowledge, competencies, skills, understanding, and attitudes whereby they could more effectively *lead the way.* thus, even though there has been advancement, if not progress, the public has proved time and again that it is not willing to support education so that it can keep pace with the annual inflation factor. Operating funds are made available grudgingly; capital funding (especially in the U.S.) is really difficult to obtain; and there is a continual discontent with education. Regardless, the struggle will continue for us all as we seek to determine the ideal hierarchy of educational values in a pluralistic, evolving North American society. We still find an ever-present lack of agreement about the purpose of, and support for, public education. These are truly two most disconcerting facts to those who have devoted their professional lives to education, and who try to find a life purpose therein.

DEVELOPING A LIFE PURPOSE

Despite the above, our task here is to motivate you, s young physical education and sport professionals (undergirded by knowledge from kinesiology), to find a life purpose in your future work in this field. Most of you may agree that potentially we have a unique role to fulfill in people's lives, but perhaps you are worried about these listings of 16 persistent historical problems that seem ever-present to us. (Also, I must confess that below I will also be discussing 10 "stances" that have to go if we are to achieve our mission.)

To counteract any concerns you may have, I should like to point out that the 16 persistent problems—the six (or probably more) social forces, the nine (or probably more) professional concerns, and the final concept of "progress" that I argued may be regarded as both a social force and a professional concern—would be present to a greater or lesser degree no matter what profession you would be entering. By that I mean that the social forces are simply present in all societies, and each profession also has its own unique set of professional concerns.

The important point, as I see it, is the enormous challenge that is present, that is inherent in physical education/kinesiology and sport by their very nature, and that if overcome can do so much to enrich the quality of life for all people everywhere. I accepted this challenge more than 50 years ago, and I have not regretted this decision for one minute. I have seen so many fine people who have indeed found a life purpose in our work that I believe firmly in our prospects for the future.

How then does a person find this life purpose? Also, what is meant by the term "life purpose?" These are good questions, and my response will be geared to making the answers as clear as one can possibly make answers to such basically subjective questions. The answer should be self-evident, but one must be ever so much more precise and offer a step-by-step analysis of how one gets *from* here *to* there. The following are the steps that I recommend: (1) determine your personal values; (2) place these values in some hierarchical order; (3) relate your personal values as best possible to the values and norms of your culture within a world perspective; (4) analyze your own abilities and interests while ascertaining the needs and interests of the time; and (5) choose a life purpose for yourself and nurture it so that maximum energy for living will result.

It has been so difficult recently to decide upon *personal* values. The home and the church have run into serious difficulty coping with this problem, and the school and the university have been slow to fill the gap. Since the days of the ancient Greeks, savants have been plagued by whether education should be both rational and moral. Is a commitment to moral values caught or taught? Do you teach about it, or do you teach a commitment of value? (Brubacher, 1977, p. 73). Further, it is very easy to confuse means and ends along the way toward the achievement of a set of personal values. For example, are the following terms regarded as means or ends or both: sound health, religious faith, knowledge, truth, recognition, service to others, creativity, personality traits, pleasure, and capacity and opportunity to profit from a life long education in an evolving democratic society?

For some unexplained reason we go at this most important aspect of our development in a typically haphazard manner. If a child has a mother and a father who are able to spend a large amount of time with him or her, and these people are intelligent, sensitive, and dedicated to the task, that young person is most fortunate indeed. This is true because it is during these formative years that a person's sense of life gets off to a good, bad, or indifferent beginning. Rand discusses this succinctly in *The Romantic Manifesto* when she explains that religion offers humans a myth or allegory, stating that there is a supernatural recorder from whom none of a human's deeds can be hidden. She states, "That myth is true, not existentially, but psychologically, The merciless recorder is the integrating mechanism of a man's subconscious; the record is his *sense of life* (1969, p. 31).

To paraphrase Rand's sequence of ideas, this sense of life is a preconceptual, emotional, subconsciously integrated appraisal of existence, of the human, and of that person's emotional response and character essence. Thus, before a person has a chance to study philosophy—if ever she does in today's world—choices are made, value judgments are formed, emotions are experienced, and an implicit view of life is acquired. If the person has the opportunity subsequently to develop rational powers, the hope is generally that reason will act as the programmer of his or her "emotional computer," and then the earlier sense of life may develop into a rational philosophy. If we do not make the necessary effort to develop rationality, or never have the opportunity to understand that we need to develop such rationality as the basis for the possible future emergence of a life purpose, then chance takes over. The person then tends to become a machine without a driver that is "integrating blindly, incongruously, and at random" (p. 33).

The *hierarchy of values,* whether arrived at implicitly or explicitly, indicates what is important to a particular person, and thereby serves as a bridge between the individual's metaphysics (belief about the nature of reality) and ethics (system of values). If a person's basic values are integrated, then a sense of life is integrated as well. The goal is "a fully integrated personality, a man whose mind and emotions are in harmony; whose sense of life matches his convictions" (Rand, 1969, p. 36). Of course, this sense of life continues on in an automatic fashion, but the hope is that thereafter the enlightened person will derive value judgements conceptually from an *explicit* metaphysics.

The third step involves *relating personal values* in the best possible fashion to *the values and norms of the culture* in which one resides, keeping it all within a world perspective. The relationship between personal and societal values should be reasonably consistent or serious difficulties may arise. Proceeding on the assumption that the various subsystems of the general action system of a society together compose a hierarchy of control and conditioning, our cultural values (i.e., social, scientific, artistic, educational, sport) determine the state of our culture in the long run if the action system is functioning properly. Thus, our societal values in this evolving democratic North American culture determine a pattern or configuration that in turn basically programs the entire societal action system.

In a classification of the fundamental values of the social system of the United States—actually an attempt to perceive the self-orientation in relationship to what is called a "collectivity orientation"—the United States is viewed as being more achievement oriented, universalistic, equalitarian, and self-oriented than, for example, Canada. However, the value differences are really not great, and any differences are probably due to "varying origins in their political systems and national identities, varying religious traditions, and varying frontier experiences" (Lipset, 1973, pp. 4–5). Our problem as individuals is, therefore, the question whether we should work within *our* system and its ascribed values, or we should seek to change these values (or possibly move elsewhere if the possibility of change is remote and we can accept the status quo to at least a reasonable degree).

In *analyzing one's own abilities and interests* while ascertaining the needs and interests of the time, the individual may move closer to the selection of a life purpose by asking such questions as (1) What is it I want to do more than anything else in the world? (2) Will my work give me the greatest amount of satisfaction? and (3) Will I be able to follow through with my initial decision tentatively before eventually making a final choice?

Here it seems appropriate to state that a life purpose is much more than the mere choice of, and efforts to fulfill the demands of, a job or occupation. It involves even more than the choice of, and following through with, a profession. A profession is a means to an end. We must ask what that end, that goal, is. This leads to the thought that the term "vocation" would be more appropriate here, because it means a "calling" (based on its Latin derivation). With a calling we encounter immediately the idea of accomplishing something of significance for the total movement of human life on this planet.

Frankly, I am still hopeful that this idea has validity even today despite the turmoil, unrest, and economic instability all around us. Such a hope embodies a type of philosophical meliorism that—starting from where you are and working with deep conviction and commitment to improve the quality of life—equates nicely with Berelson and Steiner's "behavioral science image" of man and woman. The image envisions the human as a creature who is continually and continuously adapting reality to his or her own ends (1964, pp. 662–667). Within this context a person should inquire as to what kind of striving gives life its greatest meaning. (Here I point out that the idea of sacrificing yourself for some cause with no thought of any enjoyment in the effort—a "hair-shirt" approach—is definitely not the best approach. I believe it can be argued that you must really enjoy yourself, even if through vicarious satisfaction, to effect the most fruitful results from your work.)

If you are thinking at this point that it would be interesting to try to narrow down the list of possibilities in a search for a life purpose for yourself—if you haven't found one already—I would like to recommend that the following techniques be explored: (1) read widely and try to observe first hand (and ask questions about) as many different occupations as you can; (2) think reflectively while also practicing a bit of "self-examination and soul-searching" about your inner nature and desires; (3) talk the results over and listen to the thoughts of close relatives, friends, and associates who may have insights about you and who may have your best interests at heart; and (4) enact a process of self-measurement and evaluation by reviewing the qualities necessary for entry and success listed at the end of this book's Prologue (keeping in mind, also, that there are agencies that will test your qualifications).

At this point you should *choose a life purpose* (at least tentatively). Keep in mind that you must begin immediately to *nurture it* to promote its effective development. Actually you are confronted here at once with a "move-it-or-lose-it" ultimatum. Talk your choice through with your closest friend; even write it out so that you will comprehend it more thoroughly. A life purpose ought to grow and flourish. It should be reviewed annually—and revised if necessary. A person needs to re-dedicate himself or herself from time to time. Certain immediate objectives, and even a long-range goal, may change or alter somewhat, of course, but the purpose you have chosen needs to be fostered by the development of a strong, personal attitude (psychologically speaking) about it. Possessing such an attitude will help to avoid any gradual surrendering to the shifting currents within the on-rushing, changing society.

A young person will often find it difficult to hold true to a chosen vocation. The purpose may have to be guarded against a variety of ills that may appear from time to time along the way. Other career opportunities may present themselves that will seem to hold out a hope of greater material reward or more rapid success. It is true that success for some comes more quickly than for others. Further, there will always be ways to make more money—or even just some extra money—that will in time detract from the overall accomplishment of your avowed life purpose. In the field of teaching and coaching, for example, success may come only after long years of dedicated effort to a cause. Youth may be long gone n such instances, and we all know of occasions when recognition comes after a person's (perhaps untimely) death. Although a statement such as this cannot be proved by mathematics, I believe that the course of human history has indeed been shaped by personalities who have held to a high purpose on behalf of humankind over a period of years.

As we nurture a life purpose, we must guard that the means do not become confused with the end, that we do not become bogged down by so-called instrumentalities. So many people seem to spend time getting ready to live that they never quite get around to living itself. I am convinced that the joy comes from travelling hopefully along the way, and that we should therefore enjoy ourselves because it's later than we think. We should be truly searching for that Aristotelian Golden Mean between fanaticism and egomania, on the one hand, and lackadaisical apathy, on the other. A person cannot ignore the conditions that must be met to fulfill a life purpose, and yet he or she should not ignore the important interests of friends, colleagues, and associates. The challenge, truly a case of delicate balancing, is to be sufficiently passionate about one's purpose in life while avoiding the sad pitfall of fanaticism. Particularly important in achieving this delicate and difficult golden mean that will allow accomplishment of one's life purpose, is the attainment of a battery of knowledge, competencies, skills, attitudes, and conditions. In this era of specialization, the following seems to prevail: (1) knowledge equates with power; (2) competence is needed to meet both the general and specific demands of life; (3) skills are required to solve the problems of varying complexity faced each day, not to mention the ability to distinguish between the extraordinary and what is ordinary (or even nonsense); (4) an attitude is needed that exhibits care and concern for humanity—love for fellowman everywhere; and (5) a condition of health is required that permits the maintenance of the vigor and the development of the endurance needed to accomplish one's chosen life purpose. Good luck to you (and it does seem true that luck often enters the picture along the way)!

A FORMULA FOR HAPPINESS AND SUCCESS

Accomplishing one's chosen life purpose is, of course, highly important for any person. However, at this point we should broaden our outlook to inquire about what might be a formula for happiness and success in North American society. In offering this list of "ingredients," admittedly normative and unscientific, no effort has been made to present the eight aspects of the formula in any hierarchical order. My position is simply that these ingredients, applied to a degree or extent that must be personally determined, will enable a person to obtain the values most cherished in this culture. These values will accordingly contribute to the vague, intangible goals of happiness and success. My belief is that achieving competence (i.e., adequacy or sufficiency) in each of these following eight aspects of modern-day living is possible:

1. A life purpose based on one's choice of profession (which should be fulfilled passionately but not fanatically).
2. A broad general education that should result in an inquiring mind.
3. Desirable personality and character traits (which are the result of nature, nurture, and unplanned experiences).
4. Intensive, specialized professional preparation (which should prepare the individual for the highest type of position available in accordance with his or her potential).
5. Successful human relations (which may involve the home and family and other social groups).
6. Developing an approach to exercise and physical recreation (which should achieve continuing physical fitness and bring enjoyment through free play).
7. Creative educational/recreational participation (which may be carried out to a desired degree in social, communicative, aesthetic and creative, and "learning" recreational interests).
8. Community service (which should make a contribution to the goals of community living—interpreted as involvement locally, regionally, nationally, and internationally, or in combinations of these). (See Zeigler, 1979a, pp. 15–16).

TEN STANCES THAT HAVE TO BE CHANGED

In addition to the achievement of one's life purpose, including the elusive "happiness and success" components, I have mentioned above a number of times in different ways that the road ahead in this profession will not always be smooth for you. Over and above the 16 (or more) social forces and professional concerns, there are a number of prevailing philosophical positions or stances (held by a significant number of people) that should be changed. This is necessary if we ever hope to eliminate the present credibility gaps that exists between many practicing professionals and so many of the young people and adults that we hope to serve. (Please compare these with a similar listing in Chapter 1.)

My analysis of the profession of sport and physical education, or physical education/kinesiology as we have designated it for the purposes of this text, revealed that it is suffering from what Walter Kaufmann identified as "decidophobia"—the fear of making autonomous decisions without the aid of "crutches" such as political ideologies, philosophical positions, most religions, microscopic deviational maneuvers, and other "Band-Aids of life" (1973, pp. 2–34). Finally, I concluded that there are at least 10 prevailing ideas in the field that have to be changed dramatically is we wish to eventually bridge the gap fully that presently exists between our occupation as a full-fledged profession, on the one hand, and that of a "not-so-glorified quasi-profession."

Idea No. 1: Our Mission in Professional Preparation Is to Prepare People to be "Jacks-of-all-Trades. In our professional preparation programs, we seem to be preparing people to be "jacks-of-all-trades." We should be preparing students who are capable of teaching humans of all ages to move efficiently and with purpose in exercise, sport, and related expressive movement. The public, as well as many professionals within the field, are having difficulty keeping up with the various images that the field is projecting presently. Without additional specialized preparation, we are basically not qualified health educators, recreation directors, or dance educators. The task for us right now is to bring our present "blurred image" into focus prior to any subsequent specialization that may occur.

Idea No. 2: It Doesn't Matter Whether Our Students Can Exhibit Motor Skill. In recent years, especially since the rise in the "disciplinary content" of our training programs, there has been a distinct tendency to down play the need for our prospective teacher/coaches to demonstrate an above-average level of motor skill in the various phases of our activities curriculum. Elevated entrance standards should be applied to both the theory and practice of human movement, along with the need for people who have knowledge and competency in the humanities, social science, and natural science aspects of general education.

Idea No. 3: Athletics Are Separate from Education. Athletics are now considered by almost all to be separate from the basic educational experience. We should be working to improve the quality of such an experience in ways that will help it to become a truly *educational* experience that can then named accordingly. At present the public seems entranced with competitive sport, and the influence of materialism at all levels seems almost insuperable. Accordingly, poor educational practices in competitive athletics are multiplying almost unchallenged.

Idea No. 4: A Lower Status for Women in the Field. The status of women in the field has improved to the point where equal opportunity has been achieved in professional association and scholarly societies. Yet in many ways they are still "second-class citizens," a status that undoubtedly has a relationship to women's place in society and accordingly within the educational structure. Although such change will not occur overnight, this situation must be made a primary objective and should be steadily rectified.

Idea No. 5: Embarrassment over the Term "Physical Education." Many people in our field appear to be embarrassed by the name "physical education." This name was fought for by our predecessors seeking to avoid the opprobrium of the term "physical training." Admittedly, it has caused embarrassment to some, and confusion to many, because it seems to imply a mind-body dichotomy that presumably does not exist. However, the time is not yet ripe for complete elimination of the term. An interim solution appears to be the use of the term "physical education and sport" (or vice versa), with the term "kinesiology" reserved for university and college units where scholarly research should take place.

Idea No. 6: Elementary School Physical Education Will Somehow Improve By Itself. It is obvious to almost all professionals that there is an urgent need for strengthening and improvement of the program of physical education at the elementary level. Somehow there is always rationalization that *others* ought to do something about this vexing problem that is so damaging to our field. We must all take some responsibility to improve this situation at the elementary level. (This is not to say that the status of secondary school physical education is adequate.)

Idea No. 7: A Solid Requirement in Physical Education Is Not Necessary Throughout Elementary and Secondary Education. Because of burgeoning demands on the school curriculum, not to mention relatively low educational test scores (internationally speaking), there is a continuing struggle to find time and money to meet these needs and deficiencies insofar as the so-called education *essentials* are concerned. This means that we must constantly be on the alert to ward off those who make the physical education program elective rather than required. We should determine what our standards are for "a physically educated person" and see to it that physical education is a school requirement until those standards are et by all who are physically capable. Adapted physical education should also be available for those who need such assistance.

Idea No. 8: The Body of Knowledge Will Somehow Emerge. Despite continuing attacks against physical education by uninformed (or misinformed) people seeking to eliminate it from, or cut it down within, the curriculum, most professional physical education and sport practitioners do not understand the great need for a more solid body of knowledge so arranged that it is readily available and steadily upgraded for the practitioner. This problem needs diagnosis and prescription so that the prognosis will look brighter for the years ahead.

Idea No. 9: Internecine Warfare at the University Level Is Healthy. In addition to the ongoing problem that often results in an organizational split at the college and university level between physical education and competitive athletics, an often unexpressed struggle (and "triangle") has developed among (1) faculty members teaching and carrying out research in the bioscience aspects of the field, (2) those attempting to strengthen the core of undergraduate and graduate programs in the social science and humanities aspects of our field, and (3) those not wishing to lose the professional emphasis within our training programs. Because of the as yet unrecognized subdisciplinary relationships possible, it is short sighted and delimiting for the entire field if any group attempts to effect arbitrary exclusion of any seemingly worth while subdisciplinary area, not to mention the shortsightedness of a stance that delimits the scope of professional training when the large majority of our trainees will eventually become practitioners who need a breath of outlook and understanding.

Idea No. 10: We Should Accept Our Second-Class Status. For a variety of reasons, physical education and sport has not been considered fully educational or academically respectable in the past. It is obvious that the field will have great difficulty achieving full status on a world wide basis in the foreseeable future. Above I have explained the ways in which I feel that this field can contribute to the improvement of the quality of life—if properly understood and implemented. The best way to make the grade would appear to be the steady improvement of the quantity and quality of scholarly endeavor, teaching coaching, and overall professional service. We should NOT readily accept our present second-class status. First-class status is "out there," if we will only improve our effort to earn it (revised from Zeigler, 1979B).

THE NEED FOR CONSENSUS

If you accept that the philosophic stances listed above have to be changed or modified, it follows that—if we ever hope to influence whatever we decide is progress in our society and in our profession—we must work for a greater amount of agreement about our professional goals. It follows, also, that these goals must be largely consonant with the values and norms that prevail in this culture. For example, any evaluation of qualitative as opposed to quantitative progress would depend upon the extent to which our physical education and sport practice approximates an agree-upon hierarchy of educational values. It is vitally important now, therefore, that we speak out intelligently, honestly, and forthrightly regarding the many recurring problems that the profession is facing.

This means, of course, that we will have to assist in the establishment of criteria for the measurement of the goals that we set. Then we will have to state (1) what elements of our work should progress; (2) what the causal factors are that will produce the desired result; (3) what the route of change should be; (4) how the elements of progress may change with time; and (5) toward which objectives and long-range goals the elements we typically promote are moving—all in all, a prodigious task.

We should be able to agree on the following at least: (1) what a desired level of physical vigor and fitness is; (2) whether we believe that a reasonably standardized program of physical education and sport should be required, and continued to a specific educational grade and/or level; (3) what attitudes toward health, ecological problems, and peace are needed for survival; (4) what amount of developmental physical activity is desirable in relation to other leisure activities; (5) who is responsible for therapeutic exercise for remedial physical defects; (6) what type of competitive sport experience is desirable for the majority of people of both sexes; and (7) to what extent educational sport and development physical activity can contribute to character and personality development. I don't believe this is too much to ask for (or expect) in a search for agreement about our professional standards (Zeigler, 1977, p. 235).

I have argued that to a considerable extent we are being downgraded and shortchanged daily by our professional colleagues from many directions and from the public at large (including many politicians as well). Why is this so, and what can we do to bring about progress toward our avowed goals? We know that a large segment of the population is sedentary and is characterized by what Herbert Spencer in the mid-1800s called "seared physical consciences." Scientists tell us that rapid behavioral evolution, that is, significant emotional, physical, and intellectual trait alteration, is at least possible with humans. The answer for us is to be able to demonstrate to people through proof what a normal "physical conscience" should be, and then to work to influence to develop the proper attitude (psychologically speaking) in an ever-greater percentages of humans striving for such achievement.

Undoubtedly there are many forces and influences threatening "good old physical education" at present. Much of our tradition, our cherished orthodoxy, and our now hoary assumptions and myths are being challenged as never before. In the years immediately ahead, such confrontation will undoubtedly continue—especially so if we don't adapt to the changing times. How we ourselves confront this opportunity for professional consolidation and progress—the attitude that we will need to foster within our profession least we be swept aside by the tidal wave of change that is threatening to sweep over us—is explained in an anecdote that described how Destiny came to an island some time ago and confronted three people—a *cynic*, a *mystic*, and a *physic* (al educator). Destiny asked, "What would you do if I told you that in exactly 30 days this island would be submerged because of the after-effects of a shifting of polar ice?" The first person, the cynic said, "Why I would eat, drink, and make love for the whole month." The second person, the mystic, said, "I would go to our sacred grove with my loved ones, make sacrifices to the gods, and then pray ceaselessly for the entire 30-day period." But the third person, the physic(al educator), thought for a while, greatly concerned, somewhat perplexed, but seriously cogitating, and then stated, "Why I might eat, drink, make love, and pray to the gods when the occasion presented itself, but my immediate plan of action would be to assemble our wisest scholars, researchers, and practitioners, along with aquatics specialists and experts in survival techniques. Together we would begin to plan, organize, staff, and work like mad 20 hours a day to figure out how to live under water!"

I am not suggesting, of course, that prospective physical educators and sport coaches take this story literally, and that we are indeed going to have to learn how to live under water. But I do believe that we are going to be inundated in the years ahead by all sorts of people from other trades, professions, and disciplines who will seek increasingly to "get into the act" that might be called "developmental physical activity in sport, exercise, and related expressive movement." I want *us* to be recognized as professionals who are leading the way in the research, analysis, teaching, coaching, and promotion of such developmental physical activity. Is this too much to ask?

If we wish to continue our progress, we will have to redouble our efforts to provide our profession with a sound body of knowledge at the same time as we sharpen our "conceptual lenses" as to exactly what our purpose is. Simultaneously we will need to improve our efforts in both undergraduate and graduate professional preparation. Finally, as a profession we will need to develop marketing techniques with a strong psychological orientation. We will have to increase public awareness of *their* need for *our* product. As we improve the motivation techniques that we employ, we will need also t strengthen our educational base and our instructional techniques. We should provide opportunities for developmental physical activity on an "easy-entry" basis, encourage continuation of reasonably vigorous activity regularly, and arrange for reinforcement reminders that carry a positive message with humor (Kisby, 1980).

A FINAL WORD

Finally, then in the words of Durant,

> The heritage that we can now more fully transmit is richer than ever before. It is richer than that of Pericles, for it includes all the Greek flowering that followed him; richer than Leonardo's, for it embraces all the French Enlighten-

> ment and its ecumenical dissemination. If progress is real despite our whining, it is not because we are born any healthier, better, or wiser than infants were in the past, but because we are born to a richer heritage, born on a higher level of that pedestal which the accumulation of knowledge and art raises as the ground and support of our being. The heritage rises, and man rises in proportion as he receives it (1968, pp. 101–102).

We in the field of physical education and kinesiology are part of this heritage. We now have a golden opportunity to enrich humankind's heritage through the involvement of a steadily increasing number of people to improve their quality of life through heightened experiences in exercise, sport, and related expressive movement. We know also that regular physical activity will enable people to live longer, more active lives. In the process there will be many opportunities for eager and enlightened young men and women to find their life purposes in such an enormous undertaking.

Obviously our duty, our responsibility as trained professionals, is to improve upon the human heritage through the experiences that developmental physical activity can provide for all people everywhere. We must work unremittingly toward the preparation of leadership that will permit our field to achieve its unique potential. This represents a concept of "progress" that is very difficult to refute.

REFERENCES

BERELSON, B., & STEINER, G. A. (1964). *Human behavior: An inventory of scientific findings.* NY: Harcourt, Brace and World.

BRUBACHER, J. S. (1977). *On the philosophy of higher education.* San Francisco: Jossey-Bass.

DURANT, W. (1953). *The pleasures of philosophy.* NY: Simon and Schuster.

DURANT, W. (1939). *The life of Greece.* NY: Simon and Schuster.

DURANT, W., & DURANT, A. (1968). *The lessons of history.* NY: Simon and Schuster.

EISLER, R. (1987). *The chalice & and blade.* NY: Harper San Francisco.

HUXLEY, A. (1964). *Tomorrow and tomorrow and tomorrow.* NY: New American Library of World Literature.

KATEB, G. (Spring, 1965). Utopia and the good life. *Daedalus,* 94: 454–473.

KAUFMAN, W. (1973). *Without guilt or justice.* NY: Dell.

KISBY, R. (1980). Conversation with Director, Sport Particip-ACTION, Toronto, Canada

LIPSET, S. M. (1973). National character. In *Reading in social psychology: Focus on Canada* (D. Koulack and D. Perlman, Eds.). Toronto: Wiles of Canada.

RAND, A. (1969). *The romantic manifesto.* NY: World.

SCHWARTZ, E. S. (1971). *Overskill: Decline of technology in modern civilization.* NY: Times Books.

SIMPSON, G. G. (1949). *The meaning of evolution.* New Haven, CT: Yale University Press.

ZEIGLER, E. F. (1977). *Physical education and sport philosophy*. Englewood Cliffs, NJ: Prentice-Hall.

ZEIGLER, E. F. (1979). Concepts of progress. In *Academy Papers, No. 13* (G. M. Scott, Ed.). Washington, DC: AAHPER.

ZEIGLER, E. F. (1979a). Developing a life purpose in the profession of sport and physical education. In *Theory into practice* (J. J. Jackson, Ed.). Victoria, Canada: University of Victoria.

ZEIGLER, E. F. (1979b). *Issues in North American physical education and sport.* Washington, DC: AAHPER.

ZEIGLER, E. F. (1979c). Physical education and sport philosophy: Foundations and definitions. *Asian J. Phys. Educ.*, 2:3:151–164.

ZEIGLER, E. F. (1989) *Sport and physical education philosophy*. Carmel, IN: Benchmark.

Index